# THE INFORMATION SECURITY DICTIONARY

*Defining the Terms that Define Security for E-Business, Internet, Information and Wireless Technology*

# THE KLUWER INTERNATIONAL SERIES IN ENGINEERING AND COMPUTER SCIENCE

# THE INFORMATION SECURITY DICTIONARY

## Defining the Terms that Define Security for E-Business, Internet, Information and Wireless Technology

*by*

**Urs E. Gattiker**
*Information Security this Week – Denmark*
*CASEScontact.org*
*EICAR.org*
*and*
*International School of New Media (ISNM)*
*University of Lübeck, Germany*

**KLUWER ACADEMIC PUBLISHERS**
**Boston / Dordrecht / London**

Distributors for North, Central and South America:
Kluwer Academic Publishers
101 Philip Drive
Assinippi Park
Norwell, Massachusetts 02061 USA
Telephone (781) 871-6600
Fax (781) 871-6528
E-Mail: <kluwer@wkap.com>

Distributors for all other countries:
Kluwer Academic Publishers Group
Post Office Box 322
3300 AH Dordrecht, THE NETHERLANDS
Telephone 31 78 6576 000
Fax 31 78 6576 474
E-Mail: <orderdept@wkap.nl>

 Electronic Services <http://www.wkap.nl>

**Library of Congress Cataloging-in-Publication**

THE INFORMATION SECURITY DICTIONARY
Defining the Terms that Define Security for E-Business, Internet, Information
and Wireless Technology by Urs E. Gattiker
ISBN: 1-4020-7889-7
E-ISBN: 1-4020-7927-3
Set ISBN: 1-4020-7998-2

This book is **dedicated to the memory of**:

# George Lermer

The dean who hired me for my first tenure-track job at the
University of Lethbridge, Alberta, Canada,
who became my mentor and dear friend.
He died March 15, 2003 while skiing at
Castle Mountain (Canadian Rockies).

# Contents

| A | 1-31 | B | 32-44 | C | 45-76 | D | 77-105 |
|---|------|---|-------|---|-------|---|--------|
| E | 106-127 | F | 128-136 | G | 137-138 | H | 139-149 |
| I | 150-182 | J | 183-189 | K | 190-192 | L | 193-198 |
| M | 199-218 | N | 219-222 | O | 223-226 | P | 227-260 |
| Q | 261-262 | R | 263-281 | S | 282-318 | T | 319-339 |
| U | 340-345 | V | 346-359 | W | 360-373 | X | 374 |
| Z | 375 | | | | | | |

---

If you would like to see a new word added to the **IT Security Dictionary**,
please write to:

Dictionary@WebUrb.com

# List of Figures

# List of Tables

# Preface

## Something for Everyone

If this book is to succeed and help readers, its cardinal virtue must be to provide a simple reference text. It should be an essential addition to an information security library. As such it should also serve the purpose of being a quick refresher for terms the reader has not seen since the days when one attended a computing science program, information security course or workshop.

As a reference work, **THE INFORMATION SECURITY DICTIONARY** provides a relatively complete and easy-to-read explanation of common security, malware, vulnerability and infrastructure protection terms, without causing much damage to the usually slim student pocketbook.

This dictionary can help non-specialist readers better understand the information security issues encountered in their work or studying for their certification examination or whilst doing a practical assignment as part of a workshop.

This book is also essential to a reference collection for an organization's system personnel. Special attention is paid to terms which most often prevent educated readers from understanding journal articles and books in cryptology, computing science, and information systems, in addition to applied fields that build on those disciplines, such as system design, security auditing, vulnerability testing, and role-based access management. The dictionary provides definitions that enable readers to get through a difficult article or passage. We do not, for the most part, directly explain how to conduct research or how to implement the terms briefly described.

The emphasis throughout, is on concepts, rather than implementations. Because the concepts are often complicated, readers may find that a definition makes sense only after it has been illustrated by an example. Thus explanations and illustrations are sometimes longer than the definitions.

Quite a few terms are included that might not meet strict definitions of "information security"—for instance, validity, reliability, attitudes, cognition, and digital divide. But they, and several others like them, are defined because they meet the main criteria for inclusion:

*The words pop up fairly often, in more than one discipline, and many people are unsure of the meaning.*

When learning any language, beginners will sometimes be frustrated because they have to look up words in the definition of the term they just looked up. By writing the definitions in ordinary English whenever possible, we have tried to keep this unavoidable annoyance to a minimum. However, there is simply no escape when defining advanced concepts that are built upon several additional basic concepts. Those terms, also defined in this dictionary:

❖ start with a capital letter (e.g., Computer Literacy), or may be simply
❖ listed in the text or, finally, be
❖ added to a term or definition in brackets in the paragraph or at the end (see also Computer Literacy).

Hence, the reader is able to find the other term quickly in order to understand the larger picture.

As in any language, in Information Security, more than one word may be used to express the same idea. In such cases, we have defined fully what we believe to be the more common term. Others are briefly defined and cross-referenced (Computer Literacy). Nonetheless, we have not tried to stipulate the "proper" labels for concepts that appear under more than one name. Neither have we specified the "correct" use of terms that are used in different ways. In short, we have attempted to be:

*inclusive and descriptive*

not exclusive and prescriptive. The goal throughout has been to provide a comprehensive dictionary of terms that will increase access to works in the engineering, medical, social and behavioral sciences.

*While not every company will use the same security tools and services, a company must use a level of security that is appropriate for safeguarding its functions. There is no such thing as 100 percent security, but striving to reduce the potential risk for a threat to materialize makes business sense.*

*Similarly, there is no free lunch. Satisfactory security for critical IT infrastructures can hardly be attained without the necessary human, technical and financial resources.*

*Finally, an important step toward greater security against threats from within and without, is achieved by talking the same language—improving communication and ultimately improving results.*

*This dictionary is a step toward developing similar meanings and a more unified interpretation of different terminology, categories and events—a crucial step toward a discipline's maturation.*

**There are rarely straightforward solutions to real world issues—especially in the field of security. This dictionary is an essential tool to help solve those real world problems by providing the foundation we need to communicate effectively amongst each other—our work vocabulary.**

*By covering situations that apply to everyone from the seasoned Systems Administrator or student of Computer Forensics, to the security curious home user, the Dictionary distinguishes itself as an indispensable reference for security-oriented individuals.*

Many events result in loss of data or damages of IT hardware and software. Theft of equipment is part of physical object management. Furthermore, environmental threats (e.g., earthquakes, floods and power surges) and software bugs are also of concern.

This glossary focuses on information, e-business, computer and wireless security as encompassing, but not necessarily limited to:

1) the protection of computer files containing digitally stored information:
   a) ensuring the accessibility of computer and network systems and, as well,
   b) protecting the integrity and confidentiality of data;
2) protecting access processes to certain operations, thereby reducing the risk for role-based access being violated or compromised.

**Statistical definitions** are included since IT security is moving rapidly toward a more established scientific discipline, which supplies research used for guidelines applied in corporate settings.

# Acknowledgements

Many people have aided my development as a researcher and student of technology and, in particular, the Internet and security. This book provides a welcome occasion for me to express my indebtedness and appreciation.

This book would have never been taken on as a task and most likely remained unfinished if I would not have passed through a stage, whereby I was trying to figure out a few things concerning my private life and professional career. Whilst reflecting and not being particularly productive, Inger Marie Giversen urged me in no uncertain terms to write these things down. She felt that I needed to clarify some of these issues and further develop the vocabulary for my own benefit. Subsequent use might even help others working in information security and striving in protecting their organization's or country's critical infrastructures. She has an uncanny ability to see and formalize things in a clear and concise fashion, also where a field of inquiry or discipline might move toward. She is a true **trail blazer** and in this case I definitely benefited from her visionary understanding of IT security in the context of September 11, bio-terrorism and the spread of medical viruses. Hence, she deserves a big thank you, yet any mistakes are mine.

Stefano Perlusz, my former Ph.D. student and dear friend, once told me while we were standing in his kitchen getting supper together that I needed to carefully focus my work and interests. Over a salmon steak, beer and a delicious salad, he urged me to either focus more on IT security and risks in information technology, or else just simply drop the ball and vanish into the sunset. I have taken his advice to heart, and worked diligently to focus more on the area of information security (http://Security.WebUrb.dk, http://www.CASESkontakt.de, http://www.CyTRAP.org for examples). Any omissions remain the sole responsibility of the author :-).

Rainer Fahs remains another fixture in my private and professional life. We are so different in more ways than one, or Ying and Yang. His experience in

IT security at the highest policy levels in international agencies and political forums, making it happen against nearly insurmountable obstacles of which one is surely politics, never ceases to amaze me. His persistence, vision and hard work with the ability to drive through all the fluff while getting to the core of the security matter is an extremely valuable talent that he has skillfully used to my benefit when analyzing my work and research. While I appreciate his vision, know-how and insights it does not come close to how much his friendship means to me.

Klaus Brunnstein was responsible for getting me into EICAR in the first place. He invited me to come to the 1994 EICAR Annual Conference in Rueschlikon, Zurich. Subsequently, Guenter Musstopf was the one who made sure I volunteered myself for several EICAR jobs over the years starting with supporting the work on the annual EICAR conference. Neither he nor Klaus bear any blame for what I did with this opportunity thereafter but I appreciate their help and support steering me in the EICAR direction.

Sarah Gordon is and remains a special person in the security field. Her flexibility, help and sometimes firmness enabled me to advance in my endeavours without getting depressed. She always made sure through her virtual contacts with me that I never really was aware in advance how difficult, dusty and stony if not sometimes outright lonely, the journey might be. If worst came to worst, we met at EICAR and shared a dinner over a nice bottle of wine.

David Harley must be thanked for helping me many times in further sharpening my ideas and keeping me from making too many maybe dumb mistakes. Besides this he has been a pleasure to write with on various projects including Viruses Revealed (Osborne/MacGraw-Hill, 2001).

Vesselin Bontchev not only showed me the ropes about viruses but, most importantly, was patient enough in explaining with humor, why working with viruses could be research (he convinced me all right!). Allan Solomon demonstrated and let me participate in a few fun jamborees. Vinny Gullotto was the one who made sure that I took marketing seriously while doing information security.

Several EICAR members and friends have helped to bring the book to completion. I cannot mention all of them, but Vlasti Broucek, Eric Chien, Shane Curson, Hervé Debar, Christoph Fischer, Mich Kabay, Jakub Kaminski, Andreas Marx, Robert Niedermeier, Christine Orshevsky, Vincent Weaver, Eddy Willems, Motoaki Yamamura, Anton Zajak have been particularly instrumental in providing guidance for portions of this book on the basis of their own disciplines. A number of their valuable suggestions have been incorporated; they have acted as unpaid research assistants and as participants in an informal seminar, as have experts from other organizations and institutions. All have endured many hours of discourse, reacting graciously to my unorthodox questions and unusual assertions. I appreciate all that they have contributed.

Special thanks also to Ian Bryant and Peter Burnett from the UK's National Infrastructure and Security Coordination Centre (NISCC) for their support.

My colleagues in the Cyberworld Awareness and Enhancement System (CASES) network, Martine Ducobu, Ruedi Rytz, Rudi Smet, Francois Thill, and Johan Timmers deserve thanks and appreciation. In this context, I also need to mention Wendy Ann Mansilla, Imram Ahmad, Fernanda Scur, Mohamadou Nassourou, VemuSaiSreenivasa Ramalingeswara (Sreenu) Rao, and also Marit Hansen and Christian Krause from the Independent Center for Privacy and Data Security - Schleswig-Holstein, all supporting and working with the CASES National Node in Germany. Thanks also to the Parchamsche Foundation for its support and our host ISNM (http://www.CASESkontakt.de).

One group to whom I owe many thanks, is my students. They have patiently reviewed and critiqued my material over the semesters. Some of this help came directly through assessment and expansion of some of the material I gave them; other support came from individuals or groups of students doing class projects, who pursued new avenues for addressing, expanding upon, and solving a potential Internet-related challenge. They were diligent and tolerant—even in situations where it took their teacher a while to understand. I truly appreciate their patience, willingness to share, and hard work.

Thank you to the reviewers of this book. They helped me find my way during a long journey. Sometimes they told me things I wanted to hear; sometimes, when I needed it, they set me straight.

Finally, I thank my friend Lars Krull who helped me fit into the Samfund by giving me the motivation speeches I needed to beef up on my Danish. Inger Marie, Charlotte & Mette deserve thanks for talking Danish to me, thereby allowing me to practice with them, while making many hilarious and no so funny mistakes :-).

Last but not least I am glad to know the BullGuard crew and especially Morten Lund, Theis Sønderggard, and Heini Zachariassen, your spirit, vision, diligence and smart work habits, deserve my greatest respect.

Copenhagen, Denmark          Zurich, Switzerland          Lüebeck, Germany

# Why is IT Security Important?

We have listed seven lessons below outlining why everyday network security is important to stakeholders, ranging from a firm's investors, employees, suppliers to consumers, citizens and children. Naturally, the reasons are neither listed according to importance nor are they all exhaustive. They serve to give the reader a short overview.

## Everybody Has Enemies

Corporations have competitors, countries have enemies and citizens have jealous neighbors. Some enemies may target us by name, others may simply want to harm another individual or enrich themselves at the cost of the victim (e.g., Identity Theft). While we may feel better by asking ourselves "Who could benefit from harming us?" we may be ignoring a risk or possible threat. This might simply be carelessness on our behalf.

## Every Enemy has One Strength

Even a consumer launching a Semantic Attack on his or her Website by spreading wrong information about the firm's products can become a major threat if picked up by many consumer groups and the media. Moreover, cyberspace attackers have proven to be better funded, smarter, and more tenacious than anyone has estimated. If we think our enemies are too weak to possibly do any harm, or will be unable to figure out our defenses and bypass them, we play ignorant or possibly negligent.

## Technology Makes Us Vulnerable

The firm's own Critical IT Infrastructure may be used for attacking its information resources. Software vulnerability or a missed vulnerability patch may

result in a successful hacking attack. Hackers succeed in making software do
things it was not intended to do. The scanner not working at the cashier's desk
due to a power outage makes it impossible to shop at the store, forcing clients to
leave without their goods. Forgetting to back-up our data makes us lose many
hours of work in case of a hard-disk crash.

## Attacks Will Strike the Technology at its Seams

Seams are the places where different technologies come together. Here attacks
can exploit weaknesses and thus succeed. When the FBI read a PGP-encrypted
mail, it was able to do so by first installing a keyboard sniffer to crack the
password (probably a weak one in the first place). Users that bypass copyright
protection mechanisms for DVD technology may do so by mimicking them
rather than breaking them.

## Technology Interdependence Exacerbates the Problem

For instance, Malicious Code has been known to use features of Microsoft Word
and Outlook to spread quickly. Moreover, a single SNMP vulnerability affects
hundreds of products. The Internet succeeded based on its interdependence but
it is also its Achilles heel.

Ever greater interdependence of systems (e.g., database with digitized medical records accessed by patient's general practitioner and emergency staff at
a regional hospital trying to access the information while providing first aid)
makes us depend ever more on these systems working properly.

## Collaboration between Public and Private
## Organizations is a Must

The software industry is **not interested in security but in selling software**.
Hence, without a commercial incentive—consumers face lack of improvement.
Neither can government do it alone without help from university and corporate
researchers. Governments can, however, do a few things to speed up the process,
while getting us moving in the right direction, such as:

- ❖ provide a financial incentive to business to improve by removing the liability ex-
  emption from software;
- ❖ supporting research that investigates new approaches for developing tools and methods for categorizing attacks and vulnerabilities (this could, but must not be limited
  to developing standards);
- ❖ setting regulations that demand regular reporting similar to that of Y2K; and

❖ encouraging public and private partnerships that foster greater awareness regarding security, trust and confidence with information and wireless technology.

If the government really wants the CEO to care, it will have to make security matter in the market place.

## Develop IT Security as a Discipline

IT Security cannot be done by just everybody. Nor may certifications offered by for-profit organizations do the trick. Instead, universities need to offer training specializing in IT Security including programs for Security Engineers and Security Researchers.

Cryptography has become a vibrant research discipline with much productive work coming out of universities and industrial research labs from around the globe. A similar outcome is needed for IT Security, in order to reduce the stress for Network Administrators who are overwhelmed if not underqualified for security tasks. Often these must be done on top of or beyond work regarding system assurance, upgrades and end-user help desks.

# About This Dictionary

The **FIRST EDITION** of the **THE INFORMATION SECURITY DICTIO-NARY** defines over 1200 of the most commonly used words in the security field, with particular attention to those terms used most often in forensics, malware, viruses, vulnerabilities, and IPv6.

If you cannot find it here, look to the links provided at the end of this book (e.g., dictionaries, utilities, regulation and newsletters worth subscribing).

A new world of words has emerged from technology's affect on the language of our modern culture. Dictionaries must tune in to the lingo of "screenagers" (defined in the new Oxford Compact English dictionary as Internet or computer-addicted teenagers) along with countless other developments in technology, fashion and pop culture.

The challenge facing an IT dictionary remains two-fold:

1) unearthing fresh, new words in the IT security field, and
2) predicting which terms will pass the test of time.

We prefer a cautious approach due to countless new words, phrases, numbers/letters and terminology mentioned in conference rooms around the world every day. Some terms may fad and fizzle within months; others continue beyond their boundaries affecting techies and home users. Therefore we have strived to maintain the balance between fresh and long-lasting terms.

Another challenge to success and making a dictionary a good tool is its definitions. Looking at a thesaurus for the word **define** shows, it can mean many things such as:

a)  To fix the bounds of; to bring to a termination; to end. To *define* controversies." *Barrow.*

b)  To determine or clearly exhibit the boundaries of; to mark the limits of; as, to define the extent of a kingdom or country.

c)  To determine with precision; to mark out with distinctness; to ascertain or exhibit clearly; as, the defining power of an optical instrument.

d)  To determine the precise signification of; to fix the meaning of; to describe accurately; to explain; to expound or interpret; as, to define a word, a phrase, or a scientific term.

(The ARTFL Project: Webster Dictonary, 1913, p. 382, online: http://machaut. uchicago.edu/cgi-bin/WEBSTER.sh?WORD=Define). Hence, we may have set boundaries where they might not necessarily be justified and avoided setting them where they are needed. We appreciate and welcome your comments, criticisms and additions.

---

If you would like to see a new word added to

THE INFORMATION SECURITY DICTIONARY, please write to:

*Dictionary@WebUrb.org*

---

# About The Author

## Urs E. Gattiker

Dr. Gattiker currently holds the Parcham Foundation Professorship in Management and Information Sciences at the **International School of New Media** (ISNM), University of Lübeck (http://www.ISNM.de).

Previous positions include **Aalborg University** School of Engineering, **Aarhus School of Business, Melbourne Business School**, the **University of Lethbridge**, the **University of the German Federal Armed Forces at Hamburg**, and the **Stanford Center for Organization Research** at Stanford University Graduate School of Business.

In 2001, Gattiker co-founded **Bullguard** (UK), and anti-virus/P2P/filtering software vendor (http://www.BullGuard.com). He is a member of the supervisory board of **KonNet GmbH** (Germany), and **Econo-Trans** (a Division of Medela AG, Switzerland).

Gattiker's books include **Technology Management and Organizations** (Sage, 1990), **The Internet as a Diverse Community–Cultural, Organizational and Political Issues** (Lawrence Erlbaum, 2001), and **Viruses Revealed** (with David Harley and Robert Slade) (Osbourne/McGraw Hill, 2001). The latter has been translated into several languages, including German (e.g., Das Anti-Viren Buch), French, Japanese, Chinese (Mandarin), Hindu and Polish (for detailed list, see http://research.weburb.net/frame/published/published.html).

He is currently finalizing **IT and Wireless Infrastructure Protection** (John Wiley) that will appear sometime in 2005: (http://research.weburb.net/frame/in_press/in_press.html). He has recently edited a book with Laurie Larwood on **Impact Analysis: How Research Can Enter Application and Make a Difference** (1999, Lawrence Erlbaum).

Gattiker has served as Chair for the **Academy of Management** Technology & Innovation and Research Methods divisions (the leading association for academics and consultants in management in the US). He is one of the founders and was an executive member of the Canadian Association for the

Management of Technology (CANMOT), now the **Innovation Management Association of Canada** (IMAC) and the Technology Management Division of the **Administrative Sciences Association of Canada** (ASAC).

Gattiker is the Scientific Director for **EICAR** (a European association of IT-security professionals), a member of the Board (http://www.EICAR.org), and acts as program chair for its annual conference and workshops (http://conference.eicar.org/). He is a member of the EU's **Internet Protocol version 6 Task Force** (IPv6) and was Chair of the **Internet Society (ISOC) European Coordinating Council** (http://www.isco-ecc.org).

Currently, he is establishing a **Warning, Advice and Reporting Point** (**WARP**) for citizens in Germany providing them with a FREE service for Threat Alerts and Security Notices about vulnerabilities, specifically tailored for home users with Windows-based operating systems (http://www.CASEScontact.org). He is also running the CyTRAP research laboratory (http://www.CyTRAP.org).

As the founder and editor of **Information Security this Week** (ISSN 1600-1869), Gattiker has managed to create an influential weekly e-newsletter about infrastructure protection and vulnerabilities/malware that includes a newsboard: (http://security.weburb.net/frame/newsboard/other/newsboard.html).

# How to Use This Dictionary

Every Dictionary follows some rules for its listings and while some explain these, others do not. No matter what the purpose, rules should help simplify things for the user and save time when working with the dictionary. The rules used here are minimal but important to know in order to save time.

1) Entries are in alphabetical order, using the word-by-word (not letter-by-letter) method. This means that, when looking up terms and expressions made up of more than one word, you should ignore spaces and hyphens between words.

2) In terms containing numbers, terms that start with a number come before the first word without a number in front (e.g., 2Closter comes before Caas).

3) When a term such as Virus has several related terms (e.g., polymorphic virus), the definitions may all be as sub-entries under virus, while under polymorphic virus the reader is simply referred to the main entry virus for further explanation. This helps non-specialist readers to find their way around faster with unfamiliar terms.

4) If a term is related, it is usually pointed out in a bracket such as (see also Virus). If the reader is referred to a sub-item of Market it would look such as (Market—Digital Divide) whereby the dash indicates that Digital Divide is a sub-item of the Market entry or such as (see Table 16A—Tariff 22), whereby Tariff 22 is a section in Table 16A.

5) When a term is also known under an abbreviation such as DDoS = Distributed Denial-of-Service Attack or WWW for World-Wide Web the reader is generally referred to the full explanation being given (e.g., WWW see World-Wide Web).

6) If additional resources are provided as linked to a term (e.g., Vulnerabilities) then the reader is referred to appendices at the end of the book referring to further material. These resources facilitate the reader's efforts regarding additional descriptions and URLs from other on-line database or software and utility tools.

7) Regardless of the above, in some cases, definitions may not be all encompassing which is to say that somewhere somebody has used another definition than provided

herein. For instance, Authentication is a term that is defined by numerous organizations, in standards and legislation. Nonetheless, they are not always meaning the same. In a case, such as privacy we have made an attempt to point out differences (e.g., privacy versus data security and 'Datenschutz'). While these efforts should take care of many problems, most certainly some nuances or different definitions have been omitted and we apologize for any inconvenience or confusion this may cause the reader.

**Abend / Application Crash**   (derived from 'abnormal end') is where an applications program aborts, or terminated abruptly and unexpectedly. One of the prime reasons for a thorough testing of an organization's applications systems is to verify that the software works as expected. A significant risk to data is that, if an application crashes it can also corrupt the data file which was open at the time.

**Absolute**   is the observed or calculated probability of an event in a population under study, as contrasted with the relative risk (see also Risk).

**Acceptable Risk**   (see also Risk) is the risk that has minimal detrimental effects or for which the benefits outweigh the potential hazards. Risk studies have provided data for how experts view various IT-related risks associated with the internet and other technologies. However, cognition-based studies indicate that what is acceptable to an expert may not be to the general public (see Table 22B).

**Acceptable Sampling**   requires division of the "universe" Population into groups or batches as they pass a specified key indicator (e.g., time of incident, severity of incidence, costs) followed by sampling of cases or sites / incidents within the sample groups (see also Sample). Hence, Statistics about Viruses, Security Incidents and other matters should be based on acceptable sampling (see also Statistical Inference).

To illustrate, some vendors offer spam calculators on their website to help potential clients figure out the costs per employee and annum caused by such nuisance mail. These 'calculators' assume that roughly 40% of a firm's email

A

is spam. Justification for this percentage is that "typically 30–60%, based on XYZ Research" is spam and the costs this creates for the firm is "...based on spending 3 seconds per spam email for 220 paid workdays per year."

But such numbers must be backed up with using Acceptable Sampling (see also sample. These may include but are not be limited to:

- user statistics (e.g., per work week and employee), such as:
  —number of email s received per work week per employee,
  —number of hours spent per work day responding to email,
- size of firm,
- industry firm is in (e.g., manufacturing versus banking),
- location of workplace (e.g., country and/or region), and
- socio-demographic data about users (e.g., education, type of job held, income, gender & race).

All the above information provides important sampling parameters that enable a decision-maker to determine if the numbers created make any sense. Using a very simple filter program some of us get barely 10% spam and we do not even have to look at it (see also Sample).

Hence, without information about the sampling used, calculations offered by vendors and IT outsourcing services for email and Virus scanning are difficult to understand if not meaningless. Assumptions made are hard to follow, suggesting that marketing concerns let to throwing cautiousness into the wind, thereby not following proper procedures required for sound statistics. Hence, IT security requires Acceptable Sampling to raise credibility and acceptability of figures generated by industry especially regarding justification of costs and Damages (see also Sample, Statistics).

**Access** to a system or computer can be given in two ways (see also Authentication):

**Physical Access**    is the process of obtaining use of a computer system on a physical level—for example by sitting down at a keyboard—or of being able to enter specific area(s) of the organization where the main computer systems are located.

**Logical Access**    is being able to enter, modify, delete, or inspect, records and data held on a computer system by means of providing an ID and password (if required)

But neither physical nor logical access is enough (see also Role-Based Access). An attacker may want access to a process or files (see also Process and IT Security)

**Authorized Access**    means the person's access to resources according to Role-Based Access rules.

**Unauthorized Use**    describes the situation whereby a party uses a process or data for which one was not given authority to do. Nonetheless, the user may still have gain authorized access to the system while using a process for which one has not been granted Role-Based Access.

**Unauthorized Access**    represents the person's access to system resources, files or databases one does not have authority to do. Hence, the individual could gain access from the home PC to the network (unauthorized), while using a database for which one is authorized.

**Unauthorized Use**    implies that the person has gained access (authorized or unauthorized) and is now using system resources for which one does not have authorization.

Figure 1 outlines a simple model of how various tools can be used to access or use system resources and processes resulting in various outcomes that are not desirable for the owner of the system.

**Access Control**    refers to the rules and deployment mechanisms which control access to information systems, and physical access to premises. Access control can be managed through Passwords and Biometrics as well as other means.

**Access Control List (ACL)**    is a method that a computer's operating system uses to determine the users' individual access rights and privileges to folders / directories and files on a given system. Common privileges allow a user to:

- read a file (or all the files in a folder / directory),
- to write / update the file or files, and
- to run (execute) the file (if it is an executable file, or program).

**Role-Based Access**    see Role-Based Access Control

**Access Control Matrix**    means preparing a system permitting to bring together user and the system's available resources. Preparing a matrix requires the following steps

1) A broad level of groups of resources that share the same or similar security objectives is established based on requirements for Confidentiality, Integrity, Availability, User Accountability, Authentication and Audit (Compliance) (CIA-UAA). The resources include files, directories, applications, databases, hosts services, processes and others including those protected by the operating system or by other mechanisms.

2) Users are grouped according to common security needs into functional teams and a group owner is identified who is responsible for group management

3) If necessary, naming standards for resources can be defined based on the findings under 1 & 2 above, thereby further facilitating resource groupings.

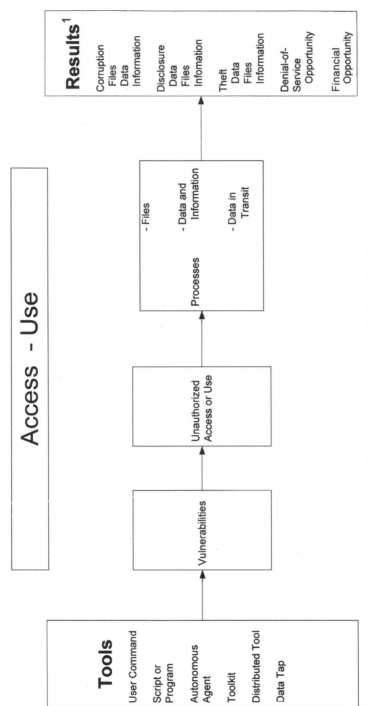

**Figure 1** Basic model about vulnerabilities resulting in unauthorized access or use of processes (see also Figures 2 and 3)

[1]Jurisdictional and legislative matters must be addressed, particularly important is specifying the types of damages and costs that might be incurred through data losses (see Tables 2A, 2B, 2C and 2D as well as Table 16A and 1B).

4

A

4) Now a decision can be made on the degree of access such as read, write, execute, take ownership, access control, delete, purge, modify, file scan (see also Role Based Access).

5) Balancing central security control and group administration decides about the involvement of security administration.

A corporation's access control matrix should not become a static document but, instead, regular review and improvement is a must. This matrix is closely linked to a Role-Based Access management system, whereby user roles (e.g., nurse versus private or general physician) have roles to perform requiring access and modification of data or addition of new information regarding an electronic patient file.

**Access Control Systems**   can include Biometrics that Authenticate (verify the identity of) users by means of physical characteristics, such as, face, fingerprints, voice, or eye retina pattern (see also Tables 4A – 4C).

**Access Rights**   are grouped by role name, and the rights to the use of resources is restricted to individuals authorized to assume the associated role (see also Role)

**Accident**   is an unanticipated event, commonly leading to damages on the IT infrastructure, software, databases or information. IT Security studies are beginning to show that the Risk of accidents is sometimes / often predictable; they are therefore preventable.

**Account**   is the domain of user access on a computer or network which is controlled according to a record of information that contains the user's account name, password and use restrictions.

**Canonical Account**   is one of those standard accounts that have the same password across all systems at the time they're installed. Canonical accounts not owned by end users are among the easiest avenues for breaching system or network security. These trophy accounts often protect the crown jewels of an enterprise, but they are often configured to allow easy access to anyone.

Typically they are used for system administration by software and hardware vendors but are left in their initial state because system owners don't realize that the accounts are there and vulnerable.

Canonical accounts must have their passwords changed at once to prevent abuse, but many systems have their doors propped wide open by unchanged standard passwords. Another approach, on those systems that use resource accounting and controls, is to assign a zero value to some critical feature (such as maximum allowed CPU seconds or maximum allowed session minutes) for a canonical account; such a value precludes new logons to that account until system managers reset the parameter.

**Accountability**   is the case whereby users are accountable for their use of a database or system resource by authenticating themselves (task based check) and provide an audit trail about their use of resources.

**Activate**   (or trigger) describes a situation whereby, for instance, destructive routines of a virus are activated when certain conditions are being met. These could be such as a certain date or the user carrying out a pre-defined action may be all that is needed. The condition that activates the malicious payload of the Virus is called the trigger (see also Virus).

**Active Attack**   is an attack that results in an unauthorized change of files or adding data or corrupting files (see also Attack, Table 3A & 3B)

**Active OS Fingerprinting**   is conducted in order to detect the target's Operating System. It is usually done by sending specially crafted network packets and comparing them against known responses. Each operating system responds to different packet differently and even response to the ping command can give a good indication of the target OS.

   Several methods have been developed and fingerprints are widely available on the internet. The tool of the trade for this is a tool called Network Mapper (nmap). While Active OS Fingerprinting is more accurate than Passive OS Fingerprinting, it has a significant disadvantage.

   Being active, means that attackers have to send packets to the host, hence, Active versus passive Fingerprinting means risking discovery (see also Passive OS Fingerprinting).

**Active Server Content**   executes locally on the machine that runs the web server. Each script that is installed presents a potential attacker with another opportunity to discover exploitable errors, and possible compromise of the computer system. Poorly written content or errors might result in:

  1) being fooled into executing commands on the local system that provide an attacker with a wedge into the firm;
  2) leak information about the web server system that could permit an attacker to gain the insights needed to break into the system; and finally
  3) use of processing facilities as part of the run cycle and, therefore, unwillingly be part to a Denial-of-Service (DoS) attack.

   Active content checking prior to installation by a programmer is a must. Reviewing of audit logs permitting scanning for possible attempts to subvert active content is also needed. Moreover, regular checking of scripts and active content on a website for Vulnerabilities or errors made during programming is also required to reduce the Risk for a Threat being emanated.

A

**Active Server Page (ASP)** is a method used for dynamic web sites/pages that includes one or more scripts (small embedded programs) that are processed on a web server before the page is sent to the user. An ASP is somewhat similar to a server-side include or a common gateway interface (CGI) application in that it involves programs that run on the server, usually tailoring a page for the user. Typically, the script in the web page at the server uses input received as the result of the user's request for the page to access data from a database, thereafter it builds or customizes the page on the fly before sending it to the requestor.

**Active Stack Fingerprinting** see *Active OS Fingerprinting*

**ActiveX** are similar to Java applets in that ActiveX controls may be included within a web page. The control is downloaded and executed on the browser's computer in the form of a pre-compiled executable. Unfortunately, ActiveX does not enforce any form of security management technology. Hence, ActiveX control has the same level of control of the client computer as the user that is executing the browser. ActiveX controls are specific to Microsoft Internet Explorer (MSIE).

ActiveX controls are elements that can be added to web pages, thereby providing them with more functionality (e.g., animation, video, and three-dimensional browsing). The controls are written in programming languages such as Visual Basic, C or C++. They are written in a different code than the one used for the web pages itself such as HTML. They could, however, be infected with malicious code (Malware).

Whatever risks are associated with running native executables on a computer also apply to ActiveX. How security of ActiveX controls is handled is at the user's discretion who runs the browser. Without appropriate training this may be risky, justifying disabling this functionality within web browsers by setting security settings to 'high,' ActiveX is prevented from running.

**Activity Monitor** keeps an eye on employees' or students' activities, such as if they play games or surf the internet instead of doing an assignment. Monitoring may be real time whereby through continuous tracking of real time screens of the remote computers, typed **keystrokes**, visited internet sites history and, used **applications much data** are collected if required. **All such** activity is recorded onto the log file and can be done from one single computer (see also Behavior Blocker).

But some countries are very restrictive about acitivity monitoring such as eMail and surfing on the Web. The French Supreme Court ruled in October 2001 (Onos vs. Nippon France) that employers do not have the right to read their employees' e-mail or other personal computer files.

Nikon France was charged by an employee for violation of his right to workplace privacy. A worker had been fired for using the firm's computer equipment to engage in personal freelance work on the side. His activity was discovered when the firm reviewed his eMail including personal ones and correspondence stored on his computer at work.

The case, Nikon France v. Onos, is expected to have a major impact on workplace surveillance policies and the use of email in the workplace. But we believe implications go beyond France, since these regulations will affect any firm that has employees in France or does business with France. Finally, other European countries such as Italy have a similar understanding of eMail privacy at work, whereby the public and unions feel that private eMail on company computers is private.

**Acute**    could either refer to:

1) a security status effect, brief; sometimes loosely used to mean severe, or
2) exposure to a threat, brief, intense, or short-term: sometimes specifically referring to brief exposure of high intensity (see also Chronic)

**Address Resolution Protocol (ARP)**    is defined by RFC826 and provides transparent mapping between 32-bit IP address (in a case of TCP/IP v4) and 48-bit physical address.

**IPv6**    uses 128 bits for addressing (see also Internet Protocol version 6 or IPv6 for short).

**Admissible Evidence**    is evidence produced in a court of law that satisfies rules of evidence. Different jurisdictions have different requirements and specific tests may apply (for e.g., Daubert's test in the USA) (see also Forensics).

Electronic evidence is generally considered to be admissible if it was collected in the course of normal business operations (see also jurisdiction).

**ADSL**    see Asymmetrical Digital Subscriber Line

**Advanced Encryption Standard (AES)**    was initiated by the USA government during 1996 when it thought it needed a more advanced standard (see also DES and Rijdal below) (see also Tables 11A and 11B).

**Advanced Research Projects Agency (ARPA)**    see Defense Advanced Research Projects Agency (DARPA)

**Advisory**    is a service that reports after the fact or a follow-up to a previous alert or advisory (see also Alert, Briefing Notice, Scenario and Technical Note)

An advisory gives people the advantage to file things away if they are not of immediate concern. Advisories include those items that are being reported after the fact (e.g., source is other than a CERT-based one).

However, an Advisory can also become a type of Alert as is the case when CERT-CC sends out its CERT-Advisory regarding vulnerabilities, buffer overflows and others. Here, recipients are encouraged to not put the Advisory aside but instead check immediately and take the necessary steps if their systems are affected or vulnerable as outlined in the Advisory.

**Advisory and Notification Markup Language (ANML)**   is an Extensible Markup Language (XML) -based specification for describing advisories and other types of notifications. ANML is currently being developed to help in solving the inconsistent use of terminology by software vendors in their advisories.

The hope is that ANML will make it easy for applications to read these advisories. This will make way for the necessary tools to automatically update systems. Although ANML will have its biggest impact for security advisories, it can be used for any type of notification. Some examples include

- bug-fixes,
- feature enhancements,
- upgrade availability, and
- many more.

More information can be found in Appendix 1 (Opensec) and Appendix 6 under ADML

**Affect**   is how we feel about an object (e.g., IT security), often operationalized with verbal and facial expressions, other nonverbal reactions but almost never measured because relatively costly.

Also encompasses the negative connotation of words such as emotion, sentiment, affect. Affect dominates expected utility theory approaches to Risk (see also Risk, Attitudes).

Affect is the second of the three components usually used to measure attitudes (cognition, affect and conation, see Attitudes).

**Alert**   is formatted message describing a situation that may harm IT and wireless infrastructure and data in contrast to an Advisory that is usually far less urgent (see also Briefing Notice, Scenario).

Alert is issued infrequently and contains information that should be acted upon as soon as it is received, therefore, requiring a system administrator's or user's immediate action (see also Advisory, Briefing Notice, Technical Note, Vulnerabilities).

As such, an alert is breaking news but to make it of value, it should only contain verified information, otherwise it could turn out to be a hoax. This would diminish its effectiveness in the future (e.g., people treat it like an advisory instead of giving it immediate attention) (see also Hoax).

**A**

An alert sent should be ranked by its severity. This information must be part of the Subject Header of the message:

>          1 – Very Low
> 2 – Low          4 – Severe
> 3 – Moderate     5 – Red Alert/Very Severe

In general low or moderate alerts should be rarely used, unless they are hoaxes or for other reasons a mail out is required for the benefit of subscribers. The problem for the recipient of an Alert is that it is often difficult to determine how serious a threat might be involved with a Virus or Vulnerability Alert, hence a standardized system is not available while vendors tailor their ratings to their own customers (see also Virus, Tables 24E, 24F & 24G).

Alert can also be defined as a message from the Intrusion Detection System (IDS) about activity detected by the IDS (see also Threat Level Definition, Tables 24E–24G).

**Technical Alert**    provides a System Administrator or other experts with the technical information required to safeguard systems including PCs against a new discovered Vulnerability and/or Virus (see also Tables 24E–24G).

**Non-Technical Alert**    provides a home user or possibly a Small and Medium Sized Enterprise (SME) with information that is less technical but focuses on the Threat or Vulnerability while, most importantly, leading one to the source for a remedy. The latter is possibly also including a step-by-step guide for fixing the problem quickly.

Put differently, a home user or most SMEs cannot really benefit from receiving an alert or alert notice that tells him or her the following:

*Notice*

*This is a Low-Profiled Virus Notice for W32/Smibag.worm.*

*Justification*

*This W32/Smibag.worm has been deemed Low-Profiled due to Media Attention at <http://joongangdaily.joins.com/200309/27/200309270241188639900090609061. html>. W32/Smibag.worm is referred to as Smess within the article.*

*Read About It*

*Information about W32/Smibag.worm is located on VIL at:*

*http://vil.nai.com/vil/content/v_100692.htm*

*Detection*

*W32/Smibag.worm was first discovered on 09/26/2003 and detection will be added to the 4296 dat files (Release Date: 10/01/2003).*

*If you suspect you have W32/Smibag.worm, please submit a sample to http://www.webimmune.net.*

Algorithm 11

In fact it is very unlikely that with all the Spam, the number of important emails and alerts a person receives he or she may even study such type of email carefully. Similarly, a Short-Messaging-System (SMS) type Alert whereby a person receives the SMS whilst riding on the public transport system, seems of little benefit unless the recipient is an expert that can call the appropriate system people and guide their efforts, while being away riding a train.

**Preventive Alert**   see Prevention

**Algorithm**   pronounced AL-go-rith-um is a procedure or formula for solving a problem. The word derives from the name of the mathematician, Mohammed ibn-Musa al-Khwarizmi, who was part of the royal court in Baghdad and who lived from about 780 to 850. Al-Khwarizmi's work is the likely source for the word *algebra* as well.

Algorithm is any well-defined procedure (does not have to be computational) that takes some value or set of values as input and produces some value or set of values as output.

It is a technique that comes with a guarantee. The technique for rational function integration is an algorithm because it always produces the answer, without exception. Differentiation is an algorithm—given an elementary function, you can always find its derivative. Algorithms can be fast or slow, but the important thing is the guarantee. In some sense, an algorithm is a 'predictable heuristic,' whereby one cannot tell if a heuristic will work, before one tries it, but one knows in advance what the output of an algorithm will be.

In computing terms, algorithm is a sequence of computational steps that transform the input to the output.

A computer program can be viewed as an elaborate algorithm. In mathematics and computer science, an algorithm usually means a small procedure that solves a recurrent problem.

In this context the term **Virus Algorithm** means a set of operations or a procedure designed to create a virus problem.

In the context of **Digital Signatures** or **Encryption**, the algorithm describes how the signature or text is encrypted using mathematical formulas

Another example is the **Condensation** algorithm (**Con**ditional **Dens**ity Propag**ation**) that allows quite general representations of probability. The simplicity of the **Condensation** algorithm also allows the use of non-linear motion models more complex than those commonly used in Kalman filters. Using the statistical technique of *importance sampling* it is possible to build a **Condensation** tracker which runs in real time tracking a dancer or a hand as they move.

Computing the greatest common divisor of two numbers (positive integers) one obtains the **Euclidean Algorithm**.

**Alias**  is an alternative name for a virus or a person surfing on the Internet. There is no absolute naming convention for computer viruses. Some may have a number of aliases whereby vendors differ, resulting in considerable confusion for users (see Viors, Researcher–Virus).

**American Standard Code for Information Interchange** see ASCII

**Anatomy of attack**  is set of steps that are conducted by hacker in his or her attack. *The Hacker* first collects general information about target *footprinting*. Then hacker proceeds to scanning and enumeration. Finally he or she attempts one of the following:

- all of system hacking,
- network hacking, and/or
- software hacking.

**Anomaly Based Intrusion Detection Systems (AB-IDS)**  are matching collected data against a "normal" situation.

These types of systems are capable of discovering known attacks. Unfortunately, they are also known to have quite substantial amounts of *False-Positives*.

**Anomaly Detection Model**  systematically looks for activities that are different from the user's or the system's usual behavior, thereby possibly helping in detecting intrusions.

**Anonymous Remailer**  permits the hiding of the message and the sender's identity, thereby making it untraceable mail. Untraceable mail relies on mixes. This means that computers process each message before delivering it, in order to hide the correspondence between received message and the delivered on.

The above creates an anonymous channel between the actual sender and the receiver. A mix delivers the messages received within a given time period in lexicographic order, while assuring that each message is processed only once. This way, traffic analysis is more difficult (see also Digital Pseudonym).

**Anti-Virus Researcher**  see Research, Theory, Methodology

**Anycast**  is used in Internet Protocol Version 6 (IPv6) as a method of updating routing tables. One host initiates an update of a router table for a group of hosts, sending the data to the nearest host. That host then sends the message on to its nearest router until all the routing tables in that group are updated

Anycast supports service-oriented address assignments in IPv6 networks. The Anycast address is not determined by the location of node, but by the type of service presented at the node. In Anycast communication, the client can automatically obtain the appropriate node corresponding to a specific service without knowledge of the location of the server (see also http://www.ietf.org/internet-drafts/draft-ietf-ipngwg-ipv6-anycast-analysis-02.txt, June 2003)

IPv6 can determine which gateway host is closest and sends the packets to that host as though it were a unicast communication. In turn, that host can Anycast to another host in the group until all routing tables are updated (see also Denial of Service attack—internet routers).

**Apache** is a freely available multiplatform web server. It is currently the most commonly used server on internet connected sites. Its genesis was in early 1995 when developers of some high visibility web sites decided to pool their patches and enhancements to the NCSA / 1.3 server to create a patchy server. The project has since gained considerable momentum.

**Application Based Intrusion Detection Systems** (**Application Based IDS**) are built in to the application and usually work on a principle of anomaly detection and/or of audit log trails.

**Application Level Gateway** could be a Firewall system (see also Firewall) whereby processes are used that permit maintaining complete TCP connection state and sequencing. Application level firewalls may re-address traffic so that outgoing traffic appears to have originated from the firewall, instead of the internal host system.

**Application Service Provider (ASP)** are service firms who seek to lease their software packages over the Internet, whereby clients sign on to a subscription-based mode (e.g., monthly fee for using the software or service by so many users and hosts, or systems). ASP hosts a firm's software applications remotely on servers.

**Architecture** can be defined as the attributes of a (computing) system as seen by the programmer, or the conceptual structure and functional behavior, as distinct from the organization of data flows and controls, the logic design, and the physical implementation

**Technical Architecture** refers to the core computing / information resources such as Linux servers running on HP hardware.

**Application Architecture** defines the foundational database upon which the majority of business applications are built. For example an organization's applications architecture could be an Oracle relational database (running on the UNIX servers identified above in the technical architecture) for business applications, Star Office, and SOT Office 2002 for all office and inter-organization communications.

**Archive** is data storage for non-current records. Care must be exercised to ensure that the records retained meet legal requirements should it ever be necessary to produce these records in a court of law (see also Record).

Computer scientists at the National Institute of Standardization of Technology (USA) were launching an effort to develop specifications for "archival quality" CD and DVD media during Fall 2004.

This was done in the hope that "archival quality" would permit government agencies to ensure during the procurement process that sufficiently robust media would be purchased for their long-term archiving needs. In particular, 50 years and longer is a key issue.

Currently, CD and DVD media do not meet such requirements for posterity and quality regarding content replay and storage.

**Individual Archiving** means that for legal reasons (see Jurisdiction) organizations must be able to provide copies of emails and other materials to protect their interests in subsequent law suits (e.g., Table 5C). But a smart user proceeds cautiously and also archives all eMails.

For an individual it is advisable to keep in mind that anything written in a chat forum, posted on a newsgroup or website (e.g., presentation given at a conference), eMail sent/received or a messenger service is probably archived somewhere. In turn, such information can be retrieved sometime down the line by a supporter or an adversary quite easily if need be. A web-based e-mail service by such organizations as Swissinfo.org or Yahoo! allow one to send a friend a personal eMail to his or her account on a similar service about a work-related topic that one might not want to have archived by the employer. For this reason, many employers do not permit using such services from work.

To illustrate further about the usefulness of archiving one's own eMail, most countries require a firm to keep any documentation for 10 years beyond the year it happened. Similarly, citizens must be able to provide receipts for tax audits up to 7 years or more after having filed an annual return to which this receipt might apply to. Accordingly, it is necessary to manage and store one's eMail (sent and received) and keep it for at least 10 years thereafter.

This can be accomplished by:

1) using folders and sub-folders, such as country and within country A have sub-folders such as government, business and within each of these further depending upon need;

2) with the help of filters, whereby each incoming or outgoing eMail is already transferred into the appropriate folder;

3) doing regular backup of the eMail at the same time other directories are being backed-up; and

4) burning a CD and archiving the CD with the eMails at least 2 times a year (e.g., May 1 and Nov 1).

All the above will help to refresh a boss' mind about severance package or harassment if need be or just to give a colleague a friendly reminder about a deadline he or she agreed to. Hence, it is advisable to burn a CD even of one's work eMail (e.g., from one's PC at work) and store it in a safe place. For security reasons, a fired employee is no longer permitted to access any IT resources and equipment after having been told that he or she is let go. Accordingly, all access to vital eMail written during one's tenure is no longer accessible unless the firm is ordered by the court to do so (see Table 5D).

**ARPAnet**   is the name of the original internet funded by ARPA (see also Advanced Research Projects Agency).

**ARP**   see Address Resolution Protocol

**ASCII (American Standard Code for Information Interchange)**   is a series of standards used to identify simple characters (numbers, letters, etc.) where each character is represented by a numerical code. Each character is assigned a 7-bit code, whereby the bit has a minimum unit of data, 0 (zero) or 1. ASCII files can be created using simple text editors.

ASCII is a universal computer code for English letters and characters. Computers store all information as binary numbers, regardless of what make or brand the computer is. ASCII also refers to a protocol for copying files from one computer to another over a network, in which neither computer checks for any errors that might have been caused by static or other problems. The difficulty with ASCII is twofold:

1) all special fonts and elements used in a document typed using one software (e.g., WordPerfect) will be lost when the file / document is saved in ASCII format and than reloaded by somebody else into WordPerfect (or even Microsoft Word for that matter), and

2) special characters such as those used in German cannot be transferred by ASCII (e.g., ü is transferred as a blank and an ue must be typed instead). Besides German, for many languages (e.g., Chinese and Japanese), this represents a real problem.

For the above reasons, a new source called Unicode was developed (see also Unicode).

As 8 bit codes only allow for 256 separate characters, a single 8-bit encoding is not suitable for all text requirements. Even western alphabets have many 'characters', and once languages of China, and Braille are included there are many thousands of characters that are needed. Of course, within a given domain, an implicit assumption of a particular character set could be made. This leads to multiple 8-bit codes. But it doesn't work for those character sets where more than 256 characters are needed in the same context.

Both 7-bit ASCII and the various 8-bit extensions of it can be considered to be subsets of Unicode. One does not need to know the above level of detail, but it is important to see why ASCII is insufficient, and why a standard is required for character encodings (see also Unicode).

**ASP**   see Application Service Provider and Active Server Page.

**Asset Value**   describes the value of an asset such as an information system and / or a database the firm currently has. Investments undertaken using technical and non-technical measures (e.g., firewall and better use by employees of accepted security measures available), can be compared to the costs incurred if the asset is damaged or possibly even lost (see also Damages, Disaster Recovery Plan).

Table 1 outlines how the value of information is determined. As importantly, who needs the information and how training may help to improve security of such data are also addressed.

**Table 1:**  Value of Information—Asset Approach

| Factors | Description of Factor |
| --- | --- |
| Data | In the simplest scenario, the firm has insured the Risks for loosing data. In such a case, the insurer will have to determine with the help of the organization what type of Risks are involved and the value data that might have gotten lost. |
|  | Similarly, a death insurance premium is based on the calculated risks a person has to die abruptly (e.g., sky diver versus a person jogging), in combination with the person's earning power. This enables one to arrive at a premium that will be offered to a particular group of individuals (e.g., car insurance for older men versus younger ones). |
|  | For data, the risk of loosing such data and their worth or their value to the organization must be determined. For instance, if customer data are lost, can backup restore most of these lost data and minimize loss, such as data generated between last backup and when the disaster struck. In turn, all these factors will be used determine the premiums it would take to make such a type of insurance offers coverage that is worthwhile, from an insurance carrier as well as the insured party's perspective. |
| Stakeholders | The more parties require access to information due to their role played in producing a particular service (e.g., nurse to patient record to check history or blood type), the more valuable information will be (see Table 5A). |
|  | If an electronic patient record cannot be accessed, it may be difficult to perform surgery unless a backup is made available within minutes or a paper print-out can be looked at instead by the physician. |
| Training | Provides the basic Skills needed by managers and staff to help with pro-active defense efforts about the firm's CIP and its strategic importance as well as how security can be increased by modifying user behaviors. In turn this will permit users to exhibit the behavior and vigilance required for strengthening security efforts–creating synergies (see also Table 7B). |

**Note.** The more difficult it is to obtain data and the more stakeholders need access to the information to perform their tasks such as subcontractors or suppliers, the more valuable information becomes to a firm and its partners. Workers have also to be trained to take advantage in an appropriate manner of the information resources provided.

**Table 2A:** Value of Information—Hard Costs

| Equation | Description of Factor |
|---|---|
| | The focus here is on calculating what it would cost to get a compromised database running again or if need be, re-create the information stored in the damaged database, or the passwords that gotten stolen in the password file. |
| | The more stakeholders depend on the availability of a resource, IT system or data, as well as the training needed to take advantage of the technology all increases the value of the data (see Table 1) |
| (1) $\sum \text{Costs} = \sum \text{HC} + \sum \text{SC}$ | Where **HC** are the **hard costs** (e.g., human resource costs for working hours lost and overtime needed to cope with the backlog of unprocessed work amassing rapidly on one's desk) and **SC** are the **soft costs** (e.g., opportunity costs due to downtime of machine/system). |
| (2) $\sum \text{Costs} = \sum \text{HC(FC + VC)} + \sum \text{SC(FC + VC)}$ | • **FC** are **fixed costs** (e.g., fixed charge by computer service to do a "house call", based on Shadow Pricing)<br>• **VC** are **variable costs** (e.g., hours not being able to work due to personal computer being down or hard disk crashed) |
| | **Hard Costs** may also entail costs for new hardware and software required to fix the problem.<br>    **Incurred costs by a patient** are usually **HC** and **VC**, i.e., sometimes we can calculate them and they are variable.<br>    For instance, if a hacker alters a patient's record, correcting the record on the database costs (e.g., system expert's time) but, most importantly, the patient's life may be at stake if given the wrong blood or drugs during emergency treatment. Hence, the difficulty will be to determine the likelihood of such outcomes (death due to wrong treatment, latter was caused by party gaining illegitimate access to data and altering it incorrectly) as well as the value of damages caused to the patient by such outomes.<br>    **Shadow pricing** is a concept used by economists to determine the price for a product and/or service for which the firm may not have a clear idea or formula for calculating realistic costs. Here economists suggest we look at the market price for the product/service we need.<br>    In the case of wrong information or illegitimate access to the medical database, the patient and/or the patients physician may both claim damages against the party managing the database on behalf of the government. Here previous product liability and/or malpractice lawsuits may help in determining the costs. |

(Cont.)

**A**

**Table 2A:** (Cont.)

| Equation | Description of Factor |
|---|---|
| | In turn, these figures from previous lawsuits in conjunction with the likelihood of such outcomes represent a shadow price for the **fixed costs** (FC) incurred by the firm to fix a medical problem/disaster. For instance, a patient may suit the hospital because inaccessibility of the digitized medical records due to a system break down may have harmed the person. |

**Note.** Hard costs still require Shadow Pricing to obtain all the costs.

Variable and fixed costs as part of the Soft Costs may also contain opportunity costs. When an e-commerce site is down, the firm may loose business or sales.

Table 2A provides a simple model in how hard costs that are incurred for generating data can be calculated, for instance, in the case of electronic patient records. Even if internal records are not available, Shadow Pricing can be used to arrive at these costs.

Table 2B presents a systematic way in how Soft Costs can be calculated. This is a difficult process. Table 2B provides the basis permitting an organization to thoroughly assess what it will take to re-create data lost during a hard-disk failure. Another example might be the costs incurred by the productive time being lost. This could be due to an unstable Window operating system on PC that tends to crash, thereby requiring a reboot of the machine.

Table 2C outlines how the Asset Value of information can be calculated based on having arrived at the total hard costs as well as the total soft costs.

For a more general approach see also Table 2D and Assurance below.

**Assessment** is a systematic review process of information system assets whereby an examining the information acquisition and review process of information (e.g., about following policies or ping attacks) is undertaken. This process is designed to assist the system owner to determine how best to use resources to protect information stored on organizational systems.

**Assurance** is a measure of confidence that the security features of an information system accurately mediates and enforces the security policy as well as the security measures undertaken to protect information Assets.

With the help of the Asset calculations (see also Tables 2A–2B) the firm than has to determine which measures it wants to take to further safeguard information Assets. Moreover, it also needs to calculate the costs of these measures and how effective they are (Cost and Benefit Analysis, cf. Table A.2C)

Table 2D outlines in four distinct steps what a firm can do to get value for its Assurance efforts regarding Critical Infrastructure Protection (CIP).

**Table 2B:** Value of Information—Soft Costs

| Equation | Description of Factor |
|---|---|
| | Soft costs (SC) (see Equations 1 and 2) are more difficult to calculate than the hard costs (HC) since we have to determine the value of information which in itself is a subjective process. For instance, |
| | 1) what is the value to the firm (i.e. medical database administrator or health agency) of a password file with 1200 accounts? |
| | 2) How much does it cost the firm or medical community including patients if the database is down for eight hours during the night and medical personnel are unable to access it to provide emergency health care, and neither are these records available on paper? |
| | 3) What are the costs for lost data/files due to a failure of a hard-disk for a notebook computer in a doctor's office assuming that the last back-up was done 12 hours ago? |
| | 4) What are the costs of lost material (e.g., sentences typed using a word processing program between the last automatic update and the system crash) because of random system crashes. For instance, Windows may crash requiring the user to reboot the system. In turn, productive work time is being lost every time this happens (PS. On average Windows crashes more than once a day, see GATES). |
| | 5) How dependable is the firm on the IS, asset and property that could be damaged because of a threat or a vulnerability? Could medical or sales personnel perform important work when the system is down? |
| (3) $\sum$ Soft Costs (SC) = $\sum$ FC (CF + R&D/C) + $\sum$ VC (OC + NR&D/C + AC) | In Equation 3, **CF** are the **confidence costs** incurred by the "disaster." Accordingly, every time a system is being shut down or data is being lost, users (e.g., doctors, nurses, sales representatives, purchasing clerks) loose confidence and require additional measures to feel safe. |
| | The organization has to put effort into reassuring users of the Reliability of the system. Again, this takes human effort and other resources that cost money. |
| | **R&D/C** are the **research and development costs/expenditures** that the firm incurs if data is lost from laboratory work due to a system or hard-disk crash. |
| | If we look at the **VC** part of Equation 3, **OC** represents the **opportunity costs** incurred due to the disaster (e.g., crashed system disk) where medical personnel could perform surgery needed by a patient instead of trying to keep a patient stable until receiving data from the patient's medical file. |

(Cont.)

**Table 2B:** (Cont.)

| Equation | Description of Factor |
|---|---|
| | **NR&D/C** are the **new research and development costs** which must be absorbed by the firm in order to either re-establish the medical database.<br><br>**AC** are the **additional costs** a firm may incur such as training/support of employees for retooling recovered system/data files, as well as the costs of lost productivity (e.g., health professionals are unable to perform their tasks because of system down-time, also dependability on the system). |

**Note.** The above provides a schema for arriving at the total soft costs incurred by the organization to create information (e.g., complete electronic patient records of all patients treated the last 12 months). There are no hard and fast rules for determining Soft Costs, hence it will take some time to assess these to get a better fell what Disaster Recovery measures might be necessary.

**Table 2C:** Asset Value of Data/Information or Object

| Equation | Description of Factor |
|---|---|
| | Once the Soft Costs as well as the Hard Costs have been calculated with the help of Equations 1–3 in Tables 2a–2b, the Asset Value of the object can than be obtained. |
| (4) $\sum$ Asset Value of the Object(AVO) $=$ | **AVO** represents the **asset value of the object** (e.g., data file, software, web page system and much more). |
| Equation 1 + AVO (SP + CAI) | **Shadow Pricing (SP)** plays an important role here whenever internal costing is difficult. For instance, internal or transfer pricing may not reflect market prices. Hence, shadow pricing is being used to arrive at realistic costs (see also Tables 2A and 2B).<br><br>**Cost accounting (CA)** may be used to determine the **Investment (I)** required to design and implement various components of the system. This applies to components that were developed in-house. Those also represent a value that needs to be included in the calculation. |

**Note.** The above represents the final steps that must be undertaken to arrive at the asset value, in turn permitting the organization to determine the information security investments justify to protect the informational asset. For further information see also Table 15C regarding costs and benefits of an Intrusion Detection System (IDS).

**Table 2D:** Assurance: Security—Costs and Benefits

| *What Can Be Done –* *Effective Steps* | *Value Firm Gets for Money Spent* |
|---|---|

Based on the Asset Value calculated (see Tables 2A–2C), the firm gets an insight about the type of costs that it may incur in case of a disaster. In turn, this should enable management to authorize the release of required additional human and financial resources for protecting the Assets that are under threat. Such decisions should help in reducing the risk for vulnerabilities being exploited, while possible threats materializing in a disaster.

| | |
|---|---|
| 1) Dedicate a staff person to maintain security systems such as:<br>—Firewalls,<br>—Anti-virus software,<br>—Passwords,<br>—Digital signatures,<br>—Loggers, and<br>—Vulnerability patches | This is a low cost option that provides great value for the amount of money spent. This individual is also responsible for installing the Patches in a timely fashion (see also Patches).<br><br>A Security Engineer will also free system personnel from doing their primary tasks well, thereby making sure that all systems are running smoothly. |
| 2) Develop and monitor security policies | Data protection, privacy, private email and other policies or items regarding security policies must be implemented in the organization.<br><br>Regular random checks are needed to assure that these policies achieve the tasks or objectives they were implemented for. |
| 3) Conducting regular security and penetration assessments and audits | Regular testing by Security Engineer and outsiders for vulnerabilities or script errors made, whilst updating certain resources (e.g., firm's webpage) should be done regularly to minimize Risks. |
| 4) Educating staff about security policies and security matters Promoting security awareness companywide | Similar to a fire drill, employees must have checklist on what to do if certain things happen (e.g., virus infection), and security drills enable workers to test these procedures to be ready when the "real" disaster happens (see also Table 17C and 17D).<br><br>This also requires that staff have a better understanding about security policies, how they are being monitored and why certain rules may apply<br><br>Employees comprehending the efforts as outlined above are the key, in order to reduce the risk of policy violations and behavior that can exacerbate vulnerabilities, risks and threats. |

**Note.** There are many more steps that can be done in addition to the above but these provide a high return for investment and are, therefore, included in the table. Most important is that first the firm tries to determine the value of information assets and what it will cost if downtime occurs or information is being corrupted, ends in the wrong hands or lost.

If these deliberations were done and results have been written down, it will be relatively easy to justify the few resources needed to realize the four approaches as outlined in the Table.

If information has not been assigned a value, implementing the above steps will be difficult because accountants will have a difficult time understanding and justifying the expenses incurred by these actions.

**A**

**Asymmetrical Digital Subscriber Line (ADSL)**   allows voice, video and data to be transmitted over a single telephone line at up to 6.144 megabits per second (Mbps) in a single direction, with significantly slower speeds in the other direction. Accordingly, it is very appropriate for downloading large amounts of data but for certain applications, such as video-conferencing, other technologies work better [see also Very-High-bit-rate Digital Subscriber Line (VDSL), Discrete Multi-Tone (DMT) modulation, Quadrature Amplitude Modulation (QAM-VDSL)].

**Attack**   is a single unauthorized access attempt, or unauthorized use attempt, regardless of success. Success may or may not result in the alteration, releasing or denying of data. The likelihood of success depends on the effectiveness of implemented security measures that reduce the risk and probability for a threat resulting in a compromised system (see also Figures 1–3). Computer networks make it easier to start attacks and speed their dissemination, or for one anonymous individual to reach vast numbers of people at virtually no cost.

Defending against Attacks means engineering in a world ruled by Satan's Law. The differences between Attacks and Accidents are intent, intelligence, and control. Things go wrong because there is a malicious and intelligent adversary trying to force things to go wrong (see Security Engineering)

Table 3A outlines a taxonomy of the attacks that can be launched against information resources and infrastructure. The types of attacks that are of greatest concerns to Security Engineers are:

**Syntactic Attacks**   threatening the operating logic of computers and networks (see Table 3A for a definition, Incident).

**Semantic Attacks**   involve misinformation in written or verbal language regarding the attacked (see Table A.3A for definition).

Graphically, Syntactic and/or Semantic Attacks involving Information and Webpage content are outlined in Figure 2. Similarly the organization needs to apply:

- Primary Prevention = reduce risk for and incidence of access,
- Secondary Prevention = shortening unauthorized access and use, and
- Tertiary Prevention = reducing number & impact of complications (see also Prevention)

Unauthorized Access does not automatically result in Unauthorized Use because depending on how the access was gained, Role-Based Access may very much limit the privileges the user may have attained by cracking a particular password (see also Prevention).

**Table 3A:** Taxonomy of Attacks

| | Description of Attack |
|---|---|
| Physical | These are made against the computers, wires, and electronics. These were the first kinds of attacks the internet defended itself against. Distributed protocols reduce the dependency on any one computer. Redundancy removes single points of failure. Physical outages caused by power failure, data or other scenarios have caused problems. Nonetheless, these kind of problems are known, understood and can be solved or protected against. |
| Syntactic | These are against the operating logic of computers and networks. This second wave of attacks target vulnerabilities in software products, problems with cryptographic algorithms and protocols, and denial-of-service vulnerabilities. This is a moving target and requires constant vigilance on part of security people. While we have a pretty good idea about the problem here, detection and response processes suggest that our measures of security have not improved much over the last few years. This type of attack contains pretty much over 90% of what has occurred recently including media attention given. |
| Semantic | These target the way we assign meaning to content. In our society, people tend to believe what they read in newspapers or on the web. Most often we fail to corroborate the veracity of that information, by examining the credentials of the site, finding alternate opinions, and so on. Even if one were, it still depends if the writer from newspaper B verified the information presented as fact or truth by the reporter writing in newspaper A. The success of Hoaxes would suggest that much information is getting amplified and eventually being taken as the truth. A person with malicious intent can achieve the same. |

Falsifying input into a computer process can be much more devastating than a physcial or syntactic attack, simply because the computer cannot demand all the corroborating input that people have instinctively come to rely on. Indeed, computers are often incapable of deciding what the "corroborating input" would be, or how to go about using it in any meaningful way. Hence, falsifying book sale records, stock prices or epidemological data about a medical virus can result in books becoming 'bestsellers', stocks falling significantly due to automatic sell order further exacerbating the effect and people possibly panicking about a disease.

It seems quite likely that Semantic Attacks will be more serious than Physical or Syntactic Attacks. They cannot be dismissed with cryptographic magic wands of "digital signatures," "authentication," or "integrity." What makes Semantic Attacks so devastating is that they directly target the human/computer interface. This is the most insecure interface on the internet. Only amateurs attack machines; skillful Hackers or professionals target people. And any possible reduction in the Risk of such a Threat materializing requires putting the user at the core of any possible counter strategy, not the math problem (see also Information Warfare).

**Note.** The above provides a general description of the three types of attacks against IT infrastructures (see also Table 3b, Figures 1–3).

Physical and Syntactic Attacks may have embedded in them certain attribute that could help in classifying these attacks. Table A.3B outlines these possibilities ranging from Strategic to Jump Point to Scumware. Because there is no established and adhered to list of Attack Attributes, this list may change over time (see Table 3B) [see also Short Message Service (SMS) Flood].

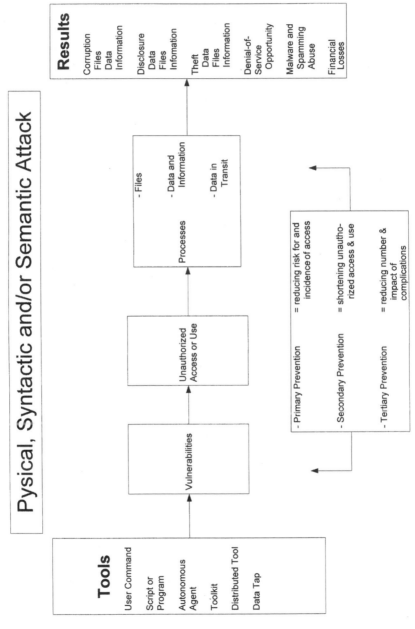

## Pysical, Syntactic and/or Semantic Attack

**Tools**

User Command

Script or
Program

Autonomous
Agent

Toolkit

Distributed Tool

Data Tap

Vulnerabilities → Unauthorized Access or Use → Processes

- Files

- Data and
  Information

- Data in
  Transit

- Primary Prevention    = reducing risk for and
                          incidence of access

- Secondary Prevention  = shortening unautho-
                          rized access & use

- Tertiary Prevention   = reducing number &
                          impact of
                          complications

**Results**

Corruption
Files
Data
Information

Disclosure
Data
Files
Infomation

Theft
Data
Files
Information

Denial-of-
Service
Opportunity

Malware and
Spamming
Abuse

Financial
Losses

**Figure 2**  Prevention mechanisms for reducing unauthorized access or use.

# Pysical, Syntactic and/or Semantic Attack

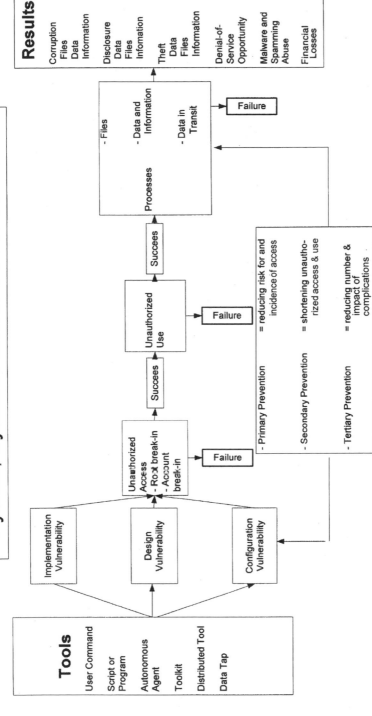

* Failure may result in an unsuccessful attempt for access. or use. Encryption may not prevent the stealing of data but attacker may be unable to decipher information.

**Figure 3** Attack resulting in unauthorized access and use of processes with various results as outcome thereoff - Awarenness and Prevention are key for increasing security.

25

A

A

**Table 3B:** Attributes of Attacks

| Attribute of Attack | Description |
|---|---|
| | The description below suggest that any of these can be embedded in a:<br>—physical or<br>—syntactic<br><br>attack as described in Table 3A. |
| Collateral Damage | These have identified a third party as the target but their spillover affects another party, hence a virus may have been sent to a colleague who inadvertently had it also sent to other team members by using addresses listed in the email program |
| Exploit | Uses a specific instance of a Vulnerability or loophole. The Love Bug worm could be described as exploiting the fact that Windows 32-bit (Win32) systems use only the final filename extension as an indicator of file type, and the default installation of Windows Script Host with Windows 98, Windows 2000, and Internet Explorer 5 and higher. |
| Integrity | These types may try to reduce the firm's credibility by launching an anti-Web site or cyber squatting efforts on domain names. |
| Jump Point | These are exemplified by Distributed Denial of Service (DDoS) attacks, whereby a large target is attacked through numerous systems. This could occur through P2P file sharing whereby thousands of home systems are being used to attack a major system. The network traffic from all these systems to one IP address makes the latter confused and possibly shutting down. |
| Leapfrog | Means that userid and password information was obtained illicitly from one host to compromise another host such as Telnetting through several hosts in order to preclude a trace, a standard cracker procedure (see also Cracker). |
| Negative Acknowledgement | Means using a penetration technique that capitalizes on the potential weakness in an operating system. It does not handle asynchronous interrupts properly, thereby leaving the system in an unprotected state during such interrupts. |
| Random Skirmish | Here automated tools are being used to scan large numbers of IP addresses, looking for holes and open ports to be exploited resulting in numerous 'skirmishes.' |
| Scumware | This type is software or program code that may alter webpage content or re-route visitors to another webpage (see also Scumware). |
| Strategic Effort | The attacker identified a specific target, this could be an information system, a firm or an individual |
| Replay or Forgery Attack | Whereby an attacker could trick the server into authenticating the attacker using the same authentication data as a valid user. Replay attacks can be prevented by encrypting IP traffic. |

**Note.** Except for strategic and integrity attribute of an attack, the above attributes do not apply to semantic attacks.

**Table 3C:** Elements of Attacks

| Element | Description |
| --- | --- |
| | Each attack has some elements ensconced. Below is a list provided without any order of importance or completeness. Each of the taxonomies (Table 3A) and their attributes (Table 3B) (e.g., Random Skirmish as part of a Semantic Attack) may encompass certain elements. |
| | Every element may have to be described (e.g., characteristics) to further understand an Attack. |
| Method | What methods are being used for the Attack (see also Tables 3A and especially Table 3B)? |
| Tool | The types of tools being used for the Attack (e.g., Sniffer and/or self-propagating Worm)? |
| Target | Is the Attack pursuing a particular target or is it acting non-preferentially (e.g., virus infects all vulnerable hosts it can find)? |
| Criticality | Is the target part of the organization's Critical Infrastructure? |
| Risk and Worry | Is there a Risk (i.e. probability of and perceived Risk) that the Attack will succeed (see Tables 22B–22D)? |
| Outcomes | Based on the above, what are the chances that the Attacker's planned outcomes will materialize and what are other possible ones? |
| Costs | What are the financial considerations and possible ramifications (e.g., service level agreements require compensation) (see Asset Value, Tables 2A–2C, Tables 7A–7B)? |
| Human | Are humans involved directly in the Attack or only indirectly (e.g., by having released a program that is now being spread automatically). Is it a single party or a group of people (see also Motive). |
| Motive | What is the objective for the Attacker(s) (e.g., criminal, mischievous, malicious and/or political)? |

**Note.** The above elements should be addressed to all types of Attacks (see Table 3A).

**Attitudes** are generally seen as a disposition to respond in a **favorable** or **unfavorable manner** to an object. They may be made up of beliefs and feelings that lead an individual to respond consistently to people, ideas, and situations

In the context of security, what attitudes employees have toward the Risk of Threats, Vulnerabilities or their possible consequences if they are realized may affect their behavior regarding cautionary strategies followed in order to reduce the Risks, for Vulnerabilities to be exploited (see also Threat).

Attitudes are not directly observed but, rather, they are hypothetical constructs. They are thus measured indirectly, and apart from the requirement of targeting like-dislike judgments, any formulation can be used in the operationalization of attitudes. To simplify the measurement, it is useful to refer to

**A**

attitude structures. A tripartite structure is often used for measuring attitudes, and goes back at least to Plato. It discriminates three components, namely:

1) cognition, formed by perceptions and beliefs;
2) affect, by feelings and emotional reactions (see also Affect); and
3) conation, by intentions and overt behaviors

**Attributes**   are the person's characteristics (e.g., being tall and skinny).

In the context here Attributes can be defined as the characteristics assigned to all files and directories. The attributes could be Read only, Archive, Hidden or System.

**Audit**   is the process whereby records and activities are examined to ensure compliance with established controls, policy, and operational procedures. Internal or external audits often recommend possible changes in controls, policy, or procedures to further safeguard information resources (see also Authorization, see also Table 4A–4C, 5C & Table 6).

**Audit Log or Audit Trail**   details chronologically how system resources have been used and what amendments were made to records. The information collected includes but is not limited to:

- user login,
- file access,
- file alterations,
- process execution,
- other activities

and whether any actual or attempted security violations occurred, legitimate or unauthorized (see also Table 6).

The majority of commercial systems feature the creation of an audit log. The latter permits subsequent review of all system activity, and provides details about which User performed which action to which files, and when. Failing to produce an audit log means that the activities on the system are 'lost'. The information collected through an Audit Log or Audit Trail can then be used in the event of system recovery being required.

**Vulnerability Audit**   means that IT assets are scanned for known vulnerabilities and weaknesses. Security scans may be scheduled and these tests may include suggested fixed or mitigation steps. Such Vulnerability scans may be used to test Firewall and Intrustion Dedection Systems (IDSs) and Audit data may be compared to benchmarks, Metrics for additional information.

**Authentication**   results in positively verifying the identity of a user, device, or another entity in an information system. This is often a prerequisite for allowing access to resources offered by a system (see also Access, Password, Tables 4A–4C).

One element that contributes to the reliability of individual authentication is good password management practices (see also Password). In an area of high risk, stronger authentication may be required such as:

- **Asymmetric Keys**—see Access Control
- **Biometrics**—see Biometrics
- **Cryptographic Tokens**—see Cryptography
- **Digital Certificates**—see Digital Certificate
- **Smart Cards**—see Smart Card
- **One-Time Password Generators**—where password can be used once only.

Stronger authentication relies on combining **one or more** of the following:

- password / Pin or something else user knows,
- token or other means, that is something user has, and finally,
- biometrics or other technique enabling system to identify who the person is.

The above means may be used to verify the true source of a message or data. But all approaches have their weak spots and combinations of measures are usually more effective (see also Table 4A–4C).

In case of electronic voting, the term refers to verification that an electronic ballot really comes from the person it claims to have been initiated by, and not from an imposter (see also Tables 10A and 10B).

**Authentication Header (AH)** is the field that follows the IP header in an IP datagram. It provides authentication and integrity checking for the datagram.

**Autonomous Agents** is a program or program fragment which operates independently from the user to exploit vulnerabilities.

**Autopsy Forensic Browser (autopsy)** is a graphical front-end for *The @Stake Sleuth Kit (TASK)*.

**Authorization** is the process whereby an individual approves an event or action. Audit Trails must, therefore, identify both the creator and the authorizer of new or amended data, files or records (see also Audit Log or Audit Trail, Record).

It is probably most effective to have one person change or amend records, while another authorizes these actions (see also Table 5C).

**Auto Dial-Back** is designed to ensure that 'dial up' links to the organization's communications network may only be accessed from approved / registered external phone numbers. The computer holds a list / register of user IDs and

A

passwords together with telephone numbers. When a remote call is received from one of these users the computer checks that ID and password match and then cuts off the connection and dials back to the 'registered' telephone number held in the computer files.

To overcome the mobility issue, mobile phone numbers may be registered as well, permitting staff to connecting their mobile to their notebook, while connecting to the system (see also Bluetooth, Wireless).

**Automated Security Incident Measurement (ASIM)**   permits the monitoring of network traffic and the collecting of information on targeted unit networks by detecting unauthorized activity on the network.

**Automated Security Monitoring**   are all the security features needed to provide an acceptable level of protection for hardware, software, as well as classified, or critical data, material, or processes in the system.

**Availability**   is the property that data, information, as well as the necessary systems, are all accessible and useable on a timely basis as required to perform various tasks. An example might be where medical personnel must have access to electronic patient records during a massive power outage (see also Table 5—Confidentiality, Integrity, and Availability).

**Awareness**   (noun of aware) means having or showing realization, perception, or knowledge. Aware implies vigilance in observing or alertness in drawing inferences from what one experiences such as being aware of changes in the Threat level of computer Viruses.

Teaching users about security is not an easy task. Security professionals tend to be more comfortable fiddling with firewalls or installing intrusion-detection systems than educating end users about safe computing practices.

Moreover, management doesn't usually expect security professionals to be skilled communicators.

Obviously, having employees with solid technical skills is important, but the importance of communicating Security Policy to end users is critical because it helps improve users' cooperation in security initiatives and therefore should not be given short shrift.

As security teams focus on Policy and Audit/compliance, the success of those security initiatives depends on obtaining cooperation from end users, customers, citizens, management, and IT experts.

**Security Awareness**   is a term used to describe the understanding of security requirements and methods. For instance, governments may operate security awareness programs to making home users aware about:

- the need for information security,
- the threats to information security and, most importantly,

A

- the methods for maintaining, and
- improving information security, while
- becoming vigilant about their home information/system(s) security level(s).

Security awareness and security awareness training should be built into the Security Policy and organization adheres to and, thereby being part of the contract of employment (see Table 23D).

Home and corporate users must understand and be able to distinguish between safety measures and procedures and those things involving Security (see Table 23A, 23B, and 23C for a definition of these terms).

If a user is Aware of the inherent Risks (see Table 22B) linked to certain actions, Worry may motivate him or her to take the necessary steps for Prevention, thereby reducing Damages and much other outcomes that are not desirable (e.g., loss of data, Privacy violations). Finally, Security Awareness is a continuous effort that requires Learning and refreshing people's memories to enable them to comply with Policies (see also Audit).

**B2B**   see Business to Business

**B2C**   see Business to Consumer

**Backdoor**   is a hidden feature of an application prepared by its designer or maintainers. The backdoor gives the programmer special privileges for running the application. These privileges are not available to the user.

The motivation for such holes is not always sinister; some operating systems, for example, come out of the box with privileged accounts intended for use by field service technicians or the vendor's maintenance programmers. But we are not sure if such an account should be called backdoor – in our understanding, backdoor is a hidden feature. Yes, these accounts were sometimes hidden, Microsoft NT 3.51 and then they could be called backdoors, but generally they are not hidden.

**Back Orifice (BO)**   is probably most successful hacking tool ever written for hacking Microsoft Windows 9x systems. Back Orifice 2000 (BO2K) targets Microsoft Windows 2000 computers.

**Backup**   (see also Restore Data) is the process where copies of computer files are taken in order to allow recreation of the original, should the need arise. A backup is a spare copy of a file, file system, or other resource for use in the event of failure or loss of the original.

Backup copies must be kept at a different site or in a fire-resistant safe/ location. Hence, backups of a notebook's hard-disk should be stored on a network drive and subsequently backed up from there.

**Backup Power Generator**   (see also Uninterruptible Power Supply—UPS)

**Batch Files** are files usually describing automated sequence of commands. These are used in mainframe operations where even special languages were developed for creation of batches. Shell scripts known in the UNIX world can also be considered in some cases as batch files. In MS-DOS and MS Windows context, these files are characterized by a .BAT extension. These text files contain MS-DOS commands, one on each line of the file that are processed in sequential order, for example when the computer is booted (e.g., Autoexec.bat).

**Behavior Blocker** is similar to an Activity Monitor. It not only alerts users to unusual or dangerous operations, but more importantly, restricts them from doing certain operations.

**Bell-La Padula Security Model (BLPSM)** is a model of computer security policy that outlines the formal set of access controls that should be used to provide users access based on information sensitivity and subject authorizations.

**Benchmarking** is generally understood as comparing the performance of a system, unit or organization against other similar types of systems, units or organizations. Key indicators used depend on the purpose but a Security Audit may use benchmarking methods to compare the performance of one unit to other similar ones to establish a lower and upper level of Security Risks, Vulnerabilities and possible Threats and successful system Penetrations.

Developing a benchmarking definition is the first step for implementing a company-wide, formal benchmarking methodology for improving business performance. This tool defines what benchmarking is and what the benefits will be for the organization including its goals and objectives with this program (see also Metrics).

One of the biggest mistakes occurs when beginning the benchmarking endeavor by only looking to benchmark someone within one's own industry. While this is also interesting it seems more fruitful in benchmarking an organization that is well known for being a good model (e.g., customer service, IT security and logistics). Sometimes this is also referred to as Best Practices, exemplary practices, business excellence.

Lack of enthusiasm, lack of commitment, and a lack of implementation can leave participants dissatisfied. Finally, Benchmarking focuses on the **past** and not necessarily the **future**, hence, the firm is trying to improve to catch up. Instead, it might be better making several quick and small steps forward into the right direction, helping the firm to stay ahead of competition (see also Metrics, Quality).

**Bench testing** is the procedure whereby verification of the software is undertaken making sure that it performs in accordance with System Requirements (see also System Requirement).

B

Can also be testing of new/revised software by the developers. Bench testing is a critical step in the software development process and precedes the more 'formal' User Acceptance process and testing.

Bench testing should verify that the software performs in accordance with system requirements.

**Berkeley Internet Name Domain (BIND)**   see Domain Name

**Best Practice**   are well working practices usually in an industry and/or field, such as information technology, and have culminated in successful results (see also Benchmarking). However, they can vary from country to country, from region to region and even within countries from organization to organization.

Best Practice codes or standards in an industry are used in order to help promote consistency and therefore, Trust and Confidence regarding the internet by citizens and customers.

Best Practices can be a published document which sets out technical specifications or other criteria necessary to ensure that a material, or method will consistently do the job it is intended to. Best Practice standards play an important role in the spread of e-Commerce by establishing common platforms, languages and protocols that are available to anyone to use, ensuring that systems are interoperable (see also Standards).

In the case of Damages (see Tables 2D and 15C) or Liability (see also Table 16A) demonstrating the use of Best Practice measures for Hardening the Operating System and taking other precautionary measures to improve security may be required to proof to a court that the organization has taken the necessary or standard steps to protect its information Assets against intrusion, unauthorized use and launching attacks against other systems (see also Testing - Testing and Liability).

**Bibra Integrity Model**   is a formal security model for the integrity of subjects and objectives in a system.

**BIND**   see Domain Name

**Binders**   are programs permitting hackers to 'bind' two or more programs together resuling in a single .EXE file. Hence, harmless .EXE animations, e-greetings or other such files could have a Trojan horse inserted (see also Trojan Horse) (see also Figure 5).

The only way to stop an executable from harming a PC or system is to run it in a proactive 'sandbox' environment and monitor its behavior for malicious activity in real-time.

**BIOS**   (Basic Input/Output System) contains the instructions for the computer stored on one of its chips and used by the operating system to access the hardware in the computer. The Bios also controls the flow of data to/from the operating system and peripheral devices, such as printer, hard disk, keyboard and mouse.

**Biometrics**    identification systems are based on the recognition of unique morphological characteristics of each individual, so that only the physical presence of the person will allow access to the system. Numerous biometric parameters are available such as:

- facial,
- iris,
- fingerprints,
- hand and finger geometry,
- signature and
- voice recognition.

Although iris recognition has stronger security credentials, fingerprints are often preferred due to the maturity of the technology (see also Access Control, Smart Cards).

As Table 4A outlines, Retina Scan, Iris Scan and Hand Geometry are most accurate and both, the **False Rejection Rate** (FRR) and the **False Acceptance Rate** (FAR) are quite low for these Authentication measures based on Biometrics.

In Table 4B other measures are outlined that can be used for Access Control. Often a system may use a Magnetic Swipe Card and a Keypad Entry System to give an employee access to a restricted office area or a database. Some of the time a system such as the ones outlined in Table 4B may also be combined with one of those described and explained in Table 4C. Unfortunately, all the one's in Table 4C do have, however, some severe weaknesses that limit their Reliability and Validity. In particular the FRR and FAR may not be satisfactory.

For instance, during May 2002 a Japanese group of researchers reported that using fake fingerprints fashioned from gelatin were able to fool biometric fingerprint readers 80% of the time. The researchers also devised a way to create fake fingerprints from fingerprints left on glass surfaces.

What is interesting is that the material needed to make this work, was purchased at a neighborhood store and cost less than Euro 11. This attack is a classic **replay** (or **forgery**) attack. Unfortunately, replays are not unique to fingerprints but are a fundamental Vulnerability of all Biometrics (see also Table 3B).

The American Civil Liberties Union (ACLU) published a report during May 2002 about the inaccuracy of tests using facial recognition technology at the Palm Beach (FL) International Airport. The technology failed to correctly identify faces more than half of the time. The recognition rate went down when people wore glasses, turned their heads, or were moving.

**Table 4A:** Biometrics and Authentication - Access Controls

| Factors | Description of Factor | |
|---|---|---|
| | **How it Works** | **Effectiveness** |
| Retina Scan Cost of Device: $2–2,500 | Device projects a low-intensity infrared light through the pupil and onto the retina. Patterns of the retina's blood vessels are measured at over 400 points to generate a 96-bute template | Considered the most accurate and reliable of the biometric technology. Regarded as virtually impossible to replicate the image produced by a human retina. FRRs can be 0.1% and FARs about 0.0001% (1 in 1,000,000). |
| Iris Scan Cost of Device: $3,500–5,000 | Based on the unique visible characteristics of the eye's iris, the colored ring that surrounds the pupil. Every eye's iris is different from another | Considered one of the more secure identity verification methods, the odds of two different irises returning identical templates is 1 in $10^{52}$. Technology cannot be foiled by wearing contact lenses or an artificial eye FRR about 6% and FAR between 1–2% |
| Hand Geometry Cost of Device: $2–4,000 | Collects over 90 automated measurements of many dimensions of the hand and fingers | FAR and FRR of less than 0.1%. |

**Note.**  Retina Scan, combined with Proximity Cards and a Keypad Entry System whereby every person that requires access has a unique alphanumeric code, should work well for a restricted area (see also Table 2B).

Hand Geometry and Proximity Cards with a Keypad Entry System are less intrusive than the above and should suffice for most workplaces. These approaches can also be used in conjunction with password navigation through a virtual world or by using a single image (e.g., anatomical drawing of the bones of the body whereby a special sequence must be identified) to further strengthen security (see Table 20A—Picture and Password).

Critical measures for comparing authentication instruments are:

1) FAR is the False Acceptance Rate, and
2) FRR is the False Rejection Rate (FRR)

The above explains why some of the measures outlined in Table 4C may not be satisfactory for Authentication purposes.

Strong authentication requires at least two forms of evidence (something only one person has, knows, is, or can do), of which at least one is implemented in such a way as to resist replay. Searching for the perfect authenticator such as:

• easy to use,
• can be reconciled at a distance,
• easy to enroll,

**Table 4B:** Authentication - Access Controls

| Factors | Description of Factor | |
| --- | --- | --- |
| **Combination** | **How it Works** | **Effectiveness** |
| Magnetic Swipe Cards Cost of Reader: $150–300, each card about $1 | Inserting or swiping a uniquely coded access card through a reader. | Does not verify person, it only confirms that the individual has a card. Not acceptable as a stand-alone system. |
| Proximity Cards Cost of Reader: $750, each card about $5 | Contains an embedded ratio frequency (RF) antenna that constantly transmits a low-level fixed RF signal | Does not verify person, it only confirms that the individual has a card. Not acceptable as a stand-alone system. |
| Smart Cards Cost of Reader: $20 and higher, each card about $3–35 | Increasingly used in one-to-one verification applications comparing a user's biometric data such as a fingerprint or hand geometry with the biometric template stored on the smart card. | Does verify person is the individual as claimed but there are problems that question the merit of this system.[1] |
| Keypad Entry Systems Cost of Device: $ 250 and up | Users can enter by first entering a passcode (a PIN or special code). Usually used in conjunction with an ID card and card reader | Keypad-only system requires a passcode that may be inadvertently shared with others or "stolen" If used in conjunction with a card reader, individual must also present something they have, namely the authorized card to gain entry. |

**Note.** Retina Scan, combined with Proximity Cards and a Keypad Entry System whereby every person that requires access has a unique alphanumeric code, works well for a restricted area (see also Table 2A and 2C). Hand Geometry and Proximity Cards with a Keypad Entry System is less intrusive than the above and should suffice for most workplaces.

Often a Keypad Entry System with an ID card and card reader is all that is needed for most workplaces to be secured enough.

Critical measures for comparing authentication instruments are:

1) FAR is the False Acceptance Rate, and

2) FRR is the False Rejection Rate (FRR)

[1] With Smart Cards, if biometric data is being used such as a fingerprint a new problem arises. Namely the problem with fingerprinting is also that as long as fingerprinting equipment cannot detect the **difference between a live finger and a dummy**, biometric fingerprint sensors should not be used in combination with identity cards or any medium to high security applications such as a patient's digitized medial records.

Identity cards with fingerprint biometrics are in fact weaker than cards without it illustrated by these two examples:

1. Suppose, because of the fingerprint check, there is no longer visual identification by a security guard. Accordingly, if the fingerprint matches with the template in the card, then access is granted if it is a valid and not a blacklisted card.

    For the person whose card is blacklisted, he or she can purchase a valid identity card with matching dummy fingerprint (only 15 minutes work) and still get access without anyone noticing this.

2. All else held constant, visual identification is still used and in case of doubt (the look-alike problem of two individuals) then the fingerprint will be checked.

    When the photo on the identity card and the person do not really match and the official asks for fingerprint verification, most likely the positive result of the fingerprint scan will prevail. That is, the "OK" from the technical fingerprint system will remove any (legitimate) doubt.

    The combination of identity cards and biometric fingerprint sensors results in Risks of which not many people are aware (see also Table 4C).

**B**

**Table 4C:** Biometrics and Authentication: Less Effective Access Controls

| *Factors* | *Description of Factor* | |
|---|---|---|
| | **How it Works** | **Effectiveness** |
| Fingerprint Scan Cost of Device: $1–3,000 plus $4 software fee for each user enrolled | Fingerprint recognition uses the impressions made by the unique, minute, ridge formations or patterns found on the fingertips. | FRR of 0.01% claimed by vendors but tests show nearly 50% |
| Facial Recognition Cost of Device: $15,000 but each entry point also needs a software licence in the range of $650–4,500 each | This system captures facial images from video cameras and generates templates for comparing a live facial scan of an individual to a stored template. | Testing shows about 51% correctly matched and identified images. |
| Speaker Verification Cost of Device: $70–250 per enrolled user | Based on a created voice template using the unique characteristics of an individual's vocal tract, resulting in differences in the cadence, pitch, and tone of a person's voice. Often used for telephony and call centers | Equal error rates between 1–6% when fixed set of enrolled pass phrases are used. |
| Signature Recognition Cost of Device: $375 for a signature recognition tablet | Uses personal rhythm, acceleration, and pressure flow. | Not very reliable |

**Note.** The methods described in this table do not appear to justify the costs compared to the security and accuracy of methods offered. These appear more effective while offering a better return on investment (ROI) than those in Table 4A and 4B. Nonetheless, final decision has to be made considering the circumstances the identification system will be used for. (For further approaches see also Table 20A.)

Critical measures for comparing authentication instruments are:

1) FAR is the False Acceptance Rate, and
2) FRR is the False Rejection Rate (FRR)

- cannot be forgotten, lost, stolen or copied, and
- easy to implement

means looking for the impossible.

**Biometrics and Economics** means that in reality the high total cost of ownership for a biometric or smartcard infrastructure prevents the majority of individuals and small businesses from implementing them as authentication measures (see Tables 4A–4C for costs).

Internet sites are forced to rely on information to which only one person should have access, usually a Username and Password system. But the reality is that online environments should be treated as hostile (see also Identity Theft—Authentication).

**Bit** is the smallest unit of data and its value can be either 0 (zero) or 1 (one). All data are coded in bits.

Hard disks/memories are designed to store data in bit multiples called, such as:

- Bytes – B (8 bits)
- Kilobytes – KB (1024 Bytes)
- Megabytes – MB (1024 Kilobytes is a small novel or a 3.5 inch floppy disk contains 1.5 Megabytes), or
- Gigabytes – GB (1024 Megabytes)

Put differently:

- 1 Exabyte = 1,000,000,000,000,000,000 bytes or $10^{18}$ bytes (2 Exabytes represent the total volume of information generated during 1999 - see Information),
- 1 Petabyte = 1,000 terabytes (1,024,000,000 Megabytes or 2 Petabytes are all USA academic research libraries combined),
- 1 Terabyte = 1,000 Gigabytes (1,024,000 Megabytes or 1,000,000,000,000 Bytes or $10^{12}$ bytes, 500,000 tress made into paper and printed, 2 terabytes is what an academic research library may contain),
- 1 Gigabyte = 1,024 Megabytes (one pick-up truck with books)

A retailer such as Wal-Mart is already storing over 200 terabytes of data including information from its customers and suppliers.

The world's largest print library is the USA's Library of Congress in Washington, containing about:

- 26,000,000 (19 million books and other print collections) represent about
- 10,000,000,000,000 (10 terabytes of information, "Tera" means 1 trillion - 1 followed by 12 zeros.)

The above is quite a bit of information but compared to the Internet Archive (WayBack Machine) it is not that much. The Internet Archive goes back to 1996 and contains:

- more than 100 terabytes of data and is growing by
- 10 to 12 terabytes a month

More on this topic can also be found under Information - Quantity Produced per Year.

**Bitloss** occurs when data bits are lost during transmission. Bit loss can be counteracted by use of Control Totals (see also Control Total).

**Blackhat**   is another term for Hacker. However, the term blackhat is usually used for a skilled hacker only.

**Blended Attack**   is sometimes used to describe Cybercrime (see Cybercrime, Hybrid Threat or also Blended Threat—Table 24D).

**Blended Threat**   see Hybrid Threat (also Table 24D)

**Bloatware**   means software with minimal functionality, requring a disproportionate amount of disk space and memory. This term is very common in the Windows world.

**Block Cipher**   is an encryption scheme in which data are divided into fixed-size blocks (often 64 bits), each of which is encrypted independently of the others. Complete independence of blocks is cryptographically undesirable, so usually a block cipher will be used in a chaining or feedback mode in which the output from one block affects the way the next is encrypted (see also Tables 11A and 11B).

**Bluetooth**   is short-range radio that can be stuck on anything, including a mobile phone or computer as well a ticket barrier, or a trolley full of supermarket goods. In turn, users can use the technology to connect various devices (e.g., computer and stereo) or pay at the train waving their Bluetooth enabled technology (e.g., card or mobile phone) to have the fare added to their monthly bill (see also Cybercash, Auto Dial-Back).
    Bluetooth was named after a 10th century Danish King, Harald Bluetooth. The standard was founded by Ericsson in 1994 but it was joined by Nokia, IBM and Intel in 1998 to form the Bluetooth Special Interest Group that campaigns for further Bluetooth adoption (see Wireless).

**Blue Screen of Death (BSOD)**   is a term used in relations to Microsoft Windows operating systems. Some crashes of these systems appear as a blues screen with white hexadecimal text (part of memory dump). Many users consider this a useless information, however it can be often used to detect misbehaving programs (often not from Microsoft) causing these fatal crashes.

**Bomb**   is a general synonym for software crashes or operating system failures. It is also used in relation to specially crafted segment of program code, often executed at specific time—see Time Bomb.

**Bot**   see Robot

**Boot**   means starting up a PC or server. Comes from the recognition that starting up a system is a process, whereby a piece of 'boostrap' code in the BIOS of the computer is needed. It starts the load-up of the operating system.

**B**

**Boot Sector** is the first logical sector of a disk. In a floppy disk it is situated on side 0 (the top), cylinder 0 (the outside), sector 1 (the first sector). On the hard disk, the boot sector is found on the first logical sector of the disk.

**Boot Disk** allows the user to start the PC or server when one cannot do so from the hard drive. These disks can also be used when a PC has been deliberately configured by technical staff to refuse to run without the Key Disk present, a simple security feature.

**Bottleneck** is a place where the problems, usually related to speed, occur. Such problems many include but not be limited to:

* not enough of memory,
* not enough of processor speed, or
* small transfer rate of network connection in a case of distributed systems.

**Bottlenecking** see Email Bombing

**Breach** is the successful penetration or defeat of security controls, thereby exposing information assets or system components unduly. In fact, a Breach could result in a Penetration of a system.

**Brief** describes a short document (e.g., 2–10 pages double-spaced text is probably about the maximum) outlining in non-technical language certain security related parameters such as Benchmarks, good practice or guidelines for pro-active defense efforts that reduce the risk for security disasters to materialize (see also Advisory, Alert, Report, Scenario).

A brief is intended to give a non-technical person a concise and explicit overview of an important aspect of IT and wireless security. As such, a brief from security staff is an important first step in alerting readers (e.g., policy makers) to a security area that requires further attention (see Alert, Awareness).

**Briefing Notice** may entail general information or advice to maintain good security practices including such as details of software Vulnerabilities and patches (see also Alert, Advisory, Technical Note).

**Broadband** is high-speed internet access. Broadband may be delivered to private households with Asymmetrical Digital Subscriber Line (ADSL), Digital Subscriber Line (DSL), Cable TV lines, Fixed Wireless Access or even satellite supported broadband in more remote areas.

From a security perspective, the consequence of many households having access to the internet with ever faster broadband connections is that the number of computers with static (and what's worse often dynamic) IP addresses and more or less permanent connections to the internet is increasing rapidly. This is likely to increase the Risk for Viruses and Malicious Code in spreading at a high and sustainable rate. Hence, countermeasures may fail to penetrate the population at a rate allowing the situation to be controlled (e.g., DDoS attacks through P2P networks, or sharing music files containing malicious codes that coul launche a remote Attack).

For instance, W97M/Groov.A virus shows that the virus spreads slowly but has had rapid increase in infections at various points in time in the past, even though all anti-virus systems are capable of detecting and removing the virus. The uptake and use of anti-virus protection does appear insufficient to prevent W97M/Groov.A or other viruses such as SirCam or Klez.H from spreading at a high and sustainable rate long afterwards. Broadband connections for households will further exacerbate this problem (see also Market—Digital Divide).

**Routers, and Broadband for Home Users and Small and Medium Sized Enterprises (SMEs)** exacerbates this challenge. For instance on August 21, the University of Wisconsin-Madison revealed that beginning in May 2003, it discovered being the recipient of a continuous large scale flood of inbound Internet traffic destined for one of the campus' public Network Time Protocol (NTP) servers.

NTP servers are used to synchronize computer clocks on the Internet. The flood traffic rate was hundreds-of-thousands of packets-per-second, and hundreds of megabits-per-second. The problems are far from being resolved.

The university determined the sources of this flooding were literally hundreds of thousands of real Internet hosts throughout the world. What was thought to be a malicious distributed denial-of-service (DDoS) attack, turned out to be a serious flaw in the design of hundreds of thousands of NetGear platinum products, including the RP614 and MR814.

These are low-cost Internet routers targeted for **residential use** and they had serious design flaws. The university reported 500,000 unique NetGear sources queried the Wisconsin time server in just ONE DAY, while NetGear has reported that 707,147 of its products might be affected by the problem. Questions that must be addressed, especially considering the ever greater use of Broadband connections are as follows:

1) What does this unintentional Denial-of-Service flood indicate about the viability of some public Internet services?

2) Can the Internet routing infrastructure be improved to enable less disruptive solutions to such problems?

3) Are incidents such as this a likely side-effect of ubiquitous, low-cost, perhaps even disposable Internet hosts?

4) Are the manufacturer, vendor, Internet operations, and user communities willing and able to cooperate to address such problems?

5) Would product liability for the manufacturer of such defect products help to address this issue, and

6) Are **home users** and SMEs liable for these attacks?

Answers to these questions are especially important with the rapid diffusion of Broadband services and routers for residential use, permitting home users to have their own servers with web pages and other services online all-the-time (see also Jurisdiction, Table 16A).

**Broadband Wireless** see Fixed Wireless Access (see also Broadband, Cable, Asymmetrical Digital Subscriber Line—ADSL, Digital Subscriber Line—DSL).

**Browser** is an access tool to the WWW that uses hyperlinks to access remote information. Browsing is using the browser to look at the information on the WWW. Cruising and surfing are synonymous with browsing.

Besides Netscape/Mozilla, Internet Explorer, Opera there are many more browsers such as Crazy Browser, 23rdBrowser, and WebView Pro Browser.

**Brute Force Password Cracking** is a process of trying to guess users' passwords. This can be done either by using available utilities, completely by hand or by using Social Engineering.

**Buffer overflow** occurs when program does not adequately check input data for appropriate length. Unexpected input can then "overflow" onto another portion of the CPU execution stack. If it is carefully crafted it can lead into execution of any code.

**Bug** is an unwanted property of program code or piece of hardware that could cause malfunctioning or slowing of processing. It can also be defined as an error in the design and implementation of a program making it do something neither the user nor the program's author wanted it to do.

**Bulletin Board System(s) (BBS)** are a type of online computer service that functions as an electronic notice board. Users can read or post messages, download programs, and play online games. Some functions of a BBS are similar to that of the internet, but on a smaller scale.

**Business Continuity Plan (BCP)** is a plan to ensure that the essential business functions of the organization are able to continue (or re-start) in the event of unforeseen circumstances; normally a disaster of some sort (see also Critical Infrastructure Protection or CIP).

The BCP follows the Disaster Recovery Plan (see also Crisis Management and Disaster Recovery Plan). BCP identifies the critical people and their roles and functions while the BCP is in force, information, systems, and other infrastructures (e.g., telephones, servers, SMS gateways) that are required to enable the business to operate again fully.

The BCP lays out a detailed plan which, if called upon, should be executed to assure minimum additional disruption after a massive computer Virus Attack or disaster.

Companies that do not have clear business continuity plans remain very vulnerable. Good recovery from a disaster is, however, contingent upon people, processes and training. Finally, management awareness may be the main weakness in business continuity planning. Doing the basics well is they key, whereby if one says one will take his or her data off site within 24 hours of a calamity, one must make sure that this is being done.

Hence, fire drills or 'dress rehearsals' by simulating various disaster scenarios will permit the organization to be in a better position, while recovering faster after a disaster. Hence, business continuity and disaster recovery plans need to be exercised so that kinks may be worked out before the crisis hits.

**Business Software Alliance (BSA)**    see Illegal Software

**Byte(s)**    see Bit

**Bypass**    occurs when a process is being avoided by using an alternative method to access the target computer or information system (see also System Redundancy).

**C2**  is the acronym for Command and Control (see also Command and Control Warfare)

**C2 Attack**  represents a defender's successful efforts for denying information to, influencing, degrading or destroying the adversary's C2 system.

**C2-Protect**  means the defender is maintaining effective command and control by either negating the adversary's effort to influence, degrade, or even destroy the friendly C2 system. However, instead of pro-active defense, this could result in a pre-emptive strike by the friendly C2 against a possible adversary. It raises ethical and moral issues (see also Table 6B).

**Cable**  means the TV cable that delivers programs to a subscriber's TV set. It can also offer internet access and even telephone services (see also Broad band, Wireless Local Loop—WLL).

**Cable Modem**  can also provide internet access for subscribers, the line is 200 times as fast as a normal telephone line, about 70 times as fast as ISDN (see also Digital Divide, Tables 18A & 18B).

Hence, cable companies around the world are offering their subscribers internet access (if permitted by law) in addition to television channels and phone services.

Disadvantage from a security perspective is that the modem is always on (i.e. one is always online unless the computer and/or cable modem is switched off). Furthermore, anybody can connect to the service, no username and password is needed once the service is activated. Hence, if a family member visits, he or she can simply connect the computer and surf, this can be either an advantage (i.e. convenience) or a disadvantage (i.e. possibly less secure) (see also Asynchronous Digital Subscriber Line—ADSL, Fixed Wireless Access, Market).

**Cache**   comes from the French word cacher meaning to press, hide or form.

**Disk Cache**   is a temporary storage place that a computer can use to store a file after reading it from the hard drive. For instance, telling a computer to open a MP3 file, it may take several seconds for it to locate and read the file into memory from the PCs hard drive. However, if the computer stores the file in the Disk Cache, the next time one wishes to open the same file, data can be retrieved from the disk cache rather than loading it from the hard drive.

One definition refers to a *Disk Cache* specifically as: hard disk-based memory used to store accessed web pages. This technique enables the browser load the stored pages from the cache rather than from the network. That is why clicking the 'Back' button on a browser usually retrieves a page nearly instantaneously. The virtual memory system that comes with Microsoft Windows is also another example of disk caching to increase performance.

**File Cache**   is used to store the locations of frequently used files for quick reference. When open a file that is stored on a hard drive, the computer will first check for the file name (and location) in the file cache. If it finds this information, the computer can jump immediately to the correct place on a hard drive without having to search in the file allocation table (a type of table of contents for a computer's hard drive). Because read/write heads on a hard drive have to physically move across the disk to search for them, it takes time for the computer to search the hard drive for files, that is why using the cache is faster

ISPs may also be required to pay copyright fees when caching in the near future (see also Table 16A—Tariff 22).

**Processor cache**   can be described as a small area of the memory used to store the next batch of instructions that will be used in the computing process. By reducing read access to the hard drive, it allows the speed of the processes to be increased.

**Web Cache**   is closely related to Disk Caching and occurs between web servers and a client or many clients. It watches requests for HTML pages, images and files to come by, saving a copy for itself. Then, if there is another request for the same object, it will use the copy that it has, instead of asking the origin server for it again.

This type of caching may, however, infringe upon copyrights and publishers and music distributors are trying to find a solution for this problem [see also Tables 7A and 16A).

**Candidate or CAN**   see Common Vulnerabilities and Exposures—CVE

**Canonical Account**   see Account

**Capacity Planning**   is the determination of the overall size, performance and resilience of a computer or system and should consider:

- the expected storage capacity of the system and the amount of data retrieved, created and stored within a given cycle;
- the number of on line processes and the estimated likely contention;
- the required performance and response required from both the system and the network to meet end-to-end performance standards;
- the level of resilience required and the and the planned cycle of usage—peaks, troughs and average;
- the impact of security measures on performance such as encryption of and decryption of all emails;
- the need for $24 \times 7$ operations and the acceptability of downing the system for maintenance and other remedial work.

With the exponential increase in use through the internet, predicting volume of traffice or load is nearly impossible. Because other servers could be down, Capacity Planning must consider the possibility of real overloads (see also Downing the System, Load and Resilience. Denial of Service Attack).

**CAST**   is a symmetric key block cipher (see also Encryption)

**Call Forwarding Fakery**   means the attacker uses call forwarding to defeat systems using dial back for penetrating security measures.

**Canonical Password**   (see Password and Table 20A)

**CERT**   is the **Computer Emergency Response Team**. Besides military and defense CERTs, educational ones have also been established.
   AusCERT (Australia), CERT-IT (Italy), CERT-NL (academic) & GOVCERT-NL (govt.) (The Netherlands) and DFN CERT (Germany) are just a few of these whose primary focus is on internet security, and vulnerabilities in their respective countries.
   Large firms have established CERTs that provide this service for internal and external clients (e.g., Alcatel, IBM, Siemens, and TDC). Others exist to serve governmental agencies and departments only (e.g., BSI / GISA in Germany).
   Also, while some CERTs believe they are a CERT, critics point out that some may only be Warning, Advice and Reporting Points (WARP). Hence, differences in scope, mission and talent available in a CERT vary widely.

**CERT®/ CC-CERT®**   Coordination Center, formerly known as the Computer Emergency Response Team Coordination Center at Carnegie Mellon University. After an internet Worm incident in November, 1988, the DARPA established the CERT Coordination Center (CERT / CC) (see also Forum of Incidence Response and Security Team—FIRST)

Table 5A describes the different types of CERTs that might exist as well as other organizations focusing on services and help regarding Information Security. The descriptions provided in Table 5A are more general.

In contrast to Table 5A, descriptions in Table 5B are specific and focus on particular types of organizations that exist today. Nonetheless, these represent a selection only and many more may exist.

Table 5B indicates that beside public and private partnerships, various models exist to assure payment of different activities. The latter is determined by stakeholders that have particular demands (see also Critical Infrastructure Protection—CIP).

**Computer Security Incident Response Team (CSIRT)**  is a service organization that is responsible for receiving, reviewing, and responding to computer security Incident reports and activity.

A CSIRT usually performs these services for a defined constituency or a group of stakeholders. These could a firm or a government agency or a client that pays and subscribes to such a service.

**Certificate**   see Digital Certificate and Certification Authority

**Certification Authority**   is a trusted third party clearing house issueing Digital Certificates and Digital Signatures. For firms, the certificates include the corporation's name, a serial number, and an expiration date. A public key is also enclosed to allow others to decrypt the message. The digital signature of the certificate-issuing authority is also part of this, permitting the recipient to verify that the certificate is valid (see also Digital Certificate and Digital Signature, Cryptography-Management).

The challenge is that in some countries, the government may require that the Key Recovery facilities *must be exercised* within its national borders. For instance, how this may affect citizens who have a Digital Signature to do e-government business with their local government when wanting to do a transaction with the EU or EC or another EU member state's agency still needs to be addressed. Will these other governments accept that the KR facility is exercised in Denmark instead of, for instance, France?

**CGI**   see Common Gateway Interface

**CGI Script**   see Common Gateway Interface

**Chain Letter**   asks the recipient to forward multiple copies to people he or she knows. If people follow the demand, circulation increases in a geometric

**Table 5A:** Critical Information Infrastructure Protection (CIIP)—Information Sharing Approaches

| Type[1] | Location | Focus | Client or Stakeholder | Funding |
|---|---|---|---|---|
| Organisations[2] | | | | |
| Option 1–CERT & CSIRT | University | Applied Research & Technical Services | University and Public (e.g., Funding Agencies) | Public, possibly also Private |
| Option 2–CERT-CSIRTS | Government | Technical Services & Support | Government agencies ser-ving its departments | Public |
| Option 3–CERT-CSIRTS | Private | Technical Services & Support | Corporate (internal or clients may subscribe for a fee to the service) | Private |
| Others | | | | |
| WARP | Industry, Home-Users in a Region | Prevention & Support | Members volunteer and contribute | Minimal seed funding |
| ISAC | Industry | Prevention and Support | Members pay for services | Funding from subscriptions |
| MSPs | Private | Monitoring of systems, technical, patching & other services | Subscribers | Private |
| Vendors | Private | Product Support | Subscribers | Private |

Note. The above represents a simplified general overview of some of the ways information security and/or engineering is provided by the above organizations including paid for services, self-help, advice and awareness raising. Sharing of information may range from tactical, strategic to Incident and Vulnerability data from multiple organizations and across sectors as well as across international networks.

Some have argued that there are five main types of information sharing that are needed, namely, (1) best practice publications, (2) baseline monitoring, (3) Incident information, (4) Vulnerability information and (5) technical insights and Research findings.

[1] The **abbreviations** used in the Table are as follows:

—Computer Emergency Response Team (CERT)–Computer Security Incidence Response Team (CSIRT) are usually charged with analyzing and responding to security threats and attacks. Often quasi-public organizations, CERTs are partially and sometimes fully funded by the government.

—Incident Security Awareness Cooperation (ISAC) is usually a service offered for a subscription to firms, often within an industry.

—Warning, Advice & Reporting Point (WARP) is a more self-help type group that may be a region or even a city

—Managed Security Providers (MSPs) are private firms that offer various types of services including monitoring of systems to organizations for a subscription fee.

[2] Option 1–Option 3 does not represent any type of ranking whatsoever, simply different ways of establishing and running such type of organization.

**Table 5B:** Critical Information Infrastructure Protection (CIIP)—Trusted Information Sharing Network

| Type[1] | Location | Focus | Client or Stakeholder | Funding |
|---|---|---|---|---|
| CASES | Cross-National Government | Prevention and Awareness Raising | CASES National Nodes–helping Citizens and Small and Medium-Sized Enterprises (SMEs) | Public/Private Partnerships Minimal funding from participating governments, firms and/or universities |
| FIRST | Among CERTS and CSIRTS | Exchange of Ideas | Members | Minimal funding from participants |
| Gov CERTS[2] | Several countries | Exchanging of Ideas | Members | Minimal funding from participants |
| TERENA | Cross-national amongst CSIRTS | Applied Research | CSIRTS | Minimal funding from participants |

**Note.** The above represents a simplified general overview of how trusted information sharing may occur across national borders. The above listing is neither in any order of importance nor all inclusive.

Again, a CASES National Node or a National CERT may act as the trusted linking pin for national organizations, hence a WARP for Small and Medium-Sized Enterprises in country A may be linked to its counterpart in country B directly and indirectly to others in country B through its National CERT. The latter is again linked to the National CERT in country B.

So while some linkages can be formalized, many might evolve over time as does Trust. The latter is unlikely to be dictated via regulation.

[1] The abbreviations used in the Table are as follows (see also Table 5A for further definitions):

—Computer Emergency Response Team (CERT)–Computer Security Incidence Response Team (CSIRT)
—Cyberworld Security Enhancement Project (CASES)
—Forum of Incidence Response and Security Team (FIRST)
—Trans European Research and Education Networking Associations (TERENA)

[2] A country may also have an information sharing network amongst its CERTS, such as the CERT Bund organization in Germany.

progress. However, a chain letter:

- does neither have to contain fraudulent, mythological material;
- nor include a 'replicative mechanism' (an appeal to forward the message) (see also Figure 5); nor
- contain an appeal to pass it on to everyone in the known universe (or even the recipient's entire address book), such as:

*Schicke diese Mail min. an 5 freundliche und intelligente FRAUEN und bereite ihnen hierdurch einen schönen Tag! (send this mail to a minimum of (5) five friendly and intelligent WOMEN and make their day more enjoyable herewith!)*

A Chain Letter may also follow the tripartite model of embracing:

- hook (e.g., appeal on recipient's greed and interest in making money fast);
- threat (e.g., fear of technology such as a virus hoax); and / or
- request (e.g., appeal on reader's sympathy as in the case of a cancer victim hoax).

The request could be the objective of the chain letter as is the case in:

1) pyramid scheme where person is asked to forward money;
2) Virus hoaxes where recipient is asked to help others by disseminating information (see also Virus); and
3) mydek type Hoaxes where person is asked to generate money for medical or other type of research by forwarding identical messages.

The difference between an Urban Legend and a Chain Letter may be that the latter includes an explicit replicative mechanism.

**Chain Reaction**   in form of a self-sustaining nuclear one was first initiated and controlled by humans on December 2, 1942. A chain reaction can be of various types, but nuclear chain reactions are the best known. A line of dominoes falling after the first one has been pushed is an example of a **mechanical chain reaction**; a pile of wood burning after it has been kindled is an example of a **chemical chain reaction**. In the latter case each piece of wood, as it burns, must release enough heat to bring nearby pieces to the kindling point. The wood, therefore, must be piled close enough together so that little heat is lost to the surrounding air.

In the case of the fission of a nucleus, the reaction is begun by the absorption of a slow neutron. When one atom fissions, a certain amount of energy is released, along with (let us say) two neutrons. If those extra neutrons cause two more atoms to fission, then twice as much energy is released along with four more neutrons. The new neutrons may cause another four atoms to fission, adding four times as much energy and eight more neutrons; so the total energy grows, doubling with each new generation of neutrons. The result is a stupendous release of energy.

**Information Security Chain Reaction**   could be a scenario whereby a falling tree branch falls on some power lines and, in combination with several other problems, causes a cascading failure. In 1990, a similar event with an AT&T switch touched off a **chain reaction** that shut down long-distance communications across the United States.

Not regularly and immediately fixing Vulnerabilities with available Patches, while having employees not following certain procedures can exacerbate a Virus or Worm problem. For instance, in September 2001, the Nimda **virus** worms its way into servers and networks internet-wide, hitting the financial industry especially hard.

C

Forgetting using a virus checker (e.g., a young woman not checking the pedestrian light and running across a red light) because one is in a hurry (because there was a bus she wanted on Kingston Road) causes the computer to be infected (causes a huge traffic tangle), sending out the Virus to everybody in the user's email address book forcing recipients to delete the email or get infected (forcing drivers to avoid a chain reaction crash).

**Information System Chain Reaction**   may involve a mechanical chain reaction (e.g., a branch interrupting power), and/or be a chemical chain reaction (e.g., power interruption results in a fluctuating power supply, resulting in a burned fuse, shutting system down), while a human chain reaction (e.g., trying to stop a mechanical chain reaction by turning the wrong switch) could all exacerbate the problem.

**Challenge Handshake**   see Handshake (see also Circuit Level Gateway)

**Checksum**   is a mathematical method whereby the individual binary values of a string of storage locations on a computer's hard drive are summed up, and the total is then retained for future reference. On subsequent accesses, the summing procedure is repeated, and the total compared to the one derived previously.

A difference indicates that an element of stored data has changed during the intervening period. Agreement provides a high degree of assurance (but not total assurance) that data have not been changed during the intervening period.

A check sum is also used to verify that a network transmission has been successful. If the counts agree, it is safe to assume that the transmission was completed correctly (see also Editor and Integrity of Data).

**Check_Password**   is a program used for cracking VMS passwords.

**Chernobyl Packet**   (also called Kamikaze Packet) is a network packet that induces a broadcast storm and possible network meltdown. This could be an IP Ethernet datagram passing through a gateway with both source and destination Ethernet and IP address set as the respective broadcast addresses for the sub-networks being gated between.

**Chronic**   could refer to a(n):

1) IT security-related state, lasting a long time, or,
2) Referring to exposure, prolonged or long-term, often with specific reference to low intensity

One could also define 'chronic' as an IT security condition that lasts 3 months or longer.

**CIT**   see Critical Infrastructure Protection

**CIIP**    see Critical Infrastructure Protection

**CIP**    see Critical Infrastructure Protection

**Cipher**    means any encryption algorithm. Ciphers can be classified according to whether they are symmetric or public key algorithms (asymmetric), and by whether they operate on their data as a stream or divided into blocks (see also Encryption, Tables 11A and 11B).

**Circuit Level Gateway**    is a type of firewall that validates TCP and UDP sessions before opening a connection. After a handshake has been created and processed, everything is passed through until session is terminated (see also Handshake).

**Click Wrap Agreement**    checks if a user meets certain requirements, by clicking on the I Agree button, the user has agreed to complete terms of use agreement including another confirmation that the user meets certain requirements (e.g., working at an educational institutions or being located in a country the product can and may be used). To complete the agreement, the user may again be required to scroll to the bottom of the agreement and click on the "I Agree" icon [see also End User License Agreement (EULA), Jurisdiction].

This is also sometimes called a Shrink Wrap Agreement, whereby ripping off the shrink wrap around the software implies that the user will take advantage of the software according to the conditions stipulated by the vendor (see also License).

**Cluster viruses**    (see Virus and also Tables 24F, 24G, 25 and 29)

**CMOS**    see Computer Metal Oxide Semiconductor

**Code**    is human (source) or machine (object) readable programming. Viruses are often referred to as code, since they are not complete but, instead, attach themselves to programs (see also Figure 5).
Code of Conduct may consist of

- Principles
- Rules

The Principles provide parties guidelines for behaviour that is according to the Rules. The Principles are used as a grounding for the Rules that culminate into a Code. The latter guides or even governs services, products and other activities by members.

A Code of Conduct is usually adopted or ratified by the membership (see also EICAR—Code of Conduct) to provide guidance and rules to all members—those in research, public practice, in industry, government, and in education—in the discharging of their professional responsibilities (see also Morals, Ethics).

**Compliance**  depends primarily on members' understanding and voluntary actions, secondarily on reinforcement by peers and public opinion, and ultimately on disciplinary proceedings, when necessary, against members who fail to comply with the Rules.

**Code Red**  was one of the first Blended Threats (see Table 24D) (see Nimda) that launched DoS attacks, defaced web servers, and its variant, CodeRed II, left Trojan horses behind for later execution. CodeRed was processed in memory–not on a hard disk–allowing it to slip past some anti-virus products.

**Cognition**  is what we think about an object. It is not observed directly, but there exist conventional ways to measure cognitions. Often the term is operationalized such as beliefs about principles, propositions, ideas accepted as truth without positive proof (see also Attitudes, Risk).

**Collaborative Application Software**  enables groups of users to work together by sharing information and processes through a variety of applications

**Collective Invention**  see Invention

**Command and Conrol Warfare (C2W)**  is an integrated use of electronic warfare, military deception, operations security, and also physical destruction. These activities are supported by intelligence in order to deny information or degrade or destroy adversary command and control capabilities. Friendly C2 activities are protected C2W is an application of information operations in military operations and a subset of information warfare. Hence, it can be offensive and defensive raising ethical questions for non military applications if ever used (see also C2, Information Warfare).

**Commercial Off the Shelf (COTS) Software**  represents a standard product, not developed by a vendor neither for a particular application nor according to user specifications.

Using COTS software components to build systems has been proposed as a means of developing software with reduced risk and cost while increasing functionality and capability of the system. Building a system based on COTS components involves buying a set of pre-existing, proven components, building extensions to satisfy local requirements, and gluing the components together. The advantages claimed are that the COTS components are honed in the competitive marketplace resulting in increased capability, reliability, and functionality for the end user over what would be available from custom built components. COTS software components from different vendors are expected to be integrated easily, work in a wide range of environments, and support extensions and tailoring to local requirements.

Some organizations find that using COTS software carries a high risk and expense during development, deployment, and during the ongoing evolution and maintenance of the system. Systems using COTS components are neither necessarily easy to build, support, nor maintain. The problems encountered may be related to the processes an organization uses to build systems, in the technologies used to construct the system, and in the way systems containing COTS components evolve.

Finally, in the case of COTS or mass-market software, the end customer might be the alpha, beta and/or final product tester. Unfortunately, there is little if anything done providing the user real assurance that a system is going to do what it should do (see also Tables 24A & 24E).

**Common Gateway Interface (CGI)** is a programming interface for World Wide Web *(WWW)* servers. It was the only way of creating dynamic web pages in the past. Poor design and wrong usage have been reasons for many vulnerabilities in CGI and CGI based applications.

**CGI Script** permits dynamic and interactive web pages but are also most vulnerable part of the web server besides the underlying host security.

**Common Vulnerabilities and Exposures (CVE)** numbers identify fully verified vulnerabilities and provide a description of the vulnerability they refer to such as associated attack range and damage potential. A list of the vulnerable software names and version numbers, as well as links to vulnerability advisory and patch information is also provided on the CVE database (see also Candidate—CAN) (for a link to the database see also Appendix 1).

CVE is a community-wide effort to standardize the names of vulnerabilities and other types of security exposures. For more information about CVE, see Appendix 1. The CVE database is publicly available for download. Each entry consists of

- an officially assigned name,
- a brief description, and
- references to information related to the vulnerability.

The database is offered in text, HTML, and CSV formats. Although this is nice for human consumption, applications attempting to filter out relevant information will have a hard time parsing these formats. OpenSec offers the CVE database in XML format (see also Appendix 1).

Finally there are efforts underway to build if not improve on CVE as outlined in Appendix 6B.

**Candidate or CAN** entries are candidates for Common Vulnerabilities and Exposures (CVE) entries that are not yet fully verified to be included but are under consideration to be entered in the CVE dictionary.

**Communicable Malware** is a disease due to a specific infectious agent or its malicious codes that arises through transmission of that agent or its products from an infected host, system, PC to a susceptible host. This can either occur directly or indirectly through an intermediate computer or IT host or the system environment (see also Virus, Transmission of Infection).

**Component**    describes one of the parts that make up a computer or network.

**Compromise**    is the intrusion into a computer system that could result in unauthorized disclosure, modification or destruction of sensitive information.

**COMPUSEC**    (see Computer Security)

**Computer**    is the device that consists of one or more associated processing and peripheral units, controlled by internally stored programs. It can perform substantial computations including numerous arithmetic and logic operations without human intervention during execution. It could be a standalone PC or else a connected PC with other PCs (e.g., see also Wireless LAN) or mainframes.

**Computer-Aided Thematic Analysis (CATA)**    see also Ethnography.

**Computer Crime**    (or Information System Crime) is defined by many state, provincial and national laws as deliberate actions to steal, damage, or destroy computer data without authorization, as well as accessing a information or computer systems and/or accounts without authorization (see also Damages). When looking at a computer crime one may distinguish between:

1) Computer as the target—such as an unauthorized Intrusion, Attack
2) Computer as the instrumentality of the crime—illegally copying music files using Peer-to-Peer (P2P) systems on the internet (see Copyright)
3) Computer being incidental to other crimes—such as, using email to communicate plans for a bank heist; and
4) Computer prevalence resulting in crimes (e.g., somebody stealing computers from an office).

In the context of the dictionary, we are primarily interested defining Computer Crime as Computer, Information or a System being the target (see EpiSystemology, Evidence, Forensics, Jurisdiction).

**Incident Reporting**    may be interpreted as crime (e.g., according to the USA computer crime law) since one can go to jail for simply telling potential victims that their data is vulnerable. For instance, by explaining how a vulnerability works and why customer data were at risk, prosecutors could assert that the security expert 'impaired the integrity' of the affected network. This case is currently going to a Federal Appellate Court in the USA to determine whether this interpretation of the law is to stand.

If the interpretation is upheld in upper court, this could mean a dramatic decline in postings to Bugtraq, Secunia, CERT, and other public forums for vulnerabilities.

In the above case, the government argued that the Secret Squirrel's missive itself-whether posted on his own webpage or emailed to Tornado's (the firm selling the software with the vulnerability) customers (or, presumably, posted to any other public source, such as Bugtraq) "impaired the integrity" of Tornado's computers or network. The government argued that the message was incorrect, useful to would-be attackers, and was intentionally designed to give Tornado trouble.

Because McDanel (defendant) revealed the flaw publicly (having previously revealed it privately to Tornado to no avail) he could be prosecuted, because, according to the government, "the public now knew about a flaw in the Tornado system, how that flaw worked, what that flaw could get somebody who exploited the flaw, and in fact a how-to manual about how to exploit that flaw".

But the government here has stretched the federal computer crime statute to include not only attacks on computers or networks, but the dissemination of information about Vulnerabilities. They've expanding the definition of "impairing the integrity" of such affected systems. This is a dangerously slippery slope.

Under the theory articulated by the government, the transmission of any information that can be used by others to impair the integrity of a computer system (or cause loss of reputation) if done without authorisation (and who would authorise it?) is a federal crime.

The law requires the impairment to be "intentional," but under USA case law a person is presumed to intend "the natural and probably consequences of his or her actions." Revealing the vulnerability will embarrass the company, and this fact alone "impairs the integrity" of the network, according to the government's theory.

If one were to come into a lawyer's office and ask his or her legal opinion about whether one should reveal a vulnerability under this interpretation of "impairing the integrity" of a computer, the lawyer would most certainly have to advise the person that it was a federal felony to do so.

What would help is for the USA Congress and the European Commission (EC) to produce stringent guidelines in form of a law, directive or whatever for prosecutors about what kinds of conduct "impairs" integrity, and therefore runs afoul of the criminal law. These guidelines should be binding on all Prosecutors so there is a clear understanding about what people in McDanel's (he is the defendant in this case—year 2003) position are permitted to do.

A Code of Conduct for security specialists with clear guidelines on what they can do when a company or entity refuses to fix a Vulnerability would be helpful as well. Until then, as the canny desk sergeant in Hill Street Blues used to say, "Let's be careful out there."

**Computer Ergonomics:**    Applies to such things as workstation design, readability of screen and movement of keyboard or tilting of screen to adjust to the human's motor needs (e.g., avoid eye fatigue) (see also ergonomics further below).

**Computer Emergency Response Team**    (see CERT)

**Computer Forensics**    (see Forensics)

**Computer Fraud**    describes crimes involving deliberate misrepresentation or alteration of data in order to obtain something of value.

**Computer Incident Advisory Capability**    (CIAC) is the agency that helps the USA Department of Energy to keep its IT resources safe. Its mission is to apply "...cyber security expertise to prevent, detect, react to, and recover from cyber incidents for DOE/NNSA" (National Nuclear Security Administration) "and other national stakeholders." (http://www.ciac.org)

**Computer or Information Security Law**    is mostly an eclectic amalgamation of concepts from existing law, which are applied to the relatively new technologies of computer hardware and software, email , and the Internet.

Hackers who use a modem to enter a computer without authorization and either (1) use its services or (2) alter records are committing a crime similar to burglary, but the traditional notion of burglary *requires* the criminal personally to enter the victim's premises, which is not satisfied in the case of entry via data to/from a modem. Therefore, new laws were enacted to define Computer Crimes.

I believe it might have been preferable to change the definitions in existing concepts, instead of creating new one.

**Computer Metal Oxide Semiconductor**    (CMOS) is a section of the RAM memory containing important data, such as date and time of the computer clock, and its configuration settings. A battery that is housed on the computer motherboard powers the CMOS. While a virus can overwrite information on the CMOS, it can neither infect nor reside in it.

**Computer Mouse:**    A "mouse" is a pointing device to select items on a video screen. It is a small box set atop wheels or ball bearings. Rolling the mouse on the table will cause analogous movements of the cursor on the video display. Buttons protruding from the top of the mouse can be used to select certain commands and actions.

**Computer Network Attack**    involves operations to disrupt, deny, degrade, or destroy information resident in computer networks and information systems.

**Computer Security (COMPUSEC)**   was the engineering discipline to ensure secure operation on a stand alone computers when the security of the
Communication Systems (COMSEC) still was a discipline of its own. In
today's Information Technology systems both, COMPUSEC and COMSEC
are integrated together with network security into Information Technology
Security (see IT Security), sometimes also referred to as Information Systems
Security or recently just Information Security.

**Computer Security Incident**   is a breach of compromise of a security policy.
Where such policy does not exist, a Computer Security Incident will mostly
be recognized as an attempted or successful intrusion into an automated
information system (AIS).

**Computer Security Intrusion**   represents any event of unauthorized access
to an automated information system (AIS) (see also Figures 2 and 3).

**Computer Virus**   see Virus

**Computer Virology**   see Virology

**Confidence**   see Trust

**Confidence Level**   see Table 15B (see also Statistical Inference)

**Confidentiality**   is the property that data or information is not made available
or disclosed to unauthorized, parties (e.g., individuals, organizations and
processes). Hence, a health insurer cannot get access to medical files as such
but only to information pertaining to a particular bill submitted electronically
for reimbursement (see also Email Signature—Confidentiality).

**Confidentiality, Integrity, Availability of Data, User Accountability, Au-
thentication and Audit (CIA-UAA)**   ensure that confidentiality, integrity
and availability of data and system resources are secured, while users are accountable for adding, deleting and viewing of information. Confidentiality,
Integrity and Availability (CIA) are often referred to as the "Fundamental
Security Objectives." In modern IT environments, in particular the internet
environment, "Accountability" has become another fundamental security objective. As well Authentication is needed to make sure the person is who he or
she claims to be (e.g., Biometrics) while without the Audit function, however,
there is no assurance for Compliance (e.g., see Policy) nor can the organization provide a paper trail indicating it has done enough to meet best practice
standards. The latter may be the only way to avoid a huge fine in a lawsuit
which is to say unless the firm can proof it met best practice standards it may
be liable for a DDOS attack originating from its servers (e.g., see Appendix
5—Swiss Law link).

　　Confidentiality, Integrity, Availability of Data, User Accountability, Authentication and Auditing (CIA-UAA) is outlined in Table 5C.

**Table 5C:** Confidentiality, Integrity, Availability of Data, User Accountability, Authentication and Audit (CIA-UAA)

| Categories | Description | Example of Property |
|---|---|---|
| Confidentiality of Data | Is the property that data or information is not made available or disclosed to unauthorized, parties (e.g., individuals, organizations and processes). | Medical data is not being disclosed to others, such as employers, thereby making the identification of the patient possible. |
| Integrity of Data | Is the property that data and information has not been modified or altered in an unauthorized manner? | Unauthorized personnel are unable to alter medical records, while changes made by others are tracked and recorded. |
| Availability of Data | Is the property that data and information, as well as the necessary systems, are all accessible and useable on a timely basis as required to perform various tasks. | Medical personnel must get access to patient files even during a massive power outage, when backup electricity generators may have to be used to guarantee availability of data. |
| User Accountability | Is the property that accessing data for informational or other use, including its alteration or other processes is being logged and monitored, thereby enabling the firm to generate a trail of information about access if an audit requires this. | Accountability, requires that policy compliance (see Table 6) by users is monitored, thereby making their enforcement feasible. Agreements made with other stakeholders (e.g., patients or investors) regarding such things as privacy, confidentiality and quality of services provided (see also Tables 7A and 7B) must be monitored. |
| Authentication | Is the property that before one can access the data the system ensures that users are who they claim they are. | Authentication requires that some type of identification is used to make sure that the user is really the person he or she claims to be through such mechanisms as log ins, Passwords and Biometrics. |
| Audit | Is the property that the system will record important events, to allow later tracking of what happened (for example, to catch or file documents with a court against an attacker). | This means that the system is able to create the necessary trail of events that will enable the organization to produce any documentation needed in case of subsequent demands such as a lawsuit. |

Most frameworks do not specify Accountability, Authentication nor Audit specifically. However, such cases as the one where New York's Attorney General put Merrill Lynch on trial for emails sent between analysts and bankers, suggests that use of data, generating information from these, while communicating the latter via emails to others can increase the firm's liability (see also Table 7A).

(Cont.)

**Table 5C:** (cont.)

| Categories | Description | Example of Property |
|---|---|---|
| | Credit Suisse First Boston (CSFB), Salomon Smith Barney, Morgan Stanley and Goldman Sachs were put through the paces in part, because policy requirements (e.g., separation of research and investment banking) were not monitored closely enough. User Accountability and Audit played a major role when New York Attorney-General Eliot Spitzer released a series of internal emails on April 8, 2003, showing how Merrill Lynch analysts privately disparaged as "crap" companies they were publicly recommending.<br><br>Audit trails must identify the authorizer (see Authorization) of new or amended data, files or records (see Audit, Forensics), hence, User Accountability is crucial to be able to show that Confidentiality, Integrity and Availability have been protected adequately (see also Table 7A).<br><br>Put differently to achieve satisfactory Confidentiality, Integrity and Availability (CIA) levels, User Accountability and Authentication are a must. Moreover, recent legal disputes suggest that without the necessary mechanisms permitting a comprehensive Audit, the firm may be unable to show beyond reasonable doubt that it has delivered the CIA levels required by legislation. However, the latter requires User Accountability features and satisfactory Authentication mechanisms to satisfy a court. | |

**Note.** The above represents a simple categorization of issues that must be addressed to achieve a certain level of security for any property owned by the organization ranging from customer to patient records stored digitally.

Demonstrating Confidentiality and Accountability in a court may require a system that addresses User Accoun-tability and Authentication while providing the necessary Audit trial in case proof must be supplied to a judge (see also Table 21B).

Table 5C outlines CIA-UAA in more detail. Recent court cases also indicate that User Accountability is becoming an ever more important concept to produce the records sometimes required in court cases as well as the audit trail permitting the accused or suing party to make its case.

As the email cases in the USA regarding banking services indicate CIA-UAA requires that an audit can be performed and such activity would reveal the necessary information, such as is required for Confidentiality, Integrity, Availability of Data, User Accountability and Authentication.

**Configuration Vulnerability** results from an error in the configuration of a system, such as having system accounts with default passwords, or having 'world write' permission for new files, or having vulnerable services enabled (e.g., attachments are opened by default).

**Content Filtering** see Filtering.

**Continuous Innovation** see Invention

**Control–Baseline for IT Security** is made up of the key control measures and procedures that should be used when planning for security management activities or undertaking reviews of systems or sites (see also Information Security Policy, Policies). These key controls are outlined in Table 6 below.

**Table 6:** A Baseline for Security-Taxonomy of Policies for Enhancing and Supporting Critical Infrastructure Protection (CIP) Efforts

| Type of Policy | Description of Policy |
|---|---|
| Information Security | Ensures that corporation is clear on the relevant security objectives, while executives have given approval and support for the various policies regarding Critical Infrastructure Protection (CIP) |
| Allocation of Information Security Responsibilities | Staff and / or departments agreed on who is responsible for security functions while staff performing these has been identified and allocated according to need and specifications. |
| Training | Provides the basic Skills needed by managers and staff about the firm's CIP and its strategic importance as well as how security can be increased by modifying user behaviors. In turn this will permit users to exhibit the behavior and vigilance required for strengthening security efforts–creating synergies. |
| Reporting of Security Incidents | A standardized system and preset Reporting Format can empower users to easily and systematically report in a very timely fashion internal incidents to dedicated parties such as a group's super user. Latter may than immediately inform Security Engineer who, within a pre-set time limit forwards verified information to the appropriate agency such as a Computer Emergency Response Team–CERT. |
| Malware and Anti-Virus Controls | Necessitates the use of mail gateway anti-virus scanning software and desktop counterpart mechanisms enabling this threat. Specific user behaviors must be outlined (e.g., not opening attachments automatically unless having verified that sender did actually ship the attachment). |
| Disaster Management Plan | Outlines various contingency plans that are continuously updated to giving responsibilities and processes to identified parties for who does what, when and how during a particular disaster affecting critical infrastructures in the IT domain. |
| Property and Copyrights | Must be observed and promulgated by the firm. Compliance to these rules is monitored to reduce the possibilities of violations such as unauthorized use of software or pirated software. Software use inventories must indicate who uses which software, check-ups have to permit the tallying up of licenses used versus purchased ones. |
| Data Security, and Protection | Records from various stakeholders including but not limited to customers, suppliers, employees, and shareholders must be safeguarded against unauthorized use (see Table 5C, CIA-UAA). |
| Data Protection and Privacy / Other Legislation | The organization must be pro-active to legislative developments and changes, including implementing directives and regulations handed out by the European Commission, USA agencies and others for being able to act globally (see Appendix—Legislation) |
| Hardware/Software including PDAs and Mobile Communication Devices | Related to Property and Copyrights but if Personal Digital Assistants (PDAs) are not supported, explaining reason must be given. Departments set standards for any hardware including PDA, and mobile phone security and synchronization, and should not allow users to install their own synchronization products on their devices. |
| Compliance with Security Policies | Effective security management requires the regular review of compliance with security policy reviewing Accountability of system or information users. |

**Note.** The above policies may be very short or somewhat longer. Regardless of length without being enforced based on publicly known and understood performance standards, policies will fail to be effective (see also Policy and Table 16).

**Objectives** formulated must be quantifiable, thereby making them easier to be measured. Satisfactory adherence to property and copyrights is hard to measure. However, stating that successful implementation of the hardware policy means that less than 3% of PDA's have non-authorized synchronization software installed is a start.

Table 6 outlines that to achieve any baseline in security; policies need to be formulated outlining the minimum acceptable standards. Hence, every security or data protection policy has to also address the how, when, why, where and what questions.

**Control Total** is the value that can be compared against the sum of a batch of items being checked against loss of data in transit. The safest way of using control totals is to send the control total message at a different time, and by a different route to the master message (see also Bitloss).

**Cookies** are **data files** that are stored on a hard disk by some web sites. Whenever visiting a Website, it tries to access this cookie enabling users to enter the site according to one's preferences (e.g., first page shows news, email and horoscope). Cookies may also store one's password to access a site unless the user prevents the browser from doing so, a must for any security-minded user. Additional information is collected from subsequent browsing on the web site, to further personalize one's browsing experience on this web site (e.g., customer profile).

Cookies are accessible to a particular Website only and cannot be used by other Websites to gain information about the user (see also Table 18A, about Malicious code).

**Consequence Analyzers** see Disruption Management

**Copyright** protects a person's property rights by giving him or her right to charge for viewing a film or listening to music. However, all entertainment media on the internet is just bits, ones and zeros. Bits can easily and repeatedly be copied. Hence, a digital text, music, video or other type of file can be copied as often as the user would like. This characteristic of the digital world makes the internet different from copying trying to copy Patek Philippe watch or a Ferrari automobile (see also License and Table 7A).

Because there are no political boundaries on the Internet, it is difficult to enforce Copyright legislation regarding digital content. Even trying to control copyright by using an encryption scheme as done to protect Digital Versatile Disk (DVD) may work in a limited sense only, since it can and already has been broken.

A business model could be used whereby clients are charged for early releases, interactive entertainment, convenience and other means that consumers feel are desirable and worth paying for. In other cases, content may be used as advertising such as done with emailed newsletters or printed industry-type magazines distributed for free to any interested party or qualified readers. Nonetheless, digital files cannot be made 'uncopyable'. The internet is not the death of copyright. However, business models that respect the realities of the internet instead of fighting them, will likely be more successful than other models (see also Illegal Software, Open Source).

Finally, we need to differentiate between the genuinely new and deserving of Patent protection and the bread-and-butter business of software development for which copyright protection is more than adequate (see also Table 16A).

We can distinguish copyrights from patents as follows:

* Copyrights protects against wanton plagiarism, while
* Patents cover ideas, have to be applied for and cost money.

**Copyright—Database Content**   Our focus has been on the ownership of creative material in the worlds of music and film (e.g., remember Napster?). But a less visible fight over the ownership of data deserves attention. The internet has boosted the market for data, including raw materials of creation.

Those who use those data to create new things ranging from scientific inventions to new commercial services on the web are battling to ensure that naked facts stay largely in the public domain.

For instance, a Toronto man spent years developing a site with thousands of images, only to have a Dutch competitor copy the images and repost them. During May 2001, the man was turning to EU Database protection laws for help, since copyright law was and still is of little assistance for the public domain works.

Bidder's Edge collected information about what was being auctioned any-where online. It than made that information available in one place, similar to a Meta search engine, permitting users to search for an item on several auction sites at once. But a California district court found Bidder's Edge had trespassed on eBay's site to collect that information. Bidder's Edge went out of business before the preliminary injunction could be appealed.

Krak, a publisher of maps in Denmark offers people the choice to find addresses, phone numbers, email and fax information, including a map to drive to the address online. Some of the information is collected from users who register, but most comes from phone directories and the government's national registry database, where every person's legal home address is listed. This could infringe upon:

• a person's right for privacy, since the individual may have given the right to the phone company to list his or her name, address and phone number in the phone directory, but not given permission to Krak to put it online in their directory—hence, Krak may be violating EU privacy laws;

- Krak copied the information and reposted the data on its site, hence this act could be judged as representing wholesale theft from other databases.

In the USA, the rights of database providers are tightly circumscribed by a 1991 Supreme Court ruling that says raw facts in a database cannot be owned and protected under copyright law. In the Feist v Rural Telephone Service Co decision, the court stated that the phone book information is public and since Feist did re-compile it in a format differing from the original, no copyright infringement occurred.

While databases should be protected against wholesale theft, it is difficult to decide when facts are taken but transformed into something new and useful to consumers. "Who should own the facts?" is a difficult question considering the new technologies.

**Email Subscription–Copyright Infringement** could occur if an employee re-distributes a report by email paid for with a subscription (e.g., research, and news). For instance, in Lowry's Reports v. Legg Mason 2003 the federal court in Maryland ruled that a company is liable for copyright infringement after one of its employees posted a subscription email report to a company intranet. The employee paid for a single email subscription but later posted it on the intranet and sent it via email to several co-workers (see also Table 16A).

**Cost** are the expenses occurred to remedy a problem or the expenditures incurred to reduce the risk for certain threats with, if materialized, severe consequences for the harmed.

Particularly in the context of IT security it is important to assess what the basis for certain cost estimates might be such as the financial costs of having a system infected by the Nimda Virus. Hence, Reliability and Validity of Measures and Reporting are of concern. Recall bias (i.e. remembering things selectively) may affect survey responses by system administrators about effects caused by Malware the last 12 months.

Hence the following issues must be considered:

- Reliability of measure–(see Reliability) particularly if data are based on survey responses by an administrator and/or actual log files;
- Validity of measure–(see Validity);
- Data gathering mechanisms–is an issue whereby it is important to know how data were gathered (Data Collection Method) and Reporting Mechanism

The cost issues are also outlined in details in Tables 1, 2A, 2B and 2C as well as under Damages (see also Tables 7A–7C).

**Cost–Benefit Analysis (CBA)** offers a systematic way of (1) identifying all potential gains and losses from a proposal that are (2) converted into monetary units, and (3) compared on the basis of decision rules to determine if the proposal is desirable from the organization's stand-point.

A comprehensive evaluation of an IT security project will take into account the potential effect on both human lives and the environment. Once all this information has been quantified, and compared using such methods as Net Present Value, Internal Rate of Return, and / or cost-benefit ratios, management and security personnel have to decide whether the proposal for beefing up Critical Infrastructure Protection is beneficial from the firm, its stakeholders and society's point-of-view (see also Tables 2A, 2B, 2C & Tables 7A, 7B and 7C).

**Corruption of Information**   takes place when accidentally or deliberately (maybe unauthorized) alterations of data on a computer or network are being made.

**Countermeasures**   describe any action, device, procedure, technique, or other means that reduce the vulnerability of an automated information system. Countermeasures often aim at specific threats and vulnerabilities and may use techniques as well as activities traditionally seen as part of security.

**Country-of-Origin**   see Jurisdiction (also Table 16A).

**Covert Channel**   is being used when cooperating processes transfer information in a manner that violates the system's Security Policy.

**Crack**   represents a popular hacking tool used to decode encrypted passwords, while system administrators may use it to assess weak user passwords.

**Cracker**   is a person dedicated to breaking all types of protection systems, especially those of software and / or information systems. Forms of predatory and malicious behavior are embodied by crackers. Hence, they cause damage or losses requiring restitution to the property owner by damaging files, copying and distributing proprietary information to others (see also Hacker, Cyberpunk).

A cracker will be gathering all information possible about the network or systems that are to be cracked. The first part of this information may be obtained through, for instance, the web server and its publicly known address. From this IP, an attacker could establish if there are more systems in the same IP range belonging to the same company, or consult the server DNS to locate other resources.

Based on this, public servers must be placed in a different IP range from that used by the rest of the servers in the company (e.g. the proxy), thereby ensuring that they are completely separate.

Once the attacker has a list of machines the type of system, services, and versions can then be established. Using scanners or devices that examine all ports in all the machines and 'interrogate' them—if possible- are tools being used to obtain this information.

Accordingly, when configuring servers, only essential services should be active, and precautions should be taken with those that by default, leave more than one port open.

**CRC**   see Cyclic Redundancy Check

**Crime**   see Computer Crime

**Critical Infrastructure Protection (CIP)**   tries to coordinate efforts to protect critical infrastructure that may include but not be limited to information technology and utility grids (e.g., electricity). Critical Infrastructure may include essential services such as telecommunication, finance/banking, food production, transport and logistics, energy and utilities as well as critical government services.

One also should consider that in many countries much of the Critical Infrastructure (e.g., electricity, gas distribution and shipping) is privately owned.

Critical Infrastructure Protection may also include Emergency Preparedness. Its mission is usually to enhance the safety and security of citizens or users in their physical and cyber environments.
Mandates could be such as:

- to provide a comprehensive approach to protecting critical infrastructure—the key physical and cyber components of the energy and utilities, communications, services, transportation, safety and government sectors; and
- to be a government's primary agency for ensuring national civil emergency preparedness–for all types of emergencies.

Protecting critical infrastructure and responding to emergencies is often a shared responsibility in a country between public agencies (e.g., police, and emergency services) and organizations (e.g., utilities), requiring the full co-operation and effort of these parties, municipalities and the private sector (see also Disaster Recovery Plan).

CIP is closely linked issues regarding Redundancy of System design as well as Business Continuity Planning in a case of a disaster.

**Critical Information Infrastructure (CII)**   may include the information technology component (e.g., hardware, software and data) of essential services, such as telecommunication, finance/banking, food production, transport and logistics, energy and utilities as well as critical government services (see also Table 5A–5C) .

One also should consider that in many countries much of the CII for essential services such as electricity supply lines are is privately owned.

CII may be vulnerable to an outside dimension that comes from disruption through natural disasters, accidents and mismanagement as well as deliberate Attack with criminal intent. An inside dimension is Safety and System-related issues including Complexity (see Tables 13A, 13B & 13C).

**Critical Information Infrastructure Protection (CIIP)** is similar to CIP but it specifically focuses on information systems and technology. CIIP requires that critical functions such as signalling for trains runs separately from the system that is used for corporate emails. This was not the case when a worm penetrated CSX Corp.'s computer system August 2003, shutting down train signaling and dispatching systems in the eastern US, according to a CSX spokesperson, while SBB (the Swiss Federal Railways) had problems providing satisfactory e-commerce services such as making reservations and printing tickets online due to the LovSan/Blaster worm.

Accordingly, mission critical systems should only be connected to the internet almost entirely for monitoring and remote management. If monitoring is required than these systems must be isolated on a subnet with a closed firewall that allows a port to be opened and a few packets to go out, or else mission critical systems need to be completely disconnected from the general network and allow management data to be sent entirely through out of band communication such as a dedicated link or telephone excluding auto answer modems. This apparently is not yet accomplished everywhere but is required if we are serious about CIIP (see also Redundancy of System).

Many physical critical infrastructures have a spatial element that can be bounded and defined, thereby permitting its protection. In contrast, CIIP deals with information technology and systems that are technically complex, largely abstract and worst, not easily understood. Hence, Risk management is not well developed and suffers from many uncertainties (e.g., Damages). Technological changes in the CIIP domain are rapid and difficult to track.

For many sectors, information infrastructures are recognized as a common critical cross-sectoral dependency. This dependency is not only significant but as information and its protection is becoming increasingly the base platform for industry sectors, dependencies increase and are making thereby systems and industries more vulnerable in case of an Attack (see also Disaster, Business Continuity Planning, Redundancy of System).

**CRM**   see Customer Relationship Management

**Cryptanalysis**   entails operations undertaken for converting encrypted information to plain text without initial knowledge of the crypto-algorithm and / or key employed during the encryption process.

**Cryptographer**   is an individual who is active in the field of cryptography, (see also Steganography).

Cryptographers can be found working at universities or in firms including consultancies (see also Security Engineer).

**Cryptographer-Researcher** is an individual who is active in the field of cryptography as defined above but also doing Research, writing and publishing papers, and sometimes writing his or her own algorithms and protocols. Such work advances our knowledge and, most importantly, understanding of cryptographic issues whilst findings / results produced from such work can be used to build theory and generalize to other settings (see also Research).

**Cryptographer–Implementer** is an individual that implements cryptography in software and hardware products. However, implementers are not Cryptographers, they are usually individuals who build secure systems that use cryptography (see also Security Engineer, Virus Engineer, Research).

**Cryptographic Hash Function** is a process whereby a value (referred to as a hashword) is being computed from a particular data unit. This is done so that if the hashword is protected, manipulation of data is detectable.

**Cryptography** consists of the encryption or encoding of a clear text into an unreadable one for anyone not having the key to carry out the corresponding decryption (see also Data Encryption Standard, Digital Signature, Key Recovery).

Historically, Information Theory and Cryptography are closely intertwined, although cryptography is an older discipline. Claude Shannon's foundation of information theory was motivated in part by his work on secrecy coding during the World War II. His 1949 paper "Communication theory of secrecy systems" can be seen as the first paper triggering the transition of Cryptography from an art to a mathematical science.

Cryptographers have been advocating open source ideals calling it "using public algorithms and protocols" for a long time. One reason put forward is that cryptography is hard to do right. An effective way to know if something was done correctly is to be able to examine it.

In the cryptographic context, two algorithms can be that one is secure whilst the other is not. Unfortunately, both can work perfectly by encrypting and decrypting efficiently and providing a nice user interface, while never crashing either. However, the only way to tell good cryptography from bad cryptography is to have it examined. Hence, this has nothing to do with functionality but, instead everything with security (see also Encryption).

To illustrate, the Advanced Encryption Standard (AES) had five final contenders. Before the winner Rijndael was chosen as the standard, the world's best cryptographers spent thousands of hours evaluating it and the other four. No firm, no matter how rich, can afford that kind of evaluation. And since AES is free for all types of uses, there's no reason for a company to even bother creating its own standard. Open cryptography is not only better, it is cheaper and more secure (see also Algorithm, Encryption and Tables 11A and 11B).

In most cases, open standards provide more security than closed ones because of them being put under scrutiny and testing by many security engineers around the globe (see also Tables 11A and 11B). However, some would probably counter-argue this statement by possibly stating something similar to:

—one cannot proof such a statement since one does not have access to the "closed" algorithms, and

—it depends very much on the cryptanalytic to be applied.

Nonetheless, resolving the above may take more than a book and cannot be done here.

**Crypto-Hacking**   is hacking the mathematics of cryptography. While it represents hacking, it requires the knowledge of advanced mathematics to attack and possibly break cryptography. Cryptographic algorithms might be secure but the key-generating procedures might not. Accordingly, a Crypto-Hacking attack might not result in one being able to break a cryptographic system but, instead, how it is used. Hence, while the algorithm might be secure, unfortunately, the method to produce keys for the algorithm has a weakness that could be resulting in not as many possible keys as there should be. Again allowing Crypto-Hackers to break the random number generators used to supply cryptographic keys (see also Hacker).

Using information about timing, power consumption, and radiation of a device when it executes a cryptographic algorithm, Crypto-Hackers have been able to break smart cards and other "secure" tokens. These are called "side-channel attacks."

There isn't much underground Crypto-Hacking going on because of the mathematical skills required to do it. There are a few programs that take advantage of poor passwords in UNIX and NT, or poor pass-phrases in PGP, thereby making it feasible to break the encryption. However, there are really not any tools that allow for serious Crypto-Hacking, simply because too much mathematical expertise would be required to use them anyway.

**Cryptology**   is the science which deals with hidden, disguised, or encrypted communications (see also Tables 11A and 11B).

**CSIRT**   see CERT (see also Tables 5A–5C listing other organizations of this type and form)

**Cutover**   is the point at which a new program or system, takes over or is going live.

**CVE**   see Common Vulnerabilities and Exposures (see also Appendix 1 for web link)

**Cyber Alert**    see CERT (Tables 5A–5C).

**Cybercash**    represents money digitally and requires an electronic system with virtual credit used worldwide. Cybercash is not really cash but instead represents an obligation that the issuer has incurred to pay a monetary amount at some future date. In contrast to cash, which a merchant must accept for payment by law, using a stored-value card for settling one's bill can be rejected by the store owner.

C

While hard cash is symmetrical, digital cash is not. A Euro 5 bill purchases Euro 5 worth of goods: but digital cash has costs that must be recovered. In the US, PayPal (launched October 1999) has been very successful as the main payment method for users of eBay, the country's dominant internet auction site. Pay Pal charges about Euro 1.10 for cross-border payments (e.g., USA to Europe), while banks charge Euro 17 (since July 2003, charge within Euro area is the same as domestic, i.e. for German Mastercard owners, no payment fee will be imposed for online purchases or goods purchased during vacation in France). Hence, digital cash may become very attractive for consumers for cross-border payments (e.g., Denmark to Singapore) (see also Mobile Payments)

**Cybercrime**    describes illegal activities that involve the exploitation of access and use of network or system processes from within or outside the corporation. Two types of Attacks are prevalent:

1) Techno-Crime with the intent to copy, steal, prevent access, corrupt or otherwise deface or damage part of all computer systems including unauthorized use of processes requiring IT resources

2) Techno-Vandalism includes but is not limited to Website defacement, obtaining unauthorized access and use to data that is subsequently revealed to others without prior permission. Tight internal security, allied to strong technical safeguards should prevent the vast majority of such incidents.

Cybercrime also depends on what type of Attack has been undertaken by the culprit (see also Tables 3A and 3B.

Often Cybercrime combines "traditional" crime activity with IT related crime that is sometimes called Blended Attack.

The law tries to prevent harm to the material or psychological interest of others.

**Differential Association Theory**    (Sutherland, 1947) states that delinquency is rooted in normative conflict. Consequently, modern society contains conflicting structures of norms and behaviours as well as definitions of appropriate behaviour that give rise to crime. At the individual level, Sutherland maintained that normative conflict is translated into individual acts of delinquency through differential association learned through communication and primarily in intimate groups. In short, the actions my friends think justify the means will influence my reasoning.

**Social Control Theory** (Hirschi, 1969) denies the existence of normative conflict. Instead it posts a single conventional moral order in society and assumes that the motivation for delinquency is invariant across people. Instead of asking "why do some people violate the law and social norms?," control theory asks "why do most people refrain from law and moral code violations?" Hirschi's answer is that they are dissuaded by strong bonds to conventional society such as attachment to friends, involvement in the community and belief in what is right and wrong.

We know that strong social bonds (e.g., what would my friends think if I do this) influence the reasoning process for deciding if exhibiting some action is appropriate or not. Trying to explain delinquency in white and black youths in the USA, Matsueda and Heimer (1987) reported that differential association theory "is supported over social control theory."

Consequently, a person's Moral framework of **what is right and wrong when working with computers** and any technology may be explained by association theory. In turn, what may be correct as far as copying software or working with a virus for fun or hacking a computer system may depend largely upon one's friends own values, behaviours and norms or what they think is right or wrong. Hence, **whom you keep company with may help in explaining why diverse end-user groups pursue different actions which may or may not harm others** such as sharing illegally copied music or pirated software.

The above helps in assessing what external governors (e.g., social control) people may be submitted to that would bring them to act legally. Additionally, it is of interest to understand how such **external governors** may influence the person's reasoning process, thereby helping in answering **what brings people to act in moral ways or immoral ways** (e.g., pirating software by making an illegal copy from a friend's licensed version and installing it on one's own machine) that is addressed by Cognitive Developmental Theory.

**Cognitive Developmental Theory**   (Nucci, 1981, Turiel 1983, applied to viruses, software, newsboards by Gattiker and Kelley, 2001 divides social events into three domains of knowledge, namely:

1) **personal domain** that is outside the realm of societal regulation and moral concern (i.e. one's own business);
2) **conventional domain** are acts which have interpersonal consequences but are not harmful moral, such as wearing jeans instead of formal clothing to a ball and, therefore violating social conventions and, finally,

3) **moral domain** includes acts where the harm is intrinsic to the act/behaviour, children and adults who will reason that the act is universally wrong, even in another country (e.g., hitting another child at the playground)

The principal interest here is whether people assessing certain behaviours related to computer technology take a *moralizing* or a *permissive* stance toward these acts. People have notions of freedom from external constraints, ideas about the human construction of rules and laws, and issue of who is to be included in the moral domain. Accordingly, if a person chooses to write a computer virus and then proceeds to test it with the scanner program on his/her own machine this is not harmful to others. Similar, downloading a computer virus program from a bulletin board (BB) or an electronic discussion list (EDL) is not necessarily harmful to others, since the virus will, if activated affect one's own machine. However, convention may suggest not to do this because there is a potential that the virus could accidentally spread, hence the person may be playing with fire. Finally, releasing a virus into the wild is harmful to others and, therefore, morally wrong (see also Justice).
But things become complex when:

- 29 % of Internet users use file-share software (i.e. 35 million Americans)
- 26 million Americans allow others to download music & other data files from their computers, most often these individuals are between 18–29 years old.
- 18 to 29 year olds are least worried about copyrights, with 72 % saying they are not concerned.
- 61% of respondents (i.e. Americans) between 30–49 years old are not concerned about copyright infringement,
- 82% of full-time students say they are not worried

But if Differential Theory applies (i.e. it matters who's company one keeps), college students in the USA are so much exposed to others pirating software and music that what according to Moral Development Theory might have been considered immoral or wrong a few years back, such as illegally copying software and music, is now part of the conventional domain (i.e. one should not do it but many if not most do while the music industry is fighting a loosing battle). For interesting info on this see Appendix 3 (Crime, Copyright and Privacy Issues links).

**Cyber Crime Convention**    The Council of Europe's, Convention on Cybercrime was developed by the European Commission and published on 22/23 November 2001 in Budapest. The convention "Illegal Interference" or "Data / System Interference" is the first international "Framework" for definitions on illegal activities, such as "Illegal Access". Though the Convention was also adopted by countries outside the EU, it is still awaiting ratification of the EU Member States in order to become international law.

**Cyberpunks** embody behaviors similar to what we define as Crackers and phone phreaks but, in addition, they use technology to damage, destroy or capitalize on the data they find (e.g., for profit). Most importantly, cyberpunks use their know how to gain more information which, in turn, increases their influence, power and potential threat upon others' information world. Most of this activity is done at somebody else's expense by, for example, breaking and entering into an organization's voice mail system. Gaining unauthorized access and using IT resources and process while not being authorized to do so (see also Identity Theft, Hackers, Crackers, see also Figures 1 and 2).

Similar to the things we learned in Economics 101, demand and supply of goods are related. Accordingly, *cyberpunks can be compared to "fences"* in New York who sell stolen merchandise at very "attractive" prices. As long as there is a consumer who is willing to go home with a "good" deal, even if it is at the expense of the victim whose apartment / car was broken into, then the supply will continue. If we stop purchasing from fences supply will drop; if cyberpunks find no demand for their illegally acquired information and, therefore fail to sell their goods, supply will be reduced (see also Hackers and Crackers).

Finally, providing individual cyberpunks with five minutes of fame does further reinforce the cool image or status the individual is striving for within his or her social group. Lack of attaining fame, status or other benefits (e.g., being on a TV show) will also help reduce the supply of cyberpunks.

**Cyber-users:** Epitomize individuals who use computers, phones and cyberspace to derive jobs and exceed current limitations of technology and reality without performing implicit or explicit violations of current laws and ethical as well as moral standards held by society. The interesting thing is that the information highway offers *cyber-users* to both consume (e.g., sign-on at a commercial information provider such as CompuServe) and broadcast / produce information on today's information highway (e.g., edit and distribute electronic newsletter, join on-line discussion groups, administer a list server of electronic addresses).

**Cyberspace** represents the world of connected computers and systems.

**Cyberterrorism** is a term that has been used if not abused by many but general agreement seem to be that the term but it is rooted in the term terrorism.

**Terrorism** can be defined in various ways such as done by the USA State Department:

"premeditated, politically motivated violence perpetrated against non-combatant targets by subnational groups or clandestine agents, usually intended to influence an audience."

However, the Federal Bureau of Investigation (FBI) defines the term slightly different as:

"The unlawful use of force or violence, committed by a group(s) of two or more individuals, against persons or property, to intimidate or coerce a government, the civilian population, or any segment thereof, in furtherance of political or social objectives."

Both of the above definitions have the simple common denominator of violence and the ascribed motive of invoking terror. However the FBI definition qualifies the terrorist violence as unlawful, whereby lawful violence with similar motivation of invoking terror would not fall under the definition of terrorism. The United Nations assembly came up with a even more general definition:

1. Strongly condemns all acts, methods and practices of terrorism as criminal and unjustifiable, wherever and by whomsoever committed;
2. Reiterates that criminal acts intended or calculated to provoke a state of terror in the general public, a group of persons or particular persons for political purposes are in any circumstance unjustifiable, whatever the considerations of a political, philosophical, ideological, racial, ethnic, religious, or other nature that may be invoked to justify them (General Assembly Resolution 51/210 Measures to eliminate international terrorism, 1999).

The above nationally specific definitions of terrorism allow for the furtherance of the agendas of the respective government and its power structure, such as the dominant legalistic and nation state-based structures. However, law is simply politics dressed in a different garb. The UN's definition struggles to balance the competing visions of what constitutes terrorism and is quite borad. It simply equates violence with instilling fear and being directed towards fulfilment of political ends as terrorism.

The definition put forward by Ayatulla Ali Taskhiri from Iran illustrates this point by focusing more on oppositional resistance and the violent struggle against perceived injustices (see Justice).

"Terrorism is an act carried out to achieve an inhuman and corrupt (mufsid) objective, and involving [sic] threat to security of any kind, and violation of rights acknowledged by religion and mankind" (Taskhiri, Ayatullah Shaikh Muhammad Ali, 1987. Towards a definition of terrorism, *Al-Tawhid*, 5:1).

The Ayatullah in his discussion of the concept leaves struggles against colonialism, imperialism, despotism, racism and international agression as falling outside the definition of terrorism. Important is also that non-combatants or civilians Rights are not clearly defined in his concept of terrorism. Naturally, the developing world sybjectivity of the Ayatullah and the revolutionary background may influence his engagement with this concept.

Accordingly, Cyberterrorism as a concept is hard to define whereby geographical factors (e.g., country A versus country B) and political agendas will influence the definition. Hence, the term seems of little use for Information Security purposes and a focus on Cybercrime would be more beneficial for system administrators, policy-makers and End-Users.

**Cybercrime Activities**   represents a group of Hackers defacing websites or bringing an eCommerce site to a halt using various means of Attacks. Such behavior cannot be seen as undertaking Cyberterrorism activities but simply behaving in ways that might be construed as representing Cybercrime activities (see also Attack).

**Cyberterrorist Attack**  is not clearly defined in the literature, except that information technology is ensconced in such an Attack (also Tables 3A and 3B)

**Cyberterrorism Group**   practices or has significant elements that are involved in Cyberterrorism.

**Cyberterrorism Threat**   see Threat (also Tables 24A–24G).

**Well-Being and Terrorist Attacks**   can cause stress and anxiety in the civil population of all ages, ethnicities, and geographical locations. By enabling State authorities to better understand and ameliorate human emotional, behavioral, and cognitive responses to terrorism as well as other disasters, your legislation takes the important step of recognizing the impact psychology can have in such instances.

If we understand better how attitudes and beliefs about terrorism affect consumer confidence, trust, population mobility, and decisions about children, job behaviors, and attitudes about the internet, e-commerce and security.

There is a wealth of research to draw from on the subjects of fear, resilience, and responses to terror and trauma. Evidence based studies on the response to 9/11 attacks in 2001 in the USA have taught us that there are factors to deal with beyond the degree of exposure or loss from the trauma that need to be dealt with. For example, early disengagement (e.g. giving up, engaging in denial) from scientifically validated coping efforts such as behavioral therapy was found to be a forerunner of ongoing distress symptoms. At the same time, those who engaged in "active" coping in the immediate aftermath of the attacks were associated with lower levels of stress in response to the 9/11 attacks.

**Cyclic Redundancy Check (CRC)**   is a technique used to determine file integrity through the generation of a CRC algorithm. The CRC algorithm calculates the CRC of the file in question. This way a protection system can be established, whereby if something changes, the CRC also changes. This permits the detection of any possible modifications.

**Daily Digest**   happens in cases where all incoming email is collected and sent out in one message to each user on a list covering a 24-hour period (see also Listserver and Moderated Listserver).

**Damages**   are difficult to define in the context of the internet and bytes and data. However, the Swiss made a first attempt in coming up with a legal instrument which should help in protecting one's data as well as information. Swiss legal infrastructure about data safety / security and computer viruses changed when article 144bis—Damaging of data was becoming part of the country's criminal code while coming into force on Jan 1995 which states:

1. *Anyone, who without authorization deletes, modifies or renders useless electronically or similarly saved or transmitted data, will, if a complaint is filed, be punished with imprisonment for a term of up to 3 years or a fine of up to 40,000 Swiss Francs.*
   *If the person charged has caused considerable damage, the imprisonment will be for a term of up to 5 years. The crime will be prosecuted ex officio.*
2. *Anyone who creates, imports, distributes, promotes, offers, or circulates in any way programs that he / she knows or has to presume to be used for purposes according to item 1 listed above, or gives instructions to create such programs, will be punished with the imprisonment for a term of up to 3 years or a fine of up to 40,000 Swiss Francs.*
   *If the person charged acted for gain, the imprisonment will be for a term of up to 5 years (English translation by Claudio Figerio, who was instrumental in the legislative process, presented at EICAR 1995, Rüschlikon / Zurich, p. 2).*

While the above provides a quite comprehensive legal framework for damages, to quantify these in monetary terms is often difficult (e.g., hours of work lost, and potential lost sales). A possible framework helping one structure these issues is outlined in Tables 2A, 2B, and 2C, as well as Tables 7A–7B.

Nonetheless, Damages are from a legal standpoint not measured purely in terms of adverse changes to systems. Damage can also be measured in terms of the time and costs needed to respond to Worm or Virus infections.

**Legal Issues—Viruses**    means that various states handle criminal acts different including the distribution of software viruses or software piracy. For instance, May 1, 2002, a district court judge in New Jersey sentenced David L. Smith to 20 months in federal prison for writing and releasing the notorious Melissa virus. Smith's judgement required him to serve 3 years of supervised release, during which he could not use the Internet, computer networks, or bulletin boards unless authorized by the court. May 6, 2002 he was sentenced in a New Jersey court to 10 years in prison on state charges, but he will serve only a 20-month federal sentence handed down May 1 (see above). Smith had pleaded guilty in 1999 to a state charge of computer theft and to a federal charge of sending a damaging computer program (see also Cyberpunk, Damages, Virus)

The author of the Kournikova virus was appealing his sentence of 150 hours of community service given to him by a Dutch court, nonetheless, ultimately he served. Regardless, the two verdicts do raise such issues as:

1) the lack of severity exhibited in the sentencing imposed by the NL judge makes a mockery out of the law but, worse
2) if being 'clueless' as he claims is a valid defence for overt acts, then the law in The Netherlands is not even worth the paper it was written on.

If we compare the Kournikova case to David Smith's Melissa verdict (20 months in Federal prison, 20 years in state prison, latter one he does not have to do, plus community service and supervision after jail sentence and $5,000 fine), the Dutch verdict is very light indeed.

**Legal Issues–Damages**—While these two verdicts are very different, in both cases millions of Euros of damages were caused by these acts. For instance, some estimates claim that the Melissa worm caused more than $80 million in damages (see also Asset, Tables 2A–2C, Table 7A).

But in case of software violations, judges seem to have less difficulty in setting rather draconian verdicts to prevent others from doing the same. For instance, Barry Erickson, a former Symantec software engineer, was sentenced to nearly three years in prison for providing copy protection removal technology to a software piracy group known as DrinkOrDie in early May 2002. As apart of his plea, Erickson agreed that his action caused damages of $2.5–$5 millions. Following his prison sentence, Erickson began to serve two years of supervised release.

The above illustrates drastically that at least in the US, software piracy with relatively small damages compared to those caused by computer viruses, results in quite severe jail sentencing.

During Spring 2002, a court in the USA threw out a case about virus damages, stating that the firm (i.e. victim) could not really prove that it had incurred any damages from a virus spread by an ex-employee. The court approved the costs for having to clean the hard-drives but felt that this did not go beyond $5,000, hence no damages could be awarded (what about lost employee time). This raises two issues for the USA, EU and other countries:

1) Why is a criminal act such as writing and distributing a computer virus dealt with less severely than copyright or property right infringements caused by software piracy;
2) How can it be that countries and judges look at software outcomes so differently in Netherlands than in the USA, and
3) how can judges come to the conclusion that damages caused from a Virus attack are minimal—do we have difficulty in measuring these in economic terms (see also Asset Value, Costs, Damagers, Measurement, Validity, and Tables 2A, 2B, and 2C)

Hence, the EC's current attempts to set a clearer stage for sentencing concerning cybercrime and criminal acts involving IT appears needed (see Appendix 4 for links to regulatory EU documents on cybercrime). Nonetheless, putting much greater value on software property rights versus malicious acts causing millions of damages is somewhat strange (see also, Asset Value, Jurisdiction, Malware, Virus).

Table 7A outlines what steps are needed to provide the information and data required to convince a judge or other parties about the possible damages an unauthorized Inrusion or a Virus may have caused the organization (see also Asset Value and Tables 2a–2C, 6).

However, since September 2001, anti-terrorism legislation has been strengthened. For instance, in Switzerland, the following article is now part of its anti-terrorism laws:

"Whilst conducting business or activities that are part of an organization's purpose, illegal activity or a crime may be undertaken and due to organizational difficulties this act may not be attributable to a particular person, than the illegal activity or the crime will be attributed to the organization itself. The fine can be up to Sfr. 5 million" (Art. 100quater StGB) (English translation by author, no warranties whatsoever) (law was put into force October 2003, see also Appendix 5 for link to law in German, French and Italian).

**Table 7A:** Damages—Using the Asset and Policy Document Approach to Quantify Losses

| Factors | Description of Factor |
| --- | --- |
| | Below are some suggestions on what the firm should have documented in one way or another. |
| Value of Data | This includes soft and hard costs (see Table 1, Tables 2A – 2C) as well as Return on Investment (ROI) (see Table 15C). |
| Policies | Which policies may have been violated by the stakeholder and/or employees, could this result in liability (see Table 6 & 21A). |
| Copyright and Property Rights | Software inventory permits control over who uses which software, while check-ups permit the tallying up of licenses used versus purchased ones (see Table 6)<br><br>Database rights for information collected must not go beyond what could be considered fair use, while the facts taken have to be transformed into something new and useful to clients.<br><br>Disk Caching may infringe upon another party's copyright or property rights. Since most large Internet Service Provider's (ISP's)cache highly popular webpages to reduce traffic while increasing access for their subscribers (e.g., news pages), this issue is an international one that awaits a solution that is practical and sensible (see also Tarif 22, Table 16). |
| Audit Trail | Is organization able to produce audit trail indicating when, where, how and by whom data, information or IT resource was being used (see Tables 4A, 4B & 5D)<br><br>Hence, policy compliance must be documented by having data about when and how audits were conducted and how violations where dealt with. |
| All else considered equal (ceteris paribus) | The greater the Value of Data (see Tables 2A- 2C, 7A) the more likely the number of parties wanting to justify their access (e.g., medical records—health professionals, insurance carriers, employers and so on). In turn, the potential Risk for a Threat culminating into a violation of the CIA-UAA of these data increases substantially.<br><br>Accordingly, the higher the value of data, the more resources must be used effectively to reduce the Risks for having these data's CIA-UAA violated. |

**Note.** Unless a firm can produce detailed answers to the above issues it will be difficult to claim damages caused by others affecting critical infrastructure in the IT domain.

The above suggests that in the Swiss context, if a firm's servers are being misused for a Distributed Denial-of-Service (DDoS) Attack and the originator cannot be found, it will be held liable and possibly have to pay a large fine. Nonetheless, what can be expected as satisfactory standard and reducing of risk of having one's servers or information technology misused for illegal acts by a third party still requires that such a standard is known, judges understand the issues at hand and so on (see Appendix 5—Swiss Law for full text of this legislation).

**Dark Web Site**   is typically hosted off-site but is only activated under certain circumstances. Hosting off-site eliminates the Vulnerability produced by a building casualty. This serves many purposes, including customer relations, public relations, emergency communications, and situational awareness.

**Darknets**   are a collection of networks and technologies used to share digital and other content or objects (e.g., software programs, songs, movies, and books) and have substantial non-infringing uses. The darknet is not a separate physical network but an application and protocol layer riding on existing networks.

D

Darknets offer distributed object storage, whereby today's Darknets do not rely upon any centralized server or service—a peer just needs the IP address of one or a few participating peers to be able to reach any host on the Darknet.

Also important is that with the open protocol, anyone can write a client application for a particular Darknet. Second, Gnutella is not really "run" by anyone: it is an open protocol and anyone can write a Gnutella client application.

Members-only darknets are popping up to protect file sharing from prying eyes. Innovation in Darknet technology is coming from many different directions.

How do darknets work? People who want to build a Darknet will start by installing on their computers specialised software, which they can buy or often download free on the Internet.

Then individuals who want to form their own group swap passwords of digital keys so their computers can communicate with each other. The data shuttling between computers are often encrypted, a security feature similar to that used for online credit card transactions, making darknets more secure than typical corporate intranets.

Microsoft has been using the name 'darknet' to refer to the overlay networks of point to point filesharing in their Digital Rights Management (DRM) position papers in conferences.

In cases of infringing uses and sharing of digital content such as music, an MP3 file purchased on a Website is as useful as the version acquired through a Darknet. A securely DRM-wrapped song is, however, less attractive. Hence, selling unprotected objects is more attractive for the user and requires that **vendors need to rethink their revenue models**.

**Convenience and low cost is a more likely succeeding revenue model** than additional security from vendors making the use of content more cumbersome for users only (see Spoof, Copyright, Jurisdiction).

**DARPA**   see Department of Defense Advanced Research Projects Agency (DARPA)

**Data**   are the collection of items of information such as the representations of facts, concepts, or instructions in a manner suitable for communication, interpretation, or processing by employees or by automatic means. Data can be in the form of files in a computers volatile or non-volatile memory, in a data storage (see Bit) device (e.g., tape), or in the form of data in transit across a transmission medium (see also Data Classification, Reliability, Validity). **Note:** The singular of data is *datum*. A writer's sloppiness can result in that the plural noun is accompanied by a singular verb.

**Data Aggregation**   is the case when combining seemingly innocuous data to get confidential information.

**Database**   is a large collection of data organized for rapid search and retrieval for indexing, updating, and retrieval purposes (see also Copyright—Databases).

**Data Capture**   is the process of entering data into a computer manually (e.g., keyboard or by scanner) or automatically (e.g., system is receiving transmission from another program or server)

**Data Classification**   means that the owner has assigned a level of sensitivity to data being created, amended, enhanced, stored, or transmitted. The classification of data should then determine the extent to which these data need to be controlled / secured. It may also be indicative of the value of data in terms of assets (see also Asset Value) from:

- highly secret (highly sensitive such as pending mergers, new designs, strategies) where loss of information would seriously damage the firm,
- highly confidential (critical to firms ongoing operations),
- proprietary (loss may endanger know-how and patents),
- internal use only (workers only), and
- public documents (for clients)

**Data Dictionary**   is a list and description of all the files, fields, and variables used in a computer system.

**Data Diddling**   is the altering of data in an unauthorized fashion before, during, or after input into a computer system. (see also Data Interference, Table 5, Confidentiality)

**Data Driven Attack**   is a form of attack that is encoded in innocuous seeming data that is executed by a user or a process to implement an attack. Such an attack could go through a firewall in data form and then launch an attack against a system behind the firewall. (see also Trojan)

**Data Encryption Standard (DES)** has been the most popular encryption algorithm of the past twenty-five years. Originally developed at IBM Corporation, it was chosen by the US' National Bureau of Standards (NBS) as the government-standard encryption algorithm in 1976. Since then, it has become a domestic and international encryption standard, and has been used in thousands of applications. Concerns about its short key length have dogged the algorithm since the beginning, and in 1998 a brute-force machine capable of breaking DES was built. Today, modifications to DES, such as triple-DES, ensure that it will remain secure for the foreseeable future (see also Rijndael and AES, Table 11A & 11B).

**Data in Transit** are packets of data that are being transmitted across the network.

**Data Interference** (Council of Europe, Convention on Cyber Crime 22 Nov 2001)
Article 4—Data interference
". . . when committed intentionally, the damaging, deletion, deterioration, alteration or suppression of computer data without right."

**Data Leakage** could be described as a case whereby an none-Authorized party downloads information to some storage-type technology (e.g., USB drive or memory stick) and than takes it out of the building (see also Security Breach)

**Data Mart** is a database of information collected from operational and other systems, made available to a group of users. The presence of a Data Mart often suggests the presence of a Data Warehouse. A Data Mart is introduced for tactical reasons and directed at meeting an immediate business need (see also Data Warehouse).

**Data Mining** a term coined by IBM means gathering information from various data sources such as:

1) looking for relationships and correlations still to be discovered based on customer data, cookies, accounting information and many more available in corporate databases, and
2) finding the information by using the Web.

**Data Protection** requires that the organization safeguard its organizational records to meet confidentiality, integrity, availability and accountability of data and their use by authorized system users (see also Confidentiality, Integrity, Availability, and User Accountability,—CIA-UAA, Security of Media)

**Data Safe**   is made of heavy, fire-resistant, tamper-resistant, magnetically in-ert, materials, usually dual controlled. They are designed for the safe keeping of computer media, including master program media, 'mission critical' soft-ware, and top security data files.

Safes come with a rating such as "30TL"–30 minutes, tools or "60TLTR"–60 minutes, tools and torch. This indicates that a professional safecracker, with safecracking tools and an oxyacetylene torch, will need an hour to break open the safe. If the alarm doesn't sound, bringing the guards within that timeframe, the safe is worthless. Accordingly, while the safe buys time, the latter must be spent wisely to protect data from thives.

**Data Safety**   see Data Protection

**Data Scope**   see Data

**Data Storage**   see Bit

**Data Tap**   is a device external to a network that can 'listen' to the traffic on that particular network by detecting and reading the bit-patterns of data passing down the communication line and interpreting / translating these patterns into readable alphanumeric characters.

Some devices are capable of detecting / reading the electromagnetic radia-tion emitted directly by computers without the need to 'tap' a communications line (see also TEMPEST, "Van Eck Radiation").

**Data Transmission Rate**   is the speed by which data is being transferred from point a to b. If one where to compare technologies according to how much time it would take to transfer a Mega Byte (MB) in seconds, transmission of 1 MB from A to B would take the following number of seconds:

- 163 for GPRS cellular/mobile phone,
- 146 for analogue phone modem,
- 128 for ISDN card,
- 4 with a UMTS mobile phone,
- 1.5 with a W-Lan card using the 802.11b standard,
- 0.08 with a Fast Ethernet,
- 0.008 with a Gigabit Ethernet, and
- less than 0.001 seconds using a Gigabit Ethernet fiberoptics cable.

Data Transmission Rates will further improve with fibre optics whereby each fibre can carry up to 160 different wave lengths.

Early 2004, transmission standards of 10 Gigabits per second are common, while 40 are technically feasible. In tests, several terabits (1 terabit = 1,000 Gigabits) have already been transferred during **each second**. One Terabit is comparable to the content of 1,200 CDs.

**Data Warehouse**  is a database whose sole purpose is to store and execute searches upon, substantial volumes of corporate data. A data warehouse is not, or should not be, a larger version of the organization's current transaction processing system. A Data Warehouse should be a separate data store that is optimised for the type of data and queries envisaged (see also Data Mart).

**DDoS**  see Distributed Denial of Service Attack (see also Denial of Service Attack).

**Debugging**  illustrates the tracing and fixing of faults (bugs) in computer software and, occasionally, hardware (see also Bug).

**Decoupling**  means thanks to the internet, business processes can be decoupled in order to create large efficiency gains. The internet not only connects systems, processes and companies to each other but possibly, more important, is that system and business processes can be decoupled. Hence different types of functionality and expertise will be decoupled or separated from each other and relocated to make the most of specialization. While some firms may provide IT infrastructure and services, highly focused informational appliances for end-users may also emerge.

Decoupling can mean that processes are centralized in a location that provides certain advantages, such as lower labor costs to provide software maintenance remotely (e.g., India). Front-end activities are than managed closer to the local market. Moreover, disaggregation of industry value chains into networks of specialized firms called business webs or value networks. Hence, a large such as Cisco may offer a family of products and augments these with specialized products and services from a network of partners. The internet allows firms to resolve the debate between

- specialization versus generalization,
- centralization versus decentralization and, finally,
- scale versus focus

by giving firms the opportunity to decouple systems, processes and divisions. Decoupling helps us to go beyond these seemingly irreconcilable conflicts and unlock new value for the organization (see also E-Commerce).

**Outsourcing and Decoupling**  allows a firm to outsource certain IT security, software maintenance or processing related activities. For instance, updating software according to alerts and advisories *relevant to the systems used by the firm* could be done remotely by experts. How such an approach might reduce Risks and Threats from cumulating into damages should be shown by Metrics and a Cost Benefit Analysis (see Tables 2A–2D, Table 6 & Tables 15A–15C). While this approach might not be cheaper at first, reduced Risk should be worth the initially higher price, often for Small and Medium-Sized Enterprises (SMEs), it is impossible to keep abreast all the new vulnerabilities while installing the relevant patches quickly enough.

In turn, the firm continues focusing on its specialized mission, such as providing a service that is perceived as giving high quality at good value by customers, while being quite profitable.

**Security and Decoupling**   also means that vital systems must be kept separate from others, such that if one part is affected by a disaster such as a computer Worm or Virus, the others work without being affected. Hence, when the Sobig Virus on a PC at the Swiss National Post Office affected the system on October 7, 2003, it not only forced the email system down to a crawl but much worse, the online banking system was also affected including many money machines all across the country and preventing customers from paying their bills at the service counters in post offices. Not having a system that checks and Audits if all PCs are patched for Vulnerabilities was the first mistake but much worse seems that the Post Office forget the basic rule to separate Critical Cystems from each other.

**Decryption:**   Denotes the process of retrieving the plain text from the cipher-text (see also Encryption, also Tables 10A and 10B).

**Default**   is the standard setting a system or software package comes with and most likely to be chosen by most users if they had to, thereby allowing software to work 'out of the box' without requiring users to first figure out many options. But as Microsoft has shown, too many options set at defaults that ignore standard security precautions can be a nightmare for users and system administrators alike (e.g., Microsoft Outlook—things got better during 2002 though).

**Default Password**   see Password

**Defense**   in IT security is also linked to the baseline of IT security. Once the standards have been established (see Table 7A), the firm also needs to determine how to put into place the checks and balances.

Table 7B outlines how defenses could be used starting from passive defense moving toward active defense. As Clausewitz, a famous German general is attributed of having said something to the effect that if you entrench yourself behind strong fortifications, you compel the enemy to seek a solution elsewhere. Accordingly, defense must be able to cope with a moving target otherwise attacking forces may circumvent the fortification as happened with the Maginot line during the 2$^{nd}$ World War in Europe (German's went around the French fortified trenches via Belgium and the rest is history).

Table 7B outlines what defense might entail to thwart an attack (see also Table 2D and Attack Figures 2a–2c). Of particular intrest are also the

**Table 7B:** Defense—What it Might Entail

| Factors | Description of Factor |
|---------|----------------------|
| | The military's notion of defense distinguishes between passive and active defense, as well as counter attack. Below these terms are described and their link to critical infrastructure protection (CIP) and information technology resources and data are outlined. Defense is closely linked to the issues addressed in Table 6A. |
| Passive Defense or Maginot type Defense | The Maginot Line was built between 1929 and 1940 in order to protect France from her longtime enemy, Germany, and to defend the traditional invasion routes across her Eastern frontier. With the Maginot Line France hoped to gain time for the French army to mobilize and to make up for a potentially disastrous shortfall of manpower predicted for the late 1930s. Most of all, it was built to provide a place behind which the French army could hide, a so-called "Great Wall" of France where the nation could feel secure in its doctrine which would become known as the "Maginot" mentality.<br><br>Putting into place some type of defense in the information technology sector (e.g., anti-virus software and spam filter) is a requirement but may not be good enough to fend off an attack by a group of hackers.<br><br>Most of us must rely at least to a large extent on passive defenses. We carry our gas masks, we move in the dark and we encrypt our communications. We also make sure that every notebook or home PC has updated anti-virus software, as well as a firewall installed. Naturally, the latter is configured to reveal the minimum amount of information about our PC or corporate networks. |
| Active Defense | This type of defense is designed to take out the attacker. Anti-tank gun fire that eliminates attacking tanks might be one way. This is harder than passive defense, but can be much more effective if it encompasses a technical and behavioral dimension.<br><br>Intrusion Detection Systems (IDSs) and Honeypots provide alarms that can alert defenders of an attack in progress. Managed Security Monitoring services can filter these alarms and provide expert response when a network is under attack. Vigilant, adaptive, relentless, expert intelligent network defense is far more effective than static security products.<br><br>Active-defense also focuses on Social Engineering by training users accordingly. Information Security is a job for all not just management, hence it requires that employees do their share such as refraining from opening attachments without making sure that it was sent by the individual who is in the Sender field. Moreover, providing others system access under one's password is a not acceptable.<br><br>How much information really ought to be made public in one's email such as phone number, snail mail address as well as if the firm's web site should list a directory of employees is an issue, especially considering the increasing occurrence of Identity Theft. In most instances, it is not necessary to provide such data, while increasing the Risk for misuse of such information. |

(Cont.)

**Table 7B:** (Cont.)

| Factors | Description of Factor |
|---|---|
| | This type of defense also requires the use of a Demilitarized Zone (DMZ). |
| Pro-Active Defense | Pro-active defense builds on the above and tries to address issues such as Social Engineering by educating users accordingly by **raising awareness** and putting policies in place for improving **prevention**. One example might be getting users to refrain from opening attachments without beforehand confirming that the known sender actually mailed this document. Not installing unauthorized Screensavers and other software on machines and understanding Security Policy while being able to follow it as an employee is vital for an effective Pro-Active Defense. |
| | Put into place mechanisms that permit fast response against attacks from within and outside the firm, automatic if possible. |
| | Policies must be developed, implemented and enforced, whilst audits provide the organization with information about the weakest links and appropriateness of measures taken. |
| | Guidelines, benchmarks and other key indicators are developed, deployed and regularly reported when testing defense mechanisms. Such information is than also used as feedback for further improving pro-active security-related behavior by employees and home users. |

**Note.** Many firms and government organizations focus on Active Defense while Pro-Active Defense appears the minimum acceptable level to protect data. Moreover, awareness raising sometimes requires training or communicating security to employees, thereby necessitating resources beyond just hardware and software.

definition of Passive, Active, pro-Active defense as well as Counter Attack in Table 7B.

Table 7C outlines how an escalation of defense efforts might look like such as Counter Attacks and Strikeback. Ethical and policy concerns regarding such approaches are discussed as well.

**Defense Advanced Research Projects Agency (DARPA)**   originally provided the resources for the launch of the internet (see also ARPA for a definition) (see Department of Defense ARPA).

**Defense In-Depth**   (see Table 6A and Multi Layered Security)

**Definition and Exchange Format(s) (DEF)**   is a common data format and common exchange procedures being used for sharing information required for handling incidents. Such format permits exchanging information involving known and new types of incidents. DEF permits exchange of data to be formatted and shared in machine-readable form.

Appendix 6 B outlines the various efforts that are currently being undertaken by various constituencies regarding the improvement of DEFs for

**Table 7C:** Defense—Possible Escalations

| Factors | Description of Factor |
|---|---|
| Counter Attack | This type of attack means turning the tables and attacking the attacker. Against the tank assault, it could involve attacking the tanks by air before they reach the deployment area. It may even involve the bombing of their fuel and repair depots, and ammunition storage facilities. Hence, the defender is trying to remove the attacker's tools to launch. |
| | In the information technology (IT) domain, prosecution is currently the only way to use counter attack legally against a system perpetrator. Hence, it is used after the attack for putting the accused and subsequently found guilty party into jail. Unfortunately, it can only be done after the fact such as web site defacement has already occurred and resulted in damages for the attacked. |
| | Counterattack and vigilante justice are wrong, both legally and morally (see also Table 16B). While victims of attack are allowed to defend themselves, they are not permitted to take the law into their own hands and attack back. This has to be addressed by a country's legal system (e.g., police, prosecutors and legislation). |
| Strikeback | In system engineering terms, strikeback could occur in a situation with a positive loop whereby each component responds with an increased reaction to the response of the other component, and so the problem gets worse and worse. |
| | For instance, a firewall may have an option for a finger attack. Hence, if one were to enable such an option, the firewall might recognize an attack. For instance, an employee from a supplier A visiting firm B and trying to log onto the system of his employer, firm A, thinking he or she was authorized to do so. Firm A's firewall would than initiate a retaliatory finger attack against the supposed originator of the attack, firm B's system. |
| | In this example, the firewall A initiating the finger attack is waiting for the other firewall B to stop. The problem cannot be resolved by the firewalls themselves; termination requires external intelligence and intervention. |
| | Finally, in a sense, the problem is a kind of race condition, since it does not occur unless the communicating systems have the misfortune to pick partners with the same configuration. For instance, all you need is a message to be sent by someone who happens to turn on their own out-of-office auto-reply and you have a mailstorm brewing. |
| | Your autoreply sparks their autoreply which sparks another autoreply from your mailbox and so on until a server crashes or someone notices the flurry of useless email. |
| | In the strikeback firewall option, the internet pipe may be filled with attack and counterattack data, effectively cutting both companies off the Net until an administrator at one of the companies shuts down their firewall, ending the data storm. |
| | The above suggests that setting a system to strikeback if certain conditions are met is likely to be counter-productive, |

**Note.** The line between defense and offense can blur, as some counterattack targets are less clearly associated with a specific attack on a specific target and more geared toward denying the attacker the ability to wage war in general.

sharing data about software, web and system Vulnerabilities (see also Reporting Format, Reporting Mechanism).

**Degaussing**   see Security of Media

**Demilitarized Zone (DMZ)**   is a separate and shielded or 'cut off' system from the main corporate network, containing technical equipment such as the Webpage. This further protects the main system from being accessed by external parties or via the Internet

The term comes from the buffer zone that was set up between North Korea and South Korea following their war in the early 1950s. A DMZ is not a single security component; it signifies a capability. Within the DMZ one can find:

- firewalls,
- choke and access routers, and also
- front-end and back-end servers.

Essentially, the DMZ provides multi-layer filtering and screening to completely block off access to the corporate network and data. And, even where a legitimate and authorised external query requests corporate data, no direct connection will be permitted from the external client, only a back-end server will issue the request (which may require additional authentication) from the internal corporate network. How much data may be accessible from the outside is also depending on asset values that may be represented by these data (see also Asset Value).

**Demon Dialler**   (also called War Dialler) is a program that repeatedly calls the same phone number. While it is benign and legitimate for access to a BBS, it can be malicious when being used as a Denial of Service (DoS) Attack.

Sometimes a Demon Dialler may also be used for automatically dialing large banks of phone numbers and collecting details. The purpose of this activity is to hack/break into dial-up, PBX and other systems. It is worth note that Demon Dialling is outlawed in many countries.

**Denial of Service (DoS) Attack**   is considered to take place only when access to a computer or network resource is *intentionally* blocked or degraded as a result of malicious action taken by another user. While these attacks could damage data directly or permanently they do not have to. However, they intentionally compromise the *availability* of the resources. An attacker carries out a denial-of-service attack by making a resource inoperative, by taking up so much of a shared resource that none of the resource is left for other users, or by degraded the resource so that it is less valuable to users. Those shared resources are reached through processes and can include other processes, shared files, disk space, percentage of CPU, modems, etc.

DoS is an attack based on the principles of the *TCP Three-way Handshake* exploitation. It was very popular in late 1990s. Flooding system by specially crafted packets from one host could disable its networking capabilities and in some cases even force it to reboot. Majority of the exploitable holes were patched and this form of attack is nowadays nearly impossible

DoS Attacks over the internet can be directed against three types of targets: a user, a host computer, or a network. An attacker must begin a denial-of-service attack by using tools to exploit vulnerabilities and then either obtain unauthorized access to an appropriate process or group of processes, or to use a process in an unauthorized way. The attacker then completes the attack by using some method to destroy files, degrade processes, degrade storage capability, or cause a shutdown of a process or of the system.

Denial of service tools, such as Trin00, Tribe Flood Network and Stacheldraht, are readily available on the internet and that they are easy to use. Given the apparent number of script kiddies that have the ability to break into machines and install these tools, getting an army of zombie machines together is becoming child's play.

**DoS on the 13 Internet Root Servers**    occurred October 2002. These root servers run the master directory for lookups that match domain names with their corresponding IP addresses. Below the root servers are the servers that support top-level domains such as .com, .net and .org, and below the top-level domain servers are hosts of Web sites

During a Distributed DoS attack, a hacker hijacks machines across the Internet and uses them to send a flood of requests to a server until it becomes overwhelmed and stops functioning.

October 2002 the root servers were under a Distributed DoS attack for about an hour, causing several servers to stop being available to regular Internet traffic. However, the remaining root servers withstood the attack and ensured that the Internet's overall performance was not degraded. Nonetheless, this was the most serious hacker attack ever on this key piece of the Internet infrastructure, and it was an eye-opener for the root-server operators.

Without the root servers, the Internet cannot function. Named by the letters A through M, the root servers are operated by U.S. government agencies, universities, nonprofit organizations and companies such as VeriSign. Of the original 13 root servers, 10 are located in the U.S., one in Asia and two in Europe.

With Anycast, a routing technique, the root server operators are replicating these servers around the world.

Four of the root-server operators—including the Internet Software Consortium and VeriSign—have mirrored their root servers. There are now 34 locations worldwide with root servers or replicas deployed.

Using this technique, Internet addresses are more like 800 numbers that get routed to call centers. There are...more root servers scattered around the network than there used to be. It's not necessarily that the servers are more available but that these data are more distributed.

As extra root servers are deployed using Anycast, the root server system acquires additional capacity if another Distributed DoS attack occurs. Today the root server system is much better equipped to respond to this type of attack than it was in October 2002, because of Anycast and concurrent hardware and software upgrades.

**Denial of Service through Psychological Manipulation (PsychoDoS)**   chips away at corporate resources and confidence, thereby undermining an organization's ability to use the resources on which it relies on.

For instance, Spring 2002 hackers sent messages telling victims that their systems were infected (not true), and instructing the victim to go to a certain website and download the software or risk being banned from the Instant Messaging system. Users downloading as asked were actually tricked and got malicious software onto their computers that could then be used to launch a Distributed Denial of Service (DDoS) attack. (see also Distributed Denial-of-Service Attack, Social Engineering, Virus—Virus Hoax).

**Department of Defense Advanced Research Projects Agency (DARPA)**   is the USA Department of Defense's (DoDs) research agency that funded, through their Information Processing Techniques Office (IPTO), the development of the original Internet.

DARPA manages and directs selected basic and applied research and development projects for DoD, and pursues research and technology where risk and payoff are supposed to be high, while success may provide advances for traditional military roles and missions.

**Derf**   is the act of exploiting a terminal that someone else has left logged on while being away from one's desk.

**DES**   see Data Encryption Standard

**Design Vulnerability**   see Vulnerability of Design

**Desktop Personal Computer**—also called Desktop is a term normally used to distinguish it from notebooks, portable PCs and palm tops.

In Windows, the screen visible on the computer monitor is known as the desktop (your working place) and can be used to store programs and data as if it were a normal directory / folder. It is generally considered better practice to use the desktop as a place to store links to files and programs, rather than the files and programs themselves. This is partly because of the risk of accidental deletion, but—more importantly to companies—to avoid such files being visible to any curious passer-by.

**Development Library**   is an area of the computer systems' fixed storage space that is set aside for the development of software, thereby helping in minimizing or even avoiding the possibility of conflict between an existing program and a new version.

**Development Machine**   is a smaller system than the main one with similar configuration used for creating new or amending software, testing such software to ensure reliability and avoiding possible security effects on the main system being compromised by conflict between different versions of the same program. If no such machine is available, the Development Library may serve a similar purpose.

**DHTML**   see HyperText Markup Language

**Dial-up**   is using a computer modem to dial up an internet connection via the phone lines (see also Asymmetrical Digital Subscriber Line–ADSL or Digital Subscriber Line—DSL, Broadband and Cable).

**Dial-Back**   see Auto Dial-Back

**Digital Certificates**   is the electronic version of an ID card that establishes one's credentials and authenticates a person's connection when performing e-commerce or e-government transactions.

To obtain Digital Certificate an organization or individual must apply to a Certifications Authority which is responsible for validating and ensuring the authenticity of requesting organization. The Certificate will identify the name of the organization, a serial number, the validity date ("from / to") and the organization's Public Key where encryption to / from that organization is required.

In addition, the Digital Certificate will also contain the Digital Signature of the Certification Authority to allow any recipient to confirm the authenticity of the Digital Certificate.

A global standard (X. 509 Public Key Infrastructure for the Internet) defines the requirements for Digital Certificates and the major Certificate Authorities conform to this. Such standards, and the integrity of the Certificate Authorities are vital for the establishment of 'digital trust', without which e-Commerce will never attain its full potential.

**Digital Divide**   see Market

**Digital Forensics**   also called **Computer Forensics** was supposedly coined back in 1991 in the first training session held by the International Association of Computer Specialists (IACIS) in Portland, Oregon. Forensics is the extension of the techniques used in audit and police investigations to the world of bits. It will gain in importance as Information Security is recognized as a threat to organizations, governments and citizens.

Digital Forensics deals with the application of law to computer science and some refer to it as Forensic Computer Science. Computer forensics has been somewhat naively been described as the autopsy of a computer hard disk drive because specialized software tools and techniques are required to analyze the various levels at which computer data is stored after the fact. The discipline deals with the:

—preservation,
—identification,
—acquisition,
—extraction,
—documentation,
—safeguarding and
—analysis of

computer AND information network, infrastructure as well as information and data evidence that the findings can be used in a court of law.

Tools used to accomplish the above are usually software. To assure Reliability of results, different tools should be used by different investigators to allow cross-validation of data. Validity and Sampling issues are very important for assuring and maintaining the integrity of the results.

Some of the tools that stand out are Firewire, faster machines and Gig E. In 1999, the common practice to image a single drive machine was to turn off the computer, boot from a controlled floppy disk and send the image to a 2GB Jaz drive. In practice, an 8 GB HDD would have taken about 8–10 hours. Using Firewire, one may now image the same drive in 15–20 minutes. The major choke point of imaging single drive machines is the speed of the hard drive being imaged.

Accordingly, Forensics is more than getting data off the hard disk of a PC or server (see also Network Forensics below).

**Immature Science** means that the discipline's Paradigm, vocabulary, Methodology and so on are not yet well defined nor shared by all 'experts.' This certainly applies to Computer Forensics, whereby two experts most likely define the discipline in different ways and, as importantly, using different Methodology, approaches, tools and standards when doing their work (see also EpiSystemiology, Securmatics).

However, Digital Forensics can borrow much of its methodology or systematic approaches from such well established areas as Criminal Forensics as well as Environmental Forensics. Hence, while much is different information produced must convince a judge of the merit of the case and for this, it is not always necessary to re-invent the wheel.

**Microsoft Word**   documents are notorious for containing private information in file headers, therefore a bonanza for Forensic experts. The British government of Tony Blair learned this lesson the hard way.

During the week of June 23, 2003 Alistair Campbell, Blair's Director of Communications and Strategy, was in the hot seat in British Parliament hearings explaining what roles four of his employees played in the creation of a plagiarized dossier on Iraq which the UK government published in February 2003.

The names of these four employees were found hidden inside of a Microsoft Word file of the Iraq dossier which was posted on the 10 Downing Street web site for use by the press.

The "dodgy dossier" as it became known in the British press raised serious questions about the quality of British intelligence before the second Iraq war. Worst was that the same document was used by USA intelligence sources to prepare a paper for President Bush which the latter used during a press conference to justify the country's stance on the Iraq war.

Nonetheless, the lack of extensive use of Computer Forensics in the evidence published by the UK's independent inquiry (chaired by Judge Powell) into the presumed suicide of David Kelly again suggests that Computer Forensics still lacks credibility. This might be related to its maturity level (see also Evidence, Immature Science, Jurisdiction).

**Network Forensics**   is much more complex than just "the autopsy of a computer hard disk drive." For instance, Forensics tools for Windows are different than those required for networks. One may be able to handle limited analysis of DOS/Windows-based desktop and laptop PCs, but managing forensics on an HP 9000 with a terabyte of RAID-5 disk attached is out of the question. What about clustered disk farms and, even, servers with very large disks attached. Basically, examining a 2TB server requires a 2+TB server to examine the data and much patience.

Accordingly, Forensics has become a buzzword, but many forensic 'experts' have limited understanding what an attack looks like on a victim computer. They may neither know much about the attack itself nor how to manage an Intrusion Detection System (IDS).

Forensics is more than getting data off the hard disk of a PC or server. Comprehensive Forensics includes, but is not limited to Network Forensics and studying an entire attack from the attacker to the victim and beyond, while collecting the evidence accordingly.

**Methodology**   is still such that neither a common body of knowledge nor training does allow investigators to use similar methods when investigating a case. Lacking are:

testable theories,
peer reviewed methodologies and tools, and
replicable empirical research.

These standards that are the characteristics of an established or mature scientific discipline are not being met by today's Forensics. Unfortunately, a lack of standards and training can result in bad case law, guilty parties escaping prosecution and innocent parties being 'railroaded ' into incarceration.

To illustrate, in one instance a USA federal investigator was told to image a single drive Windows 2000 server. Instead of creating a digital image of the physical drive, the individual converted the file system from Fat 32 to NTFS, then made a logical backup of the drive. Accordingly, this act had destroyed the original evidence and damaged the court case. Standard procedure would have been to boot from a controlled floppy, create a physical image of the drive and send it to another hard drive without writing a thing to the victim drive. But than again, established standards are the characteristic of a mature science, which Forensics is not.

**Digital Information Management**   see Digital Rights Management (DRM)

**Digital Privacy**   see Privacy

**Digital Pseudonym**   is defined as the public key used to verify the signature done by the anonymous holder of the correspondent private key.

Digital Pseudonyms are certified by an authority upon users' requests. Certified pseudonyms are inserted in a list called roster. An authority receives the requests of certification of digital pseudonyms and inserts the pseudonyms that are accepted in the roster. Every request encloses a special message with no source address but a return address containing the proposed public key $P_v$ (pseudonym).

**Digital Rights Management (DRM)**   (sometimes also called Digital Information Management) lets a document owner define how recipients can handle documents in terms of forwarding, copying, and printing them. Also allows the DRM holder to determine expiration dates for those permissions. A document owner can also designate sections of a document that only certain people can change, force the use of revision marks for changes, and force the use of certain formatting and styles. Microsoft has integrated the same type of functionality into Office Excel 2003 and Office Outlook 2003.

To enable users to take advantage of DRM features in Office 2003, Windows Rights Management Services (RMS) for Windows Server 2003 has to be implemented first on the network. RMS is based on the Extensible Rights Markup Language (XrML), which is a method for defining rights and policies.

**Digital Signature** uses public-key algorithm to generate a digital signature, which is a block of data used to create some authentication (see also Signatures). When a judge sees a digital signature, he or she does not know anything about the signatory's intentions. He doesn't know if the person agreed to the document as one being presented with a notarized signature. Nor do we know if the signatory ever saw the signed document. The problem is that:

1) while a digital signature authenticates the document up to the point of the signing computer,
2) it does not authenticate the link between that computer and the individual.

Digital signatures prove, mathematically, that a secret value known as the private key was present in a computer at the time the person's signature was calculated. It is a small step from that inferring that the individual entered that key into the computer at the time of signing. But it is a much larger step to assume that the individual actually intended a particular document to be signed. And without a tamperproof computer trusted by the signing individual, one can expect "digital signature experts" to show up in court contesting a lot of digital signatures (see also Tables 10A and 10B).

**Public Key (PKI)** is used to verify that the signature was really generated using the corresponding private key. Public keys are often registered with a third party and can be downloaded so the person can check if the key is genuine. (See also Digital Signatures).

**Public Key Infrastructure** is needed as a means of generating and managing the encryption keys is required. It is the use and management of cryptographic keys-a public key and a private key-for the secure transmission and authentication of data across public networks. Vendor systems do, however, differ (Key Recovery, Encryption-Authorization).

**Private key:** The party initiating the sending of the document with the signature generated this key; it is needed to generate the digital signature. (See also Encryption and Tables 11A and 11B).

**Digital Subscriber Line (DSL)** is offered by phone companies to primarily private subscribers to achieve higher speeds than offered by a Asymmetrical Digital Subscriber Line—ADSL (see also Broadband and Cable, Satellite Broadband Access, Wireless Local Loop).

**Digital Versatile Disk (DVD)** is a technology using both sides of the disk, thereby being able to store a full length feature movie on a single CD size of up to approximately 17GB (see also Archive)

**Digital Watermark**   is a unique identifier being part of a digital document. The watermark is invisible to the human eye but a computer can analyze the document and extract the hidden data. The watermark cannot be removed.

The primary use of such marks is to allow different marks to be used when the document is copied to different persons and thereby establish an Audit Trail should there be any leakage of information.

**Disable**   means preventing hardware or software from functioning properly by, for instance, switching of a piece of equipment, or disconnecting power. Shareware or a trail version of promotional vendor software may come 'crippled' by, for instance, not permitting printing or saving of created files.

**Disassembly**   is the process used by anti-virus technicians to convert a virus into recognizable patterns that will permit the anti-virus programs to detect new malicious codes.

**Disaster Recovery Plan**   deals with the immediate crisis and tries to secure critical IT infrastructure by preventing further spread or continuation of the crisis such as a computer virus or a denial of service attack (see also Business Continuity Plan, Critical Infrastructure Protection).

The Disaster Recovery Plan is needed to make sure that when the disaster strucks, people are being taken to safety quickly, or the further spread of a Virus or Trojan horse can be prevented. Also, with the help of the Business Continuity Plan, systems can go online again immediately if need be or else within the time frame planned and agreed upon beforehand (see also Asset Value, Disruption Management).

**Disclaimer**   is often attached to **every mailed out** email message, similar to a signature and may look like this:

*SEULS LES DOCUMENTS SIGNES PAR LE CONSEIL DE L'IBPT OU UN DE SES DELEGUES ENGAGENT L'INSTITUT.*

*ENKEL DE DOCUMENTEN DIE DOOR DE RAAD VAN HET BIPT OF DOOR EEN VAN DE GEVOLMACHTIGDEN ERVAN ONDERTEKEND ZIJN VERBINDEN HET INSTITUUT.*

*NUR DIE DOKUMENTE DIE DURCH DEN RAT DES BIPT ODER EINER SEINER VERTRETER UNTERZEICHNET WERDEN BINDEN DAS INSTITUT.*

*ONLY THE DOCUMENTS SIGNED BY THE BIPT COUNCIL OR BY ONE OF ITS REPRESENTATIVES COMMIT THE INSTITUTE*

The above is short as far as disclaimers go. Nonetheless, having to have the disclaimer added to every single email in four languages makes getting messages from an employee working for this firm longer than need be.

However, the above disclaimer as compared to the one below (German and English) can still be seen as short:

*Diese Information ist ausschliesslich fuer die adressierte Person oder Organisation bestimmt und koennte vertrauliches und/oder privilegiertes Material enthalten. Personen oder Organisationen, fuer die diese Information nicht bestimmt ist, ist es nicht gestattet, diese zu lesen, erneut zu uebertragen, zu verbreiten, anderweitig zu verwenden oder sich durch sie veranlasst zu sehen, Massnahmen irgendeiner Art zu ergreifen. Sollten Sie diese Nachricht irrtuemlich erhalten haben, bitten wir Sie, sich mit dem Absender in Verbindung zu setzen und das Material von Ihrem Computer zu loeschen.*

*Sie haben uns gebeten, mit Ihnen ueber das Internet per E-Mail zu korrespondieren.*

*Unbeschadet dessen ist allein die von uns unterzeichnete schriftliche Fassung verbindlich.*

*Wir weisen darauf hin, dass derartige Nachrichten mit und ohne Zutun von Dritten verloren gehen, veraendert oder verfaelscht werden koennen. Herkoemmliche E-Mails sind nicht gegen den Zugriff von Dritten geschuetzt und deshalb ist auch die Vertraulichkeit unter Umstaenden nicht gewahrt. Wir haften deshalb nicht fuer die Unversehrtheit von E-Mails nachdem sie unseren Herrschaftsbereich verlassen haben und koennen Ihnen hieraus entstehende Schaeden nicht ersetzen. Sollte trotz der von uns verwendeten Virus-Schutz-Programmen durch die Zusendung von E-Mails ein Virus in Ihre Systeme gelangen, haften wir nicht fuer eventuell hieraus entstehende Schaeden. Dieser Haftungsausschluss gilt nur soweit gesetzlich zulaessig.*

*English:*

*The information transmitted is intended only for the person or entity to which it is addressed and may contain confidential and/or privileged material. Any review, retransmission, dissemination or other use of, or taking of any action in reliance upon, this information by persons or entities other than the intended recipient is prohibited. If you received this in error, please contact the sender and delete the material from any computer.*

*You have asked us to correspond with you via the internet per email.*

*However, the written version signed by us is the only authoritative version.*

*We draw your attention to the fact that such messages can be lost, changed or falsified, with or without any interference by third persons. Normal email s are not protected against access by third persons and, therefore, their confidentiality may not be assured in certain circumstances. We cannot be responsible for the integrity of emails after they have left our sphere of control. We shall not, therefore, indemnify you for any damages resulting out of these circumstances. If, despite our use of anti-virus software, a virus enters your systems in connection with the sending of the email, you may not hold us liable for any damages that may possibly arise in that connection. We will accept liability which by law we cannot exclude.*

The above seems like overkill but it comes from a law office which might explain it. Easier might be just to have something similar to:

Disclaimer applies to this message—see http://disclaimer.XYZ.com

The above option takes one line and saves space and bandwidth. For further details on this issue see also Warranty Disclaimer, and Jurisdiction and Email Signature.

**Discontinuous Innovation**   see Invention

**Discrete Multi-Tone (DMT)**   modulation is offered for Very high-speed Digital Subscriber Line (VDSL) applications. It presents a number of advantages for the VDSL environment, including but not limited to:

—Excellent performance, even under extreme channel and noise conditions,
—Robust performance when line conditions change, and
—Interoperability with ADSL, the most widely deployed DSL.

But some suggest that using Quadrature Amplitude Modulation (Qam)-VDSL, instead of DMT is more advantageous regarding protecting against channel and noise conditions as well as cost and speed considerations.

**Disinfection**   describes the killing of infectious agents outside the body (or program) by direct exposure to chemical or physical agents. In computer virus terminology this means removing a virus Code from the infected file or system.

Because standard conventions do not exist about what constitutes disinfection in the IT security field and amongst vendors, deletion of the infected object is usually considered the best form of disinfection.

Problems may occur when one anti-virus program deletes the last few digits of a computer virus for making it inoperable versus another a few at the beginning (see also EICAR Test File). Hence, while

• program A cleans the last digits of a virus,
• program B may clean the first few digits/characters of a virus.

Hence, program A may claim that a virus has been cleaned while program B may claim the machine has been infected by a virus.

**Generic Disinfection**   represents using heuristics rather than virus-specific techniques for disinfection.

**Generic Scan String**   matches more than one virus and while sometimes being questioned, these can detect an unknown virus very effectively (see also Signature)

**Disk Cache**   see Cache

**Disk Compression**   works by creating a "virtual disk" that is a large file that contains the compressed file(s). Unfortunately, scanning a compressed disk or file without the compression software running will typically hide viruses from a scanner (see also File Compression).

**Disposal of Media**   see Security of Media

**Disruption Management**   can be defined as a scenario, whereby a particular situation requires a sufficiently large deviation from normal procedures or plans, that they have to be changed substantially. I can be seen as part of a comprehensive Disaster Recovery Plan and Business Continuity Plan to secure quick reinstalling of services afer a disaster (e.g., 9/11 or earthquake).

Disruption management requires that a plan is designed in such a way that during the day of disruption, it can be adjusted to take last-minute changes into account. Else the plan incorporates and outlines the implementation steps of alternatives well ahead of potential problems.

A plan, such as coping with the possible Y2k disruption required that the plan was adjusted to take into account changing circumstances. This is typically called the **tracking process**. On the day of operation, the plan is implemented and the operation is monitored during execution. If the observed situation deviates marginally, no immediate action may be required to continue the operation. A substantial deviation (e.g., due to unfeasibility of plan or costs and benefits of running operation according to the plan changes), however, a disruption has occurred.

Intervention may be needed to resolve the inconsistencies resulting from the disruption or to decrease costs while improving benefits or revenues.

Consequence analyzers are tools based on software that may help decision-makers to simulate the effect of potential strategies. Also they help in developing a better understanding of the effect of different types of strategies (e.g., keep database running by all means, return to plan as fast as possible, or shut down the virtual private network for 24 hours)

Interventions can be expected or unexpected when a higher password is needed to perform a task or an error message informs a user about a printer error stopping a print job. A log of unexpected interventions should be main tained and reviewed at intervals to check if a pattern is developing with a particular program, user, or piece of equipment, which may require some repair, fix, or other corrective action.

**Distributed Denial-of-Service Attack**   (DDoS) is a distributed version of DoS. Many hosts are used to send packets to a target host. This way the host is flooded by a high amount of traffic and similar results to DoS are achieved (see also Denial-of-Service Attack—DoS).

Administrators should check any systems connected to the internet frequently for the presence of DDoS software that could be used to attack other networks by following the steps as outlined in Table 8.

Moreover, unnecessary ports should be closed. For instance, during August 2003 MSBlaster took advantage of known vulnerable network ports in Windows, ports that should have been closed.

**Table 8:** Distributed Denial-of-Service Attack (DDoS)—Tools to Reduce the Risk for a Successful DDoS

| Name of Category | Definition |
| --- | --- |
| Frequency | Use updated anti-virus software enabling the detection of file signatures on gateways, servers or PCs. However, updating once a week may be sufficient, whilst daily updates may not warrant the disruption or work services required considering the possible gains.<br><br>Even during a new virus attack, an anti-virus scanner's heuristics may detect a new version of a virus in the wild. Hence, while a subsequent update of virus signatures is advisable, panic and immediate update is not necessary. However, some programs may require an immediate update because heuristics do not yet detect a newly detected virus in the wild (e.g., Bugbear was such an example). |
| Scanners | DDoS network scanners such as the Remote Intrusion Detection Tool to check networks for the presence of DDoS file signatures (see also Resources—Software and Tools) |
| Host-Based System | Having installed a host based system for intrusion detection to detect the possible host compromise and the installation of Malicious Software |
| Integrity Tool | Using a file system integrity tool to check for changes made to key system files that could have been altered by Trojan Horse software |
| Monitoring Traffic | Software enabling monitoring of network traffice including intrusion detection systems (see Resources—Tools and Software) |
| Firewalls | Installed Firewalls enabling the blocking and logging of any communications to or from any DDoS software and Trojan Horse programs such as.<br><br>1.  activity on TCP ports 1524, 6665-6669, 16600, 27444, 27665, 31,335, 65000, or<br><br>2.  ICMP Echo and Echo Reply packets |
| Vulnerability Testing Tool | Using a tool that permits testing of network and internet gateways including servers for vulnerabilities that are known to exist but that can be eliminated. |
| Vulnerability Testing Tool–Web Page Programming | Automatic testing of web-page scripts that might be updated several times a day for programming mistakes that might inadvertently increase the system's vulnerability for attacks. |

**Note.** The above Table provides an overview. What is becoming an increasing problem is to assure that scripts on web pages are not allowing hackers to exploit errors that might harm the firm's Critical Information Infrastructure (CII). See also Tables 13A–13C.

Blaster made use of Internet port 135 to spread itself and so many ISP's followed advice from the US Department of Homeland Security (DHS) to shut down incoming traffic on this port. A good interim measure except that port 135 is also used by Outlook and Exchange Server to communicate.

Unfortunately, if a firm uses the Microsoft Exchange Server, blocking port 135 may result in its road warriors being unable to collect Outlook mail while on the road. Outlook does not provide an error message about the problem, instead one simply fails to connect very inconvenient for Microsoft Outlook customers and Exchange Server administrators.

During Fall 2003 Microsoft started to recommend blocking port 135 but, unfortunately, failed to combine that new recommendation with a note about the effect for existing customers.

The above illustrate that system complexity or inter-linkage (see Systems) can trigger side-effects due to security measures that cause interruptions.

**Distributed Tools** are distributed to multiple hosts that care then coordinated to perform an attack on a target host simultaneously after some delay.

**Distributed Processing** means two or more computers in geographically separate locations. For instance, mirroring between sites is a contingency plan for sudden disaster. If one computer fails or is disabled, the remaining computer(s) can still carry the load without disruption to users and without loss or corruption of data.

**DDL** see Dynamic Link Library

**DMZ** see Demilitarized Zone

**DNS** see Domain Name System

**DNS Spoofing** see Domain Name System

**Document** represents information regardless of physical form or characteristics. Often it is used interchangeably with record. A document could be an individual record or an item or non-record materials or of personal papers.

**Documentary Materials** encompasses records and non-record materials. It refers to all media on which information is recorded, regardless of the nature of the medium or the method or circumstances of recording.

**Domain** is a name is associated with an organization to help identify systems uniquely—also a sub-tree under a location in a domain name tree.

**Domain Name** is a part of the *fully qualified domain name* (FQDN) after first dot in the name. Fore example is hosts name is foo.mydomain.net then domain name is mydomain.net.

**Domain Name System (DNS)** is the internet system that relates domain names with IP addresses

**Domain Name System (DNS) Database** is a distributed database used to map *IP address* to *host names* and vice versa. For example one host can be identified by numerical address IP address 130.227.165.197 and symbolic host name conference.eicar.org

**Doman Name System (DNS) Interrogation**    is a process of exploring *DNS database*.

**Domain Name System (DNS) Spoofing**    means that by corrupting the name service cache of an attacked system or else by compromising a domain name server for a valid domain, the attacking system assumes the DNS name of the compromised/victimized system.

**Domains of Information Security Space (DISS)**    see Securematics, Table 23D

**DOS**    (Disk Operating System) was Microsoft's first operating system for PCs. It was massively used until about 1995 when it began to be substituted by more complex operating systems, such as Windows 95/98 and 2000.

**DoS**    see Denial-of-Service Attack (DoS)

**Down Time**    is the amount of time a system is down during a given period due to crashes, system problems and scheduled maintenance work. The downtime log lists when, why and what system was not available to users, enabling at regular intervals the identifying of any recurring problems and failure patterns (see also Patch, User Acceptance Testing).

System crashes with Windows including XP and later versions are regular resulting in unnecessary Down Time. For instance, while writing the dictionary, several times files got corrupted and when trying to reload the file, Word shut down asking me if I wanted to send a report to Microsoft (see also Stability).

The reports obviously accumulate in some database. We hope that if one bin piles up with similar crash memos, the coders get to work.

Exactly how many notifications does Microsoft get? Nobody knows for sure, but based on comments Bill Gates made at a July 2003 meeting for analysts, the number must be astronomical. Some facts:

- Gates said that 5% of Windows machines crash, on average, TWICE DAILY
- 10% of Windows machines crash DAILY or any given machine will crash about THREE X a month.

According to StatMarket.com, as of March 2003, Windows XP had:

a)  33.41% of global market share among operating systems, if we assume

b)  35% for simplicity's sake, this works out to a minimum of 30 billion Windows system crashes per year.

This is the SAME number as:

- gallons of fresh water California wastes because of mismanagement,
- the dollar total for the Enron scam, and
- worldwide cost of SARS.

We are partial to the number ZERO, and think that maybe that should be the target for Microsoft.

Finally, after sending in a report, one usually gets provided with some information what might have caused the crash—but more often than not, the report is useless for the user or why should a driver have to be replaced (as requested by Windows) when until last night it worked properly?

Incidentally, after you replaced the driver, guess what, Windows crashes again... claiming the driver must be replaced as happened to me last week... hmm... its always a driver or maybe Windows :-(

**Downing the System** is usually done for maintenance, installation of new hardware, loading new software or other work required to keep the system run smoothly. This should be done during times were the system is unlikely to be used, such as during weekends or public holidays (see also Capacity Planning, Load and Resilience).

**Driver** is a small interface program that permits a computer to communicate with a peripheral device, such as a printer or a scanner. The driver will be automatically installed when one connects the device to the PC; hence the need for a CD-ROM or floppy disk when installing such peripherals.

**Dropper** is a program that has been modified in order to install the virus on the system under attack.

**DSA** see Digital Signature Algorithm

**DVD** see Digital Versatile Disk

**Dual Control** is based on the premise that for a breach to be committed, both parties would need to be in collusion since both are required to complete the process

**Nested Dual Control Access** means that, for instance, two pairs of people are required to enable access for higher level authorization password required to permit the entry of data created or amended by another person.

Some vendors have started to sell 'trusted operation systems' that enforce requirement for dual control and the separation of duties, to provide substantially greater Information Security.

**Dumb Terminal** or Visual Display Terminal (VDT) is a terminal that consists of a keyboard and display screen being used to enter and transmit data to, or display data from, a computer or server to which it is connected. In contrast to a PC, it has no independent processing or storage capability, hence it cannot function as a stand-alone device.

**Dynamic Link Library (DLL)** is an exectuable file containing routines that canb e accessed by one or more Windows executables.

**Early Warning Information System (EWIS)** (see also Early Warning System) assists experts and policy makers in assessing desired options for:

1) early warnings and alerts about malicious code, vulnerabilities and bugs;
2) access to threat assessment & trend analysis including statistics;
3) providing of a service for incident response support (e.g., helpdesk); and
4) access to approved educational/training products

An effective early warning system's activities encompass but are not limited to helping reduce risks and vulnerabilities exploited through intrusion, data theft, hacking, malicious code and other attacks by focusing on four themes, namely:

- Network information security,
- Cybercrime,
- Privacy/data protection, and
- Critical infrastructure protection (CIP)

**Early Warning System (EWS)** for **IT Security Surveillance** is based on a specific procedure to detect as early as possible any departure from usual or normal observed frequency of phenomena. For example, the routine monitoring of internet traffic or traffic patterns on various networks or servers can be used as an early warning system for the identification of possible denial-of-service (DoS) attacks.

**Earnings** see Revenues

**Eavesdropping on Emanations**  is the listening to electromagnetic signals surrounding computer and network equipment (see also Van Eck Radiation and also Tempest).

**e-Biz**  see e-Commerce

**e-Business**  see e-Commerce

**e-Commerce**  can be divided into two general types (see also Decoupling), namely:

1) Business to Consumer / Customer (B2C)
2) Business to Business (B2B)

It is usually an electronic transaction whereby the parties agree, confirm, and initiate both payment and transfer of goods with a click of the mouse. However, in the B2B context it is often to support communication, information exchange, just-in-time efforts and logistics, instead of activating a large order with a mouse click (see also Decoupling).

B2C usually requires the acceptance of credit cards, cybercash or using cash-on-delivery (e.g., in some countries done by the post office) to complete the transaction (see also Cybercash)

**e-Government**  is the public's efforts to bring dealings with the government online, thereby enabling citizens to conduct most of their businesses (e.g., ordering a passport) online. Accordingly, while the UK wants every government transaction to be offered online by 2005, Denmark has chosen to provide all of its citizens with digital signatures to enable them to do all their transactions online (see also Digital Signatures).

Pushing e-Government initiatives requires satisfactory IT security of information, data and protection of people's privacy which can be a challenge. For instance in 2002, Canada's Auditor General released a report in which it stated that government sites do not seem to do well as far as privacy and data security are concerned. His 2003 report acknowledged some improvements but did not yet give e-Government sites a passing grade. Quite likely, other governments may have to improve on this score as well.

As Table 9 suggests, putting down a policy about e-government and IT initiatives is important. The hard work follows thereafter. Providing every citizen with a digital signature is a start but, without addressing the issues in Table 9, it is unlikely to improve service for citizens. Accordingly, governments will have to learn how to manage the changed relationships with their citizens and business thanks to e-government. Also, Identity Theft may become an issue thanks to increased use of digital signatures by citizens interacting with the government.

**Table 9:** E-Government

| Category | Definition |
|---|---|
| **E-Government** Could be described as: | • Transforming government to be more citizen-centered, <br> • Permitting government to provide better services at lower costs, and in some European countries, <br> • To compensate for lower staff levels that could occur within a few years due to large employee cohorts' retiring (i.e. aging population), while keeping service levels high and, as importantly, cutting costs. |
| **Information View** Results in the following: | 1) eliminating the need to collect the same or similar information more than once within a department or government; and <br> 2) providing government programs with access to information collected by other programs, especially where this would improve the efficiency and effectiveness of government service delivery <br><br> all without possible weakening citizens' Privacy and Data Protection. |
| **Work Processes** Are likely to change as follows: | A) single window / seamless service so that common clients can get delivery through a single window free of functional and organizational barriers, <br> B) streamlining the process by moving from task-oriented to service-oriented delivery, <br> C) providing citizens with choices about how government services are delivered, <br> D) consistency, whereby similar types of work activities performed by different agencies will be done the same way, <br> E) location and time independence, thereby giving citizens access anyplace at anytime to government services, and <br> F) continuous improvement of services with measurements embedded in the service process by measuring progress, customer needs and client satisfaction using Benchmarking and Metrics. |

**Note.** This categorization outlines the information improvements and changes in work processes. Achieving the latter is necessary to attain any effective type of e-government benefitting stakeholders such as citizens and firms.

Governments everywhere are trying to get onto the E-Government bandwagon. Nonetheless, at best E-Government will increase accessibility, convenience and service levels for citizens (e.g., filing an application in the evening when offices are closed), at the worst it will fail to do so. Realizing cost savings on top is an unlikely event.

Until 2002, in most countries beside the USA, Identity Theft was not much of an issue. Germany tried to accelerate the use of digital signatures by citizens and government agencies, after spending millions of Euros the project is so far considered a failure. Moreover, the UK's e-Envoy office is also reporting problems with digitizing government services there.

A study surveying a sample of 1,000 Swiss internet users during May 2003 revealed they would appreciate the possibility through e-government services to:

- 83% would like the opportunity change their address with the community office online (Swiss have to register and de-register when moving house within and to another community, this usually takes a trip or two to the community government offices one resides in);
- 65% would want to be able to apply for jobs online,
- 72% would want to be able to vote online even though various studies in Europe and the USA suggest that security and authentication is problem regarding electronic voting (see see E-Voting) (Swiss vote several times each year in national, cantonal and local referendums),
- over 50% would value a simple, informative e-Government service portal that offers secure services,
- 75% also were concerned about security regarding providing personal data online

The above findings are not anything new but simply indicate that Swiss citizens want e-Government initiatives to facilitate their administratively required interactions with the government ranging from getting a license, being registered or even doing taxation work online.

More important with the above findings is that even during 2003, it appears that Switzerland and many other nations were still far awary from succeeding with their digitizing efforts to the fullest. Accordingly, e-Government may still be a long time in the making (e.g., see also e-Voting). Moreover, to maintain Trust and Confidence, the Risk for disasters (e.g., with citizen data) must be reduced as much as possible, since one disaster may wipe out any progress made by having citizens simply refuse to use e-Government services.

**e-Mail**   see EMail

**e-Voting**   encompasses the management of the traditional voting procedure by means of feasible automatic procedures executed with the help of information systems. An Internet-based election system uses electronic ballots that allow voters to transmit their ballot to election officials. There are three ways in which e-Voting can be supported and in many cases they might run concurrently:

- **Polling Place Internet Voting** describes the situation where terminals permitting the casting of one's vote are available. Election officials guarantee the voters' authentication. Voters have to go to polling stations but the tallying process is automated.
- **Kiosk Voting** are located in popular and convenient areas for citizens to cast their vote by using tamper-resistant voting terminals.
- **Remote Internet Voting** is unsupervised casting of ballots over the internet using a computer not necessarily owned and operated by election personnel.

The above is intended to make internet voting secure by limiting fraud, coercion, and wrong tally. If the security infrastructure of registration and authentication is used improperly, it might be exploited for frauds such as adding votes of ghosts and ineligible voters.

As Table 10A suggests, various criteria must be met to make e-Voting secure. For instance, if Digital Signatures are used, the question arises if for every election new keys must be distributed and verified and authenticated

**Table 10A:** Criteria for an Electronic Voting (E-Voting) System—Voters and Votes

| Name of Category | Definition of Category |
|---|---|
| Voter Eligibility | Only authorized voters can take part in the voting process. The internet voter registration system must, therefore, verify the voters' eligibility. Determining citizenship, correct age, current legal residence, as well as the fact that the person is still alive needs to be checked. Precaution against possible identity theft is also necessary. Registration card, or Social Security Number may be incorrect, stolen or unaccounted for. |
| Voter Authentication | Verification of the true source of a message meaning that verification of the electronic ballot assures that the person is really who one claims to be and not just from someone trying to electronically impersonate that individual. |
| Vote Uniqueness | Voters are not able to vote more than once during a particular election. |
| Vote Integrity | Votes cannot be modified, forged, or deleted without detection. |
| Vote Accuracy | Votes may not be altered, duplicated, or removed undetectably, nor should invalid votes be tabulated in a final tally. Election systems must record votes correctly and make the count unassailable. |

**Note.** This taxonomy provides an overview of what might be needed to secure a safe voting system via the internet. While it includes the major categories of concerns, it is not all inclusive.

This taxonomy could also be applied to trust and e-commerce, since the term voter could be replaced with the word customer, and the verb vote, with purchase or purchasing to make the definitions more applicable to e-commerce.

Also, a software-based solution may require the person to do e-voting from a particular PC connected to the internet. A hardware-based solution (e.g., using also Biometric measures) may permit the individual to vote or purchase from any machine that enables secure identification and authentication using Biometric measures and tools. (see also Tables 4A, 4B & 4C).

(i.e. costly for government) or if a person's verified Digital Signature from a Trusted Authority can be used as often as needed. For instance, same public key the person uses with all other transactions with the government (e.g., to get a passport, file tax return and change of address) is also used in the voting process.

Table 10B also outlines how the election system and its voting process must be designed to address some of the issues such as Verrifiability and Cost Efficiency.

Regardless of the above efforts, like traditional ballot voting, e-Voting can also be rigged and in most countries regulatory steps are still needed to make e-Voting an eligible procedure for national elections, or referendums (e.g., California's regulator cases of electorates having to vote on a proposition) (see also Table 10B).

Finally, privacy including Information-Theoretic Privacy, Fail-Safe Privacy and Computational Privacy must all be address (see all terms explain as sub-headings under Privacy).

**Editor**   is a program that allows a user to create, view, and amend, the contents of certain types of files. There are several types of editors, the most common being Text Editors, and Hex (Hexadecimal) Editors.

Editors work at the lowest level, either in ASCII (Text Editor) or directly with disk contents (Hex Editor). Although text Editors, such as Notepad in Windows are common, Hex Editors can do considerable damage to the contents of computer files, which may not be recoverable.

Accordingly, a Word Processor can edit its own files, but is not considered an Editor in this context (see also Hexadecimal Editor).

**EICAR**   (European Institute for Computer Anti-Virus Research) was founded in 1991 by anti-virus experts. Today its focus has expanded into IT security issues in general. Membership consists of experts from universities, governments, vendors and users interested in reducing Risks, Vulnerabilities, Threats, and Malicious Code infections of systems and software, addressing Jurisdiction and regulatory issues, while advancing Critical Infrastructure Protection.

Members must adhere to EICAR's Code of Conduct, membership is open to all. The association is registered in Munich and holds annual meetings (http://www.EICAR.org) (see also Table 16B).

**EICAR Standard Anti-Virus Test File**   is a .COM file that can be used to test whether anti-virus software is active and working properly. It is safe to pass around, because it is not a virus, and does not include any fragments of viral code. Most products react to it as if it were a virus (though they typically report it with an obvious name, such as "EICAR-AV-Test").

**Table 10B:** Criteria for an Electronic Voting (E-Voting) System–Election System and Process

| Name of Category | Definition of Category |
|---|---|
| Election Integrity and Privacy | Privacy must be secured for the voter casting a ballot, while the ability for anyone to audit the election for verifiability and the security of the system must be secured.<br>    Hence, data must be protected from undetected modification by unauthorized persons, by using, for instance, a cryptographic hash or digital signature. |
| Verifiability and Auditability | Votes cast must be counted and attributed correctly. Once a vote is cast, an unalterable record must be created, thereby ensuring a verifiable electronic audit trail. |
| Reliability | Ability of the system to perform and not show difficulty to perform reliably due to design, implementation or configuration mistakes of the e-voting system(s) (see also Reliability) |
| Secrecy and Anonymity | Secrecy must be provided, while the vote is en route to the election registrar and individual's voting behavior cannot be determined nor can voters proof how they voted subsequent to casting their vote electronically. |
| Simplicity and Transparency | Citizens must be able to view and understand how elections are conducted and how the voting process occurs. Casting should be easy and simple. |
| Cost Efficiency | E-voting should be affordable and cost efficient compared to other methods. |
| Law and Regulation | Election regulation must be such that electronic voting is permissible. For instance, some countries require the physical presence when voting, hence only voting kiosk-type solutions at a voting station may be feasible unless regulation is changed.<br>    Other countries already permit absentee ballots via surface mail and may, therefore, require limited regulatory adjustments only to make internet-based voting feasible. |

*Note.* This taxonomy provides an overview of what might be needed to secure a safe voting system via the internet. While it includes the major categories of concerns, it is not all inclusive.

This taxonomy could also be applied to trust and e-commerce, since the term voter could be replaced with the word customer, and the verb vote, with purchase or purchasing to make the definitions more applicable to e-commerce.

Also, a software-based solution may require the person to do e-voting from a particular PC connected to the internet. A hardware-based solution (e.g., using also Biometric measures) may permit the individual to vote or purchase from any machine that enables secure identification and authentication using Biometric measures and tools.

The file is a legitimate DOS program, and produces sensible results when run (it prints the message "EICAR-STANDARD-ANTIVIRUS-TEST-FILE").

**Electro Smog or Electrosmog**    derives from the word smog [see also Wireless, Multiple-In, Multiple-Out (MIMO)].

**Smog** is general defined as a fog made heavier and darker by smoke and chemical fumes that can also be defined as a photochemical haze caused by the action of solar ultraviolet radiation on atmosphere polluted with hydro-carbons and oxides of nitrogen from automobile exhaust.

The term Electrosmog is usually not defined in a general dictionary (e.g., Webster). It is the non-ionising electromagnetic pollution of technical origin which, in contrast to 'classical' smog **escapes detection by the human senses**. It can have:

• thermal effects—heating of biological tissue

Basis of current safety guidelines–critical value for cellular phones is 2W/kg by the International Commission on Non-Ionising Radiation while the German Ministry for the Environment recommends 0.6 W/kg. To illus-trate, GSM phones, such as a Nokia 6210 has 1.19 W/kg and the newer Nokia 8850 is rated with 0.22 W/kg.

Extensive use of a cellular phone can result in microwave-alike heating of the brain that change the brain's functions and result in head tumors, skin changes, headaches and cataract eye disease. Furthermore,

• non-thermal effects–pulsed radiation and extremely low frequencies on the human organism, humans' sensitivity against stroboscobic character and the periodicity of the signal (not addressed by existing safety guidelines) are also matters of concern.

Measurement is W/Sqm (Watt per square meter) with a recommendation of 10 MicroWatt per square meter (10 Micro W/Sqm). Standards vary widely such as Germany with 4.5, Austria, 0.001 and Russia with 0.02 W/Sqm [see also Wireless, Multiple-In, Multiple-Out (MIMO)].

Pulsed frequencies are close to the frequencies of human cells. This could result in these cells changing their information while the electroencephalo-gram (EEG) that measures the brain waves is also altered. Blood pressure during resting can be increased due to exposure and the permeability of the brain-blood barrier is also changed, while sleep disruptions are also possible.

Electro Smog is an issue for any apartment or office having electricity plugs and lines, being located near power lines, as well as wireless anten-nas. Additionally using cellular phones as well as cordless ones at home may increase one's exposure to electro smog [see also Wireless, Multiple-In, Multiple-Out (MIMO)].

**Wireless Access** in hotels, coffee shops, airports and many more places exposes users and innocent bystanders (e.g., babies) to non-thermal effects that could result in long-term health effects about which we are still uncertain at this time.

Finally, how such access and electrosmog through wireless LANs, cellular phones and cordless phones might affect workers is still unclear. But likely a few regulatory developments will be forthcoming, while liability cases will enter some USA courts soon.

**Electronic Attack**   see Electronic Warfare

**Electronic Mail**   see EMail

**Electronic Protection**   see Electronic Warfare

**Electronic Recordkeeping System**   describes a system in which records are collected, organized, and categorized to facilitate their preservation, retrieval, use, and disposition.

**Electronic Shredding**   (see also Security of Media—Magnetic Overwrite, Degaussing) addresses the issue that when a file is deleted from a hard drive, it is just removed from sight. The reference to the file's data is deleted, contents remain on the drive until overwritten by other data. Hence, such information can be retrieved (see also eMail—Delete).

A file is stored in *clusters* that are placed on the hard drive's platters wherever the operating system can find space. The system for keeping track of clusters involves three main elements:

1) File system—stores low-level information about which clusters on the platters are available for writing and which ones belong to which file.
2) Directory structure or hard drive folders—these special files that contain an entry for each file and subdirectory inside them. It is a metaphor since folders do not actually contain anything, they are just file directories.
3) Actual data—stored information on hard disk.

When deleting a file, the operating system informs the file system that the file's clusters are now available. It writes a special one-character code to the beginning of the directory entry for that file to mark the file as deleted. However, the file's directory information, unless overwritten, is still stored in the directory. Accordingly, the file's data still exist on the disk. Someone looking a the disk using low-level software tools can read the files that were actually deleted.

Electronic Shredding may consist of four distinct operations:

1) Data bit locations or file's data clusters must be overwritten with a pattern, such as binary zeros, verification that it has occurred is necessary;
2) Renaming the file with a randomly generated name, thereby destroying the file's original name in its directory entry;
3) Truncating the file to 0 (zero) bytes in length, in order to discard the file's size and starting cluster number; and
4) Deleting and renaming the truncated file.

On a hard drive, each bit is stored as a *magnetic transition*. If a bit is polarized one way, it is a 1, if the other way, it is a 0 (zero). The disk's read-write head applies a specific signal strength when it writes a bit. The signal is not always strong enough to saturate the magnetic media. The absolute strength of a given bit's magnetization can be affected by what was there before. Accordingly, a 1 replacing a 0 (zero) may be a bit weaker than a 1 replacing a 1. Using special hardware to detect the absolute strength of the recorded signal, it is possible to deduce what a given bit's previous state might have been. This is especially true if data were overwritten by a known pattern, such as all 0s (zeros), all 1s, or a single 8-bit value repeated over and over again (see also Forensics).

In order to eliminate this ghosting, the region must be rerecorded several times using different data each time. Hence, this destroys any correlation with the region's original contents.

The above steps must be repeated based on the Risk Assessment requirements but overwriting multiple times with varying bit patterns (Security of Media) is the most effective approach.

Finally with recycling becoming mandatory under the European Union's Waste Electrical and Electronic Equipment Directive (EU-WEEED), Electronic Degaussing is becoming a paramount concern in the Security of Media domain. Specifically, after such hardware has left the organization to be re-used, data may end up with parties who are not authorized to see it (see also Memory Stick, such as 'new one' containing patient records).

**Electronic Voting**   see E-Voting

**Electronic Warfare**   is usually military action (sometimes initiated by terrorists instead) involving the use of electromagnetic and directed energy to either control the electromagnetic spectrum or attack the enemy. The three major categories of Electronic Warfare are:

1) **Electronic Attack** involves the use of electromagnetic, directed energy, or anti-radiation weapons to attack personnel, facilities, or equipment. The intent is to degrading, neutralize, or destroy enemy combat capability.

   Such activities may include actions taken in order to prevent or reduce the other party's effective us of the electromagnetic spectrum. This is accomplished by using jamming and electromagnetic deception or the use of weapons that apply electromagnetic or directed energy as their primary destructive mechanism (e.g., lasers, radio frequency, and particle beams).

2) **Electronic Protection** encompasses actions undertaken to protect personnel, facilities, and also equipment from any effects of electronic attack (on purpose or unintentional) that might degrade, neturalize, or even destroy friendly combat capability.

3) **Electronic Warfare Support (ES)** involves actions guided toward searching for, intercepting, identifying, and locating sources of intentional or unintentional radiated electromagnetic energy for the purpose of immediate threat recognition. Electronic Warfare Support does, therefore, provide the information required for immediate decisions involving Electronic Warfare activities and other tactical actions such as homing, targeting, and threat avoidance. Hence, ES can also be used to produce signals intelligence.

**Electrosmog**   see Eletro Smog (above)

**eMail**   or Electronic Mail–is an electronically transmitted message which arrives as a computer file on a user's PC or the corporation's server. Originally conceived as a simple means of sending short messages from one computer to another, the Simple Mail Transfer Protocol (SMTP) was introduced without security in mind.

Whilst standards have been agreed for the attachment of files to eMail messages, be aware that such files can contain Malicious Code such as a Virus.

eMail is insecure because:

1) Message can purport to have been sent from an individual, whilst it was sent from somebody else, possible misrepresentation;
2) The From field may have been modified to indicate a sender that is fallacious or does not exist;
3) Because there is no Authentication, the eMail can be opened by anyone unless it is encrypted (see also Encryption);
4) When sending eMail, the sender has no guarantee that the recipient has received it after passing through multiple computer nodes to get to the final destination, hence, without requesting safe receipt there is little guarantee (see also Disclaimer); and
5) eMail is not a legal document unless sent using a digital signature but by 2002, EU member states and the USA (some states) begun accepting documents with Digital Signatures as legally binding documents.

**Deleting eMail—NOT**   goes against the common wisdom, but unless one is really concerned about the size of one's mailbox or the performance of the eMail program, one must not delete eMail.

Once one empties the Trash or Deleted Items folder it's exceedingly difficult (in most cases impossible) to resurrect an eMail, and it's all too easy to toss out a vital piece of correspondence together with the spam. In fact, if one has the eMail program set up to empty the trash automatically when exiting the program, it's almost certain one day one is going to eliminate a message one really should have kept (see also Table 6—Audit, also Jurisdiction).

One preferred method of managing email is to sort it into folders and sub-folders either immediately after dealing with each item or having it pre-sourted by using filters most programs offers. Plonking the unwanted stuff into the Deleted Items folder, and emptying that every few days is safer than getting rid of emails.

**Email–Delete-** When one deletes email, such as spam, in one's eMail program/software (e.g., Eudora, Mozilla, Outlook), it doesn't get zapped immediately. Instead, it is first shunted to the Deleted Items or Trash folder from which one can retrieve it if need be. Once one empties the Trash or Deleted Items folder the e-Mails are gone for good.

Nonetheless, although the deleted eMails are now out of reach, the eMail program does not reclaim the space used by those eMails until one *compacts* the mail folders.

Compacting mail folders does not only permit one to regain wasted hard disk space, but often it will make the eMail program run faster and may reduce the risk of mail folders becoming damaged.

**eMail Bombing** (sometimes called bottlenecking) is characterized by abusers repeatedly sending an identical eMail message to a particular address. It involves material being sent electronically to a organization's access points (typically EMail servers) in such large quantities that the system becomes blocked, and genuine business material cannot get through (see also Bottlenecking).

**eMail Signature** or .sig ('dot sig'), refers to the optional footer text appended to the end of each outward email. Normally, a signature file includes the sender's name, and other contact details, such as telephone number and web site address (see also Disclaimer).

Revealing too much information to too many parties including phone and fax numbers may also increase the Risk for Identity Theft.

The eMail Signature may also have Privacy information included and/or a disclaimer, such as:

---

### Internet Email Confidentiality Footer

Privileged / Confidential Information may be contained in this message. If you are not the addressee indicated in this message (or responsible for delivery of the message to such person), you may not copy or deliver this message to anyone. In such case, you should destroy this message, and notify us immediately. If you or your employer does not consent to internet email messages of this kind, please advise us immediately. Opinions, conclusions and other information expressed in this message are not given or endorsed by my firm or employer unless otherwise indicated by an authorized representative independent of this message.

---

**eMail Spamming**   (see Spam)

**eMail Spoofing**   may occur in different forms but usually works like this: a
user receives email that appears to have originated from one source when it
actually was sent from another source.

Email spoofing is often an attempt to trick the user into making a damaging
statement or releasing sensitive information such as Passwords.

**Emoticons**   are a clever combination of keyboard characters to punctuate a
message with just the right spirit. To read them, one has to tilt one's head
slightly to the left, such as :-) indicating a smiley ☺.

**Encapsulating Security Payload (ESA)**   is a mechanism that if applied provides confidentiality and integrity protection to IP datagrams.

**Encryption**   is the process of conversion of an easily understood format (text)
into another format apparently lacking sense because it is encoded. The
encrypted text is called ciphertext (see also Overhead).

In the Encryption context, Algorithms use a key to control encryption and
decryption (See Algorithm), two categories are used:

- **Symmetric (or Secret-key):** Uses the same key for encryption & decryption, or
  the latter key is easily derived from the encryption key (see also Algorithms).
- **Asymmetric (or Public key):** A different key is used for encrypting and decrypting a message; accordingly, the decrypting key cannot be derived from the
  encrypting key. (See also Algorithms, Tables 11A and 11B).

A majority of cryptographic products are software rather than hardware
based. Moreover, many are communications-oriented rather than data storage
oriented; they heavily tend towards secure electronic mail, IP security (IPsec),
and Virtual Private Network applications.

In 1999 a report identified 805 hardware and / or software products incorporating cryptography manufactured in 35 countries outside the United
States. Most were manufactured in these countries in that order:

United Kingdom, followed by Germany, Canada, Australia, Switzerland,
Sweden, the Netherlands, and Israel.

Other countries accounted for slightly more than a quarter of the world's
total of encryption products. Table 11A outlines some of the algorithms that
have been used based on the DES standard.

Table 11B outlines the various standards that were submitted for testing
and examination. These finalists were part of the tests being undertaken to
select the Advanced Encryption Standard (AES) Rijndael (see Table 11B).

**Homomorphic Encryption**   is a cryptographic technique in which the sum
of two encrypted values is equal to the encrypted sum of the values. The
signature operation in public key cryptography is an exponentiation operation
using the private key as the exponent.

**Table 11A:** Encryption-Decryption Algorithms[1]

| Name of Algorithm | Description of Algorithm |
|---|---|
| DES—Data Encryption Standard–US | Has been the most popular encryption algorithm of the past twenty-five years. Originally developed at IBM Corporation, it was chosen by the USA National Bureau of Standards (NBS, now renamed the National Institute of Standards and Technology, or NIST) as the government-standard encryption algorithm in 1976. Since then, it has become a domestic and international encryption standard, and has been used in thousands of applications. Concerns about its short key length have dogged the algorithm since the beginning, and in 1998 a brute-force machine capable of breaking DES was built. Today, modifications to DES, such as triple-DES, ensure that it will remain secure for the foreseeable future. |
| | DES is a block cipher, meaning that it encrypts and decrypts data in blocks: 64-bit blocks. DES is an iterated cipher, meaning that it contains 16 iterations (called rounds) of a simpler cipher. |
| DSA (Digital Signature Algorithm) | Was mandated by the Federal Information Processing Standard FIPS 186 (US). This is a public key system, but unlike RSA or IDEA, it can only be used for making signatures. |
| IDEA (International Data Encryption Algorithm) | A private key encryption-decryption algorithm that uses a key that is twice the length of a DES key. This symmetric key lock cipher algorithm was developed by Xuejia Lai and James Massey in 1991. |
| RSA (Rives, Shamir, Adleman) | Is a public key crypto system for both encryption and authentication, it was invented in 1977 by Ron Rives, Adi Shamir, and Leanard Adleman it works as follows: |

1) Taking two large primes, $p$ and $q$ and finding their product $n = pq$; $n$ is called the modulus;

2) Choosing a number, $e$, less than $n$ and relatively prime to $(p - 1)(q - 1)$, which means that $e$ and $(p - 1)(q - 1)$ have no common factors except 1.

3) Looking for another number $d$, such that $(ed - 1)$ is divisible by $(p - 1)(q - 1)$

The values $e$ and $d$ are called the public and private exponents, respectively.

- public key is the pair $(n, e)$;
- private key is $(n, d)$

The factors $p$ and $q$ can be kept with the private key, or else they are simply destroyed. Voters are not able to vote more than one.

**Note.** This table lists a few of the most popular DES algorithms.

[1] Algorithm is usually a mathematical formula or set of steps for solving a particular problem. In the Virus context an algorithm is a set of operations or a procedure designed to solve the Virus inflicted problem (see Algorithm for more information on this).

In the context of Digital Signatures or Encryption, the algorithm describes how the signature or text is encrypted using mathematical formulas (see also Algorithm).

**Table 11B:** Encryption-Decryption Algorithms[1]

| Name of Algorithm | Description of Algorithm |
|---|---|
| AES—Advanced Encryption Standard | In 1997, National Institute of Standards (NIST), a USA organization solicited algorithms for the AES, to replace DES as a government encryption standard. It received 15 submissions, 10 were from outside the US, namely Australia, Belgium, Canada, Costa Rica, England, France, Germany, Israel, Japan, Korea.<br><br>NIST chose five as finalists during summer 1999 and declared the winner during late 2000. The finalists are listed below. |
| Mars | This finalist was submitted by a group of researchers at IBM. But it is not very good in hardware tests, slow on Intel chips and Algorithms do not fit on a small smart card (e.g., costing .25 cents). Hence, making it not very practical for internet applications |
| RC6 | Submitted by RSA Data Security (including Ron Rivest), RC6 has apparently similar weaknesses as Mars. |
| Rijndael (AES) | Comes from a group of Cryptographers in Belgium including Joan Daemen (Proton World Internationl) and Vincent Rijmen (Catholic University-Leuven). Fastest in software (with Twofish) and Hardware test (with Serpent) (http://csrc.nist.gov/CryptoToolkit/aes/rijndael/Rijndael.pdf)<br><br>After extensive tests, it was chosen as the new AES standard |
| Serpent | Was fathered by Ross Anderson, Eli Biham, and Lars Knudsen. In hardware tests fastest with Rijndael, in software slowest everywhere. |
| Twofish | Comes from Counterpane Systems and Bruce Schneier. Fastest in software tests with Rindael. |

Comparing symmetric and public-key keys is a lot like comparing apples and oranges. Schneier recommends 128-bit symmetric keys because they are just as fast at 64-bit keys.

However, doubling the key size for public keys roughly corresponds to a six-times speed slowdown in software. This might not matter with PGP, but it will make client-server applications like SSL slow to a crawl.

**Note.** This table outlines the algorithms that were in the final test round used to select the new AES algorithm, Rijndael was the winner.

[1] Algorithm is usually a mathematical formula or set of steps for solving a particular problem. In the Virus context an algorithm is a set of operations or a procedure designed to solve the Virus inflicted problem.

In the context of Digital Signatures or Encryption, the algorithm describes how the signature or text is encrypted using mathematical formulas (see also Algorithm).

**Persistent Encryption** means that information stored in a system such as a database is protected through a code that is required for making the information readable to employees and others.

**Ending date**    represents the last date where an incident has occurred and been recorded.

**End of Day (EoD)**    means a set or routines, or programs performed / run during the early hours of the morning or whenever there is the least amount of demand upon resources by users including customers. These routines could include:

* taking backups,
* running interest accruals on closing balances,
* checking files' integrity, and
* updating the anti-virus software.

**End User License Agreement (EULA)**   is a legally binding contract between the developer or publisher of a software program (or application) and the purchaser of that software. The purchaser does not own the software, but has merely a right to use it in accordance with the license agreement (see also Tables 16A and 16B).

During software installation, the EULA is usually shown and one is required to Accept or Refuse the terms (see also Click Wrap Agreement).

In some cases, the EULA is written on the outside of the packaging with the breaking of the seal to the CD, indicating acceptance of the EULA.

In all cases, the EULA is the contract which users ignore at their peril; and whilst most EULAs contain broadly similar clauses and restrictions, it is important to confirm these before committing your organization (see also Jurisdiction).

**Enforced Path**   means that if data or systems are classified as sensitive or requiring restricted physical access, an enforced path is applied. Hence, the system administrator configures access as being restricted to a specific workstation or range of workstations.

Enforcing the path will provide added security because it reduces the risk of unauthorized access. This is especially true, when the workstation is within a secure zone, requiring physical access codes and / or keys.

**Enterprise Resource Planning (ERP)**   are applications that help automate and optimise resources including people, cash, capital, materials and facilities, by tracking routing, and analysing information about these assets.

**ERP Software**   provides integration between all aspects of a company's business—accounting, distribution, manufacturing, human resources, customer relationship management, and more. ERP uses relational databases and fourth generation programming languages (see Programming).

ERP software originally defined manufacturing software but is now used to define the main business management system used across industries.

**Enumeration**   is the activity aiming at collection of information about users, shares, banners on particular host or network.

**EpiSystemiology in IT Security**   comes from "Epi"-upon, "systos"-the systems, "logos"-study of. The logical, systematic approach to understanding the complexities of security issues with information technology, databases and security engineering and End-User Computing within the Domains of Information Security Space (DISS).

This new discipline builds on epistemiology which focuses on the logic of observation and the methods to quantify these observations in populations (groups) of individuals (see also Sample). Epidemiology is the study of the distribution of health-related states or events in specified populations and the application of this study to the control of security problems. EpiSystemiology brings this approach into IT Security and includes:

1) the methods for measuring the information security of groups such as users and clients and for determining the attributes and exposures that influence security;
2) the study of the occurrence of security events in their natural habitat rather than the controlled environment of the laboratory; and
3) the methods for the quantitative study of the distribution, variation, and determinants of security-related outcomes in specific groups (Populations) of individuals, networks and systems
4) the application of the above to the diagnosis, treatment, and prevention of such outcomes as:

- Attacks (see Tables 3A and 3b),
- Damages of Information Assets (see Tables 2A–2D, Tables 7A–7C),
- Down Time of Information Assets (see also Tables 13A–13C),
- Incidents (see Table 13C),
- Penetration (see Figure 3, Tables 15A–15C),
- Threats (see Tables 24B–24D),
- violation of Confidentiality, Integrity and Availability of Data as well as User Accountability, Authentication and Auditing (CIA-UAA) procedures (see Table 5D),
- Vulnerabilities (see Table 24E and 26), and
- Risks and their management (see Table 22H–22E)

EpiSystemilogy in IT Security provides the library of data required to establish patterns and to verify theories which, in turn, can be used to develop Methodologies needed to acquire the Evidence to confirm or disconfirm or even proof Damages (see Tables 2A–2D, Tables 7A–7B) or other undesirable events.

**Descriptive (Observational) EpiSystemiology in IT Security**   is the description of the patterns of occurrence of health-related states or events in groups; answering the questions of

- Who,
- What
- Where, and
- When

Descriptive EpiSystemiology is usually one of the first things done at the scene of a IT security disaster or after a virus outbreak (see also Sample, Statistics).

**Analytical EpiSystemiology in IT Security**   is the design, execution and analysis of studies in groups to evaluate potential associations between risk factors and IT security outcomes to answer the question

- Why

One popular way is to use meta-analysis to compare the effects of a number of studies (see also Host, Non-Receptive Host and Receptive Host)

**E**

**Clinical EpiSystemiology in IT Security**   is the application of the logical and quantitative concepts and methods of EpiSystemilogy to problems (diagnostic, prognostic, change process, and preventive) encountered in the delivery of security care to information resources (e.g., Systems, hardware, software and Users). The population aspect of EpidSystemiology is present because individual systems are members of conceptual populations of information systems or applications. This makes it a basic science for IT Security Engineering and management.

**Infectious Disease EpiSystemiology in IT Security**   is classical anti-virus research that studies the dynamic factors involved in the transmission of infectious agents (i.e. computer Viruses) in populations of networks, systems and PCs (see Tables 24E and 24F). Some include the products of the application of the methods of this discipline, the natural history of a virus family such as information about how each disease (e.g., macro Viruses) spreads through groups and how a case of that disease develops in a host system or computer.

**EPROM—** Erasable Permanent Read Only Memory chip, containing firmware programs.

**Erasable Permanent Read Only Memory**   see EPROM

**Ergonomics**   is a science concerned with the study of the functional relationships between human beings and technology such as computers. Ergonomics considers the characteristics of people when designing and arranging technology and work space, thereby helping to increase the effectiveness and safety of interaction. The concern is primarily with physical and sensory-motor aspects of humans and not intellectual aspects. Ergonomics is one facet of the person-computer interface (see also Person-Computer Interface).

**ERP**   see Enterprise Resource Planning

**Error Log**   records any abnormal activity on application software, usually in
simple / plain text (ASCII). Each (main) application generates its own logs,
and it is the responsibility of Systems Operations to retrieve and scrutinize
them for any processing errors (see also Evidence / Log under Forensics).

**Escrow**   is a legal provision whereby a developer deposits the source code
for software at a trusted third party. Hence, in case of the firm's demise, the
source code is made available to licensed / registered users, thereby enabling
its ongoing maintenance.

**Ethernet Sniffing**   requires software to listen to the Ethernet interface for
packets. Listening can be done using keywords or other criteria. If the packet
fits the criteria (e.g., password, username are words contained in it) it is
getting logged to a file.

**Ethics**   see Justice (see also Code of Conduct, EICAR Code of Conduct)

**Ethnography**   uses direct, systematic observation, such as becoming a partic-
ipant in a social system to describe social or cultural life-based phenomena.
     In case of interviewing, the latter is fully transcribed. These records can
than studied for identifying themes or patterns. One approach is to take topical
segments from an interview and sort them into themes or categories. Similar
approach can be done with archival data such as court records or minutes
from past meetings (see also Methodology).

**Computer-Aided Thematic Analysis (CATA)**   requires that the researcher
initially defines working categories, thereafter similar ideas or observations
are brought into proximity (see also Statistics, Validity).

**European Institute for Computer Anti-Virus Research   (EICAR)** see
EICAR

**European Committee for Standardization   (CEN)** see Appendix 6

**Excess Privileges**   occurs when a user obtains capability on a system beyond
that authorized.

**Executable–(.exe)**   refers to a file that can be 'run' by a computer, usually
identified with an exe suffix, executables are created when their source code
is compiled and bound to the operating system upon which it is to be run.

**Expert**   is an individual that has developed the expertise through formal training and / or informal training as well as practical experience. Often a status of
an expert may also depend on how much credibility and insight is attributed
to the individual by influential or powerful others.

The media may fail to discriminate between experts in:

1) anti-Virus,
2) computing,
3) Forensics,
4) Intrusion Detection,
5) Hacking,
6) people who know a little more than they do, and
7) virus-writers.

It is obvious that a security expert may neither be an anti-virus expert nor an Intrusion Detection one (see also Domains of Information Security Space—DISS).

**Expiry Date**   depicts the point in time by which an event must take place (e.g., updating software) (see also Starting Date).

**Exploit**   see Attack and Tables 3A and 3B

**Exposure**   can be defined as:

1) Proximity and / or contact with a source of a disease agent or computer virus in such a manner that effective transmission of the harmful effects of the agent / virus may occur.
2) The amount of a factor to which a group of computer or system users were exposed to such as number of disinfected files or deleted infected attachments by virus scanner, therefore preventing these to reach final recipients.

Users of Microsoft operating systems and software have a great chance for exposure to virus infection, due to the number of possible viruses for these platforms, and also the built-in functionality that virus writers can utilize (see also Down Time). The ubiquitousness of Microsoft products makes the effect for a virus writer also highly attractive due to the large number of possible targets (e.g., users of Outlook Express).

Some also suggest that this term is synonymous with Exploit (see also Attack and Table 3B)

**Extensive Mark-up Language (XML)**   is the first building bloc for a Semantic Web. Invisible to the human viewer, XML tags can be used to describe how information on a page is structured, allowing visiting computers to read and act on it without human invention.

XML describes data in terms of its content. In that respect XML is a markup language that has significant potential for the capture and onward processing of data directly from web pages. The real significance of this is that Business to Business data transfer is greatly facilitated by XML as neither party needs to write interfaces to each other's systems; they merely need to be able to accept and process XML.

Unlike Hyper Text Mark-up Language (HTML) which is a single predefined language, XML is a metalanguage. Hence, it is a language for describing other languages. Therefore, visiting computers need to be familiar with the specific XML language before then can interpret the web page or document. Hence, a computer can refer to an XML "schema" located elsewhere on the web.

**Extranet**   helps the organization to link the outside world such as suppliers and customers with a private intranet. While this is similar to the internet, access is controlled and restricted to particular groups, similar to the Intranet. Accordingly, an Extranet web server can be accessed by all the participants involved in a project (e.g., various engineers and the firm developing a new product), but not by anyone else. In this example, the Extranet provides project management functions for the work in progress and the work teams involved. The security is increased; however, breaches can still occur (e.g., cyberpunk getting hold of a password or access to a server who, with a password, is given access to the Extranet) (see also Internet, Intranet and Virtual Private Network—VPN).

**Event**   is an action targeted toward an object or system with the intention to cause a change of state (status) of the target.

**Evidence**   is made up of the available facts which support a belief or proposition. It is a fact or the facts presented before a court, such as a statement of a witness, an object, security logs, information from a user's hard-drive (e.g., to show storing illegal material such as music files) that bears on or establishes a point in question (see also Table 16A).

**Evidence-based Information Security Management (EBISM)**   is the conscious, explicit and judicious use of current best evidence in making decisions about the IT security for a system, network or PC. It means integrating specific expertise about the system, network or PC with the best available external evidence from systematic research (see EpiSystemology in IT Security).

- **Specific expertise** refers to the IT scurity engineer's cumulated experience, education and skills.
- The system administrator, user, manager or any other client group brings to the encounter his, her or their own **values**. The best Evidence is usually found in relevant research in IT Security that has been conducted using sound Methodology
- The **Evidence** by itself does not make a decision for the security expert but it can help support the security care process (see also Table 16B).

The full integration of these three components into security decisions enhances the opportunity for optimal outcomes such as reduced risks and better security. The practice of EBISM is usually triggered by encounters with security situations that generate questions about the effects of Prevention, the utility of Testing, the prognosis of security risks, or the costs of security disasters (see Tables 2A–2D, Table 7A).

**Evaluating the Evidence** identifies criteria for determining the Validity and Reliability of data provided with a study or an investigation using various Methodologies such as one based on Computer Forensics. Evidence may also be used for generating the proof required to establish the fact that a Computer Crime may have occurred.

**Sufficient Evidence** is required to go forward for a court trial or into Arbitration on the charges made against the defendant regarding an IT Security event (e.g., spreading a virus, unauthorized system access, downloading of pornographic files).

The degree and type of Evidence required does often depend upon issues of Jurisdiction that is in which country the accused may be charged with what type of Crime.

**Insufficient Evidence** could occur whereby the evidence provided is not clear enough (i.e. valid and reliable, based on data acquired) justifying the accusation of a party to having caused an undesirable event.

For instance, estimates about damages caused by Viruses, Worms or Hacking Attacks are not always believable and range from $5,000 to 50,000 (about same in Euros) per PC for such Virus outbreaks such as Slammer or Sobig. At the same time, judges have been known to through out cases against people who distributed a Virus in a firm regarding Damages, claiming that apart from cleaning some hard-disks the firm could not provide Sufficient Evidence of damages. Cleaning hard-disk was, however, not costing more than $500, therefore, resulting in the firm not having a case according to the law (see Damages for more info, Table 6).

**Burden of Proof** is the necessity or duty of affirmatively proving a fact or facts in a dispute. Hence, it is important to provide Reliable and Valid evidence, especially if the victimized party (e.g., home user) wants to proof that he or she has suffered damages through a computer virus. In turn, an organization requires a systematic approach to develop the costs (e.g., Tables 2A–2D) to arrive at the quantified losses it suffered from (e.g., Asset Value).

**Fallback Procedures** are those business procedures and measures, undertaken in case of a disaster or other pre-specified event triggering the execution of the Business Continuity Plan, Contingency Plan or other Disaster Management related activities.

**False Negative** occurs when an actual intrusive action happened but the system fails to detect it or simply allows it to pass as a non-intrusive behavior. Similarly if a virus was activated by a user action on the PC but the software failed to detect it, a False Negative occurred (see also False Positive).

**False Positive** may happen when the system classifies an action as anomalous (possible intrusion) or as a computer virus even though the action is legitimate or the file does not contain a virus (see also Anomaly Based Intrusion Detection Systems).

**Fast Active queue management Scalable Transmission (FAST) Control Protocol** can squeeze more horsepower out of high-speed internet connections-up to 6,000 times more. FAST Control Protocol software continually checks the flow of data packets and then squeezes the maximum amount of data through the connection to achieve the highest possible efficiency. For example,

- a typical broadband internet connection utilizes only about 27% of the available bandwidth, but a
- FAST connection can reach 95% efficiency.

The software modifies the standard internet communications protocol called TCP but runs standard applications and has to be installed only on the web server side.

During 2003 tests using off-the-shelf hardware, speeds of more than 8 Giga bits per second (Gbps) were achieved. Such speeds could allow users to download a movie in a few seconds, making the technology of particular interest to entertainment web sites and companies.

There is a catch, however FAST can only take advantage of the raw speed of the network, hence, having a slow network connection slows things down. Currently, the only technical bottlenecks to implementing FAST, are Gigabit Ethernet cards.

Windows servers need not apply. For now, FAST runs only on Linux.

Finally, how much this will help attackers in Spoofing systems (see Peer-to-Peer) and exploiting vulnerabilities is still a guess.

**FAT**   see File Allocation Table

**Fault Tolerance**   is a systems ability to continue normal operation despite the presence of hardware or software faults.

**File**   is a collection of records or data designated by name and considered as a unit by a user.

**File Allocation Table (FAT)**   is the file system native to the DOS operating system. It can be described as an "index" to the contents of the disk that controls the location of all the files on the disk.

**File Cache**   see Cache

**File Compression**   is a form of encryption performed on files or folders to minimize the space they take on disk. Usually done manually, as opposed to the automated Disk Compression. This form of encryption means that a virus might be able to hide but most anti-virus program can now scan inside normally compressed files, sometimes even inside nested compressed files (i.e. files that were compressed and then put inside a larger file or folder that was compressed thereafter). Unfortunately, scanning inside compressed files is not always Reliable.

**File Infector**   is a Virus that attaches itself with, a file, usually a program file or it overwrites program code. It can also insert itself into free space within a program that exists in portable executable (PE) files, or even in the middel of a file, although this is not as common (see also Virus, Worm, Table 27).

Sometimes the File Infector class of virus is also used to refer to programs that do not physically attach themselves to files but, instead, associate themselves with program filenames. The term is not usually applied to macro viruses, even though these do, in a Sense, infect files (see also Virus, Figure 5).

**File Transfer Protocol (FTP)**   is a program that enables users to transfer files between computers on a network.

**Filtering**   can be done in various ways to assure that Spam, Hoaxes, Viruses and other Malware do not reach users or at least as much as possible is filtered out (see also, Heuristics).

Often, Filtering may be done at the internet gateway or mail server, in front of a Firewall as well as directly on the user's PC (see also Content Filtering and Filtering Software).

**Content Filtering** is primarily used for filtering incoming email messages as well as against hostile code embedded in various files attached to an email or downloaded from a website. Recently, using filtering for restricting access to certain websites has also been used but benefits may be more than offset by various types of costs (see also Spam Filtering).

Content filtering is nearest to virus-specific detection when it focuses on very specific lexical objects such as:

- prescribed web sites,
- domains, and
- source addresses

However, it is more common for such tools to:

- using fuzzier matching techniques,
- looking for strings suggestive of pornography
- fraud, or
- hoax material

to mention a few examples (see also Heuristic, Spam, Virus).

**Filtering Software**   allows the systems operator to prevent users from accessing certain sites. Much Filtering Software packages are limited to one language and suffer from great inaccuracy. This is in part due to the Internet's rapid change whereby new sites pop up all the time, hence, blocking web sites is simply inadequate to filter Spam. Hence, Bayesian algorithms offer a better way of filtering (see also Spam—Statistical Filtering). Scanners that search picture file for undesirable content such as pornography are more successful. Filtering does, however, raise issues concerning civil liberties (e.g., if using it in a public library on 'adult only' designated terminals) (see also Traffic Analsysis, Spam, Spam Filtering).

**Firewall** consists of a set of related programs, located at a network gateway server. A firewall is a combination of hardware and software used to implement a security policy governing the network traffic between two or more networks. Some of that traffic may be under the administrator's control (e.g., organization's networks) and some of which may be out of the system administrator's control (e.g., the Internet).

Firewalls determine whether to block or allow network traffic by looking at TCP7IP packet headers to determine if these are in accordance with predetermined security policy. However, a firewall does neither have the capability to recognize malicious code (Malware, Virus), nor any means for preventing its transfer to a target system.

A Firewall usually protects the resources of a private network from users from other networks. A network firewall commonly serves as a primary line of defense against external threats to an organization's computer systems, networks, and critical information. Firewalls can also be used to partition an organization's internal networks, reducing the risk from insider attacks.

There are three types of firewalls:

1) **Pack Filter**—filters the contents of the IP packet header, therefore, limited to the source and destination address as well as the TCP/UDP port number. Filter does not check content of message/data;

2) **Circuit Filter or Circuit Level Gateway**—applies packet filtering but verifies information based on TCP or UDP packet header information as well. Hence, it can make a better decision if the individual packets form part of a valid TCP sequence. Creates a handshake, and once that takes place passes everything through until the session is ended. Still it has no knowledge of which user is requesting access to services; and

3) **Application Filter**—uses proxies to apply filter rules based on the data content and sometimes the user. A dedicated program called a *'proxy'* or *'proxy server'* is used to effect the application filter policy rules. Commonly used application filter is the web proxy. It can be used to restrict the internal (or Intranet) web pages that are published out to the internet (see Proxy Server).

As Table 12 outlines, Functional Requirements represent the minimum required of a firewall product. But nonetheless, Firewalls do also have some weaknesses that must be considered carefully to reduce possible Risks to acceptable levels. Moreover, they require careful fine-tuning to make sure that Spam or other undesirable content or access of outside web pages can be performed effectively.

**Firewall Code** is put into a switch or other piece of equipment to make sure that the users can not do any damage. The construction of a firewall is not only a question of defensive coding but also of interface presentation, so that users are less likely to possibly damage something.

**Table 12:** Firewalls

| Tasks | | Description |
|---|---|---|
| Functional Requirements | | A) All communication traffic to and from the internal network must be routed through the firewall as the only route into and out of the intranet.<br>B) By default, the firewall should deny all connections to (and sometimes from) the internal network. Only explicitly authorized connections should be allowed.<br>C) The firewall must offer a trusted path for its management via a physically secure dedicated management console with an identification and authentication system. Else, an approved, remote, cryptographically protected system is also possible.<br>D) In order to detect breaches of the firewall's security and attempted network intrusions, sufficient audit capability must be provided including real time alarms. |
| Risks[1] and Vulnerabilities[2] | (1) New Applications | In case of new applications via the internet, protocols, services or ports used may not adhere to the initial security policy and may, therefore, not work correctly. Also the design may not account for the use of intermediary firewalls and require that the workstation connects directly to the internet. A firewall policy has to be updated in order to make room for new applications or simplifying certain on-line services. Security and user freedom have to be carefully balanced. |
| | (2) Backdoor | A user with a Firewall may connect to the internet via a modem from home. That computer can be attacked and used as an entry point to the whole internal network (Backdoor). The firewall may neither be able to detect this type of intrusion nor can it do anything about it. |
| | (3) Internal Attack | Because Firewalls are located and work as an external port for internet connections, they are not involved in operations carried out within the internal network. |
| | (4) Malicious Code | Firewalls generally restrict the use of certain protocols, services or ports. However, they cannot recognize the level of danger of the data that goes through them. Here using an anti-virus solution helps limiting the risk from Malicious Software and Viruses entering the network. Most anti-virus software is compatible with the majority of Content Vectoring Protocol (CVP) Firewalls. |

(cont.)

**Table 12:** (cont.)

| Fine Tuning | Rejecting Advertising | Some Firewalls offer: |
|---|---|---|
| | | 1) **High**—blocks all advertising; |
| | | 2) **Medium**—blocks pop-up ads and advertising that does not load within a user-stipulated time frame; and |
| | | 3) **Off**—lets all advertising pass through. |
| | | Ad-blocking software can perform the same function without firewall capabilities (see also Revenues). |

*Note.* This outlines some of the functional tasks performed by a Firewall, as well as what risks a network still faces when such technology is being used. Furthermore, how fine-tuning may affect what traffic can flow to and from the users on the network is also discussed.
[1] For a definition of the term Risk see Tables 22A, 22B, 22C, & 22D.
[2] For a more extensive definition of the term Vulnerability see text and also Tables 20C, 20D, and 22E.

**Home User or System** should also be running an individual software firewall like BullGuard, Symantec, ZoneAlarm and/or be placed behind a home router/firewall/NAT device. These devices are widely available for less than Euros 100.

The Firewall should be configured to only allow traffic to pass that one is expecting. Most home users browse the web and send and receive email. For those purposes, home users only need to allow traffic on TCP ports

- 80 (HTTP),
- 443 (HTTPS),
- 25 (SMTP outgoing email),
- 110 (POP3 incoming email), and
- potentially DNS.

If one regularly utilizes additional internet services, such as

- FTP (port 20) or
- telnet (port 23),

these should be opened as well. If they are not used, leaving them open is taking an unnecessary Risk for new infections that could exploit some as yet unknown flaw or vulnerabilities through these ports.

However, during Summer 2003 Blaster made use of Internet port 135 to spread itself while blocking it made it impossible for road warriors to collect their mail from outside the intranet whilst traveling (see Distributed Denial-of-Service Attack—DDoS Attack for more details). Hence, blocking ports must not interfere with other services and System Complexity issues must be addressed before blocking a port.

A big problem for many IT departments is users who have **corporate laptops** that get infected when **taken home** and attached to an insecure network. However, this can partially if not fully be fixed with a Patch System (see also Tables 20C & 20D).

**Network Level Firewall** examines traffic at the network protocol (IP) packet level

**Firmware**   often takes the form of a device which is attached to, or built into, a computer, such as a ROM chip. It performs some software function but is not a program in the sense of being installed and run from the computer's storage media. Hence, it is located in the middle of the conceptual continuum between hardware and software.

**Fishbowl**   means to contain, isolate and monitor an unauthorized user within a system, thereby permitting one to gain information about the user.

**Fit for Purpose**   is a general expression places an onus of responsibility upon the vendor to ensure that its solution is (indeed) fit for the purpose which the client expects and pays for. In the information security context it is wise to remind suppliers in the requirements that the solution must be fit for purpose.

**FIRST**   see Forum of Incident Response and Security Teams (see also Table 5A & 5B).

**Fix**   describes an operational expedient that may be necessary if there is an urgent need to amend or repair data, or solve a software bug problem.

**Fixed-Wireless Access**   [also called fixed (antenna/tower) to multipoint system (i.e., antennas on clients' homes)], provides high-speed internet access often with 3–11 km of range from tower antenna. For instance, a base antenna may have has six sectors that can provide 32 megabits each to clients. In total, a base station has 480 megabits of bandwidth to be sold to numerous clients (see also Wireless, Table 27).

Fixed Wireless Access runs in the 3.5 GHz with 11–12 km range from tower antenna and 26 GHz with 5–6 km range from base antenna.

**Flag**   is a message indication, alerting the user that certain actions should be taken (e.g., disk defragmentation is high requiring utility program to run). Flags may be generated manually or automatically, depending on circumstances. In the case of the stock monitoring this would be automatic. Automatic flags serve a useful purpose in drawing users' attention to situations which otherwise may be overlooked (e.g., your anti-virus software has not been updated for the last five days, do you want to update now?).

**Flamed:**   A virulent and often largely personal attack against the author of a posting on the Internet. Flaming occurs more frequently than is probably desirable.

**Flood** means accessing a target repeatedly in order to overload the target's capacity.

**Forensics** see Digital Forensics

**Fork Bomb** see Logic Bomb

**Footprinting** is the art of gathering target information before actual hacking. It is the equivalent to the preparation bank robbers would do before actual robbery. The more hacker knows about the target the better (see also Operational System (OS) Footprinting, Active OS Footprinting, Passive OS Footprinting).

**Foreseeability** see Jurisdiction

**Forum of Incident Response and Security Teams (FIRST)** is a coalition that brings together a variety of computer security incident response teams from government, commercial, and academic organizations including but not limited to CERTs. FIRST aims to foster cooperation and coordination in incident prevention, to prompt rapid reaction to incidents, and to promote information sharing among members and the community at large (see Table 5A).

**FTP** see File Transfer Protocol

**Freeware** is software that was provided by its originator for free to the community. Independent developers may give away small programs to establish a reputation for useful software, which then enables them to charge. Cover disks attached to a computer magazine often contain Freeware.

Staff should not be permitted to install Freeware on corporate machine, unless such programs have been tested in a secure environment and approved by system personnel to avoid problems with other system software (e.g., possible access conflicts) and hardware (see also Shareware).

In summary, Freeware is software distributed for free on the web. Unlike Shareware, Freeware is FREE.

**Freeze** occurs when an application no longer accepts any input, neither from the keyboard nor the mouse.

Occasionally, a frozen application will return to normal. For instance, the problem may have been related to (say) a disk write command that did not execute, resulting in an time out, but with control returned to the user.

Unfortunately, applications that freeze may also crash the operating system, especially of a PC. However, freezes followed by the need to re-boot and the possible loss of all current data are becoming less common for PC users.

Nonetheless, Windows XP still freezes and crashes on average more than one time a day for many users, resulting in lost productivity and work time (see Down Time for statistics on this).

**Functional Requirements Specifications**   are listed in a document, detailing what is required of an installation to meet the business needs of users. As a basic principle, developments within commercial enterprises should be user-driven. We could schematize it as follows:

1) Functional Specifications/Requirements are developed with users,
2) Technical Specifications are based on the functional specifications, security and business process demands, and
3) Request for Proposal is developed based on the above information outlining exactly what is needed (acceptable system).

F

**Generic Disinfection**   see Disinfection

**Generic Scan String**   see Disinfection

**Germ**   see Virus and Tables 18A, 18B, 18C

**Ghost**   is an identity that does not relate to a real person. It is not unheard of for staff with the necessary IT skills to create a fictitious user with a password, enabling them to access the system with impunity, since an audit trail will lead nowhere. Ghosts may also appear on the payroll, courtesy of a user who has the power to create new files in the personnel and payroll systems.

The creation of user profiles and the granting of logical access rights is a high security function and must be strictly monitored, preferably with dual controls for creation and authorization (Dual Control, Role-Based Access).

**Ghost Positive** occurs when the virus scanner detects viral traces that are reported as a full-blown viral infection. This can occur if another product has done an incomplete disinfection earlier on (Virus).

**Gopher**   is a menu-driven program that gives access to hundreds of other databases and services on the Internet. They can also be used to copy gopher text files and programs to a computer. However, this program has now gotten replaced to a large extent with web access programs and file downloads as well as the File-Transfer Protocol (FTP). Web browsers usually permit the access to Gopher documents.

**Grid Computing**   is the co-ordinated, transparent and secure sharing of IT resources across geographically distributed sites. Its origin can be traced back to the early 1990s when the scientific community began looking for ways to make better use of existing computer resources, to share applications and to collaborate on projects through distributed computing

Since 2001, however, the concept of gred computing has entered IT mainstream. Grid computing sees IT resources as a utility delivered like electricity or water, a seamless infrastructure that will support collaborative working, virtual super-computing and automated web services. There are three evolutionary type of grids:

1) **Enterprise or Firm/Orgnization Grid** enables collaboration sharing of computer resources across multiple sites and geographic locations within and between corporations;

2) **Partner Grid** is an extension of the enterprise grid enabling transparent, secure and coordinated resource sharing and collaboration among partner firms; and

3) **Service or Global Grid** describes a single, internet-powered service grid that provides computing resources "on-tap" for individual access around the globe, creating one viraul computer built on open protocols with everything shared.

4) Estimates suggest that about 5% of the capacity of PCs and 20% of servers deployed by corporations are used. **An Enterprise Grid** can raise this usage level to 80–90%, saving a firm money while speeding research, and discovery, thereby reducing time to market.

**Guest**   is an occasional user of system who does not have a personal/unique user ID and password but logs on infrequently as 'Guest'. This practice is quite common in offices where staff usually work in other locations and only log on as guests to the main system when in the base office. Guest passwords may also be granted to persons temporarily associated with the organization, such as short term temporary staff, students, and trainees.

Since they are often not specific to a named individual, Guest passwords should normally allow only minimal access rights. 'Guests' are also commonly known as 'Visitors'. In no way should employees log onto the system under their user name and password to give a visitor access to the internet (e.g., reading one's Web-based email), since this is a high security risk (see Role-Based Access).

**Hacker** is an unauthorized person accessing a computer or information system. Lack of proper authorization makes the activity illegal. Hackers in the original sense were referred to as explorers who solved problems and exceeded conventional limits through trial and error situations. In turn, a hacker may inform the owner of a system about weaknesses and how they could be fixed. Nevertheless, without proper authorization the activity could be labeled *trespassing* (see also Cracker).

**Black Hat Hacker** is somebody that hacks with malicious intent and enters an information asset or system without authorization.

**White Hat Hacker** penetrates systems to test security and document weaknesses to allow organizations to improve their defenses. A more general definition would state that a White Hacker is someone who has goals that are not criminal in intent.

Nonetheless, it is an individual who gains unauthorized access to a computer system, network, program or website for the purpose of identifying and reporting security weaknesses (see also Computer Crime).

**Crypto-hacking** (see under Crypto-Hacking)

**Hacking Run** is a hack session that extends into outside normal working hours and is likely longer than 12 hours.

**Handshake** indicates an electronic exchange of signals between pieces of equipment such as fax machines or computers. This allows them to establish that each has the necessary protocols installed to allow communication between the units. Sometimes it is also used to confirm identities so that transmissions are routed to the correct destination.

**Challenge Handshake**   An extension of the normal confirmation routine is the Challenge Handshake that is a demand for proof of identity and authorization (see also Circuit Level Gateway).

**Challenge-Handshake Authentication Protocol (CHAP)**   is used to periodically verify the identity of the peer using a 3-way handshake. This is done upon initial link establishment, and MAY be repeated anytime after the link has been established.

After the Link Establishment phase is complete, the authenticator sends a "challenge" message to the peer which is a random byte-sequence as well as the identifier, a randomly generated number. The peer responds with a value calculated using a "one-way hash" function. The authenticator checks the response against its own calculation of the expected hash value. If the values match, the authentication is acknowledged; otherwise the connection SHOULD be terminated.

CHAP provides protection against playback attack through the use of an incrementally changing identifier and a variable challenge value. The use of repeated challenges is intended to limit the time of exposure to any single attack. The authentication can occur between client and server, in larger infrastructures, however, the administration of keys or passwords can be quite a big effort.

CHAP also supports the use of central server that acts as a central certification unit according to such as, the Remote Access Dial-in User Service principle. or is in control of the frequency and timing of the challenges.

**Three-way-handshake**   is a way in which is a TCP connection initialized.

**Harassment**   depicts a situation whereby one individual is carrying out actions which amount to Harassment, or which they know may be regarded by the other person as Harassment. In the IT Security context, Harassment may occur via eMail, or in chat rooms.

**Hardening (of) Operating System**   is the process of eliminating basic vulnerabilities on the operating system. It is a kind of setup checklist and is one of the first and most important considerations when securing a public access workstation or server.

Numerous steps can be taken and every operating system and version may require different ones to hardening the system. Furthermore, this goes beyond keeping a system Patched but, instead means hardening the firm's operating systems. A fully patched Windows system can be taken over without too much effort, hence the greatest lie in security is to claim that a Patched system is also secure.

Hardening of an operating system encompasses the removal of all non-essential tools, utilities and other system administration options, any which could be used to easy a Hacker's path to Information Assets. Effective hardening will assure that all security features are being activated and de-activated ones have been carefully assessed for the potential Risk they may pose to the Confidentiality, Integrity, Availability, User Accountability, Authentication and Audit (CIA-UAA) (see Table 5C) of the firm's Information Assets.

Accordingly, System Administrators must be able to safely configure a system by proofing skills before flying a plane. For instance, Liability (see also Table 16B) may be such that if the firm cannot show to have hardened its Operating Systems satisfactorily or according to Best Practice, it may be held liable if its system have been used for unauthorized activity elsewhere such as a Distributed Denial-of-Service Attack (DDoS).

**Hardware Inventory**   lists all hardware owned by the organization, showing, amongst other things:

- type,
- make,
- model,
- specifications,
- cost,
- location,
- user(s), and
- asset reference number.

**Unit Hardware Inventory**   is a detailed list of hardware in order of user (individual or department). This sheet may be used for Audit checks to confirm that any given user still has the equipment detailed and no unauthorized additions, removals, or modifications have been made.

**Health and Safety**   in the IT Security context means assuring that the working environment and the precautions taken help reduce risks for employees and critical IT infrastructures (e.g., sun glare in screen, or possible power outage).

**Help Desk**   are the people responsible for assisting non-technical staff in the use of computer systems, and resolving problems which may arise.

Staffing a Help Desk is an ulcerous job and many Help Desks perform superbly, but others do not (see also User, Role of User, Superuser).

**Heterogeneous Virus Transmission**   see Transmission

**Heuristics**   is related to the theory of probability and signal processing. For instance, heuristics are used to reduce mental effort in decision making, but they may lead to systematic biases or errors in judgment. A heuristic is a technique that works sometimes, without guarantees. We all use heuristics, because they are often simple to try (so they don't cost much if they fail), and also because they are often all we have (see also Algorithm).

**Meta-Heuristics**   are optimization Algorithms that are problem independent in a sense that they are not for specific optimization problems but rather give general frame work to design a given problem. Examples could be an ants colony based systems, genetic algorithms and hybrids.

In the **anti-Virus field** heuristics means that automated detection using more-or-less exact identification cannot be used, instead, search strings have to be rather carefully chosen, while their actual position in a message is unpredictable (see also Virus, EICAR Test File).

**Conventional Scanner Heuristic Analysis**   is a fine-grained approach that works on individual files/attachments using gateway-filtering approaches (e.g., file scanning to prevent pornographic files from reaching or being accessed by users) (see also Filtering).

**Chain Letter Heuristics**   work on passing the message on to others. The heuristic works because most chain letters are unoriginal and greedy, chiefly concerned with reaching as many people, as fast as possible, like a fast burner Virus (see Tables 18A, 18B & 25 for a definition).

**Heuristic Scan**   avoids the string search and makes it thereby possible to detect unknown Viruses by searching for and reporting suspicious code. It functions by applying common-sense rules drawn from experience when looking for Viruses (see also Spam).

**Hoax/Spoof Detection Heuristics**   was originally based on the assumption that a high match rate against the heuristics listed was sufficient proof of either fraudulent intent or complete inaccuracy. While an informed observer can hope to evaluate most alerts with considerable confidence, sometimes doubt about the quality of the information contained is needed, such as (see also Alert, Hoax):

- undated alert,
- no identifiable organization quoted as the source or the one quoted is not one with expertise in security/anti-virus,
- affected hardware not specified,

- immediate and devastating damage when the 'infected' email is openend,
- no discrimination made between opening the email, versus the attachement without executing embedded or attached code, and actually executing code,
- message claims that no means of detection or recovery are known = fairly dependable heuristic,
- virus described in terms of confusing pseudo-jargon,
- reads like a new item or press release, but there is no indication of its origin,
- does not provide pointers to further help or information
- no full details of the source of the information or contact within the originating organization for further clarification (e.g., provides verifiable digital signature)
- surfeit of upper-case letters and exclamation marks,
- consistently poor spelling, grammar, syntax and presentation,
- claims to originate from a known anti-virus vendor, and
- claim that superhackers have managed to write a program to do something that was previously thought to be impossible.

Receiving an Alert or Advisory from an unknown source requires that the above heuristics checklist is being used, for assessing if several characteristics are inherent in a message, than this may indicate a hoax/spoof.

**Malware Heuristics** is a coarser-grained approach, such as

- discarding, bouncing or quarantining all attachments, or those
- attachments with suspicious filename extension or double extension (e.g., *.tx.vbs),
- multiple instances of indentical mail,
- mail with the same Subject Header, or
- mail with identical attachments.

An effective heuristic approach for finding Malware (see also Filtering) is using hardware to automate the process. But automation entails trade-offs between transparency and service. The latter entails a degree of denial of service, since borderline traffic is discarded. Hence service is maintained at a reasonable level, but at the cost of losing some legitimate traffic.

**Spam Heuristics** means filtering by sender address (see also Spam) mapping approximately to the firewall rule-set models of:

- 'explicit deny' and
- 'explicit allow.'

Examples of these heuristics used to reduce spam are such as:

1) 'Refuse villains, allow others' meaning all mail is allowed unless the sender is blacklisted, an approach that is hardly very effective, considering that spammers use forged headers and/or disposable accounts (e.g., Hotmail); and

2) 'Allow friends, refuse others' means all mail is discarded unless the sender is white listed, again an approach that will make it impossible for a new party to be able to reach the recipient by not having his or her email white listed first.

**Hexadecimal** is a numerical system using base 16 (as opposed to the usual base 10). Hexadecimal is a useful way to express binary computer numbers in which a byte is normally expressed as having 8 bits; with 2 hexadecimal characters representing eight binary digits—aka a byte.

**Hexadecimal Editors** are commonly available 'tools' (or utilities). A minority of these allow the user to scrutinize and update the precise contents of the hard disk. They reveal the hexadecimal equivalent of the binary code in which the data is stored. They also provide an ASCII converter that allows the user to make sense of the contents.

However, because they permit searches and updates, it is possible, indeed easy, to search for an expected string/word, and then update that string with a new value (e.g. by substituting the value '5644' for '9480'). Because the number of bytes has remained the same, the data file in which this string is found, may not have been corrupted, however the Integrity of data has been destroyed, and the subsequent user of the file may have little evidence of such tapering (see also Integrity).

Moreover, such an editor is also able to reveal data believed to be safe within password protected files, or even data in files which have been deleted but have yet to be overwritten (see Electronic Shredding). Using Checksums can confirm that a file has not been tampered with, even slightly. However, more fundamentally, Hexadecimal Editors should not be installed on the organization's PCs or workstations at all (see Cheksum).

**High Speed Internet Access** see Broadband, Satellite High Speed Access, Cable, Asymmetrical Digital Subscriber Line, Digital Subscriber Line.

**Historical Cohort Analysis or Study** is a study conducted by reconstructing data about people or systems at a time or times in the past. This method uses existing records about the security or other relevant aspects (e.g., Hacking attacks) of a population as it was at some time in the past and determines the current (or subsequent) status of members of this population with respect to the condition of interest. Different levels of past exposure to risk factor(s) of interest must be identifiable for subsets of the population (e.g., Virus versus Trojan Virus Incidents).

**History of Computing**   see Waves of Computing

**Hoax Virus**   see Virus (see also Hoaxes, Heuristics and Table 18)

**Hoaxes**   rely in many cases on the gullibility and lack of technical expertise of the victims. As such they depend on the recipients' altruistic urge to warn as many people as possible about what they believe to be a genuine danger. A number of close-related or derived hoaxes (e.g., Irina, PenPal Greetings, Deeyenda, It takes Gut to Say Jesus, and Join The Crew) are 'alerts' about viruses (metaviruses) using a very similar array of 'special effects.' These are described as spreading over the internet and having some destructive effect when email or newsgroup postings are read. The hoax victim is warned not to open mail with a specirfic Subject: field and asked to pass on the warning to as many people as possible (see also Heuristics, Virus).

Recently there have been cases of hoaxes that advised users how to delete viruses from their computers. System files were deleted in these cases causing more problems than users bargained for.

**Homomorphic Encryption**   see Encryption

**Honeynet**   is a network of hosts that is specifically designed to be compromised. It is **further refinement of a Honeypot**. Highest security precautions are taken and such networks are heavily monitored. The purpose of such networks is to study Hackers' behaviors, tools, motives and possible contra measures.

**Honeypot**   is a *system* or *host* specifically designed to be compromised. Such a system seems to be attractive to Hackers, but at the same moment these are heavily monitored. The purpose of such a host is to study attacker's behavior, security tools and possible contra measures.

**Host Name**   is a name of a particular host on the network, for example conference.eicar.org. Strictly speaking, the host name is only the part that is conference. The rest is the domain name itself. Together they form FGDN (see also Domain).

**Hotspot**   provides high-speed wireless internet/network access in convenient public locations or at home. Using either a laptop computer or personal digital assistant (PDA) that is 802.11 wirelessly-enabled, users can download their email attachments, watch a live webcast, or listen to streaming audio, while sitting in a restaurant or on a park bench (see also Wireless, Fixed Wireless Access).

H

**Housekeeping** entails the routine care of a computer system (e.g., servers, PCs and notebooks), thereby ensuring that it is kept running smoothly and efficiently. It normally includes:

- routines to delete items such as temporary files (which are no longer required),
- identifying and removing of duplicates of files,
- checking the integrity of the disk records and the magnetic coatings on the disk surfaces, and
- generally tidying up the filing system, and
- backing up important files.

**Hoaxware** could be a screensaver carrying a Virus Alert with it. Sometimes, these are incorrectly identified by a particular virus scanner as virus-infected (false positive), that may then progress to a chan-letter hoax/semi-hoax (see also Hoax, Malware, Spam, Virus).

**Home page** is a document on the WWW that provides information about an individual or organization. It can be accessed through an **URL** (uniform resource locator). The URL is the address of the page indicating the WWW server on which the page is located. The page can have links to other pages on the same computer or other computers (so-called hyperlinks).

Home page is very often also incorrectly used for the name of the web ("go and see our home page"). In such an instance, the default page is displayed.

**Host** means a computer that communicates across the network (e.g., information system, PC or other IT hardware). But a host can also be a PC, information system or other IT software or hardware that affords subsistence or lodgment to an infectious agent under normal conditions (see also Infection). Some malicious code or viruses pass successive stages in alternate hosts of different systems.

- **Primary or Definite Host**, signifies were the maturation occurs, and
- **Secondary or Intermediate Host**, means those were new forms of the Malware or Virus may develop
- **Transport Hosts** are those that help spread the Malware or Virus to another system or host such as a program or a digital file.

**Non-Receptive Host (NRH)** is a PC or a network that can disinfect the Malware, thereby preventing damage or secondary infection. It could also be an isolated PC that is not connected to the network or Internet.

**Receptive Host (RH)** could be a PC that has no anti-Virus software installed or an outdated dictionary of virus signatures, thereby not discovering the virus and thereby permitting it to cause damage or being used for secondary infections.

*In an **EpiSystemiologic context**, hosts are the population or group of PCs or systems, regarding their security, design and technological characteristics of this group, being relevant to security. These are called "host factors"* (see also Infection, EpiSystemiology).

**Host Based**    is information, such as Audit data from a single host that may be used in helping detect an intruder.

**Host Based Intrusion Detection Systems (HIDS)**    see Intrusion (see Tables 15A–15C)

**Host Name**    is a name of a particular host on the network, such as, conference.eicar.org. Strictly speaking, host name is only the first part, namely, conference. The rest, eicar.org is the Domain Name.
   Host Name and Domain name together form the FQDN = Fully Qualified Domain Name.

**HTML**    see Hyper Text Mark-up Language

**HTTP**    see Hyper Text Transfer Protocol

**HTTPS**    Secure Hyper Text Transfer Protocol see Hyper Text Transfer Protocol

**Hybrid**    is the direct result of combining automated tools with the most effective, specialized skills from the Virus, Trojan, Worm and Hacker communities. No two hybrids are the same. A simple hybrid may expand a basic eMail attachment virus technique to include peer-to-peer (P2P) file communication and instant messaging (e.g., ICQ). The P2P chat network is used to transfer the hybrid through the "file send" process, persuading the unwary and curious user to run the malevolent code.
   Regardless of the exact combination of techniques, automation greatly expands an individual attacker's reach, allowing many compromised systems to methodically test and infect ever-larger number of victims. Before the Invention of the hybrid, those systems would need to have been probed individually by the attacker, one at a time, far more time-consuming and laborious than using a hybrid (see also Nimda, Domain Registry Network, Partitioning of Network).
   Having a system infected by a Hybrid also results in:

- remote access exposure of the infected machine is increased,
- evidence of infection is hidden and audit trails are removed,

- backdoors for future unauthorized access are placed,
- existing security measures are rolled back, and/or
- hiding the presence of malicious code (Malware) by moving the illicit program into "stealth," or hibernation mode, until it is needed.

Other hybrid threat activities include but are not limited to:

- clearing the system logs of evidence of infection,
- changing file and registry settings,
- reformatting or altering drives, files and data,
- corrupting databases,
- denying access to critical system functions or applications, and/or
- enabling remote access and control of the infected host/server.

**Hybrid Threat**   (or blended threats, hydra attacks, advanced worms) is an advanced, automated, attack program that self-propagates and leverages both virus techniques and intruder exploits.

- This type of threat uses multiple attack strategies and must, thereby be met with matching multi-layered defensive solutions. They may not only exploit virus possibilities but also Peer-to-Peer (P2P) chat and file swapping systems, while active intruder means exploit various weaknesses as exhibited in Active Code (see Table 24D).

A more extensive description is also given in Table 24D.

**Hype Alert**   see Alert

**Hyper Text Mark-up Language (HTML)**   is a descriptive language used for the transmission of information, graphics, sounds and animation between a client web browser and the web server using *HTTP protocol.*

HTML tags, or mark-up, used in web pages dictate how the information will be displayed, such as a headline here or italics there. However, they give no clue as to the text's meaning.

**Dynamic Hyper Text Markup Language (DHTML)**   is the combination of several browser features which, together, permit a web page to be more 'dynamic'. Dynamic in this sense means the ability for the web page to change its look and features after the page has been loaded; perhaps dependent upon the selection of various options. The recent versions of the most popular web browsers all offer DHTML support.

**Hyper Text Transfer Protocol (HTTP)**   is used for the transmission of information, graphics, sounds and animation between a client web browser and the web server. It is defined in RFC2616 and updated with RFC2817.

**Secure Hyper Text Transfer Protocol (HTTPS)**   uses HTTP but additionally activates web server security, in the form of Secure Socket Layer (SSL). This means that the communications between the client and the (host) web server are encrypted and, additionally, that the host web server may be validated by the client using a Digital Certificate on the server (see also Secure Socket Layer).

The URL for such web sites indicates that they are secure by the use of 'https://address' (rather than http://address).

Some may list this term as shttp instead of https.

H

**IBAN/IPI**   see (International Bank Account Number/International Payment Instructions)

**International Bank Account Number/International Payment Instructions (IBAN/IPI)**   is is the number to be used to reduce banking fees being charged for cross-border payments. Starting July 2003, for payments under 12'500 Euros across borders within the EU, banks had to begin charging the same fees to account holders as for such transfers for payments within the country. Hence, fees charged for cross-border payments were beginning to come down.

The IPI system was established by the European Committee for Banking Standards as a European standard. Each account owner must inform a business partner of

the International Bank Account Number (IBAN)
the Bank Identifier Code (BIC)

In effect, the IBAN is additional information put on the front of the national account number format of each country. The BIC (Bank Identifier Code), also known as the SWIFT code, identifies a bank, e.g., BANKBEBB, and is defined in ISO standard 9362.

Validation is performed by check digits and a single, simple, algorithm. The algorithm covers the whole IBAN, and ensures, for example, that individual digits are not transposed. Recognition is in two parts. The IBAN commences with the ISO 3166 two-letter country code. It is therefore easy to recognize the country in which the account is held. Within the national account identifier part of the IBAN, it is an implicit requirement of the ISO standard that the bank be unambiguously identified.

The primary aim is to use IBAN and BIC to enable the straight through processing (STP) of transactions, thereby making manual intervention unnecessary. Currently, payment of bills using IBAN and BIC is not yet possible using STP in such cases as salary payments by a German employer using accounting software to transfer the money to an employee's bank account abroad. Here, online banking facilities have to be used to make the transfer.

**Electronic Bill Presentment and Payment (EBPP)**   see Electronic Payment Initiator below

**Electronic Payment Initiator (ePI)**   is a standard data container, which is made available electronically to a potential ordering customer by a potential beneficiary. It contains the essential information about the ultimate beneficiary that is required by an ordering customer who wishes to instruct his or her financial institution to effect a fully automated domestic or cross-border credit transfer in favor of that ultimate beneficiary.

**Security**   including encryption of data to be transferred is being addressed in various working groups European Committee for Banking Standards (ECBS).

**ICMP**   see Internet Control Message Protocol

**ICMP Query**   see Internet Control Message Protocol

**Icons**   are small graphic images representing a link to a graphic, another page or a program that can be manipulated by the user. Some claim that icons are similar to visual mnemonics allowing users to control certain computer actions without having to remember the function keys or commands to be typed at the keyboard.

**IDEA**   see Encryption (for a definition see Table 11A)

**Identification**   see Authentication

**Identity Theft**   occurs when a person takes on another individual's identity to conduct actions that are very likely to harm the victim (e.g., purchase products or services with the faked identity), such as damaging his or her credit record. For instance, during May 2002, Ford Motor Credit Company authorization codes were fraudulently used to obtain 13,000 credit reports from Experian (provides credit reports and scores). Information on the reports, which were stolen over a ten-month period, includes names, addresses, social security numbers and bank and credit card account information. Ford sent certified letters to all the people affected by the security breach, advising them to get copies of their credit reports and check them for unauthorized inquiries or incorrect information (see also Privacy).

As the Ford incidence suggests, Identity Theft is a significant problem that produces horrendous consequences to its victims—and it's getting bigger. Identity theft appears tied to technology, particularly the internet, and is an increasing threat to consumer confidence in conducting business on the Internet.

The internet has proven to be a virtual bazaar for identity thieves. For instance, in the USA law enforcement web sites publish names, birth dates, social security numbers and even pictures and driver's license numbers of prison inmates and wanted criminals. Court documents available on line can contain much of the same data; bankruptcy cases can even include bank account information. Though some states are passing laws requiring that such sensitive data be edited out of public documents, much will remain to be picked over by data miners (see also Privacy).

Krak, a publisher of maps in Denmark offers people the choice to find addresses, phone numbers, email and fax information, including a map to drive to the address online. Some of the information is collected from users who register, but most comes from phone directories and the government's national registry database, where every person's legal home address is listed. This could increase a person's Risk for having his or her identity stolen. Similarly, a national CPR number used by the government also shows a person's current home address. This database can be accessed by banks and most other institutions as well. Hence, this is a problem waiting to happen and is unnecessarily increasing the risk for Identity Theft for all people listed in Krak with their CPR number and postal address (see also Phishing).

Identity Theft continues to grow in North America and is well on its way in becoming an ever greater threat in other countries and regions. The above examples illustrate that Identity Theft and our ever increasing dependency on digitized data (e.g., medical records) is making it a severe problem for citizens that must be dealt with through legislation as well as every user's vigilance.

Any efforts regarding Trust and Confidence for e-Government projects will be wiped out in an instant if a few citizens' Identity is stolen and used for illegal activities (e.g., getting prescription drugs under false pretenses). During 2003, German health insurers estimated that Identity Theft in combination with the illegal use of health insurance ID-cards were estimated to cost the public several billion Euros each year in falsified charges, abuse and misuse of health services in Germany—1,000,000,000 in Bavaria alone.

**Authentication Online**   also imposes a Risk for Identity or Information Theft, especially when typing authentication information onto forms. When online data entry is required, it is recommended to copy and paste the web page into a text processing file and, most importantly, enter these data offline.

Once all fields are completed it is possible re-paste the information into the website. If reposting does not work for some reason, than each data field on the form can be completed offline using a text file and copied thereafter from the text file for subsequent pasting into the website form. This **thwarts the use of keyboard tracers**.

**IDS**   see Intrusion Detection System

**Illegal Value Insertion**   is using values out of limits/range, thereby taking advantage of software vulnerabilities.

**Illegal Software**   means that a firm or an end-user is using software that has not been legally acquired. Accordingly, property rights of the Copyright holder have been violated. Using illegal software is a crime with severe penalties and no one is exempted. Many company directors don't realise that they are responsible for the legality of their company's software. As a result, if the corporation is caught using illegal software, they can face prison terms or fines if taken to court by the software anti-piracy group the Business Software Alliance (BSA) (see also Copyright, Table 16A).
Illegal software can take many forms, such as:

—end-user copying occurs when an end-user copies software onto more machines than there are licenses for;
—pre-loading of unlicensed software by unscrupulous suppliers on new machines without supplying customers with the necessary licenses;
—counterfeit software where software is copied and illegally sold as the genuine article;
—downloading unlicensed software over the Internet; and,
- getting the registration code needed to fully-activate a software from an internet site without paying a license fee.

**Imaging Software**   can automatically deploy the authorized disk image to hundreds or thousands of workstations provided the university or organization has adequate server speeds and network bandwidth. These products would reduce (but not eliminate) the window of exposure on public terminals. For a full explanation see also Table 20C and 20D (see also Patching).

**Impact Analysis**   requires that the owners identify the threats against, and their possible impact upon assets, if the threat resulted in a genuine incident (see also Risk). By quantifying the value of assets, the appropriate safeguards and their costs can be determined (cost and benefit) (see also Cost-Benefit Analysis, Table 1–2D).

**Implementation Vulnerability**   see Vulnerability of Implementation.

**Incident**   can be defined as any real or suspected adverse event in relation to the security of information systems or networks. Alternatively, an act of violating a security policy could also be an incident.

Incident differs from an attack in that it involves a group of attacks that can be distinguished from other incidents because of the distinctiveness of the attackers, and the degree of similarity of sites, techniques, and timing. Since incidents are made up of attacks, it is appropriate to develop taxonomy for *attacks* which can then be used within a broader classification of incidents (see also Computer Crime).

Computer security incident activity can be defined as network or host activity that potentially threatens the security of information systems and networks.

**Incident objective**   describes the purpose or end goal/objective of an incident.

**Incident Monitoring**   is an essential part of IT security and helps in identifying:

1) weaknesses in systems and products,
2) procedures that need to be reviewed,
3) where education and awareness training needs revision,
4) contingency planning requirements, and
5) alerting the larger community about emerging problems by reporting to a Computer-Emergency-Response Team (CERT) or another agency about incidents (see Incident Reporting, Incident—Non-Reporting).

**Incident—Non-Reporting**   is a case where neither internal nor security authorities, law enforcement or others are informed because the incident may create embarrassment for the user/system administrator, or it is believed to have the potential for an impact or causing a loss of customer confidence and trust. But the cost of non-reporting may be a risk of not taking advantage of an opportunity to improve and continue hardening system resources. In turn, sharpening user behavior to reduce the risk for having future incidents cannot be taken advantage off if no systematic Incident Reporting system has been put in place.

**Incident Reporting**   does not only permit the organization to develop a systematic library and resources, thereby permitting Historical Cohort Analysis/Study, but also:

1) contributors' experiences influence the policy making process;
2) provides leverage with suppliers and manufacturers for obtaining solutions to problems with various products;

3) enables the exchange of experiences without compromising the Confidentiality that is necessary for effective Security; and

4) provides the basis for a more comprehensive overall assessment of the Threat from electronic attack.

The reporting of an Incident or Vulnerability may also result in legal consequences unless some USA laws are being changed (see Computer Crime).

**Incident Reporting Process**   means that security breaches such as those caused by malicious software, computer hacking, theft, fraud, misuse of resources, software or hardware failure, and authorized disclosure of information should be documented in a reporting process.

The benefits to the individual organization of such a process outweigh potential problems caused by such an approach and, most importantly, help reducing the future Risks through such as organizational Learning, Benchmarking, continuous improvement and so on (see also Appendices 5–6).

Finally, there may be a legal requirement to put in a system for documenting an Incident Reporting Process and as well, to make sure that either the firm did take the measures expected when a mishap was discovered or proofing that such an Incident never happened before (e.g., Damages in case of a law suit).

Computer Security Incident Response Team (CSIRT) see CERT.

**Incursion**   specifies the penetration of the system by an unauthorized source. Similar to an Intrusion, the primary difference is that Incursions are classed as hostile.

Intrusion is considered hostile as well, hence one could infer that they are synonymous. However, some suggest that incursion is more used in a "physical", rather than a "logical" (intrusion) invasion.

The linguistic challenge is to try to explain when an incursion becomes an intrusion and maybe both result in an invasion (see also Intrusion, Incident).

**Induced Stress Failures**   could occur when a system is being stressed to a point of starting to produce failures.

**Infection**   is the development or forming of an infectious agent in an information system or program (see also Host). Infection is not synonymous with infectious virus disease; the result may be not very obvious to the naked eye or manifest itself clearly. One can distinguish between the Mere presence of the Malware code in the system or on the hard-drive, infection does not take place until a virus has been activated, reproduced, or made a change to the system (see also Host), accordingly, the:

**Latent** or **Sub-Clinical Infections**   that do not cause a disease but a kind of reaction, an example might be where the operating system will activate the virus during a common occurrence, such as booting the system, or if a user is loading an infected, or commonly used program (sometimes also called latent virus, see Table 25), and

Infection occurs when Malware is replicating itself and passed on to others via executing of certain processes (e.g., sending the file as attachment to addresses on the victim's email address book) or if as a Worm or Bacteria it is independent of other processes (i.e. can be launched at a pre-set event such as date) (see Figure 5).

The difficulty is to linguistically distinguish between Latent or Infections. One could argue that viral code that sits on a hard-drive or its mere presence makes it also latent. Space limits us on addressing this linguistic challenge (see also Transmission of Infection).

Latent virus means it is on a computer's hard-drive and cause damage such as after a pre-set event which could be a certain date in the calendar, unless Anti-Virus software removes the file beforehand. Similarly, a car bomb may be triggered by radio at a certain date unless it is defused by a bomb expert beforehand.

**Prepender**   is a file infector that attaches itself to the beginning of the file. However it is not an English word and it stems from pre-pending.

**Informatics**   is the science that studies the use and processing of data, information, and knowledge.

The word Informatics was born in France as l'Informatique, and it seems that it has been first employed by Jean-Dominique Warnier, the French 'father' of Software Engineering.

While the term Informatics has been in use in Europe since the 1960s, it has only recently found its way into the general vocabulary within the USA. An exception is the specialty area of medical informatics, which was defined years ago.

Today we see many specialty areas, including nursing informatics, social informatics and bioinformatics.

There is a growing interest and concern with the way in which information and information technology shape human behavior and, conversely, the way human behavior shapes our development and application of information and information technology. These interests and concerns have helped to define informatics as a domain reaching well beyond a single discipline, such as computer science.

Informatics encompasses research and Inventions from the natural, medical and social sciences, as well as humanities and engineering.

**Social Informatics**   (SI) refers to the body of research and study that examines social aspects of computerization including the roles of information technology in social and organizational change and the ways that the social organization of information technologies are influenced by social forces and social practices. Hence, SI represents the interdisciplinary study of the design, uses and consequences of information technologies

Social Informatics includes but is not limited to the studies and other analyses that are labeled as social impacts of computing, social analysis of computing, studies of computer-mediated communication (CMC), information policy, computers and society," organizational informatics, and interpretive informatics.

**Structural Informatics** is a term that was coined by Jim Brinkley in 1990 in order to capture the kind of work ranging from 3-D ultrasound reconstruction to 3-D protein structure, to work in gross anatomy. Cornelius Rosse and Jim Brinkley then applied this term to the previously-described classification of structural information, concentrating on its application in anatomy. The USA's National Library of Medicine picked up this term in their long range report that led to the Visible Human project, and Jim Brinkley expanded on the term in 1991.

Structural Informatics is founded on the hypothesis that the same methods and representations are applicable at all levels of organization, and therefore can be applied at multiple levels once the common problems are recognized.

A large amount of information in medicine or biology relates to physical structures in the body, encompassing the spatial arrangement of macromolecular complexes, cells, tissues, organs and body parts. One way to represent such information is through Structural Informatics that classifies information according to Spatial versus Symbolic (see Table 14B), as well as data versus knowledge (see Table 14B for a definition of symbolic and spatial information).

**Information** see Information Theory

**Information Architecture** is the art and science of organizing information to help people effectively fulfill their Information needs. Information architecture involves:

- investigation,
- analysis,
- design, and
- implementation

**Information Architecture—Technical** represents the set of ideas about how information in a given context should be treated philosophically and, in a general way, how it should be organized. In the context of a company making security software.

**Information Architecture—Product**  would be founded in planning whereby the focus is on using the **architecture** for a specific division, set of products, or an individual security product.

**Information Design**  focuses more narrowly on activities that support the **architecture** and planning, such as style guidelines, graphic design motifs, page design, and the **information** aspects of industrial design (labels, knobs, and other physical aspects of the user interface).

In Web site design, **information architecture** has a meaning similar to the above, but focused somewhat more narrowly on Web content as building blocks to be fit into a site's visual design and navigation scheme.

Information Architecture has to also consider Security aspects very carefully. Hence, who gets access, privacy concerns as well as many others discussed throughout this Dictionary must be addressed.

**Information Assurance**  encompasses activities that protect and defend information and systems by ensuring their Confidentiality, Integrity, Availability, User Accountability, Authentication and Audit (CIA-UAA), and also Non-Repudiation. This includes providing for restoration of systems by incorporating Critical Infrastructure Protection (CIP), detection and reaction capabilities (see also Tables 2A & B).

There is currently no international agreed definition of information assurance. Another description might be that it is the guarantee that the security objectives *to protect information in communication, information and other electronic systems, and also systems themselves, against:*

- loss of confidentiality,
- integrity and
- availability

are achieved by the selected security enforcing resources and measures. In a further state one might also develop Information Assurance according to (see also Information Theory):

- Information characteristics such as timliness and accuracy as well as information states (see also Table 14B) play a critical role (see Information Theory) for Information Assurance.
- Security countermeasures, such as policies or password protection and Security Policies (see Table 6) are an integral part of Information Assurance.
- Finally, some have argued that Information Assurance is really a sub-area of Information Security (see below).

Furthermore, Information Assurance also relates to the Domain of Information Security Space (DISS) and Securematics.

**Information Crime**  see Computer Crime

**Information Custodian** is the person responsible for overseeing and implementing the necessary safeguards to protect the information assets, at the level classified by the Information Owner.

This could be the System/Security Administrator, controlling access to a computer network; or a specific application program or even a standard filing cabinet.

**Information Operations** is the term used in the military environment to describe what the military approach to "Information Warfare" is.

**Information Operations (InfoOps) could also be defined as** the "actions taken to influence decision makers in support of political and military objectives by affecting other's information, information based processes, Command & Control (C2) Systems and Communication and Information Systems (CIS) while exploiting and protecting one's own information and/or information systems." (NATO definition 1999, source "Netherlands Annual Review of Military Studies 1999).

**Information Owner** is the individual/organization that creates, or initiates the creation or storage of the information, is the initial owner. The Information owner is responsible for ensuring that:

1) that the classification hierarchy used is appropriate for the type of information processed and has been agreed upon,

2) information is classified accordingly and an inventory listing of each type is generated and regularly updated,

3) For each document or file within the classification scheme, agreed confidentiality classifications are also appended while data accessibility is again determined by the confidentiality classification.

4) Security safeguards such as logon controls and access permissions applied by the Information Custodian assure that the levels of confidentiality are met, and

5) Checking periodically that information continues to be classified appropriately according to the scheme agreed upon and, as importantly, safeguards remain valid and fully operative.

**Information Security** uses a system of policies and/or procedures for identifying, controlling, and protecting from unauthorized disclosure, information whose protection is required (see also Domains of Information Security Space (DISS).

Information Security has gone through a radical Paradigm shift whereby the single distinction between physical and other security has been replaced by encompassing all security measures (physical, organizational, human, and electronic) in order to achieve the overall security objectives (Confidentiality,

Integrity, Accessibility of Data, User Accountability, Authentication and Audit = CIA-UAA, see also Table 5C) including Non-Repudiation.

Information Security is still a "multiparadigm" discipline, because there are several competing ways of understanding the discipline and its challenges coming from very different domains (e.g., computing science, security & software engineering, ergonomics/human factors, and end-user computing).

System Complexity is also outlined in Table 13A and explains how this may affect security. Finally, Table 13B outlines human error may play a critical part in System Safety and, as importantly, relaxing standards may exacerbate the Risks.

Moreover, System Safety may also be lowered by Complexity and language that may confuse users (see Table 13C).

Information Security also relates to Safety Engineering and Security Engineering (see Table 23B) and Security as well as Trust and Securematics (see Table 23A).

**Analogy for Information Security**    could be given by comparing it with Airport Security whereby the:

- Role of the immigration officers, inspecting credentials and deciding who is allowed in, is played by firewalls.
- Identity management is the passport office, which issues and verifies those credentials.
- Content security equates to the x-ray machines used to check luggage;
- Encryption is the diplomatic bag that ensures confidential documents are not snooped on; and, finally
- The closed circuit television monitoring all activity and spotting threats is the Intrusion Detection System (IDS).

**Information Security Guideline**    is a suggested action or recommendation to address an area of the Information Security Policy. A security guideline is not a mandatory action, and no disciplinary action should result from non-adoption. However, Information Security Guidelines are considered Best Practice and should be implemented whenever possible.

A guideline typically uses words like "should" or "may" in the definition. Guidelines are usually written for a particular environment and are used to help guide users' actions. For example, "all successful logins **should** be logged and monitored." A guideline may apply to management, administrators, end users, or a specific group within the organization.

Information Security Guidelines will usually supplement the Procedures Manuals with their adoption encouraged and promoted rather than enforced (see also Information Security Policy, Policies, Security, Wireless Local-Area Network).

**Table 13A:** System Safety and Security—System Complexity

| Category | Description of Security Problem |
| --- | --- |
| Complex Systems | can, in computing science, be defined as a collection of many simple nonlinear units that operate in parallel and interact locally with each other so as to produce emergent behavior. |
| | A complex system is not just a complicated collection of parts but is also composed of several elements interacting among them. The complexity of a system depends on: |
| | 1) the number of elements that it is comprised of, as well as |
| | 2) the number of interactions among these elements, and also |
| | 3) the complexities of the elements and their interactions. |
| | A complex system's behavior cannot be explained or predicted using linear analysis. Moreover, a critical system requires that one understands the relationships of the components being part of the system. |
| | Complex systems are prone to failure, but careful design and continued corrections of problems reduces the chance of catastrophic failure. |
| | It is impossible to design a foolproof system and designers know this; they can only try to prevent accidents that they know can occur. |
| | Complex systems should try to prevent all accidents but this requires continuous improvement and innovation. |
| | To illustrate, building clean code is getting more daunting, especially for Microsoft . The Windows XP operating system had: |
| | —50 million lines of code (a line averages 60 characters) and |
| | —grows 20% with every release. |
| | It was put together by: |
| | —7,200 people, came in |
| | —34 languages and had to support |
| | 190,000 devices  different models of digital cameras, printers, handhelds and so on. |
| | Hence, Windows XP represents a complex system with extensive interactions amongst its elements and complexities that are hard to manage for the programmers and engineers. |

**Note.** The foundation of possible industrial accidents is the complexity of the system that makes its well functioning a real challenge, while the Risk for Failure of a Safety System can result in serious repercussions, especially if the system is part of the Critical Information Infrastructure (CII) of a country.

**Information Security Incident**   is an event which appears to be a breach of the organization's Information Policy (see also Computer Crime—Incident Reporting).

Security Incidents can be of minor impact or may result in grave damage to the organization. It is therefore important that reactions to Information

**Table 13B:** System Safety and Security—Failure of Safety

| Category | Description of Security Problem |
| --- | --- |
| Failure of a Safety System | In the case of a nuclear power plant, such as the Chernobyl and Three Mile Island one, failure may be triggered by human error or negligence. |
| | For instance, the Three Mile Island accident had a glitch in the cooling system occur which triggered the start of the backup system. The backup system worked as it was designed too, however the main valve on its pump had not been realigned after routine testing had been done, as a result the valve did not work properly. The error involved was a manual **human error** in not re-aligning the valve. |
| | Serious accidents are prevented by safety systems albeit a probability always exists that a safety systems fails which could exacerbate the problem. However, such a Risk is far more acceptable than having many more accidents in complex systems such as a power plant or an information system for the New York Stock Exchange. |
| | Windows offers the average computer user the opportunity to experience failure of system on his or her own PC daily. During 2003 Bill Gates revealed to financial analysis some interesting facts, such as: |
| | —5% of Windows machines crash, on average, TWICE DAILY<br>—10% of Windows machines crash DAILY or any given machine will crash about THREE X a month |
| | According to StatMarket.com, as of March 2003, Windows XP had: |
| | —33.41% of global market share among operating systems, if we assume 35% for simplicity's sake,<br>—this works out to a minimum of 30 billion Windows system crashes per year |
| | A complex system that gets ever more complex and is unlikely to function properly soon. |
| Relaxing Safety Standards – Getting Sloppy | But safety systems work well only if we take advantage of these and understand through Awareness what they really mean and why they are important. |
| | Everyday examples in a technology based world include: |
| | —ignoring of proper car maintenance schedules,<br>—forgetting to run virus checker on Memory Stick before using it,<br>—ignoring data backup schedules, and<br>—not backing up recover information after a windows crash. |
| | These events are ignored regularly by everyday people, and are excellent examples of the relaxation of technical standards and safety precautions in action. |

**Note.** The foundation of possible industrial accidents is the complexity of the system that makes its well functioning a real challenge, while the Risk for Failure of a Safety System can result in serious repercussions, especially if the system is part of the Critical Information Infrastructure (CII) of a country.

**Table 13C:**  System Safety and Security—Human Behavior and Techno Babble

| Category | Description of Security Problem |
| --- | --- |
| Complex Systems, Sloppiness and Critical Infrastructure Protection (CIP) – Oversight and Auditing Needed | On August 30/31, 2003, Switzerland reported that in the Muensingen nuclear power plant, a pressure valve had resulted in a leak in the nuclear reactor. The system shut the plant down. |
| | No radioactive material had escaped but the check-up revealed another yet undiscovered hole. The operator argued all was safe but inquiring minds dared to ask why a safety system would turn off a reactor, if the incident was not considered serious by the system as designed by safety engineers? |
| | Why would the safety system shut the plant down if there was supposedly no problem? |
| | As importantly, why did the safety system fail to detect the first hole and shut the plant down already then? |
| | The above illustrates a case, whereby a complex system with extensive safety features and procedures is not working 100% accurately, that represents a serious Risk for the plant and citizens. Worst is that the operator does push safety events aside as non-events. This illustrates that we need more work and investment in CIP and a regulatory framework in this area. |
| | Most important seems an independent oversight and audit staff making sure that these critical systems do run safely and securely. Having complex systems that are not 100% fail-safe is one thing but increasing Risks due to operator sloppiness or carelessness is unacceptable. |
| | Hence, operator behavior and attitude is a key component for making systems work |
| Techno Babble | An example of this is the main pages in UNIX. Most are written so cryptically that it is often impossible to determine how to use a particular command without referencing many sections. The result is techno babble indecipherable even for the educated user. |
| | This problem is not limited to technology however; doctors, lawyers, and accountants as well as Brussels' European Commission bureaucrats have their own speak[1]. The point of a club is to exclude outsiders. And a classic way to do that is to keep generating baffling new jargon which only insiders can understand. |
| | Einstein is attributed of once having said something to the effect that any idiot could make something sound complex, but only the gifted were able to make something difficult seem easy. With ever more complex information systems, safety and security requires that users understand most matters in order to behave wisely, thereby reducing the Risk for a Threat or Vulnerability being exploited |

(cont.)

**Table 13C:** (cont.)

| Category | Description of Security Problem |
| --- | --- |
| | Perhaps the best way to develop information technology and software documentation using more extensive testing methods involving average users as are employed in many technology areas. |

**Note.** The Risk for having an industrial accident regarding a complex system is not reduced by using language that is incomprehensible to the average user. Additionally, people tend to ignore rules or regulations if they are not enforced (e.g., speed traps, fining violators). Similarly, to assure that Users follow Active Defense patterns (see Table 7B), regular checking and discussing of policy violations with them is necessary. Sloppiness is a high Risk behavior that must not become prevalent in how people use information technology if we want to assure its smooth running (see also Tables 22A and 22B).

The importance of CIP was illustrated during August 2003 when a power grid failure created havoc in the Eastern USA and Canada, while one evening greater London suffered and power failure in Eastern Sweden during Tuesday September 23 swapped over into Copenhagen and Odense in Denmark resulting in a total blackout, closure of airports, shut down of train lines and e-commerce servers to mention a few examples.

[1] All governments deal in jargon, but the European Union may be the world leader. Its key strategy, honed over many years, is to avoid calling anything by a name that might let an outsider guess what is being talked about. Three forms of code are particularly important: acronyms, place names and numbers. In a national bureaucracy, an informed layman with a talent for crosswords can swiftly decode an acronym. The EU, however, puts all its acronyms through a sort of linguistic Enigma machine, often using English acronyms in French documents and vice versa. This can also result in sentences such as this one: "At next month's Gymnich, the ministers will discuss furthering the Lisbon agenda, applying the Copenhagen criteria and expanding the Petersberg tasks."

Security Incidents are handled by experts following a pre-planned approach. Leaving Security Incidents to the System Administrator could be regarded as the "Wolf guarding the Sheep."

Roles and responsibilities for "Incident Handling" should be pre-defined and generally be handled by the INFOSEC Officer, who should report directly to the management of the organization (see also Disaster Management).

Where a member of staff fails to observe Information Security procedures; this is not, of itself, an Information Security incident. However, depending on the risk of the incident, disciplinary and/or improved procedures may be required (see also Incident).

**Information Security Plan**   complements the IT Plan in so far as it documents, budgets and resources the upgrades to both, hardware, software, training and procedures, in relation to Information Security (see also Security Policy, Tables 6 & 21A, Figure 4).

The driving force behind the Information Security Plan will be the Security Officer with the executive sponsor likely to be the Chief Information Officer, or the Chief Executive Officer (CEO)

**Information Security Policy**   is a set of rules, defined and set in force by the management of an organization. Management sets forth the overall security policy for employees and other members of the organization. It also defines the handling procedures for information and how this information is to be protected. This includes intellectual property rights as well as access rights to such information and the organization's IT resources. (see also Table 6).

This policy aims to reduce the risk of, and minimize the effect (or cost) of, security incidents. It establishes the ground rules under which the organization should operate its information systems. The formation of the Information Security Policy will be driven by many factors, a key one of which is risk management (see Risk, also Figure 4).

Compliance with the organization's Information Security Policy should be incorporated with both the Terms and Conditions of Employment and also a person's Job Description (see also Policies, Information Security, Security).

Furthermore, there are numerous additional policies that must be implemented to assure that information security reaches the baseline (see also Figure 4, Controls, Critical Infrastructure Protection, Submarine Warfare)

**Information Security Skills (ISS)**   see Learning, also Table 17D.

**Information Security Space**   see Securematics (Table 23A & 23B)— Domains of Information Security Space

**Information Space**   see Privacy and Tables 21B and 21C

**Information System**   can be defined as the computer, communication systems and information sources used by an organization to support its day to day operations. It includes various devices, including mobile phones and personal digital assistants (PDAs).

**Information System (IS) Protection**   see Critical Infrastructure Protection (CIP)

**Information System Owner**   is the person responsible for viewing/amending/updating the content of the information assets.

**Information System User**   is any user (individual/human) with legitimate access to an Information System utilizes the information stored on that system.

**Information Technology (IT) Protection**   see Critical Infrastructure Protection

**Information Theory**   is still at its infancy. Claude Shannon wrote a paper entitled A Mathematical Theory of Communication (1948) (http://cm.bell-labs.com/cm/ms/what/shannonday/paper.html) that was later renamed to A Mathematical Theory of Information. However, the theory addresses a small portion of Information only, particularly statistical attributes of the sender and the transmission channel but ignores the recipient of the communication.

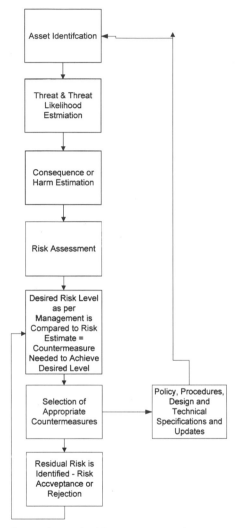

**Figure 4** A methodology for assessing security risks - a process approach.

My cellular number contains information of interest only to the person who wishes to call me. Dividing a large number into prime numbers may provide a cryptographer with the information required to decrypt an encrypted eMail. Mathematically speaking, however, these factors have always been part of a number, thereby not giving us anything new. A more extensive definition of information is given in Table 14A.

Table 14A outlines some of the concepts regarding Information Theory and while computing science feels Information Theory exist, others claim it does not encompass the whole spectrum by not fully addressing technical and social aspects as outlined in Table 14A.

**Information**    is a concept closely linked to Information Theory and requires a few definitions as well. These are provided in more detail in Table 14B (see also Privacy, Tables 21B and 21C).

**Information—Quantity Produced per Year**    is the amount of newly created information that is stored in four physical media (see link in Appendix 3–Information–How much):

- print,
- film,
- magnetic, and
- optical

The can be seen or heard in four information flows through electronic channels, namely:

telephone,
radio
television, and the
internet

A study analyzing the stock of new information recorded in storage media, and hear or seen each year in information flows reported in 2002 (using 1999 data) that the media listed under 1–4 above produced about 5 exabytes of new information in 2002.

For comparison, the USA's Library of Congress has about 10 terabytes of data (see Bit). Five exabytes of information is equivalent in size to the information contained in Library of Contress print collections.

The total is distributed as follows (see link in Appendix 3–Information–How much):

—7% for film,
—0.01% for paper,
—0.002% for optical media

Who produces all this information geographically speaking? The USA produces about

—40% of the world's new stored information, including
—33% of the world's new printed information,
—30% of its film titles,
—40% of its information stored on optical media, and about
—50% of the information stored on magnetic media.

**Table 14A:** Information Theory

| Category | Description |
|---|---|
| | Information Theory deals with measurement and transmission of information through a channel. |
| | A fundamental work in this area is Shannon's Information Theory, formerly called Communication Theory. It provides many useful tools that are based on measuring information in terms of bits or - more generally - in terms of (the minimal amount of) the complexity of structures needed to encode a given piece of information. Consequently, Shannon's theory can be applied to measure, such as the danger of obliteration of information or, equivalently, the amount of work necessary to preserve or to transmit information properly through noisy channels. |
| | In this theory, the information and the transmission channel are formulated in a probabilistic point of view. The theory established firmly that the concept of information has to be accepted as a fundamental, logically sound concept, amenable to scientific scrutiny. |
| Specified versus Non-Specified Information | Specified information is always patterned information, but patterned information is not always specified information. For specified information not just any pattern will do. We therefore distinguish between the "good" patterns and the "bad" patterns. The "good" patterns we call: |
| | **Specifications** - is an agreed target of Information Security. For instance, by first setting a target (e.g., a server with a database) and then attacking the target for penetration and unauthorized access, the pattern is given independently of the information. |
| | **Non-Specified** - is the case whereby by first attacking a server and then stating that this was the target after having successfully penetrated it, the pattern is merely read off the information. |
| Complex Specified Information (CSI) | is what all the fuss over information has been about in recent years, not just in biology, but in science generally. CSI is indispensable in our everyday lives. |
| | The 16-digit number on your VISA card is an example of CSI. The complexity of this number ensures that a would-be thief cannot randomly pick a number and have it turn out to be a valid VISA card number. What's more, the specification of this number ensures that it is your number, and not anyone else's. Even your phone number constitutes CSI. As with the VISA card number, the complexity ensures that the telephone number won't be dialed randomly (at least not too often), and the specification ensures that this number is yours and yours only. |
| | All the numbers on our bills, credit slips, and purchase orders represent CSI. CSI is the artifact of interest in most techno-thrillers. Ours is an information age, and the information that captivates us is CSI. |
| | Many of the interesting cases of specified information, however, are those in which the pattern is given *after* a possibility has been actualized. In the above example, attacking a server and successfully penetrating it and claiming it to be the target after success. |

(cont.)

**Table 14A:** (cont.)

| Category | Description |
| --- | --- |
| | It remains the case, however, that a pattern corresponding to a possibility, though formulated after the possibility has been actualized, can constitute a specification.<br>For instance, a person may receive several email messages which when viewed in the html window in Outlook each resemble a part of a pattern of a particular virus (e.g., a part of a dish set, plate, cup, bowl). Once completed the person may have a fully working Virus or a dining set for five people. This pattern therefore constitutes a specification. |

**Note.** The above table outlines some of the metaphors, components and ingredients that need precise definitions for giving us a theory of information

The world population is 6.300.000.000 people, thus almost **800 Megabytes** (see also Bite) of recorded information is produced **per person each year**. This would take about 28 meters of books to store the equivalent of 800 MB of information on paper (see also Appendix 3 for a link to more information regarding this matter).

**Information Warfare**   is a form of war, where information is the "weapon" and the target at the same time. The definition of information war depends very much from one's the point of view taken.

In the military environment, the term "Information Warfare" is synonym to "Information Operation" (see also Information Operation, Submarine Warfare)

Information Warfare can be classified using the following three categories for classification purposes:

1) Individual Privacy
2) Industrial and Economic Espionage, and
3) Global information warfare, whereby a nation is using it to fight another one

Most organizations will not need to be concerned over category 3, however, category 2 is relevant to any firm wanting to protect its confidential information. Category 2 is an issue regarding employee, customer and supplier data (see also Privacy)

**INFOSEC**   is an acronym that describes the application of security measures to protect information processed, stored or transmitted in information systems.

Protection includes measures against the primary security objectives (see also Primary Security Objectives), loss of confidentiality, integrity and availability.

**Table 14B:** Information as a Concept

| *Category* | *Description* |
| --- | --- |
| Information | is more than the physical coding used to represent it. The sender and receiver must agree in advance on conventions to represent whatever is to be communicated in the future. The field of information encompasses the |
| | a) processing, |
| | b) transmission, |
| | c) storage, |
| | d) use of information, |
| | e) and the foundations of the communication process. |
| | It specifically encompasses theoretical and certain applied aspects of coding, communications and communications networks, complexity and cryptography, detection and estimation, learning, Shannon Theory, and stochastic processes. |
| Design of Information | Complex Specified Information (CSI) is a reliable indicator of design because its recognition coincides with how we recognize intelligent causation generally. In general, to recognize intelligent causation we must establish that one from a range of competing possibilities was actualized, determine which possibilities were excluded, and then specify the possibility that was actualized. What's more, the competing possibilities that were excluded must be live possibilities, sufficiently numerous so that specifying the possibility that was actualized cannot be attributed to chance. In terms of probability, this means that the possibility that was specified is highly improbable. In terms of complexity, this means that the possibility that was specified is highly complex. All the elements in the general scheme for recognizing intelligent causation (i.e., Actualization-Exclusion-Specification) find their counterpart in complex specified information-CSI. CSI pinpoints what we need to be looking for when we detect design. |
| Coded Information | Can be found in DNA, human speech and the bee dance, it is also systematic. |
| Information Exchange | Requires that the frame of reference or context be agreed to in advance. |
| Random Processes | cannot generate Coded Information (see Table 13B); rather, they only reflect the underlying mechanistic and probabilistic properties of the components which created that physical arrangement. |
| Information Efficiency | may be denser than implied by Shannons $\log 2(n)$ equation, since a common basis of understanding exists between sender and receiver, often allowing implications with various degrees of certainty to be assumed by both parties, in addition to the raw data of the message (e.g., implied meaning or non-verbal communication). |

(cont.)

**Table 14B:** (cont.)

| Category | Description |
|---|---|
| Intention of Original Sender | must be considered since an encoding system can be devised to ensure transmission accuracy while making it impossible for an unauthorized party to understand its content. |
| Time Dimension | means that if the physical medium is not destroyed, information contained in a message can survive over time. There is, however, some flexibility as to when the receiver can interpret the information. |
| Externality of Information | means that the underlying meaning of coded information is external to the mere nature and properties of the sender. |
| Subject to Physical Law | encompasses the rule that the physical medium upon which a message is encoded is subject to such as a natural trend towards increased entropy in the long run (and thereby loss of encoded information which is dependent on a physical medium). |
| Comparative Sense of Information | results in content of messages being more easily quantified in a comparative than absolute sense. |
| Spatial Information | can be defined as information that is described in a coordinate system, in one or more dimensions. An example of a one dimension would be a molecular sequence. Two dimensions would be a 2-d image while three dimensions might be illustrated by a 3-D volume image or 3-D anatomic reconstruction (see also Structural Informatics). |
| Symbolic Information | Encompasses other kinds of structural information such as anatomic terminology, definitions, glossaries, semantic relationships. The symbolic information gives meaning to the corresponding spatial information. Symbolic Information is conventionally expressed in natural language and can be formalized for computational processing by various knowledge representation paradigms using methods of artificial intelligence (see also Structural Informatics) |

**Note.** The above table defines further the concept of information, at the core of Information Security.

There is currently no common agreement on the exact definition of INFOSEC. In some communities it is referred to as the protection of information and the systems handling the information, while other communities only refer to the protection of the information (see also Information Security).

**Infowar**   see Information Warfare

**Infrastructure Interference**   occurs when false signals are sent to a satellite or microwave system (see Critical Infrastructure Protection).

**Infrastructure Observation**   is the listening to traffic on a microwave link.

**Infrastructure Protection**   see Critical Infrastructure Protection

**Innovation**   see Invention

**Input**   means literally entering data into the information system or database either manually or using an automated procedure

**Input Overflow**   takes place when software errors resulting in the program not properly checking input bounds are taken advantage of.

**Instant Messaging**   see Short Messaging Service (SMS), also Spam-Spim

**Integrated Collaborative Environment (ICE)**   provides a framework for electronic collaboration, typically with a firm based on shared directory and messaging platforms. The core integrated functionality areas are email, group calendars, scheduling, as well as shared folders, databases, threaded discussions, and application development.

**Integrity of Data**   is the property that data and information has not been modified, altered or destroyed accidentally or in an unauthorized manner (see also Table 5).

**Integrated Services Digital Network (ISDN)**   allows voice, video and data to be transmitted over a single telephone line at speeds depending upon the network provider. In the mid 1990s ISDN offered speed of up to four times as fast as conventional 28.8 Kbps modems (up to 128 kilobits per second or Kbps.

There are two basic types of ISDN service: **Basic Rate Interface (BRI)** and **Primary Rate Interface (PRI)**. BRI consists of two 64 kb/s B channels and one 16 kb/s D channel for a total of 144 kb/s. This basic service is intended to meet the needs of most individual users.

PRI is intended for users with greater capacity requirements. Typically the channel structure is 23 B channels plus one 64 kb/s D channel for a total of 1536 kb/s.

In Europe, PRI consists of 30 B channels plus one 64 kb/s D channel for a total of 1984 kb/s.

**Interface**   is the point where interaction occurs between two systems, processes, or subjets. In computing this could be an apparatus for connecting two pieces of equipment, enabling them to operate jointly.

An Interface can be software, or hardware, such as the physical connections between a terminal and a host computer. Interfaces use an agreed protocol (language) to send and receive information from one machine to another machine, or from a machine to a human, such as the Graphical User Interface (GUI) of Microsoft Windows = Human Machine Interface HMI) [The GUI is a HMI].

**Internal Rate of Return (or Time-Adjusted Rate)**  is the rate of interest at which the present value of expected inflows or cost reductions realized with improvements of information systems and reduced downtime equals the present value of expected cash outflow of the same project (see also Revenues, Tables 2A–2D, 7A & 15C).

**International Organization for Standardization (ISO)**  is a group of organizations administering standards in their respective home countries. The aim is to establish, promote and manage standards to facilitating the international exchange of goods and services.

The term 'ISO' is derived from the Greek word 'isos' which means 'equal', which is the root of the prefix 'iso'. For example the word isobar links together areas of *equal* atmospheric pressure.

In Information Security the ISO standard 17799 has been established (see also Appendix 6 with link to standard).

**Internet**  is the world's largest collection of networks that connects various organizations in the public and private sector including households using the TCP/IP protocol suite (see also Decoupling, E-Commerce)

**Internet-Based Standards**  see Open Source Software (see also Longhorn)

**Internet Control Message Protocol**  is protocol defined by RFC 792 reporting errors and other information about IP packet processing.

**Internet Control Message Protocol Query**  is a process of extracting information from hosts and networks using different ICMP messages.

**Internet Dumping**  is practice of disconnecting a user's modem from the local call to an ISP and reconnecting it secretly to an international or premium-rate phone number. The practice is most commonly associated with adult web sites and computer programs attached to pornographic email. Victims often find out what has happened only when they receive an unusually high telephone phone bill.

During October 2003, Germany made the use of such software and charging of fees based on Internet Dumping illegal.

**Internet Penalties' Plan**  incorporates the idea of fines against people who emit viruses or worms. Hence, this affects not only those that:

- originate a virus or worm, but, most importantly,
- as well infesters who perpetuate attacks

Hence, not being protected against a viruses or worms may be interpreted as being liable or irresponsible if eventually the penalties plan goes forward.

So if you have not, maybe it is time to get your anti-virus software updated now and, most importantly, get one for your neighbor as well (see Appendix 8 for link to free anti-virus software for home users).

The plan suggests that customers who will be levied any fine will be notified by email by their ISP immediately upon the first infraction, and then daily after that. Fines will be included in the customer's ISP invoice.

**Internet Phone**   see Voice over the Internet Protocol—VOIP

**Internet Policy**   is a set of rules defining the use, rights, limits and privileges for accessing the internet on corporate assets by employees within a company or organization.

**Internet Protocol Version 6 (IPv6)**   is the "next generation" protocol designed by the Internet Engineering Task Force (IETF) to replace the current version Internet Protocol, IP Version 4 ("IPv4").

Most of today's internet uses IPv4, which is now twenty years old. IPv4 has been remarkably resilient in spite of its age, but it is beginning to have problems. Most importantly, there is a growing shortage of IPv4 addresses, which are needed by all new machines added to the Internet.

IPv6 fixes a number of problems in IPv4, such as the limited number of available IPv4 addresses. It also adds many improvements to IPv4 in areas such as routing and network autoconfiguration. IPv6 is expected to gradually replace IPv4, with the two coexisting for a number of years during a transition period (see also Anycast).

**IPv6 and Software Capability**   means that software may have to be adjusted. Hence, going through examples of text input fields it could be that these are too short to hold a valid IPv6 address such as 3ffe:1800:0:3:290: 27ff:fe14:cdee.

Necessary might also be to replacing calls to the standard library functions inet_ntoa() and inet_addr(), among others, which do not support IPv6.

On an encouraging note, however, source code that adheres to conservative coding practices and good error checking everywhere could mean that an organization's software does not crash when handling IPv6 addresses.

This all looks similar as the efforts undertaken to prepare for Y2K all over again.

**Internet Service Provider (ISP)**   describes a firm that provides access to the Internet, plus a range of standard services such as email and the hosting (running) of personal and corporate web sites.

ISPs usually charge a tariff for their services although income can be derived from various sources of advertising and portal activities.

**Inter-Rater Reliability**  see Reliability

**Intervention**  see Disruption Management, Data Interference and Cyber Crime Convention

**Intranet**  is a private computer network that uses the technology of the internet (web technology) (e.g., some browser or web software/technology) to disseminate information within an organizations network. The key concept here is privacy and security: Access to Intranets is based on proper Identification and Authentication. For instance, a department's server may be accessible to department employees only, without permitting them to receive and send mail from and to the Internet. Nevertheless, the employee may have access to another server and software to take advantage of the internet (see above) or the Extranet (see also above) (see also Virtual Private Networks—VPN).

**Internet Relay Chat (IRC)**  is a CB simulator that lets you have live keyboard chats with people around the world.

**IP Address**  is a unique numerical address assigned to each *host* on the network. In a case of IPv4, it consists of four groups of numbers separated by dot (32 bit number). For example 130.227.165.197 (see also Internet Protocol Version 6)

**IPv6**  see Internet Protocol Version 6

**Intrusion**  is an uninvited and unwelcome entry into a system by an unauthorized source similar to trespassing. Strong ID and password systems can minimize the risk of intrusion threats succeeding (see also Tables 8 and 12).
    While Incursions are always seen as Hostile, Intrusions may well be innocent, having occurred in error (see also Incursion) (see Tables 15A, 15B and 15C).

**Intrusion Detection**  the general terms and issues are outlined in Table 15A. Table 15B focuses further on terminology and how it is evolving, while 15C address financial aspects (see also Tables 2A–2D, Table 7A).

**Invalid Values on Calls**  are unanticipated requests for service resulting in violations of protection.

**Invention**  represents the genuinely new and deserving. Invention is the final output of innovation (product or process). Ultimately, an Inventor may apply for a Patent.

**Table 15A:** Intrusion Detection

| Tasks | Description |
|---|---|
| Intrusion Detection | is an activity aimed at detecting intrusion into IT infrastructure. It is very similar to security alarms in the building, rising alarms when anything suspicious happens in the IT infrastructure. |
| Intrusion Detection System (IDS) | is a specially designed software and/or hardware providing Intrusion detection. There are many types of IDS. IDS can be classified according to their three main attributes<br><br>1) where they collect data,<br><br>2) how they analyse the data and, finally,<br><br>3) how they react to such data.<br><br>Based on the place of collection of the data, IDS are classified as:<br><br>• network IDS (NIDS),<br><br>• host IDS (HIDS),<br><br>• application and packet based IDS.<br><br>The IDS has the limitation that it can only respond to an attack after detecting an intruder. However, it may be able to identify some hybrid threats. Nonetheless, it is far from a comprehensive, proactive solution, and does neither remove malicious code or Malware nor undo damage. IDS is the online burglar alarm for any network, signalling that an attack or misuse is underway. Host-based and network-based IDS remains the primary work horse for all "non-email" attack vectors. High-speed networks require gigabit (GB) capability to ensure that the IDS can keep up with the speed and immense volume of network traffic (see Data Transmission Rate). Desktop IDS is a must for all remote or mobile devices that connect to corporate networks (see also Tables 2D, 8, 12). |
| Host Based Intrusion Detection Systems (HIDS) | Collects/monitors activity on one particular host. Data collected is analysed with the aim of discovering activity matching the signature of known attack or anomaly in normal operation. |
| Network IDS (NIDS) | Collects/monitors network traffic and analyzes it to discover either anomaly in normal traffic or traffic matching signature. The example of such an IDS is SNORT. |
| Host IDS (HIDS) | Provides real-time monitoring, detection, and prevention of security breaches of a firm's critical servers. HIDS is often enabling automated policy enforcement and incident response for servers, applications, and data. Complements firewalls and other access controls. |
| Application and packet based IDS | can be viewed as refinement of a network based IDS. According to the type of analysis done on data an IDS is classified as anomaly based or pattern/finger print/signature matching based. Finally it they can have passive or active response. Each of these response types can be mixed and, accordingly, each type has its advantages and disadvantages. |
| Penetration Testing | is the evaluator's attempt to circumvent the security features of a system based on their understanding of the system design and implementation. |

**Note.** This describes some of the vocabulary used in Intrusion Detection.

**Table 15B:** Intrusion Detection System (IDS)—Evolving Terminology

| Terms | Description |
|---|---|
| Alarm | Identifies a system that has just been successfully attacked. Normally, these alarms provide the user also with diagnostic information about the context in which the attack occurred. Nonetheless, alarms may be triggered about anomalous events. IDS lingo uses the term alert and alarm interchangeably. |
| False Positive Alarm | represents a benign situation whereby the IDS made a mistake. To illustrate an IDS can raise a "SYN flood" alarm because it discovers a larger than usual number of SYN packets directed to a web server and, therefore, wrongfully concludes that it is under attack. Another example of a false-positive would be when the EICAR Testfile results in a user believing he has a virus on his hard-drive when the file simply helps vendors to assure that their anti-virus software is working properly (see EICAR Testfile). |
| False Negative Alarm | When assessing whether a screening program is appropriate, there is a particular obligation to ensure that the harms as well as the benefits are considered. Among these harms is the likelihood that false-negative results will occur.<br><br>False-negative alarm is a non-event whereby no alarm is generated when an alert-worthy condition is in effect. For instance, an IDS might fail to detect a traversal attack against the buffer directory of a web server if the hacker developed a previously unkown way of obscuring the filename that is being requested. web server buffer directory<br><br>In some cases, the consequences of these no alarm situation is difficult to assess, although false reassurance leading to diagnostic delay and subsequent security measures has been suggested. However, no IDS or IDS-related test is totally accurate (with 100% sensitivity and specificity), and false-negative results are inherent in any IDS that does not have 100% sensitivity. |
| False Noise Signal (also called Noise in IDS lingo) | Represents a false noise signal generated that cannot be distinguished from real signals. Even if the average number of false signals can be estimated through experiments, one never knows for sure which individual signal is real.<br><br>For instance, the IDS may identify a Windows/Intel-based buffer overrun against a Solaris/SPARC system that will not be affected by the attack. The IDS correctly identified an event of interest and the security engineer will react with varying levels of concerns to this event. But scanning before a firewall where one knows that it will not penetrate the firewall may be simply noise. |
| False Attack Stimulus | A stimulus that causes an IDS to trigger an alarm when no actual exploited attack has occurred.<br><br>These are frequently seen during not so well designed IDS tests or when attackers attempt to overload an IDS' alert processing capability using a tool such as Stick. Many scanning tools generate false attack stimuli. To illustrate, if a vulnerability assessment tool connects to a web server and issues a 'GET' command for a known-vulnerable CGI-bin script, it |

(cont.)

**Table 15B:** (cont.)

| Terms | Description |
| --- | --- |
| | is not the same thing as when a hacking tool connects and exercises the complete attack via the same script. |
| | Depending on the application protocols in use it may be difficult for the IDS to distinguish a stimulus that looks for a vulnerability from a stimulus that actually triggers a compromise in the system. False attack stimuli are deliberately used in some IDS testing regimens, attempting to verify the IDS' function without placing real systems at risk. When testing an IDS, the tester should mix a number of false attack stimuli with true attack stimuli. |
| | False attack stimuli generate false positives. |
| True Attack Stimulus | Could occur when a real attack is simulated using session replays of actual attacks on a vulnerable system. This type is indistinguishable for a successful attack. |
| True Attack – False Negative – Collateral Damage | In this case, a true attack occurs but the firewall is unable to detect the DoS effort (false negative), however, damages occur (e.g., router and web pages down). |
| | To illustrate, looking at a firewall log, a company's web servers might have been the victim of a DDoS (distributed denial of service) attack, and while servers might be able to handle the extra load, the router giving internet access might not. Hence, it is possible that for six minutes of a supposedly 15-minute attack, a firm's web servers could be inaccessible. |
| | A well designed DDoS attack can look like real traffic, but for that 15-minute period, traffic might have been at an order of magnitude above the usual. Worst is that the traffic can look exactly like normal web request traffic—making the requests come from different IP addresses. However, Requests could all be asking for the same page, and this can be much more than the router can handle. Hence, the router breaks down in this scenario. |
| | The above is a job for a firewall with the ability to filter out DDoS attacks. These devices use specific fingerprints to tell what constitutes an attack versus what is simply a lot of traffic. |
| | Firewalls handle bogus packets just fine, but what about floods of packets that appear legitimate. It is not always clear if a commercial firewall has a way to handle this particular scenario and many cannot handle such cleverly designed attacks. |
| | Possible in the near future we will have firewalls that are able to distinguish **fake legitimate traffic** from real legitimate traffic, thereby reducing the Risk for collateral damages for the attacked. |
| Deep Packet Inspection (DPI) | can be seen as the integration of Intrusion Detection (IDS) and Intrusion Prevention (IPS) capabilities with traditional state-of-the-art Firewall technology. |
| | The term is used to describe the capabilities of a firewall or an Intrusion Detection System (IDS) to look within the application payload of a packet or traffic stream and make decisions on the significance of these data based on the content of these data. |

(cont.)

**Table 15B:** (cont.)

| Terms | Description |
|---|---|
| | The engine that drives deep packet inspection typically includes a combination of signature-matching technology along with heuristic analysis of the data in order to determine the impact of that communication stream. While the concept of deep packet inspection sounds very nice it is not so simple to achieve in practice. The inspection engine must use a combination of signature-based analysis techniques as well as statistical, or anomaly analysis, techniques. Both of these are borrowed directly from intrusion detection technologies. |
| | In order to identify traffic at the speeds necessary to provide sufficient performance newer Application-Specific Integrated Circuit(s) (ASICs) will have to be incorporated into existing firewall designs. These ASICs, or Network Processors Units (NPUs), provide for fast discrimination of content within packets while also allowing for data classification. Deep Packet Inspection capable firewalls must not only maintain the state of the underlying network connection but also the state of the application utilizing that communication channel. |
| Confidence Level | A desired percentage of the scores (usually 95% or 99%) that would fall within a certain range of confidence limits. It is calculated by subtracting the alpha level from 1 and multiplying the result times 100, such as $100(1 - .05) = 95\%$ |
| | For instance, say a system administrator predicted that, if the vulnerability patch would not have been installed today, the attacker could have a 60% chance of successfully penetrating the system. This prediction could be qualified by saying that the administrator was 95% certain (confidence level) that the prediction was accurate plus or minus 3% (confidence interval); this means the attacker has a 95% chance of having his or her attacks succeeding between 57% and 63% of the times. |
| | For an IDS, Confidence Level is usually assigned by the author of the signatures or detection algorithms. The confidence interval indicates the level at which the IDS has correctly identified and detected an attack. |

**Note.** The above describes some of the commonly and less commonly used IDS and Intrusion Prevention vocabulary. This is likely to change and evolve further.

**Disruptive Technologies** (or **Discontinuous Innovation**) appear to offer lower product performance at the beginning such as automate part of the process compared with using the more conventional way of doing things. For instance, anti-virus software updates are being distributed centrally to all PCs and workstations connected to the Local Area Network (LAN). This can be achieved by either:

- using the 'sneaker net,' where a System Administrator may install updates manually on each machine, or

**Table 15C:** Intrusion Detection System (IDS)—Calculating Return on Investment (ROI)

| Terms | Description |
|---|---|
| $(R-S) + T = ALE$ | **R** is the **Recover** cost from the number of intrusions that occurred during a year |
| | **S** is the **Savings** gained by stopping any number of intrusions through the IDS |
| | **T** is the cost of the intrusion detection tool. |
| | Doing this equation yields the **Annual Loss Expectancy or ALE**. |
| $R - ALE = ROSI$ | To determine our **Return on Security Investment (ROSI)** we simply subtract what we expect to lose in a year (ALE) from the annual cost of intrusion (or Recover costs above). |

**Note.** This describes how the return on security investments made for an IDS could be calculated. A more in-depth but general approach is presented in Tables 2A–2C. & 7A).

* with the centralized distribution mechanism whereby patches and updates for anti-virus software are installed automatically or without System Administrator leaving his or her office.

Here the centralized distribution system was an invention that found a market that rapidly ate into the share of the more conventional Sneaker net type solution. But it was far from being Disruptive, since it built upon established and accepted ways of updating new anti-virus signatures. Nonetheless, the Invention made things easier, faster and saves labor.

In contrast, Disruptive Technologies transform markets in ways hard to understand and harder to predict. Technological progress or a Disruptive Technology/Discontinuous Innovation may also overshoot market demand or be rejected at first because it requires substantial adjustments in, for instance, production and logistics. e-Government does not just require that registration or simple forms can be filled in online, more importantly, databases must be developed that allow such entered information to be accessible by authorized government agencies. Re-entering such data defeats the purpose, hence, unless radical changes are done in the organization of this service, the benefits will be limited.

Disruptive Technologies or Discontinuous Innovation are relatively risky and can be unprofitable for the early adopters, accordingly, first mover advantage is not always genuine. Moreover, companies that follow the technology leader and Inventor may often reap bigger rewards.

However focusing on Sustaining Technologies too long can be Risky as well (see Table 22B).

**Innovation**   is the act of starting something for the first time; introducing something new and it encompasses a creation (a new device or process) resulting from study and experimentation.

Innovation is the implementation of creative ideas to produce new or improved processes or products. It also includes better ways of doing one's job and new tools that make processes more productive and effective.

Innovation has occurred when any aspect (e.g. capability, use) of a product, process or service provides an improved solution to a need.

An organization should not depend just on customers or in cases of E-Government on citizens' demand to lead innovation. Customers cannot be expected to predict new technologies and, therefore, cannot say exactly what they want. Management must also try to predict and lead customer demand (see also Market, Patent).

**Inventor**   is anyone who's involvement and contribution was essential to the development of the invention.

**Collective Invention**   could be described with Open Source Software whereby the salient features are:

- software is distributed together with the source code, and
- software can be improved and modified;

Modified versions are also redistributed under the same terms.
Collective Invention is driven and maintained by:

- reputational interests or self-interests of the programmer (i.e. to become famous for good code);
- users' solidarity to improve the code, also called overlapping interests; and
- gradual development and further improvement through trial-and-error

Collective invention is capable of promoting an effective exploration of the space of technological opportunities and of generating a rapid rate of innovation.

Collective Invention differs from user-producer interaction (Lundvall), lead-user R&D outcomes and from know-how trading (Von Hippel). It is similar to User Innovation but represents primarily the Opportunities for User Involvement facet of this type of innovation.

**Opportunities for User Involvement (OUI)**   are a vital ingredient of successful Collective Invention, especially regarding Open Source Software whereby the user (e.g., consumers or system administrators) inform each other about coding errors and continuously improve the original code. A community of users and inventors or the owner of the code may than decide if an improvement or addition to the original code is being included in the 'original' software (e.g., Linux community).

OUI can help in improving Information Security by having many users test current security features and procedures, while providing suggestions for Patches of Vulnerabilities as soon as they become known.

**Sustaining Technologies**   improve the performance of existing products along performance dimensions that have been valued by customers in the past such as, cost reductions.

It is important to continue developing Sustaining Technologies for the existing mainstream market, rather than forcing a Disruptive Technology into a market where it will not fit. However, in the context of Security, Disruptive Technologies may have to be used to significantly reduce Risks inherent in current systems such as the Windows Operating system, whereby new versions (e.g., Windows 2003 or Longhorn) do not indicate vast improvements that would give improvements regarding Security that will satisfy many System Administrators.

**IP**   see Internet Protocol

**IP Splicing**   occurs when an active, established session is intercepted and co-opted by the unauthorized user.

IP Splicing or Hijacking may occur after an authentication has been made, thereby permitting the attacker to assume the role of an already authorized users. Primary protection mechanisms against such attacks rely on encryption of the session or network layer.

**IP Spoofing**   is a method of attack in which the attacker forges the addresses on data packets sent over the internet so they appear to be coming from inside a network within which computers trust each other (see also email spoofing).

**Iron Box**   is a mechanism set up to trap an intruder, logging in over remote connections for a long enough period to permit the system to trace the intruder back. The Iron Box may include a modified shell, restricting the intruder's movements in not so obvious ways, and 'bait' files, designed to keep the intruder interested and logged on.

**ISDN**   see Integrated Services Digital Network

**IT Infrastructure**   see Critical Infrastructure Protection

**IT Security**   see Information Security

**Java** is an applications programming language developed by SUN Microsystems in 1995. Similar in look and feel to C++, Java was designed for the distributed environment of the Internet. It is based upon object orientation, and the resultant code is portable; which means that Java applications can run on many operating systems, not just the system that compiled it.

Java is a $3^{rd}$ Generation Language (GL) (see Program—Generation Language)

But some suggest that doing projects in Java may cost

1. up to five times as much because,
2. it could easily take 1.5–2.5 times as long, while
3. being harder to maintain

than a project or program that was done in a scripting language such as PHP or Perl (see Invention–meaning more Sustainable Technologies).

At least in theory, Java is a tool that has lots of power for handling problems of tremendous complexity. But this is similar to the city folks who drive to the local supermarket in their Porsche Cayenne, a Sports Utility Vehicle (SUV). A vehicle with massive abilities destined to stay mostly unused.

The SUV driver is feeling good because he or she could climb a 45-degree dirt slope if one had to. Moreover, the probability the one will and should ever do this remains the question of the year. Nonetheless, the driver (Java user) is able to give a lifestyle statement in contrast to the person driving station wagon or programming in PHP.

**J**

**Table 16A:** Jurisdiction

| Concepts | Description |
|---|---|
| Country-of-Origin | approach means that a consumer purchasing online from a website located in another country has no recourse within his or her local court system<br><br>Moreover, a judgment secured requires further proceedings in another jurisdiction, the country the website or IT system is located in. |
| Foreseeability | is a decision to determine if a reasonable person could expect the consequences of an action. Reasonable foreseeability of harm to person who is injured is a factor in deciding whether a legal duty exists.<br><br>Foreseeability enables the website owner to limit the possibility to be hauled into court by a consumer in the EU. The EU e-commerce legislation (see Appendix 4) states that a consumer has the right to bring forward a case against a web site owner at a court where he or she resides. Hence, national courts must take on jurisdiction and in such a case the website owner must meet the targeting test to avoid judgment in a jurisdiction that was excluded from being served (see below). |
| Liability | For years some security experts have been talking about the concepts of:<br><br>—downstream liability, and<br>—attractive nuisance<br><br>as being existing legal concepts that could be applied to enterprises that leave their computer systems in vulnerable condition.<br>Some experts also suggest that no additional legislation is needed in order to enforce these concepts in the Information Security domain.<br>Switzerland decided to help organizations and courts to find their way by putting legislation into place to do just that. In cases, where a perpetrator or originator of an attack or Trojan that misused the firm's system cannot be identified, the organization can be held liable. If it is shown to not have done enough for security and safeguarding its system (e.g., Best Practice), the guilty verdict may come with a hefty fine.<br>Naturally, only the future will show how much teeth this legislation has which depends upon the perseverance State Attorney's and the judges' know-how regarding IT security. For a link to this law, see Appendix 5. |
| Rome II | European Commission (EC) released a draft version of Rome II that treats internet and non-internet commerce in different ways. The draft calls for disputes to be settled in the country where the injury occurs, typically the home jurisdiction of the consumer, except where different cross-border rules have been adopted. That exception effectively creates a "carve out" for e-commerce, which is subject to the e-commerce directive's law of the supplier or web site approach. But this rule would only apply to web sites outside EU jurisdiction, since the EU e-commerce legislation allows an EU citizen to sue a web site owner from another member state at a court where the consumer lives (see Appendix 4). |

(cont.)

**Table 16A:** (cont.)

| Concepts | Description |
|---|---|
| Targeting Approach | has come more and more to the forefront in North America as well as other international forums (e.g., OECD). A targeting analysis seeks to identify the intentions of the parties and to assess the steps taken to either enter or avoid a particular jurisdiction. It lessens the reliance on effects-based analyses, the source of considerable uncertainty because internet-based activity can ordinarily be said to cause effects in most jurisdictions/countries (see also Evidence). |
| Targeting Test | depends on a core jurisdictional principle called **Foreseeability** (see above) that depends on three factors<br><br>1) **Contracts** – such as forum selection clauses found in website terms of use agreements or transaction Click Wrap Agreements permit parties to mutually determine an appropriate jurisdiction in advance of a dispute (e.g., disputes will be handled via arbitration or in country x, city y) (see also Appendix 5).<br><br>2) **Technology** – those that permit identification of geographic location (user identification based on IP address identification, self identification through attribute certificates and offline identification) may allow website owners to exclude visitors from a particular location such as France (see Yahoo! vs. France vs. France—see Zippo Test below).<br><br>3) **Actual** or **Implied Knowledge** – is a catch-all that incorporates targeting knowledge gained through the geographic location of tort victims, offline order fulfilment, financial intermediary records, and web traffic. |
| Tariff 22 | Canada—Of interest here is also that May 2002, the Federal Court of Canada ruled (Tariff 22 Decision) that **Caching** activities should not be treated as mere conduit activity and ruled that jurisdictional reach should extend to foreign based sites with a real and substantial connection to Canada. This affects Canadian ISP and others (e.g., AOL) that cache many sites' content (e.g., Google), since copyright rules apply, thereby making ISPs and other services possibly liable for royalty payments (see also Table 7A, Copyright, Cache—File Cache, Web Cache).<br><br>Caching material to speed up delivery to subscribers go beyond what is strictly necessary to communicate. Accordingly, the Federal Court of Canada ruled that caching was not protected by the intermediary exemption and that ISPs could be required to pay a royalty based on their caching activities.<br><br>Canadian internet jurisdiction law reveals that there are some differences between decisions reached by appellate courts in Ontario, British Columbia and the Federal Court. Accordingly, the Supreme Court may use this opportunity to clarify the matter by enunciating a single Canadian standard for internet jurisdiction. A decision is expected during 2004. |

(cont.)

**Table 16A:** (cont.)

| Concepts | Description |
|---|---|
| Zippo Test | (name derived from the Zippo case in the US) suggests that courts should refrain from asserting jurisdiction over passive sites, while jurisdiction over active sites is appropriate. Activity level is defined as follows: |
| | • **Active Site** whereby the user can enter data and purchase a service; and |
| | • **Passive Site** is one where interaction is minimal such as on an information-based website for sailing enthusiasts. |
| | Unfortunately, the Zippo test has been largely unhelpful by providing parties with only limited guidance and often resulting in detrimental judicial decisions from a policy perspective. In the Yahoo.com France case, Nazi memorabilia was sold on the site, the latter was governed by United States law. The French judge Gomez ordered Yahoo! to ensure that French residents could not access content that violated French law on the site. Yahoo! contested the validity of the French court's order in a California court. Nov. 2001, the court ruled in favour of Yahoo!, holding that the French judgment was unenforceable in the United States. |
| | By 2001, many courts were no longer strictly applying the Zippo standard but were, instead, starting to use other criteria to determine when assertion of jurisdiction was appropriate. Unfortunately, the Zippo test fails because: |
| | 1) Majority of websites are neither entirely passive nor completely active |
| | 2) While a site may at first be perceived as passive, using cookies or other data collection technologies behind the scenes unbeknownst to the individual user may go on and considering the value of such data, the site could be labelled as active, and also |
| | 3) Standards for what is an active or passive site are constantly shifting. |

**Note.** This describes various issues, concepts and terminology pertaining to jurisdiction (see also Table 16B).

**Java Applets** are Java applications with some security-related limitations imposed on them. These applets are downloaded to the local computer or pc. They run within a Java 'Sandbox' created by a web browser. This limits the applet's ability to perform some functions that could be considered risky. Java applets cannot:

- execute arbitrary system commands;
- write to the local file system outside of strictly designated areas (but this is browser dependent); and
- open network connections to sites other than the one from which the applet originated.

**Table 16B:** Justice, Ethics, Morality and Rights or How do these Concepts Relate to Code of Conduct

| Tasks | Description |
|---|---|
| | In this Table some terms are defined that relate to justice and ethics and some relationships to and examples about IT and information security are made (see also Table 16A) . |
| The principles of justice are founded in | 1) the ethical framework of values measuring individual and societal preferences; and |
| | 2) social morality, which represents voluntarily accepted constraints developed from the rational agreement of equals |
| | Fairness in this context may result in a social choice whereby 'who pays what' and 'who gets what' in the absence of prior agreements must be addressed, thereby calling for resolution of the distributed implications of coerced coordination. |
| Ethics | Are a system of goals, ideals, interests, and values that guide personal behavior in daily life. |
| | Ethics are the "higher order" that belongs to every culture or nationality and depict the rule that guide a person's behavior in daily life. |
| Morality | Provides an impartial constraint on the pursuit of individual interests. |
| | Moral issues involve specific topics like justice, rights, or harm, but the cultural-specific rules differ. For instance, pre-marital sex, sharing MP3 files on the internet or using pirated software is dealt with in societies depending upon culture-specific rules and understandings. |
| | How acceptable it might be to use public transport without paying the fare due or taking advantage of pirated software depends upon social norms and morality especially constraints. |
| | How a society deals with violators may be a far stronger deterrent than any law imposed consequences (e.g., Hutterites or Amish shunning a member for having stolen at a local store). |
| Rights | of a person correlate to the active or passive duties of others. If we assume that we have the right to use the firm's computer for doing private email, this implies the norm that, in turn, imposes upon others the duty of permitting us to do what we want with the technology. |
| | The principles of personal autonomy and the hedonist are aggregative principles, insofar as they assign value to the states of affairs and to the goods instrumental to them, regardless of how they are distributed among individuals. Accordingly, they establish the content of basic individual rights. |
| | The principle of inviolability means that personal autonomy and the hedonist principle cannot be pursued without some Moral constraint. Meaning, taking away from others (e.g. water or a hacker using resources without authorization) means limiting or violating their rights which could be unjust. Hence, Copyright infringement violates the copyright holders rights and is, therefore, unjust. |

(cont.)

**Table 16B:** (cont.)

| Tasks | Description |
|---|---|
| Code of Conduct | An association's or organization's code of conduct (e.g., for an employee, member or regarding IT security) is grounded in the above concepts. However, it is the **law** that provides the mechanisms for enforcing a code (e.g., by violating the code a written warning is given, $2^{nd}$ time employee is let go or fired).<br>But a code could perhaps violate local legislation. Hence, while the USA permits firms to scan eMails sent or received by employees at work, French courts have uphold employees' right to privacy concerning eMail. This even applies in case where the firm may have a strict policy that does not allow use of its facilities for sending and receiving private eMails. Accordingly, in France the organization is not allowed to check if this policy is followed, since this would violate the employee's rights. |
| Culture | The above illustrates that Codes of Conduct encompassing cultural values and norms about ethics, morals and justice including rights may be difficult in a multi-cultural or a firm that is international. Norms and values may vastly differ amongst members (see also Code of Conduct) or employees making the abiding of IT Security Policy difficult (see Table 21A).<br>Culture may also affect how employees follow the IT Security Policies (e.g., what are the norms or what is considered appropriate behavior including pilferage) (see also Tables 16A & 21A), including what type of damages certain behavior may cause to others (see Table 7A). What may be considered unjust in one culture may be perfectly okay in another. |

**Note.** The above is a summary of the issues that all are part of ethics and code of conduct issues pertaining to use of software, information systems and resources, as well as security in particular.

**Java Sandbox**    contains specific provisions to deal with potentially dangerous applets, and tries to execute them in a protected mode that severely limits the effects they can have on other applications and the host computer. The Java design team spent time worrying about malicious executables and how they can be prevented from running amok, hence the Sandbox was invented.

**JavaScript**    is an interpreted scripting language, similar in capability to Microsoft's Visual Basic, or SUN Microsystems' Perl scripting language. Java script is interpreted, not compiled, and therefore slower to execute than compiled code. It is easier to maintain and fast enough for small applications. Security risks associated with JavaScript are generally limited to Denial-of-Service (DoS) (see also Table 8) attacks, such as excessive load on the processor, or annoyance attacks (see also Active Content).

**Jurisdiction**    is the range of legal authority or power to act to enforce or pronounce judgments an area or district within which statutes apply and judgments, orders of a court, can be enforced or executed (see also Evidence).

This term is often used to reference the area over which there is a jurisdiction (e.g., traffic law in traffic court) including a geographical region (see also Click Wrap Agreement, Email Signature—Confidentiality, End User License Agreement)

Table 16A outlines the issues that are addressed under Jurisdiction including such things as Country-of-Origin, Zippo Test, Targeting Test, Tariff22 and others.

**Justice**   in essence represents our attempt to appeal to principles logically independent of any particular individuals group's, or country's specific interests, beliefs, objectives, and values.

The two major principles of justice are that it assigns

—rights and duties and that it defines the

—appropriate division of social advantages

Table 16B outlines justice and associated terminology and concepts (see also Asset Value, Code of Conduct, EICAR Code of Conduct, Jurisdiction, Computer Crime, Evidence, Forensics).

J

**Kamikaze Packet**  (see Chernobyl Packet)

**Key Escrow**  (see Key Revovery)

**Key Management**  is paramount to the security of most types of modern cryptosystms. While there is not one way of doing it, the following components may have to be part unless they add nothing to the value of the plan (see Table 17A).

As Table 17A outlines some information not included and described in the table may be considered very appropriate and may need to be added in a particular case (see also Key Recovery, Table 17B).

**Key Recovery**  (sometimes called Key Escrow) provides some form of access to plain text outside the normal channel of encryption or decryption for a third party such as a law enforcement agency (see also Key Management).

**Trusted Third Party Encryption (TTPE)**  means that private keys are either stored with a public or private agency acting in a trust capacity. The existence of a highly sensitive secret key or collection of many keys must be secured for an extended period of time. (See Certification Authority)

Implementing recovery facilities in encryption products to be used in a country may require that the product or service satisfy criteria such as those outlined in Table 17B.

Table 17B outlines what criteria must be satisfied. As the eight criteria might suggest, this requires a lot of logistical effort to satisfy the criteria.

**Table 17A:** Key Management

| Tasks | Description |
|---|---|
| Objective of Plan | Aim, scope, hardware and/software covered, policies relating to the use of the equipment, what equipment. |
| Points of Reference | Internal policy, user manuals, installation or configuration diagrams. |
| Classification of Hardware and Software | Classification of hardware/software—maximum classification of information to be protected by system (confidential, secret, etc.). |
| Hardware and Software Details | Description of configuration, interfaces and functionality, overall network topology. |
| Key Management | How will key(s) be sourced (another organization or by key generation processes or equipment), details on how key is to be physically loaded into the hardware/software cryptographic system and about how session/traffic keys are produced/distributed to the relevant parties. |
| Key Accounting | Details about number of copies of key produced/distributed, and identification of various key(s) to be produced and/or received. |
| | Also labeling and recording procedures applied for name, version and number of copies that were distributed, and the recipients of key(s) is addressed. |
| | Includes detail about cryptoperiod(s) for the various key(s), and details about how keys will be electronically/physically stored, in addition to security countermeasures used against compromise threats. |
| | The above is complemented with details about formal or informal crypto accounts are needed as well. |
| Distribution of Keys | How are these distributed electronically/physically including security details of courier(s) and how they may handle contingencies such as loss or compromise of keys. |
| Contingency | Condition under which a compromise or cryptographic key material should be declared (e.g., loss or theft, unauthorized access or extensions of cryptoperiods) as well as the reporting action required for compromise declaration should be outlined. |
| Hardware and Software Maintenance | Security measures taken to protect the integrity of the hardware/software by unauthorized maintenance staff and appropriate sanitation (Security of Media) and Electronic Shredding procedures before disposal of equipment is outlined while procedures for testing or verification of software upgrades are described. |

**Note.** This describes what steps must be taken to develop a Key Management system that works.

**Keystroke Monitoring** is audit trail software or a specially designed device, recording every key struck by a user and every character of the response that the information system returns to the user.

**Keystroke Logger** is a very useful program used by both Hackers' community and security community. It is usually stealth type of software injected

**Table 17B:** Key Recovery (KR)—Trusted Third Party Encryption (TTPE)

| Steps | Description |
|---|---|
| 1 | The KR capability can be implemented technical and/or procedurally; |
| 2 | KR facility may have to be located within a country's borders; |
| 3 | Key(s) or other material/information required to decrypt enciphered data must be accessible for the life of data including archived files with data, |
| 4 | Encrypted information must be recoverable within a reasonable timeframe; |
| 5 | KR facility cannot be altered, bypassed, disabled or otherwise rendered inoperative by a user of the product; |
| 6 | Output generated must include information sufficient for a KR agent to identify the keys or other material/information necessary to decrypt the ciphertext; |
| 7 | Audit capability is a requirement; and |
| 8 | For security purposes it may be necessary that the encryption product must allow recovery of encrypted data, in circumstances where the encryption key is unavailable due to loss, damage or failure; |
|  | Moreover, access to keys needed to decrypt the ciphertext, regardless of whether the product generated or received the ciphertext, may also be mandated. |

**Note.** This outlines some of the issues that need to be addressed or accounted for in case of implementing a Key Recovery facility.

between the keyboard and operating system in order to record every key-stroke. It is a very useful tool in *honeypots*.

**KISS**   is short for Keep It Simple, Stupid or else Keep It Short and Simple.

**Knowledge**   see Learning

**LAN**   see Local Area Network

**Latent Virus**   see Infection and Table 24

**Layered**   see Multi-Layered

**Leapfrog Attack**   see Table 3B

**Leakage**   takes place when information ends up where it should not have ended up.

**Learning**   can be definied as an unspecified change within an individual due to environmental experience that makes a change in observable behavior possible. Through learning the individual also acquires additional Knowledge. Table 17C outlines more issues regarding Learning.

**Knowledge**   is best defined by distinguishing between:

- **Declarative Knowledge** that describe a person's knowledge about something or understanding the why. This often entails theory and concepts helping explain such things as Information or programming, and
- **Procedural Knowledge** which depicts a person's knowledge about something or how to do a task (see Skills), hence how well and fast he or she can program.

**Training**   is a process whereby individuals systematically acquire Skills, rules, concepts, or attitudes that result in improved performance at work or in other situations. Effective Training stems from a systematically designed Learning atmosphere.

Table 17C also discusses scheduling of training and its effect upon learning performance.

**193**

**Table 17C:** Learning and Type of Training

| *Term* | *Description* |
|---|---|
| **Learning** | Can be described as a cognitive process |
| | 1) Phase 1 requires *controlled* processing since all cognitive or attentional resources are required by the individual to comprehend and learn the performing of an as yet unfamiliar task. Processing of two tasks occurs in serial fashion. |
| | 2) Phase 2 represents a combination of *controlled and automatic* information processes. While for certain portions of the task the individual has developed fast and effortless parallel processing of information, other task components still require full use of cognitive resources. |
| | 3) Phase 3 represents a situation in which *automatic* information processes are predominant. |
| | Thus task performance is still sensitive to memory and resource-load effects. After extensive practice an individual will reach Phase 3, enabling automatic processing when solving the problem, thereby making speed primarily dependent upon *motor ability* (e.g., typing speed). |
| | Once the individual has achieved Phase 3 (automatic processing), a shift of information processing from serial to parallel mode is possible. Consequently, the individual may perform two job-related tasks at the same time (e.g., taking a client's order over the phone and entering the information onto a computer-based order/shipping processing system). |
| | Performance improvements regarding learning are gained by a shift of information processing from a serial to a parallel mode. |
| **Intermittent Training** | gives the trainee the opportunity to practice newly acquired skills (e.g., by reviewing lessons or doing assignments at one's own/preferred time and/or speed in between lessons), thereby attaining a higher level of Automaticity. |
| | Furthermore, learning performance differences based on ability are reduced when the less able individual is given the necessary time to attain a higher speed between two seminars. |
| | The amount of time needed to improve performance will depend upon the individual's motivation and expectancy, as well as ability (e.g., *g* factor). Intermittent training allows the individual to take the necessary time between sessions to do the assignments, thereby individualizing the learning process. |
| | This approach also requires more effort of the employee who might have to study and do assignments to practice newly acquired skills or know-how in between learning sessions on his or her own time. |

(cont.)

**Table 17C:** (cont.)

| Term | Description |
|---|---|
| **Continuous Training** | such as one week full-time or a weekend executive-type training may not allow the less able student to improve his or her skills, since additional practice opportunities (e.g., on-the-job or through homework assignments) between training sessions are limited. Further, transfer of learning may not be as successful as with intermittent training. |
| | Continuous training while often desirable for various reasons for the organization is less beneficial to employees who may experience sensory overload and/or do not have the possibility to digest material, practice between sessions and, thereby, hopefully reducing performance gaps that might be primarily due to ability and intelligence. |

**Note.** The above suggests that for raising awareness about IT Security it seems more advantageous to use an intermittent approach in the firm and for home-users. Reminders and updates appear more effective than a one or two-day workshop once during a full moon. Awareness raising and prevention has to be more than a one-shot effort to reap the rewards (see also Table 21A).

**Skills**    are the proficiencies on a specific task including level of proficiency as well as the task to be accomplished such as Auditing a Patch system for all PCs used in an organization (see Table 17D for a detailed outline of the types of Skills acquired through Learning and Training).

**Information Security Skills (ISS)**    provide a Security Engineer or Expert with the competencies required to do his or her job, including the Declarative and Procedural Knowledge required to make effective decisions while reducing Risks for the Information Assets. A more detailed description is provided in Table 17D with a particular focus on Information Security Skills.

**Letterbomb**    is a piece of email containing live data intended to do Malicious things to the recipient's computer or server. Under Unix, it can also try to get part of its contents interpreted as a shell command to the mailer. This could result in a Denial of Service (DoS) attack (cf. Table 8) (see also Logic Bomb, Table 18C).

**Liability**    is the software or hardware manufacturers legal liability for errors in the product (e.g., product liability) (see also Warranty Disclaimer).

Support is growing for software companies to be held to the same liability standards as other manufacturing businesses. Microsoft, with its plethora of software holes and "deep pocket[s]" is a likely target for a liability suit (see also Disclaimer, Jurisdiction, Table 16A).

When a product fails, the vendor has a responsibility to quickly identify a way of fixing it and getting that patch out. The patch must not only fix

L

**Table 17D:** Information Security Skills (ISS)

|  | *Description* |
|---|---|
| **Skills** | can be categorized using their potential ease of transferability (e.g., to another job and/or employer) (see also Knowledge). Three defining characteristics may be used to describe skills namely: |
| | a)  skills are a wide behavioral domain in which behaviors are assumed to be complex, |
| | b)  they are gradually learned through training, and |
| | c)  attaining a goal is dependent upon motor behavior and processes. |
| | Performing certain tasks requires Knowledge (Procedural and Declarative) and their transferability to other tasks or jobs decreases from: |
| | 1)  **basic** (reading, writing and arithmetic), to |
| | 2)  **social** (e.g., interpersonal skills and the person's ability to organize his/her own effort and task performance, and possibly that of his/her peers and subordinates), |
| | 3)  **conceptual** (including planning, assessing, decision-making about task- and people-related issues, and judging or assessing tasks done by self or others), |
| | 4)  **technology** (encompasses appropriate use of technology, such as a computer, thereby preventing breakdowns/accidents), |
| | 5)  **technical** (physical ability to transform an object or item of information into something different), and finally, to a person's |
| | 6)  **task skills** (usually job-specific). |
| | The Security Engineer not only requires technical skills but also social ones to convince others about the importance of his or her work and the conceptual understanding to explain the why to others (see Research, Methodology, Security Engineer). |
| | Finally, a Security Engineer requires Procedural and Declarative Knowledge (see Knowledge) but it is necessary that Declarative Knowledge components are not neglected, otherwise skills may be applied too narrowly ignoring the complexity challenge for information systems (see Tables 13A, 13B & 13C). |
| **Information Security Skills (ISS)** | Using various means of training, Information Security Skills (ISS) are learned behaviors aquired through various means of training. ISS are needed for achieving desirable performance levels when doing job related tasks, while the content and type of Information Security Skills for doing a job is in part a relational phenomenon (i.e., how many and what type of people have or don't have the necessary skills). |

(cont.)

**Table 17D:** (cont.)

| Description |
| --- |
| Achieving satisfactory performance (during learning and, thereafter, on-the-job) hinges upon: |
| • first individual abilities (motor and cognitive process capabilities, e.g., information processing), |
| • second, the degree of substantive complexity and autonomy-control offered/required by the job and |
| • third, upon the mix of declarative and procedural knowledge the person has in basic, social, conceptual, technology, technical and task skills before training starts as well as the mix to be acquired during training. |

**Note.** This outlines some of the issues that need to be addressed or accounted for regarding type of skills and Information Security Skills in particular.

the problem, in addition, it cannot interact badly with other widely utilized applications (see also Patch).

Nonetheless, it might not be terribly valuable to litigate such problems. Arbitration may result in quicker and more satisfying solution than long, multiyear litigation (see Copyright, Table 16A).

Nonetheless, some countries (e.g., Switzerland) are trying to get a handle on this problem (see also Damages) and have put the legislative framework into place that makes Information Security a Liability issue (see Liability—Table 16A). The law puts the onus on the firm whose computers may have been misused for a Denial of Service (DOS) or other type of Attack to proof that its security measures meet industry standards (see Best Practice). Only case law will show how much teeth this legislation from October 2003 will have (see Appendix 5 for a link to the law text).

**License** is when an owner of a software provides a user with the right to use the product for a specified period, such as anti-Virus software including updates for one year, or else a particular version of a software (e.g., Ver. 3.2) (see also Click Wrap Agreement, Scumware).

To fight Scumware, some software vendors take new roads. For instance, the RadLight adware product comes with a license agreement that reads in part.

"You are not allowed to use any third party program (e.g., Ad-aware) to uninstall application bundled with RadLight. Such programs will be removed."

This may be a security concern for the organization because it may want to uninstall applications that restrict a program's features (e.g., eliminating certain type of advertising to reduce traffic). In the above example, this would mean a violation of the license agreement submitted to by using one type

L

of software in the case were another software violates this agreement (see Copyright, Jurisdiction).

**Linux**   is an Open Source Unix like Operating System.

**Listserver**   is an email 'exploder' that sends a copy of incoming email to each user on a list (see also Moderated Listserver and Daily Digest).

**Load**   see System Load

**Local Area Network (LAN)**   is a network connecting computers within a localized are such as a single building, department or site as well at households (see also Wireless LAN, Wide-Area Network).

**Log Cleaning**   is a process used by more experienced hackers to cover their own traces in the system. They sanitize system log files either by hand and/or using available tools.

**Log File**   see Evidence (see also Computer Forensic)

**Logic Bombs**   (also called **Fork Bombs**) is a program or portion thereoff that triggers or causes an application or operating system to perform when a certain logical event occurs. The code may be used to recursively spawn copies of itself, thereby eventually eating all the process table entries and effectively locking up the system (see also Virus, Table 18C).

A specific date, key combination, or internal counter are some of the most commonly used triggers that produce effects ranging from on-screen displays to the blocking of the system or the deletion of files and programs. For instance, every day at 17:00 hours it mails out a message to 10 addresses out of a person's email address database (see also Letterbomb).

A Virus may also no longer distribute itself after a certain date. For instance, the Sobig virus family expired September 10, 2003 indicating that the writer was primarily interested in studying the virus' effects on networks. However, this might change in the near future.

**Login spoofing**   is a simulation of a login program in order to obtain passwords.

**Longhorn**   is the next version of Windows being built using Web services standards. Microsoft has not said when Longhorn will be ready, but it is not expected to be shipped until late 2005 or 2006.

Microsoft's Windows is perhaps the most lucrative "volume business" the world has ever seen. But some argue that anytime an Internet-based standard is good enough, it will take over the volume business from the proprietary standard. Hence, Linux is one of those Web-based standards.

**LWAPP**   see Wireless—Lightweight Access Point Protocol

L

**Macro**  entails a series of commands grouped together as a single command to automate repetitive and/or complex tasks. Technical purists argue as to whether or not writing macros is actually programming, but from the perspective of most end users, it amounts to pretty much the same thing. Macro recording facilities are now built in to most standard business/office software packages, covering such as, word processing, spreadsheets, databases, graphics and presentations.

It is advisable that all macros created or used within an organization are checked for their function and compliance with security regulations (see also Virus—Macro Virus).

**Macro Virus**  see Virus and Table 18C & Figure 5

**Mail Spam**  see Spam

**Mainframe Computer**  once described almost any computer system, instead of a large system. Mainframes (and Supercomputers) are still being built, installed and run, but their use tends to be restricted to scientific groups and defense applications. In most commercial settings, applications require the running of several servers connecting users that way.

**Malicious Code**  see Malware, Tables 18A, 18C & 25

**Malicious Software**  see Malware, Tables 18A, 18B, 18C & 25

**Malware**  (see also Virus) encompasses all types of malicious or harmful software, such as Viruses, Trojan horses, and worms. While agreement in defining this term is still evolving some general remarks are listed below (see also Tables 18A, 18B, 18C, 25 & Figure 5).

M

**Host Program Required**   are Malware or malicious code that need a host program. Essentially, this type of Malware consists of fragments of programs that cannot exist independently of an application program, a utility that may be a macro, or a system program (see Table 18B).

**Independent Program**   is self-contained and it can be scheduled and run by the operating system (see Table 18B).

**Remote Access Tools (RATS)**   see Remote Access Tool

**Replication**   exemplifies a program that may replicate itself and spread. These are such as:

- Viruses—they are definable by their replication mechanisms, and commercial anti-virus software sooner or later detects them (see Virus and Worm) but they Need a Host Program (see also Table 18B),
- Worms these have replication mechanisms as well and they are Independent Programs (see Virus—Worms) that execute by themselves at pre-determined times or cycles (see also Table 28).
- Bacteria—these are programs that consume resources by exponentially replicating themselves. The definition is based on the way the malicious code is performing a function.

Figure 5 below provides a taxonomy for Malware and malicious programs.

As the arrows indicate in Figure 5, Logic Bombs may be part of a Virus or Worm. Similarly, a Trojan horse may also be embedded in a Virus or a Worm (See Virus).

Table 18A provides a more systematic listing of those Malicious Codes that require a Host Program versus those that are independent (see also Host).

Joke programs, fluffy screensavers and even games occupy an ambiguous niche in the anti-virus pantheon. The ambiguity reverberates into the twilight zone between Malware and hoaxware (see Hoaxware, IRC, Denial of Service Attack).

As Table 18A states (see also Figure 5), Java Cookies and ActiveX Controls can also be malicious code (see also Table 18B).

Table 20C outlines how Patches might work for anti-Virus software updates and Vulnerabilities (see Patches). Table 20D focuses on managing Patches and fighting Malware for SMEs and Home Users (see Patches)

**Manhole**   is an alternative name for a developer's Back Door into a program.

**Man-Computer Interface**   see Person-Computer Interface

**Market**   is any place where the sellers of a particular good or service can meet with the buyers of these goods and service, where there is a potential for a transaction to take place. The buyers must have something they can offer in exchange for there to be a potential transaction.

M

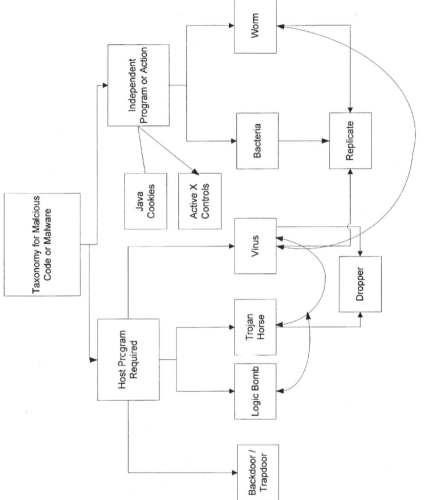

**Figure 5** Taxonomy of malicious code or malware (see also Tables 24E, 25, and 28).

**Table 18A:** Defining Malware—A Simplified Structure

|  | *Description* |
|---|---|
| Malware | encompasses any program, message or document representing a risk for the user or affected party to experience negative effects on his or her IT systems if infected or by such type of code. Malware is sometimes called Malicious Code. |
|  | The most common and dangerous type of malicious code is undoubtedly what is generically referred to as a computer virus. |
|  | Computer viruses can be further divided up into three sub-categories that could be generally defined as: |
| Virus or Computer Virus | is a program that reproduces itself by infecting other programs after it has been activated by the user, such as by double-clicking on an attachment. Some but not all Viruses damage the host computer or its data. |
| Worm | is making copies of itself or part thereoff; a worm does not need to infect programs to make copies of itself. Hence, unlike a virus, it can do damage without user intervention. |
| Trojan or Trojan Horse | is similar to a virus and enters the computer in a number of ways, thereafter it will attempt to carry out a series of actions designed to take control of the computer under attack. A Trojan may have a Virus or Worm inside. |

**Note.** This table provides the reader with a very general description. More specific information is provided in Tables 24F, 25, & 29.

**Free Market Economy**    is an economy in which the allocation for resources is determined only by their supply and the demand for them. This is mainly a theoretical concept as every country, even capitalist ones, places some restrictions on the ownership and exchange of commodities.

**Telecommunication Markets**    in most European countries are, at least theoretically, deregulated. Practically, every competitor must lay the cables for the last mile. Unfortunately, except for the former monopolist, competitors rarely do because cities and towns across the country are afraid that if firm A lays the cables, six months later firm B might want to do the same.

   Instead, the authorities are pushing for operators to get together and lay their own cables all at once. Unfortunately, this removes the possible competitive edge operator A or B might get by investing in the last mile infrastructure before any others do, thereby becoming the main competitor besides the former monpolist (e.g., France Telecom, Deutsche Telekom).

   Accordingly, most operators lease the last mile and loose between 30–60% of their revenue to the former monopolist who owns the infrastructure for the last mile.

   This revenue erosion can be reduced by having possibly four different technologies offered for providing access regarding the last mile, such as:

**M**

**Table 18B:** Vulnerabilities and Malware

| | *Description* |
|---|---|
| Today | Users tend to call every malicious program a virus, but the dangerous programs encountered these days are rarely viruses in the technical sense. More commonly, they are |
| | —worms (see also Table 18A) or<br>—Trojan horses<br>—broken messages (see below) |
| | For instance, SoBig created broken messages. These are not stopped by virus scanners because there is no virus attached to them. However, without the attached virus: |
| | —the message is being sent, and<br>—still looks like an eMail with a virus attached (i.e., it has all the traits/characteristics of a virus infected file), |
| | SoBig sends to the same address more than once, thereby creating many virus scanner replies by a PCs virus scanning software. It also creates a lot of work for scanning software at gateways and mailservers, thereby keeping information assets busy (i.e., costing money, see Tables 2A–2D). |
| | Virus writers are displaying so-called pyramid scheme strategies for spreading bad code, whereby they build on each others' efforts. To illustrate, we did not get Blaster along but, much worse, it came with the variants of Blaster a, b and c. Two new Remote Procedure Call (RPC) Worms came out right behind that using the same exploit, and finally the SoBig author chose to release an improved version of the SoBig virus. What happened during 2003 was that response teams got a big taste of what it is to deal with many threats at once. Regardless if it is a fake infection notice or simply unwanted messages, both cases represent a severe drain on resources and are thereby costly (see Damages, Tables 2A–2C). |
| | But so far, these attacks or files have maybe slowed down systems (e.g., USA Marines' network, Swiss Federal Railways, and others), resulted in closed down services (e.g., CSX—commuter trains in Washington DC got delayed) but did not carry truly damaging payloads. |
| | For instance, if a Virus, such as Blaster, would have carried a significant payload, this could have resulted in a huge problem. Similarly, if a Virus comes along that opens a back door on a server or home PC, again this could be a big problem. So far this has not yet happened but with Blended Threats (see Table 24D) things could still change to the worse. |

**Note.** This table provides the reader with a very general description comparing Vulnerabilities and malware. More information can also be found in Tables 18C, 24E, 25 & 29, as well as Figure 5.

M

**Table 18C:** Types of Malware—Categorization

| Name of Category | Name of Type or Malware[1] | Replication[2] | Definition of Category |
|---|---|---|---|

**Malware** encompasses all types of malicious or harmful software (such as Viruses, Trojan horses, and Worms) see Table 18A.

| Name of Category | Name of Type or Malware[1] | Replication[2] | Definition of Category |
|---|---|---|---|
| Host Program Required | | | Essentially, this type of malware consists of fragments of programs that cannot exist independently of an application program, a utility that may be a macro, or a system program. |
| | Trapdoor | | Secret entry point can also be defined less by mechanism than by its presumed intent. This normally is an undocumented entry point into a program (see Backdoor). |
| | Logic Bomb | | Is a program that triggers or causes an application to perform, when a certain logical event occurs. |
| | Trojan Horse | | Clandestine routine embedded in useful program. |
| | | | These are defined less by mechanism than by their presumed intent; |
| | | | These are normally detected by anti-virus and anti-Trojan programs (see Virus, Table 18A, Table 25). |
| | | | —Destructive Trojans are designed to delete certain files, format the harddisk, or carry out similar destructive action. |
| | | | —Backdoor Trojans are designed open a backdoor in the computer to let hackers enter and take remote control of it. For this reason they consist of two components: the server, installed on the machine under attack and the client, used by the hacker to control the computer. |
| | | | —Keylogger Trojans are programmed to capture the user's keystrokes. This information is stored in a special log that can be accessed by the attacker. |
| | | | —Fake Trojans, which after being run, display false error messages prompting users to enter user names and passwords which are then sent on to the creator of malicious code. |

(cont.)

**M**

**Table 18C:** (cont.)

| Name of Category | Name of Type or Malware[1] | Replication[2] | Definition of Category |
|---|---|---|---|
| | Viruses | P | Infects and/or modifies other programs to include a possibly evolved copy of itself (see also Table 18A). |
| | Dropper | | Combination of Trojan Horse and Virus |
| Independent of Host Program | | | This type of malicious code is self-contained and it can be scheduled to run by the operating system. |
| | Java Cookies | | Cookies are a combination of site identifying code used by the issuing site, and data read from your user.dat file in the Win/Cookies folder. They are used to track your movement and interests, both by the issuing site and with third party profilers such as Doubleclick. |
| | ActiveX Controls | | Can run automatically upon viewing web pages containing ActiveX Controls. |
| | Bacteria | P | A program that consumes system resources by exponentially replicating itself |
| | Worms | P | Replicates and sends copies of itself across network from one machine to another, they can be distinguished by:<br><br>• Transport (e.g., email worms spreading via email, or arbitrary protocol worms spreading via protocols, such as TC/IP sockets).<br><br>• Launching mechanisms (e.g., self-launching not requiring interaction with the victim, such as the Morris or Internet Worm, user-launched worms that require him or her to do something involving a degree of social engineering).<br><br>(see also Worm, Table 29) |

**Note.** This table categorizes Malicious Code, more information can also be found in Table 25 (Categorization of Viruses). A comparison between Virus, Worm and Trojan Horse can be found in Table 18A.

[1] A more precise definition is given elsewhere in the dictionary for each of these terms.
[2] Replication exemplifies a program that may replicate itself and spread to other systems or computers. P means possible.

M

- Cable in the past used primarily for delivering television programming, now also internet and telephony,
- Fixed Wireless Access system [also called fixed (antenna/tower) to multipoint system (i.e., antennas on clients' homes)], providing high-speed internet access (see also Electro Smog and Fixed Wireless Access),
- Electricity cables through the local utility that provide internet access and telephony besides power, and
- Telephone cables that provide fixed line telephone services and internet access often through the former telephone monopolist that owns this infrastructure in a whole region.

Of course, the above is of concern to industrialized countries where the majority of people has access to a fixed telephone line in contrast to Africa where many citizens do not.

Deregulation of telecommunication markets is an important step for **reducing** the Digital Divide, by encouraging suppliers to offer 'unlimited' or unmetered broadband Internet access at relatively low monthly subscription prices. If, however, the former telecommunication monopolist also is the largest supplier of cable-type internet access (e.g., Denmark), such a competitive market structure is unlikely thereby limiting price pressure. Even in countries where the cable providers are separate legal entities and competitors of the former telco monopolist (e.g., Switzerland), competition is limited since one cable provider sets the price for a region (e.g., 28 Euros per month), while telcos charge a bit more. In the later case, regardless of the supplier (e.g., competitors offering broadband access via telephone lines such as Tele2) the former monopolist is likely to get 30–50% of the fee for supplying the last mile.

Hence, in a practical sense this means that a monopoly is usually replaced by an oligopoly (2–3 suppliers), whereby the former monopolist telco with its last mile infrastructure competes with one cable provider with its own last mile infrastructure for a region's internet and telephone clients. Other telecommunication firms are simply re-sellers and pay a large percentage of the subscription charges as an interconnection fee to the former monopolist.

**Digital Divide**   is an issue of interest to political decision-makers in developed countries who would like to assure that many citizens have access to the internet either from home or at least public places such as libraries. In turn, this will also make the offering of E-Government services more palatable and economical.

Tables 19A and 19B outline what the possible issues are regarding digital divide. In short, they illustrate using costing that dial-up or Broadband access is relatively easy for people to obtain and afford if living in industrialized countries. In fact, many have access at work, school/university, through public

**Table 19A:** Digital Divide and Broadband Connection—Markets

|  |  | USA | CH |
|---|---|---|---|
| Dial-up @ 45K | US—unlimited local phone calls included in monthly subscription fee (30.00–$50.00) CH—about Sfr. 20 (approx. $12.50) per month service fee, every call metered. | Free to $24 | Free and metered access per minute via the phone |
| Digital Subscriber Line (DSL) | Monthly Fee | 384 KB downstream speed $30–$50 | 256 KB–2 Megabit Sfr. 34–Sfr. 80 |
| Cable | CH—Cable is generally cheaper than DSL | 512 KB to 1 megabit $40–50 | 128 KB to 2 megabit Sfr. 35–80 |

*Note.* The above compares two vastly different markets and these numbers are changing. However, digital divide cannot be addressed by just looking at prices paid for internet connections, instead it must be put into the larger framework of communication/TV expenditures (e.g., telephone, cellular, TV) as Table 18B illustrates.

USA $1.00 was roughly worth Sfr. 1.40 when these calculations were done.

libraries and from home. Hence Digital Divide may be a misnomer in most industrialized countries (see also Tables 19A, 19B, 19C).

Bridging the Digital Divide requires more than simply offering computers and Internet access. Early during 2003 a study by the {http://news.com.com/redir?destUrl=http%3A%2F%2Fwww.pewinternet. org%2F&siteId=3&old=2100-1032-997140&ontId=1023&lop=nl_ex} reported that a full 20 percent of unwired Americans said they live in homes with an Internet connection, but do not access the Net. Accordingly, technological fixes won't close the divide unless they take into account the social reasons why people aren't online.

**Market Size** must be matched with the organization, whereby the size of the organization needs to be matched to the size of the market. If only a small market exists, it may be worth creating a separate, smaller organization to serve it.

Also, an organization should not depend just on customers or in cases of E-Government on citizens' demand to lead Innovation. Customers cannot be expected to predict new technologies and therefore, cannot say exactly what they want. Management must try to predict and lead customer demand (see also Invention).

**Massaging Data** describes the re-formatting or manipulating of data from one format into another, thereby enabling another system to accept the input (e.g., processing a reservation and payment through e-commerce into the accounting and seat management systems of an airline).

M

Sometimes, data will need to be massaged to allow software to work with it such as removing extraneous characters or the addition of some control characters. Whatever the exact requirements, such manipulation of data poses a threat to the integrity of the data, and thorough System Testing is advised.

In research terms, Massaging Data means that findings (e.g., discovering trends of system failures) may not be generalizable from, that is another person may not find the same results (see Reliability) making the report invalid (see Validity) and impossible to develop a theory or general Standard (see also Research).

**Masquerading**   transpires when an individual uses the identity of another to gain access to a computer or information system.

**Master Boot Record (MBR)**   is the program stored in the boot sector of the bootable media. MBR viruses normally enter the system through a floppy disk. All floppy disks have a boot sector, regardless of whether they are bootable or not. If the computer is started with a floppy disk in drive "A:", the operating system reads the information contained in its boot sector and checks to see if it is bootable. If there is a virus in this sector, the computer reads this virus code first, and therefore, the virus is able to infect the computer (see also Host).

**MD2**   is a secure hash, or message digest algorithm developed by Ron Rivest (see also Tables 11A and 11B).

**MD5**   is another secure hash or message digest algorithm developed by Ron Rivest (see also Tables 11A and 11B).

**Media**   is the physical material storing information being fixed or removable such as hard disk, floppy disk, compact disc, digital audio tape, paper tape and many more.

**Media Virus**   see Virus (Table 19)

**Memetics**   deals with the transfer of memes (the 'unit of cultural inheritance') from brain to brain (see also Hoax, Mnemonics).

Since the early seventies several authors have tried to adopt the principle of evolution by selection to understand the continuous change in cultural behaviors. Richard Dawkins coined the term 'meme' as an analog to the biological unit of inheritance, the gene or the genetic replicator. The rather simple distinction between genetic replicators as 'genes' on the one hand, opposed to all non-genetic replicators as 'memes' has been firmly imprinted in the evolutionary thinking about cultural information.

Since its initial conception, the term 'meme' has been used under very different meanings and in very different contexts, infecting a wide variety

**Table 19B:** Digital Divide and Broadband Connection

| Category | USA | CH |
|---|---|---|
| Growth Broadband 2002–2003 | 50% | 300% |
| How do people access the internet from home? | a) 69.6 mio people are dial-up users, b) 21 mio people use cable modems to access the web (cable TV is available to 90% of USA homes) c) 9 mio people use DSL d) 9 mio or rest gets broadband from satellite, dedicated phone lines and other solutions. | a) 650,000 or about 20% of all households access web via broadband b) cable TV is available to about 63% of Swiss homes, 15% of these had broadband web access early 2004. c) 9% of all 3.8 Mio phone subscribers whose houses have broadband capability are using the technology to access the internet via DSL. |
| Trend | A June 2003 survey by marketing-research firm Ipsos-Insight reported that in the USA at: d) $40 a month, about 3% of American dial-up users would switch to DSL or cable from dial-up access, e) $30, 10% would switch to DSL; 9% to cable. f) $20, about 20% of dial-up users would switch to either DSL or cable. The above leaves 80% of the 69.6 mio dial-up users being unwilling to pay even a few dollars more for broadband than they do for their present service. | By 2007 it is estimated that about 47% of all Swiss households (1.5 Mio) will access the web via broadband connection. For comparison, it is estimated that about 27% of all German households will access the internet using broadband by 2007. |
| Marketing | a) DSL providers, looking to woo some of the country's dial-up users, cut their monthly service fees by $15 to $20 during the first six months in 2003 b) further price reductions and bundling of services (e.g., fixed monthly amount of minutes for cellular, stationary phone and internet access, such as 1000, 1500 or 2000 minutes at a fixed price) were available by early 2004. | a) Cable providers are now starting to offer telephone services as well and hope to further woo customers b) The 20 ADSL suppliers and various cable companies (each has a geographical area for itself = monopoly) are improving their bandwidth, while keeping prices stable. |

M

(cont.)

**Table 19B:** (cont.)

| Category | USA | CH |
|----------|-----|-----|
| | | c) Further price reductions can be expected, while bundling of services (e.g., cable TV, internet access, stationary and cellular) will increase. |
| Monthly Costs | In every market users are willing to spend a certain amount of money for communication, **each month**. If we assume this amount is about Euro 100 or $110 (Sfr. 150.00) we still should look at how such funds are divided (Swiss figures include all taxes, USA figures do not include the sales taxes to be added—0–15% rates depending upon state), such as: | |
| | —stationary telephone $25–$50 (unlimited local calls)<br>—wireless (incoming/outgoing calls are metered & charged) $25–40 subscription<br>—cable TV $25–$50<br>—no licensing fees to state authority for TV watching or listening to radio<br>—internet access $0–$50 | —stationary telephone SFr. 20–30 subscription (all calls metered)<br>—wireless with subscription at Sfr. 20–30 or pre-paid calling card (calls are metered & charged)<br>—cable TV Sfr. 40–Sfr. 60<br>—TV and radio licensing fees to state authority to be paid by every household about Sfr. 25<br>—metered 56K connection (about Sfr. 20 in toll charges using it primarily for email) or unlimited broadband for monthly subscription Sfr. 20–Sfr. 80. |
| Conclusion | The above indicates that Swiss customers pay a far larger sum every month for subscription fees without getting much in return except access to metered service (e.g., toll calls, mobile phone service, cable TV service, license fee for radio and TV about Sfr. 100.00).<br><br>Hence, in Switzerland as in other countries (e.g., France & Germany) there is still a lot of room for lowering prices, if subscription charges are lowered (e.g., mobile phones) similar to Denmark where subscription for mobile phones may cost as little as Euro 1.00 per month if one does not accrue any charges. Nonetheless, stationary phones still cost about Euro 15.00 per month in subscription fees in Denmark as well.<br><br>As Economics 101 suggests, having several technologies being offered to consumers to provide a service (e.g., DSL vs. broadband cable), made available by independent suppliers (e.g., several wireless companies) increases competition, thereby lowering prices.<br><br>Furthermore, bundling of services (e.g., cable TV, broadband internet and stationary phone as well as electricity) reduces administrative costs for the supplier (e.g., one bill for bundled services), again enabling the firm to lower prices. | |

(cont.)

**Table 19B:** (cont.)

| Category | USA | CH |
|---|---|---|
| | As Copenhagen has shown where TDC owns the last mile, offers DSL and owns the cable network, prices are unlikely to be as low as could be the case in the above scenario. In contrast to mobile phone service where competition is fierce (see low subscription fee) and even SMS messaging is just about 3 cents compared to Euro .15 in France when it costs providers about 2 cents per SMS according to a study released by the Union Fédérale des Consommateurs—Que Choisir in France during November 2003. Digital divide in Europe is a fuzzy concept and can be eliminated in part by increasing competition through regulation but, finally, it's the consumer's choice on how to spend his or her communication Dollar/Euro [e.g., more Short Messaging Services (SMS) or else internet broadband instead of dial-up, what shall it be?] | |

*Note.* The above outlines where we are regarding digital divide and consumers' disposable income allocated for communication and TV/radio. While consumers can make choices, regulatory decisions made in the past either facilitate or hinder these, while clearly affecting today's prices.

Accordingly, if a subscription fee must be paid just to get a line without any services this hampers market forces. In most cases, consumers pay for useage (e.g., going to the movies or eating out) except for some services that were once highly regulated (e.g., telephone, utilities) where subscription fees must be paid just to have the right to use the service.

USA $1.00 was roughly worth Sfr. 1.40 and EURO 0.90 when these calculations were done.

of disciplines. Dennett sees the human mind as being built up with memes comparable to the programming of a computer. Hull defines the meme as replicator, and adds interaction to account for evolution by natural or artificial selection. He thus describes selection processes in science and biology using exactly similar definitions.

Perhaps the most popular informal use of the term describes memes as 'viruses of the mind.' Parallels to both biological and computer Virus varieties have been drawn by Dawkins (1993, pp. 13–27, Dennett and his Critics, Blackwell Publishers).

**Memory Stick**    technology was created by Sony for audio-visual applications like digital cameras. They resemble a stick of gum and started from 4 MB but today more than 256 MB is becoming standard.

These sticks are used to store data from the hard-disk on this external instrument using the USB port on a computer to download or upload data. Because Memory Sticks can store ever larger amounts of data and are priced inexpensively, they are ever more widely used.

Memory Sticks, like hard-disks or the older five inch diskettes can pose a security risk. People may transfer data without authorization onto a Memory Stick (see also Multi-Layered Security). Discarded Memory Sticks may also

**M**

reveal confidential data as happened regarding cancer patients in the UK (see Multi-Layered Security).

**Merging of Attack Technologies**    means that attacks are getting more sophisticated by embedding several approaches in one technique.

For instance, a Virus infects the host on which it is run, but if it is also a Worm, it sends itself to other hosts via eMail. To further illustrate, the Apology worm attempts to download files from a web site in order to update its own functionality and, like a Rootkit, attempts to hide itself. Ramen attempts root compromises of Unix systems and, if it succeeds, automatically uses the compromised host as a platform for further root compromises. Hence, it is a tool that could be used to set up a Distributed Denial of Service Attack (DDoS). Accordingly distinguishing between:

- Viruses,
- Worms,
- Trojan Horses, and
- DDoS toolkits

is becoming very difficult (see also Tables 19A, & 19B) if not blurred for users and IT Security Engineers (see also Expert, Threat—Blended).

**Metadata**    describes stored data. These are data describing the structure, data elements, interrelationships, and other characteristics of electronic or computerized or digitized records.

**Methodology**    can be described as the methods being used for specific comparisons of the details of various techniques. Choice of methodology to be used for investigating an IT Security issue also requires compromises regarding depth and breadth of methodologies used. In the past, qualitative approaches were justified by providing more depth than quantitative ones, the letter providing breadth instead. Today this dichotomy seems artificial. Both methods can provide more or less breadth and depth, while blending of both may further improve the quality of the findings and their possible Validity.

Choice of method, and the nature and Quality of the results obtained depend substantially on the researcher, qualitative and/or qualitative approaches as well as data analytical methods. In the latter case, using multivariate statistics to analyze parametric data versus descriptive statistics to perform content analysis on transcribed interviews or documents affects the breadth and depth of data obtained.

Methodology is a term that is often misused/misapplied. In systems development, the tasks required to achieve the end result can be complex and usually require adoption of a disciplined and formal approach. Having perfected

M

such an approach, consulting companies and software developers will refer to their methodology. Methodology suggests an almost scientific and objective approach, which, of course, is rarely the case.

**Metrics** are measurements, collections of data about project activities, resources and deliverables. Metrics can be used to help estimate projects, measure project progress and performance, and quantify product attributes (see also Methodology, Statistics, Reliability, Validity).

For instance, the goals for a Metrics program regarding Information Security is to determine the specific metrics on which the program will be based (see also Benchmarking).

Specific Metrics that support the Quality objectives specified can be identified in the following two steps:

- Determine a set of questions which, when answered, provide the insight necessary to achieve the goals.
- Determine a set of **metrics** which can be collected and analyzed to help answer each question.

Every goal agreed upon should, thereafter be addressed using the above two steps. The result will be a set of **metrics** which support the firm's goals.

While metrics defined at this stage are quite simple, nonetheless, they are going to be used to help get the program going and to establish a baseline. Later, when the mechanics of the metrics program have been worked out, more complicated or specialized metrics can be added. It can be tempting to go overboard and measure everything right away, but this leads to information overload.

Successful metrics focus on a few key issues to achieve the initial goals such as for a 30 day period:

1. number & % of virus infected or spam-type e-mails received and stopped at mailgate,
2. number & % of e-mails with attachments received vs. sent,
3. create one or two comprehensive indices for firm's firewall(s) protecting critical systems,
4. # of violations from # of employees regarding critical security policies, and so on.

Such type of indices provide a firm with some numbers that illustrate succinctly to top management why better Metrics will help improve Quality, while permitting the firm to reap the rewards.

**Middleware** is a broad term for software that is being used to run e-business applications. It consists of application server software as well as database software. The former is used to connect eCommerce applications with the

M

mountains of crucial data on customers, suppliers and business transactions that are stored using data-base software.

**MiMail**    see Phishing

**MIMO**    see Multiple-In, Multiple-Out

**MIME**    see Multi-Purpose Internet Mail Exensions

**Mirroring**    means writing the data to more than one medium namely:

1) Writing **duplicate data to more than one device** (usually **two hard disks**), thereby protecting against data loss in the event of device failure, such as a system crash.

   This technique may be implemented in either hardware (sharing a disk controller and cables) or in software. It is a common feature of RAID systems. When this technique is used with magnetic tape storage systems, it is usually called 'twinning'.

2) A less expensive alternative, which only limits the amount of data loss (rather than eliminating the risk entirely), is to **make regular backups from a single disk to magnetic tape**.

3) An **archive or web site** which keeps **a copy of some or all of the files at another site**, so as to make them available more quickly to local users and to reduce the load on the source site.

   This type of mirroring is usually done for particular directories or files on a specific remote server, as opposed to a cache or proxy server which keeps copies of everything that has been requested through it.

4) **Archive files** from a PC on a burned CD (see also Redundancy, Mirroring).

**Mission Critical**    is a term describing activities and processes that are deemed vital to the corporation's business success and, possibly, its very existence. The term is borrowed from the military.

Hence, major application that are called Mission critical are those that if their application fails, crashes, or is otherwise unavailable to the firm, this will have a significant negative impact upon the business. Examples might be accounts/billing, customer balances, computer controlled machinery and production lines, and delivery scheduling (see also Mirroring, Redundancy).

**Misuse Detection Model**    see Rule Based Detection

**Mnemonics**    can be used to define a mnemonic or easy-to-remember name, such as in case of an access key (see also Program).

It can also be an abbreviation designed to help the user remember the menu or process for which it stands. Each Mnemonic will either run a process or take the user to another menu. For example, INDOSECI is entered for "Information Security Inquiry".

**M**

Mnemonics can also be defined as recurring concepts denoted by the same notational symbols in a classification scheme (see also Table 23C, ES$^3$ and Memetics).

**Mocking Bird**   see Virus (Trojan Horse, Table 18A)

**Mobile Payment Systems**   can be operated with the help of the telephone-billing system, whereby a person pays for a cab or a restaurant bill using one's mobile phone. The individual's monthly bill is than charged accordingly.

Downloading ring tones and logos has resulted in the first use of phone bills to pay for other small services. T-Mobile and Vodafone developed a common platform for mobile payments and are already permitting payment of internet content this way. Telstra Mobilenet permits its subscribers already to use their mobile phone at vending machines, but it is hardly hands-free and paying the cabby with such a system may be more cumbersome than using a debit or credit card (see also Bluetooth).

**Modem**   comes from **MO**dulator **DEM**odulator, a piece of communications equipment that enables a computer to send transmissions through normal telephone lines.

**Moderated Listserver**   is when the moderator views all incoming messages before they are either forwarded to each user on a list (see also Listserver and Daily Digest) or else returned to the posting party as inappropriate.

**Modify**   depicts the change of content or characteristics of a target.

**Moore's Law**   is a theorem that states that the amount of information storable on a given amount of silicon has roughly doubled every year since the technology was invented. First mentioned in 1964 by semiconductor engineer Gordon Moore, co-founder of Intel in 1968, this held until the late 1970s, at which point the doubling period slowed to 18 months. Some are now suggesting that it is taking again 24–30 months.

**Morality or Morals**   see Justice

**Multihost-Based Auditing**   takes audit data from several hosts to detect possible intrusions.

**Multi Layered Security**   is a practice that combines several different security components, such as antivirus software, firewalls and vulnerability assessment tools, to create a comprehensive and defensive barrier many times stronger than its individual parts alone.

Layered security exponentially increases the cost and difficulty of penetration for an attacker, thereby decreasing the likelihood that they would bother pursuing an organization.

M

One can use the fortress and the airport *metaphor* to describe the multi-layered concept. To illustrate, the fortress allows little movement in and out using a single-dimensioned security mechanism such as a moat and a draw-bridge. Hence, a fortress provides a reasonably secure operation, but one that has difficulty to cope with rapid events and lacks flexibility.

Conversely, the airport allows large volumes of movement using a multi-layered security strategy whereby several check-points for passport control, hand and checked-in baggage scanning, and random searches are used. Hence, multi-layered security uses **technical and behavioral means**. For instance, besides anti-virus and firewall software, user behaviors are such that they do not open email attachments, without first making sure that the individual really sent that document to them in the first place (see also Multi Level Security).

**Multi Level Networks—Systems**   are such that they provide services to users. However, not all users may have access to all data or be unaware of some highly confidential data within compartments. This could be systematized and described as follows:

1. **Multi Level Mode** whereby not all authorised system or network users are cleared to access highest classification of data, and
2. **Compartmented Mode** whereby all users are cleared to highest classification of data, but not all users are briefed for all compartments.

**Multi Level Security**   approaches security from a technical approach. Here hard-disks can be used to completely separate the different security domains, while switching from one to the other domains makes copying and/or transferring of data impossible. For a PC this means **three physically separated hard-drives** with a:

- Private domain—separates the access to and from other areas, whereby the hard-drive is operated totally separate like a PC that neither allows a network connection nor copying to or from a diskette/Memory Stick;
- Secured domain contains information that can be exchanged/shared on a separate physical network or Virtual Private Network (VPN) only, thereby limiting access to information to individuals who are part of such a network; and
- Public domain representing Internet, wireless LAN and other access where emails, web pages and word processing tasks may occur.

In the **e-health** context with **digitized patient records** the doctors notebook splits information in the above three domains. Specifically, email and web surfing is done using the public hard-disk, while exchange of patient records to the hospital is accomplished using the secured domain. The private area may contain confidential information that the patient does not want released without his or her prior consent (see also Multi Layered Security). Moreover, Memory Sticks cannot be used in the Private Domain. Memory Sticks can and have been a problem, especially if they are sold as new but the purchaser finds confidential details of 13 cancer patients as happened in the Manchester, UK area during Spring 2003 (see also Mirroring, Mission Critical, Redundancy).

**Multipartite** has traditionally described a viral program that will infect both boot sectors/MBRs and files (see also Virus, Tables 24E & 24G).

The term is now sometimes used to describe a virus that is capable of infecting using a combination of techniques, such as infecting documents, executable files, and boot sectors (see Virus—Boot Sector Virus, Table 25).

**Multiple-In, Multiple-Out (MIMO)** takes advantage of huge amounts of computing power to send signals from closely spaced antennas. Typically, Wi-Fi reaches only about 30 to 45 meters, or 100 to 150 feet, from a transmitter at 11–54 megabits a second. MIMO permits a wireless radio signal of up to 108 megabits a second and the signal can be sent over longer distances than traditional Wi-Fi.

The industry is working to define a generation of Wi-Fi that could take data rates to 200 megabits or even higher, MIMO is being proposed as the technology for that standard by Airgo, the firm that released the technology in 2003. Airgo's technology is an example of the shift to what are known as smart antennas, an approach that is being widely adopted in the wireless networking world (see also Elektro-Smog).

But Airgo faces a big challenge in winning broad support for its approach. Other companies are also striving to develop antenna technologies to improve wireless data service. These include Vivato, a wireless technology company that is using antennas to direct beams, and the leading chipmaker, Intel, which has acquired the intellectual property of another Silicon Valley MIMO company, IoSpan Wireless (see also Wireless, Table 26).

MIMO and other approaches enter a hotly contested marketplace, in the hope that Innovation resulting in new technology that, besides other advantages, offers higher speed and greater range will win customers.

**Multi-Purpose Internet Mail Extensions (MIME)** is an email protocol used to send various types of data files via email along with a regular email message. The MIME protocol defines various types of tags (specially named email headers) at the top of the mail message to specify what kind of data file is attached to the email message. Data files can include but are not limited to graphics files, audio files, and program application files.

**Secure Multi-Purpose Internet Mail Extensions (S/MIME)** is a secure version of the MIME protocol. By secure is meant that SMIME is used to encrypt and decrypt e-mail.

M

**Multi-Tasking**    describes an individual or machine doing more than one thing at a time. Humans do such multi-tasking as breathing, talking on-the-phone and typing on a keyboard, all at the same time, possibly annoying the person at the other end of the phone line as well.

It may seem that when a user is printing a file and viewing web pages on the Net, the computer is doing two things at once, but, in practice, it is handling bits of each job, one after the other, so quickly that it just looks as though they are being done at the same time. Purists maintain that true multi-tasking requires more than one processor.

As the two or more programs access memory space or need communication port access on a single processor machine—such as a PC—multi-tasking causes more hang-ups, and freezing, than any other type of operation.

Mailing out a large file with an email program and clicking on another button to compose a new message or do some other tasks in the program may result in the program freezing and requiring exiting. In such an instance all unsaved messages or lost or sometimes it may even require the rebooting of the machine (Down Time).

**Mutation Engine (MtE)**    is a widely used abbreviation for a section of code written by a virus author known as Dark Avenger. It can be attached to any virus, thereby giving the virus polymorphic features (see also Virus, Table 25).

M

**Native Format**   refers to the default format of a data file created by its associated software program. For example, Microsoft Excel® produces its output as '.xls' files by default; this is the native format of Excel. Microsoft Word® produces native files with a '.doc' extension. Whilst many programs are capable of supporting other formats, they each have their native format.

**Native Software Format**   means that a document or file is encoded for interpretation by the software application used to create it, hence an Excel file is encoded with xls and so on.

**NC**   see Netcat

**Near-Line Storage**   means data storage that is not online but can be accessed via computer without the need to manually mount the storage medium, such as tape or disk that contains the requested information. For example, data storage on media brought online through use of jukeboxes or robots (see also Robot).

**Negative Acknowledgment**   see Attack, Tables 3A and 3B

**Netcat**   (sometimes called nc) is designed to be a reliable "back-end" tool that can be used directly or easily driven by other programs and scripts.

The program is also a feature-rich network debugging and exploration tool, since it can create almost any kind of connection one might need and has several interesting built-in capabilities.

Netcat is now part of the Red Hat Power Tools collection and comes standard on SuSE Linux, Debian Linux, NetBSD, OpenBSD distributions and others.

**N**

**Netiquette** is a loose and idiosyncratic collection of rules of conduct and behavior. Life is full of etiquette and norms for various situations, such as how to behave when eating at a fancy restaurant, or when conducting a business meeting. Similarly, Netiquette tries to institutionalize and make users aware of the ropes and what type of behavior may be acceptable and what may not. Consequences are informal and one might receive a nasty response if one violates netiquette.

**Network** recites an interconnected or interrelated group of host computers, switching elements, and interconnecting branches (see also Social Network Analysis, Local Area Network-LAN).

**Network Administrator** is the individual responsible for the availability of the Network and controls its use. For smaller organizations this person may be the same as the System Administrator.

**Network Analysis** see Social Network Analysis

**Network Based** takes network traffic data along with audit data from the hosts used in order to detect intrusions.

**Network Hacking** is hacking of dial up systems, voice systems, PBX systems, Virtual Private Networking (VPN) systems and network devices.

**Network Intrusion Detection Systems (NIDS)** see Intrusion Detection

**Network Level Firewall** see Firewall

**Network Mapper (nmap)** is probably the best freely available scanning tool. It has been developed by Fyodor and is available at http://www.insecure. org/nmap. This tool accomplishes so many functions that it is impossible to list them here.

**Network Ping Sweep** is usually an automated process of mapping the network using basic utility *ping*. This utility sends ICMP ECHO (type 8) packet and expects a ICMP ECHO_REPLY (Type 0) as a sign that the target host is alive.

**Network Reconnaissance** is a process of determining the network topology.

**Network, Server and Desktop Vulnerability Scanner** see Vulnerability Scanner

**Network Services Attack** describes a situation where attacks are conducted against insecure network services to attain unauthorized access (see Attack, Tables 3A & 3B, Table 7B).

**Newsgroups** are part of Usenet and theoretically attract groups of like-minded users, enabling them to ask questions and swap information. There are Newsgroups on any subject imaginable.

Regrettably, most Newsgroups have their share of contributors whose sole mission appears to be to hurl abuse and 'flame' others' points of view.

**Nimda** is Admin spelled backwards. It was one of the first devastating Hybrids (see also Blended Threat, Table 24D) and used four means of spreading or propagation vectors (see also Virus, Table 25, Figure 5):

1) **Scanning**—infected systems scanned the network looking for unpatched Microsoft Internet Information Server (IIS) systems. Using Unicode web Taversal exploit, Nimda gained control of the target server.

2) **Email**—Nimda gathers email addresses and forwards messages to these addresses. When Nimda arrived in an email, it used a MIME exploit to execute just be reading the infected message or opening the message in a preview pane.

3) **Browsing**—visiting a Nimda-infected web server meant the user being asked to download an Outlook Express email file, containing the Worm (see Virus) as a "readme" attachment. The attachment got activated using the email technique described above

4) **Network Shares**—Allowing complete access to that system at a later date is accomplished by Nimda, having created open network shares on the target server or desktop.

Nimda was an automated Worm, using known software vulnerabilities and multiple methods of infection to spread remarkably fast (see also Code Red).

**Nmap** see Network Mapper

**Non-Receptive Host** see Host

**Non Disclosure Agreement (NDA)** is a legally binding document. It protects the confidentiality of ideas, designs, plans, concepts or other commercial material. Most often, an NDA is signed by vendors, contractors, consultants and other non-employees who may come into contact with such material (see also Copyright, Jurisdiction License, Patent, Table 16A).

**Non-Receptive Host (NRH)** see Host

**Non-Reporting** see Incidence

**Non-Repudiation** means that all parties to a transaction must be confident that the transaction is secure, the parties are who they say they are (authentication), and that the transaction is verified as final.

**N**

Systems must ensure that a party cannot subsequently **repudiate (reject)** a transaction. To protect and ensure digital trust, the parties to such systems may employ Digital Signatures, which will not only validate the sender, but will also 'time stamp' the transaction, such that it cannot be claimed subsequently that the transaction was not authorized or not valid (see also Table 5C).

**Number of sites**   entails the overall number of sites known to have reported or otherwise having been involved in an activity, security incident or other.

**Object Code**    is machine code generated by a source code language processor, such as an assembler or compiler. A file of object code may be immediately executable or it may require linking with other object code files such as libraries in order to produce a complete executable program.

**Objective**    see Incident Objective.

**Online**    is being connected to the computer network, such as the internet from home.

**Online profiling**    is the collection of detailed online behavior from uniquely identified internet users by taking advantage of such means as using cookies. Online behaviors generally refer to records about pages that were viewed and products or services purchased. Online advertisers can use profiling to better target banner advertising and mass mailings via the internet according to a user's past behavior.

**Open Microphone Listening**    is when somebody listens to a microphone that is open on the network.

**Open Source**    is code that is put into the public domain. Hence, any user can take advantage of it usually for free. Most importantly, if the code is popular many people may examine it and, therefore, assuring that security bugs are published quickly. Very nicely for users, fixes are usually available in relatively short time thereafter (see also Linux).

**Open Source Software**    and security means that Open Source is usually more secure than proprietary security. Hence, for cryptographic algorithms, security protocols, and security source code, open source is not a business model but, instead, represents smart engineering practice (see also Cryptography, Table 11A and Table 11B).

Public source software or security protocols gain credibility because people know and use them if they are useful tools for certain applications (e.g., Linux). Often, proprietary products based on open source software take up substantial shelf space in computer stores. Some marketing folks call this mindshare (see also Security).

On June 17, 2003 The Apache Server Project team and ISS issued competing security alerts for a DDoS vulnerability in Apache web servers. The Apache team claimed the ISS patch did not correct the problem. On Tuesday June 18, participants in several online forums raised these questions:

- Who is responsible for patching open source software?
- If a third party provides a source code patch, such as ISS did in the above instance, what can people who have embedded versions (without source) do to protect themselves?
- If a flaw in open source code is discovered by a third party, should it be shared with the entire open source project team? Is the whole team trustworthy?

Support is growing for software companies to be held to the same Liability standards as other manufacturing businesses. Microsoft, with its plethora of software holes and "deep pocket[s]" is a likely target for a liability suit (see also Jurisdiction).

**Internet-Based or Web-Based Standards** is open-source software such as Linux that has become good enough whereby it is taking over the volume business from the proprietary standard (e.g., Sun, Windows) (see also Longhorn, Tables 16A and 16B).

**OpenSSL**   see Secure Socket Layer (SSL)

**Open Systems Interconnection (OSI)**   are a set of internationally accepted and openly developed standards that meet the needs of network resource administration and integrated network utility.

**Operating System**   are computer programs that that are primarily or entirely concerned with controlling the computer and its associated hardware, rather than with processing work for users. Computers can operate without application software, but they cannot run without an operating system. Examples are DOS, MaxOS, Linux and Unix.

**Operating System Hardening** involves the removal of all non essential tools, utilities and other systems administration **options**, any of which could be used to ease a hacker's path to the systems. Following this, the hardening process will ensure that all appropriate security features are activated and configured correctly. Again, 'out of the box' systems will likely be set up for ease of access with access to 'root'/Administrator account. Some vendors have now recognized that a market exists for pre-hardened systems.

**Trusted Operating System** is a system that has been specially modified to be so secure as to be almost unusable. The reason for this development is due to the substantial rise in concern over the apparent ease by which hackers are able to gain access to seemingly **secure** systems, a number of vendors have developed variations on mainstream version of UNIX and Windows. These standards go well beyond the standard Operating System hardening which is advisable for all and any desktop and server systems.

However, the deployment of a Trusted Operating System, does require substantially more training of systems operations staff, because the System Administrator does no longer necessarily have 'ultimate power'. Henceforth the functions which control say, file, print or network access, are now split into separate 'sandboxes' which permit only a subset of actions to be performed by one systems administrator. It will be apparent that a substantially higher degree of coordination is required with the systems Operations team, and also a much deeper level of planning before any changes are made.

A Trusted Operating System does prevent a system from gradually being changed over time by a single system's Administrator making small changes 'here and there'. In effect the Operating System is locked down and such Trusted Systems lend themselves to any e-commerce business where maximum security is paramount such as online banking.

**Operating System (OS) Fingerprinting** is the activity of collecting information about the computer host in order to ascertain what operating system is running on target host. Every operating system has its significant attributes that enable skilled hacker and/or network professional to ascertain target's OS. The OS fingerprinting can be either passive or active (see Active OS Fingerprinting, Passive OS Fingerprinting).

**Other Sites** are those sites known to have been involved in an Incident, but that did not report the Incident.

**Outsourcing** offers companies opportunities to outsource certain production and service functions in order to reduce costs. A possible disadvantage is that scheduling and quality control becomes more difficult. Trust between supplier and client is a must. Recently, some firms have began to in-source some tasks again to avoid the above difficulties while, most importantly, giving their workers the chance to compete for such contracts. Nonetheless, while a firm may not necessarily save when outsourcing part of its IT function, additional expertise may be worth it and permit the firm to focus on core competencies instead (e.g., Outsourcing vs. in-sourcing of software, hardware and web page maintenance) (see Table 23C).

**Overhead**   refers to the load placed upon a computer or system. Encrypting and decrypting data will increase a system's overhead and reduce the resources available for other processes during the encrypt/decrypt cycle.

Sometimes, when using a broadband connection, providers fail to inform users that up to about 50 kilobytes either direction may be lost due to Overhead between the internet gateway and the user such as administration, encryption and security (e.g., Digital Subscriber Line—DSL, see also Table 19B).

**Packet** is a block of data sent over the network transmitting the identities of the sending and receiving stations, error-control information, and message.

**Packet Filtering** see Filtering

**Packet Insertion** depicts the situation whereby a forged packet of data appears from a different source (see also IP Spoofing) or fraudulent packet is inserted inside of regular packets from the same source.

**Packet Intrusion Detection System (PIDS)** is working on similar principle as a Network Intrusion Detection System (NIDS), however these systems do not think about protocols as network based do and work strictly on raw packet structure. PIDSs are currently at the beginning of their development and have yet to reach their full potential.

**Packet Sniffer** see Sniffer

**Packet Watching** see Sniffer

**Paradigm** describes a discipline's general orientation or why of seeing and interpreting subject matter. Originally, the term referred to an example in grammar showing a pattern in a conjugation or declension such as ring, rang, rung or seeing, sang, sung.

The term was introduced to the social and behavioral sciences by Thomas Kuhn. Around Einstein's time it is said that physics went through a "paradigm shift," whereby one understanding of the discipline and the world in how it is studied to a radically different approach.

**Shared Meaning**   in this context means that the vocabulary, beliefs, meanings and methods used are being shared, hence everybody talks the same language. But in Information Security, this is not always the case, such as in:

- **Forensics**—some see it as examining PCs and hard-drives with software, others as a methodology also encompassing network traffic (See Forensics)
- **Hacker**—is defined as a person doing an illegal act, nonetheless, White Hat Hacker is a term used widely in industry and sometimes associated with Authorized entering of a system versus unauthorized (e.g., to expose vulnerabilities)
- **Naming of Computer Viruses**—is an ad-hoc approach and lacks a scientific system that results in a name that contains information such as, type of code; accordingly, for customers it appears that every vendor seems to use a different name for the same virus confusing matters instead of clarifying it for home users.

The above indicates that Information Security and Security Engineering as well as Information Assurance represent terms that include similar lingo, activities, technologies, systems, methods and behaviors. Nonetheless, Mnemonics nor teaching of each is similar. This dictionary is a further effort in developing a more unified language that will help in reducing Risks & Threats while improving Security.

The problems outlined above also apply to Information Theory. While computing science is using a paper that once supposedly explained Communication Theory, it is implied that after its renaming it suffices in explaining Information Theory. However, many issues inherent in Information are not explained thoroughly, neither in this famous paper nor in other material coming out of computing science or Informatics (see Tables 14A and 14B). Hence, Information Theory is still awaiting a paradigm shift.

**Parallel Processing**   occurs when a computer uses more than one processor, either to be able to perform more than one task at the same time or to improve processing speed by breaking down one larger task between different processors. Parallel processing is not quite the same as 'Multi-Tasking' since, by definition, a single processor cannot do two things at once. It just seems that way to the user because the two things are handled one after the other so very quickly.

**Parallel running**   means when a new and existing system run side by side, using the same data, performing the same processes, and generating the same outputs to prove the suitability of the new system. This is usually the last phase of the user acceptance testing process, followed by formal acceptance if all went well (see also User Acceptance, System Requirements). Here the necessary security checks must also be done to assure that the system meets the security standards the organization needs.

**Partitioning of Network**   occurs when an Ethernet repeater or hub detects a fault on one of its ports it will isolate that port from the remainder of the network. This operation is referred to as partitioning—the network is said to be partitioned. Normally, if the repeater/hub again finds "good" data on the affected port it automatically reconnects it to the network.

Partitioning of Network should help in **minimizing the effect of Vulnerabilities** and also increase the organization's chances of securing downtime for installing Patches in critical systems.

Partitioning of Network resources is part of effective Safety Engineering as well as Security Engineering, thereby reducing the risk of a threat being realized. As importantly, this can help in reducing system interdependence and a possible cascading effect, whereby one successful attack shuts down much of the interconnected systems.

Critical Mission systems require Redundancy and this may necessitate that a web server or e-Commerce site runs totally separate of the firm's eMail system as was not the case when Blaster hit during summer 2003 and the Swiss Federal Railway's system could no longer handle selling of tickets. Similarly, the Swiss Post Office's online banking and automated teller machines went haywire on October 7. The organization claimed that all their 15,000 PCs and external access points were patched against SQL Slammer. And while the Post Office stated that critical systems were not affected, networking problems forced technical staff to switch off systems to check various things. But for customers this is not satisfactory, since neither their computer banking requests, cash withdrawals on automated tellers, nor paying at the teller inside the Post Office branches worked properly throughout the day.

Proper Partitioning would have made it unnecessary to switch all systems off and Software and Physical Partitioning can help (see also Multi Level Networks—Systems, Multi Level Security).

**Software or Logical Partitioning**   is the partitioning of a computer application's code into distinct executable programs. Logical partitioning is independent of the platforms on which an application may be deployed.

**Physical Partitioning**   is the concept where one physical computer system can be divided up into multiple mainframe operating environments utilizing software partitioning. This allows system software to partition a single physical computer into several different "virtual" computers, which can be started and stopped separately, while sharing the same hardware resources.

Physical partitions can again be divided into a greater number of partitions using software. The number of Logical Partitions within a logical volume is variable.

**Passive Attack**   see Attack and Threat (Figure 3)

**Passive Operating System (OS) Fingerprinting**   is conducted in order to detect target's operating system. This can be done by passively monitoring host (for example by collecting network traffic flowing from it) and then match characteristics of the packets against known values. This is less accurate than active OS Fingerprinting but by far less risky. Method of passive OS fingerprinting can be also used in investigation of cyber crime (see also Active OS Fingerprinting, Operating System Fingerprinting).

**Password**   is usually a string of alphanumeric characters a user will type on his or her keyboard with lower and/or uppercase letters as well and hopefully without vocals such as (19mlnMY82]. Ideally, a computer or a network has its own dictionary of common passwords, whereby a password previously used or included in the dictionary is refused by the system.

Passwords must **never** (**ever**) be written down. Neither should one use one's first, last or a family member's name nor one containing all digits or a word contained in a dictionary. Below are some additional issues that need to be remembered.

Table 20A outlines what issues need to be addressed when using passwords to access information resources.

Table 20B outlines how passwords should be chosen and the best practice approach as well as policies needed.

**Patch**   is similar to a 'Fix', it is a temporary arrangement used to overcome software problems or glitches. A patch will normally be released as a 'quick fix' prior to the next formal release of the software. Patches are usually (but not always) available on-line from the vendor's Web site. While a patch is an incremental addition to a currently running software, the software version to which it applies must be confirmed. Naturally, without first having adequately tested the update, the update cannot be performed (see also System Testing).

As the sections below illustrate, Vulnerabilities relevant to the operating system and software used in an organization or by a home-user must be installed immediately. Automatic or live updates for anti-Virus software (e.g., see Norton product from Symantec, or Bullguard's services will handle this) are also adviseable for users and when the product asks to re-start after a Patch or update was downloaded and installed, do it immediately and not 10 minutes later!

Finally, even if *you* have run Microsoft update and are patched, is your grand-mother patched, and what about your P2P pal? So you should take an hour of your time to make sure that your neighbor is patched as well and has anti-virus software installed. When someone finally releases a major Worm with a destructive payload, it will do as much financial damage as a hurricane.

**Table 20A:** Password Issues

| Issues | Description |
|---|---|
| Canonical | Could be a password set by default such as the users phone number enabling them to access their voicemail or email (see also Voice Mail). |
| Default | Is usually the password required to start newly purchased software or hardware. In any case, such passwords (e.g., default on mobile phone) should be changed immediately by the user to increase security (see also Configuration Vulnerability). |
| Forgotten or Lost | Sometimes anywhere from 10–30% of calls to a help desk are password-related. |
| Guessing | Is illustrated in a case whereby an individual tries different guesses of passwords to defeat access controls. |
| Reset | Enables users to reset their own passwords and unlock their acconts without the aid of a help desk. Typically, a user accesses a password reset application through a standard browser, Windows client or telephone (interactive voice response). Users are authenticated by a set of questions to which only they should know the answers. |
| Sniffing | Is in process when with the help of a sniffer somebody is 'listening' for a password being sent across a network unencrypted. |
| Synchronization | Aligns user passwords across multiple systems and applications. Users have to remember one password, this may eliminate 50–70% of password reset problems due to user having forgotten a password for accessing one database (see also Role-Based Access Management). |
| Single Sign-On (SSO) | Lets the user log on once to a PC or network and access multiple applications and systems using a single password. Here Role-Based Access Management is also used to further coordinate to which information resources an individual requires access to perform his or her tasks/job duties. |
| Picture and Password | Tries to address the problem that many people have trouble remembering random combinations of letters and symbols. In turn, they jot difficult passwords down near their computer or replace them with far simpler combinations, making the system vulnerable to attack. |
| | Some Experts in Security claim that the word 'password' is the most common used password, but only for systems where leaving a blank is not allowed! The approaches below are still in the development phase and some claim that it still has not be tested satisfactorily that graphical passwords will significantly (see Significance) strengthen security (see also Authentication, Tables 4B and 4C). |
| | a) **Password Navigation through virtual world** means that people become familiar with the world; then when they want to sign on, the system puts them at a random spot in the world such as a street corner, and they have to find a particular location. This builds on the fact that it is harder for a car passenger to retrace a tricky route than for the driver, thereby making Shoulder Surfing less of an issue. |

(cont.)

P

**Table 20A:** (cont.)

| Issues | Description |
|---|---|
| | b) **Single image** may also be used such as an anatomical drawing of the bones of the body. The user clicks on a few of the hundreds of locations available on the image such as a jawbone, followed by a bone in the wrist and, finally by part of the spine. Users remembering the location and order of each click have the password they need to log-on. |
| | Some Experts also point out that organizational customers might want to stick with old-fashioned passwords, primarily because the cost of training and supporting people as they learn a new system might be too costly. |

**Note.** Some basic password-related matters are outlined in this table (see also Tables 4A, 4B, 4C and 15B).

Being willing to help one's neighbor board up their windows with anti-Virus software and a Firewall, suggests that one is also willing to help them get patched.

**Bandwidth and Automatic Upgrades**   may be a problem for pushing a Patch or anti-Virus software update to users if they already experience limited bandwidth due to an attack. Bandwidth may be limited in a case where patches must be distributed after the fact. To illustrate, pushing the anti-Virus patch out to users who were already experiencing the "good Samaritan" worm alternately called Blast.D, Welchia and Nachi was a problem around August 17–23, 2003. The Worm went through networks looking for the Blaster worm, removed it and fixed it by automatically downloading the Microsoft patch.

When the worm got into the network it ate up huge amounts of Bandwidth by sending out pings to locate instances of the Blaster worm. Hence, sending out patches for Vulnerabilities or even an anti-Virus software update using an automatic feature is difficult. This is especially true, if the bandwidth is curtailed already through such an event as the Blaster worm sending out pings, as experienced and reported by the USA Navy Marine Corps in regard to its Intranet on August 19, 2003.

**Regression**—encompasses the Risk for patches describing the failure of things that worked in the past will work thereafter. For any emergency patch, there is simply no time to repeat all the tests run against the regular release. Since security patches might well involve code deep within the operating system, it's no surprise that the failure to adequately Regression test the patches may result in a major incompatibility bug escaping (see also Statistics—Regression).

**Table 20B:** Password Use, Policy and Best Practice

| Tasks | Description |
|---|---|
| Choosing | Means that we try to choose a password that makes it difficult for a colleague to guess it and a hacker to 'work out' one's password. A hacker can initiate a 'brute-force' search by trying every possible combination of letters, numbers, and other characters. A search of this sort, even processed on a computer capable of generating and testing thousands of passwords per second, could require many years to complete. So, in general, passwords should be safe; this requires that one selects them carefully. These are usually selected, such as:<br><br>a)  A standard password using English alphabet and numerals, non-case sensitive with 6-characters offers over 2 million possible combinations.<br>b)  In the case sensitive password, 'a' is not the same as 'A,' thereby doubling the number of available characters, hence a six character, case sensitive password and allowing the shifted version of the numerical keys (e.g., 5 and %) increases the number of combinations making them approach 140 million.<br><br>Each additional character increases the number of combinations exponentially, and so a 7-character, case-sensitive password would offer over a billion combinations. A human user has virtually no chance of ever identifying a 6-character password, if it was *randomly generated*. |
| Use, Policy and Best Practice | A string of characters input by a system user to substantiate their identity, and/or authority, and/or access rights, to the computer system that they wish to use. Passwords are central to all computer systems—even sophisticated systems employing fingerprints, voice recognition, or retinal scans.<br>Even having chosen an 'impossible to guess' password, one's management of the password will determine its effectiveness in safeguarding access to the system using one's user ID and password. The following best practice guidelines should be observed.<br><br>1)  Passwords chosen must be at least made up of six characters, case sensitive, including numbers and letters allowing the shifted version of the numerical keys (e.g., 5 and % is possible), thereby increasing the number of combinations making them approach 140 million, thus making the use of rule-based password cracking with the help of software much more difficult.<br>2)  Single sign-on system should be used (see Table 20A).<br>3)  All passwords needed for accessing e-commerce or e-government sites outside the firm (e.g., internet banking, submitting tax records and purchasing a book) should be stored in encrypted form on the computer (e.g., using freeware such as Whisper 32 (see also Appendices 7 & 8 or another program from a vendor). |

(cont.)

**Table 20B:** (cont.)

| Tasks | Description |
|---|---|
| | 4) Passwords of key role holders—such as System and Network administrators—should be copied and held under dual control in a fire-resistant, secure location, to enable access to the system by an authorized person in the unavoidable absence of the password holder. |
| | 5) Passwords must be changed at regular intervals, and should be chosen privately by the individual users; and although often issued initially by the IT people, the password must be changed immediately. |
| | 6) Password changes must be forced if necessary by implementing an expiry period after which a user's password will not be accepted and the next attempt to log on by that user will result in a security flash to the system console. |
| | 7) Number of failed attempts and an issue and re-issue procedure as well as possible suspension of user privileges must be established. |
| | The above should be written down in a password policy that is part of the Information Security Policy (see also Security of Media, Shoulder Surfing). |

**Note.** The above outlines how use, policy and best practice can improve password management (see also Tables 4A, 4B, 4C, 6, 15A and 23C).

Regression bugs, particularly those where new code breaks existing functionality, can easily result in a maintenance release or patch resulting in a lower (rather than higher) level of system quality. Regression bugs might be relatively rare, unfortunately, they can be very dangerous.

**Reliability and Patching** is clearly an issue. For instance, Microsoft Corp. released patches that caused problems on foreign language versions of the Windows operating system and Exchange e-mail server. As a result, Microsoft's released two further patches, MS03-045 and MS03-047, that included new patches for affected customers and additional instructions to get the patches to stick on vulnerable systems late during October 2003.

One could think that if MS continues down the path of 'let us patch this here and there' that 90% of the World's operating systems will come to a screeching halt someday. The question really is if 25% or 50% of the original code has been modified can problems be undone by simply adding another layer.

One must wonder what Risk this entails for large organizations using such systems. The Software Development Life Cycle (SDLC) points out some of these problems (see Appendix 6). The January 2003 release has information security as integral part throughout.

**Resource Drain** means a firm may spend substantial amounts of labor time and resources to install Patches. For instance, testing and thereafter installing a Patch on 500 servers and 8000 workstations is a Resource Drain for the organization. Normally, organizations need to schedule downtime in advance to deploy such Patches, but running a 24/7 service in an organization, such as a hospital, makes scheduling of downtime nearly impossible (see also Partitioning of Networks).

**Security Patch Management (SPM)** (see also Table 20C & D) is a process that every organization must have in place. The key concepts and principles of Security Patch Management include:

- **Setup** for SPM requires taking inventory and baselining the environment, as well as subscribing to:
  1) security alerts, especially those pertaining to operating systems used in the firm such as Windows XP versus Windows Server,
  2) establishing security reporting to assist with issue identification, and
  3) configuring and maintaining the patch management infrastructure.
- **Change Initiation** means that monitoring is used for identifying any security issues that should be resolved by changing the production environment. This includes but is not limited to:
  1) Reviewing several sources of information and reports to help in identifying in a timely fashion software updates and security issues (e.g., Microsoft Vulnerabilities),
  2) determining their relevance,
  3) quarantining new software updates for use in subsequent steps,
  4) testing updates and security patches in a safe and controlled environment before deployment, and
  5) initiating a response to address the security issue.

Typical SPM requires addressing the three issues raised below, namely:

**Time Lag** is getting ever shorter. For instance, SQL Slammer didn't appear until eight months after the vulnerability was announced, the worm Blaster was released within one month after the vulnerability had been reported (see also Computer Crime).

During 2003 some government agencies or larger firms required anywhere from about three to four days to push out Patches across their networks. But if the Time Lag is getting ever shorter, system administrators need a solution that cuts the process down to a few hours, if not **minutes**.

**Timeliness of Releasing a Security Patch** is often a software update or related countermeasures to a newly-identified Vulnerability by users, the vendor's own staff or others. Performing a security release includes change, release (including testing), and review (including rollback, if necessary) management.

Timeliness of Releasing Security Patch was an item for discussion when Microsoft decided to move from weekly or sometimes nearly daily releasing of patches to a monthly schedule during 2003.

What was important when addressing this was that a fair number of security issues during 2003 had been discovered "in house" at Microsoft first. If Microsoft discovers the patch first internally, the result is that the bad guys know about the vulnerability when the patch appears—so there is really no extra problem with a monthly cycle—unless someone else finds the problem in the meantime.

Where monthly release of Patches is a problem is where the exploit is disovered "outside." Sometimes there is a fix but its not being widely disseminated. In the worst case scenario, perhaps some Malware incorporating it circulates before Microsoft even starts cracking on the fix. In this scenario, of course, system administrators would clearly like the fix to be delivered as soon as possible—and indeed Microsoft's stated policy allows them to roll out the fix outside the normal monthly cycle.

Hence, the big unkown is how many bad guys will know about the security issue and the Risk of that they might exploit it, a big unkown. Only the future can tell us if a monthly roll-out of Patches provided by Microsoft is a good solution. The monthly roll-out also allows people to plan their time ahead unless of course one thinks it is possible a month will come around with no fixes from Microsoft having to be deployed!

It is true that thousands of systems cannot be patched using the 'sneaker net' but instead require Image Software to do it effectively. Nonetheless, even after that hand fixing may be required of some PCs or servers where the patch failed or those laptops where it was not installed because they were out of house. How much can go wrong here has been discussed on the NTBugTraq list (see also Table 18C).

Table 20C outlines the possibilities available for a larger organization to patch its systems using software and other means to improve the chances of having all systems patched. The challenge as mentioned is those computers that are not on site and connected to the system (e.g., home PCs and notebooks of road warriors or sales personnel). Patching of such machines when they log into the system needs to be secured to reduce the Risk on infection or Threat manifestation through such a PC.

For an SME, Partitioning of the Network is crucial because depending upon resources both human and financial ones, managing Patches could be an issue. One ministry of a European country found that more then 10% of their networked PCs did not include the latest patches when doing an Audit

**Table 20C:** Vulnerabilities and Malware—Managing Patches and Upgrades-Corporate Users

| | *Description* |
|---|---|
| | Corporates are supposedly automating the deployment of anti-virus software updates and Security Patches by delivering fixes and updates to desktops, laptops, servers and devices. Moreover, Patch dependencies and conflicts are to be resolved during these automated Patch installation processes and claim to have built-in repair, rollback and self-healing capabilities. |
| | And no, automated Security Patch Management software distributing fixes and installing them is not necessarily the solution either. Such an approach would violate the security requirement for first testing the Patch and making sure it runs properly with an organization's systems. And no, a service that provides security Patch management cannot guarantee to be able to pre-test everything for any organizational system beforehand. |
| | An automatically installed Patch that shuts down a system may be nearly as bad as a virus attack with a heavy payload. |
| Shared Internet Access and/or Workstations | raise Vulnerability issues, especially at schools and universities where students have access to computers linked to the campus networks. Reducing the Risk for tampering, such as putting a keylogger on a hard-drive, is being reduced by cloning these workstations' disks every night. Hence, every disk is being re-written with a fresh, uncontaminated copy of the entire contents of the drive. |
| | There are products available which can automatically deploy the authorized disk image to hundreds or thousands of workstations provided the university or organization has adequate server speeds and network bandwidth. These products would reduce (but not eliminate) the window of exposure on public terminals but also employees' workstations. |
| | Accordingly, users should be careful about what they reveal on public terminals as those provided in a public library. |
| Imaging Software | can facilitate patching by supporting not only preservation of data integrity and trustworthiness but, as importantly, providing a speedy mechanism for restoring functionality of a damaged system by: |
| | —restoring the disk image of the operating-system drive, —while not requiring one to re-install the software. |
| | These tools support the principle of a known-good copy of the operating system but require: |
| | 1) The image is taken immediately after installing the operating system, such as Windows, and before using—and potentially damaging—it. |
| | 2) Before installing new software such as applications, drivers, and Microsoft security updates, one can restore the original image, while |
| | 3) Subsequently installation is being done while the new image is being taken at the same time and properly documented for the next time . This is enabling one to start from a clean environment lateron if need be. |

(cont.)

P

**Table 20C:** (cont.)

| *Description* |
| --- |
| In the above way, patches are being installed on a known-good copy of the operating system. In turn, this can than be tested and subsequently installed overnight on all workstations throughout the system.<br>    Such an approach helps ensure that all patches are installed throughout the organization including updates, security patches and virus software-related changes as well (see also Patch—Timelines of Releasing a Security Patch).<br>    System administrators cannot check workstations manually nor can one expect users to keep up all-the-time. Otherwise, if audited, such systems may show that a few machines do not have known vulnerabilities and released patches installed. Hence, for larger systems Imaging Software is a viable option that saves time and helps improve the firm's Risk Management. |

**Note.** This table outlines how an organization can improve distribution of patches where Imaging Software plays an important role, an example of such a tool can, for instance, be found here: http://www.cs.utah.edu/flux/papers/frisbee-usenix03-base.html.

including addressing Patch management. These problems were of particular concern during Blaster, shutting down communication internally and externally via the Internet for just about two working days. As Table 20D suggest it might be a viable option for an SME to outsource certain things to reduce Risks.

**Enforcing Security Policy**   (see also Security Policy) may become necessary when previously addressed Vulnerabilities reoccur and might be due to such events as users installing non-authorized software on their machines. Recurring Vulnerabilities represent an increase of risk of exploitation of the organization's information assets by viruses, worms, and attack tools. The latter may remotely Scan the firm's computers for security weaknesses.

**Responding to Security Emergency**   means preparing for and responding to attacks that exploit security vulnerabilities (including those to having not yet patched the vulnerability) in the organization.

**SPM Configuration**   is also an issue (see also Tables 20C & D)

**Patent**   for an Invention is granted by government to the inventor, giving the inventor the right for a limited period to stop others from

- making,
- using, or
- selling the invention,

without the permission of the inventor (see also Copyright).

**Table 20D:** Vulnerabilities and Malware—Managing Patches and Upgrades as a Small and Medium-Sized Enterprises (SMEs) or a Home User

| | *Description* |
|---|---|
| Home Users and Small and Medium-Sized Enterprieses (SMEs) | Dial-up and Patching—means that if one does not pay regular attention to patching Windows, then one can could easily find oneself with tens of megabytes of downloads to install.<br><br>While broadband is spreading rapidly, there are still a whole lot of folks who use dial-up, and many who have no broadband options available in more remote areas but also in developing countries to mention two possibilities. Because the slow connections make it impractical for dial-up users to stay up to date on security patches, it's highly likely that a large percentage of them are out of date. This situation is a continuing security problem for all internet users and businesses.<br><br>*Windows Update—**Broadband** customers have a plethora of features to customize their patching experience. Automatic Updates will check for available updates from Microsoft's site and download them in the background, letting the user know when they are available for installation. One can schedule the system to install downloaded updates at some predetermined time, such as three o'clock in the morning.<br>*Windows Update–**Dial-Up**—there is no way to schedule the system to go out and retrieve the updates, which can be installed at some point. The closest thing to a workable solution for dial-up users is to leave the connection on at all times and then use Automatic Updates to eventually download what they need.<br><br>But leaving the connection on most of the time is impractical and increases the security Risks unnecessarily. Finally, with metered phone calls, this option is a no-starter since it becomes very expensive very quickly. Metered phone calls is a service that applies for most users outside North America. |
| Windows Update—Home Users and SMEs | While broadband is spreading rapidly, there are still a whole lot of folks who use dial-up, and many who have no broadband options available in more remote areas. Plenty of home users could not even afford to have broadband internet access considering their countries' standard-of-living possibilities, such as Latvia & Estonia, two new European Community member states.<br><br>Because the slow connections make it impractical for dial-up users to stay up to date on security patches, it's highly likely that a large percentage of them are out of date. This situation is a continuing security problem for all internet users and businesses.<br><br>Microsoft could issue periodic update CDs, being written in Windows Script Host. Than it would check a system for which updates need to be installed, apply them in the correct order and even reboot in between. At that point one would still need to check Windows Update for recent additions, but it is unlikely the home user would have an unbearably long download time. In fact, the CD could launch Windows Update at the end of its script.<br><br>This approach would benefit probably more than 50% of home users in industrialized countries and who knows how many in less developed countries who do not have broadband access (see Tables 19A and 19B for data on the 'digital divide.'<br><br>Unfortunately, Microsoft has so far been unwilling to offer this approach, thereby making dial-up users' life easier. |

**Note.** This table is a bit Windows centric but considering that more than 90% of all operating systems for home users and SMEs' PCs run on Windows, this seems justified.

The SME may also consider some other issues as outlined in 23D to reduce Risks. Most importantly might be the outsourcing of certain activities such as a firm's web site, as well as a clear Partitioning of Network(s).

When a patent is granted, the invention becomes the property of the inventor. The latter may:

* sell,
* rent, or
* license

its use to others. Patents are territorial (see also Invention).

We need to differentiate between the genuinely new and deserving of patent protection and the bread-and-butter business of software development for which copyright protection is more than adequate (Jurisdiction, License, Liability).

*Copyright protects against wanton plagiarism*, **patents cover ideas**, have to be applied for and cost money. By analogy with literature, if there are only a handful of original storylines, once each had been patented, the novel would make no further progress depriving us of Harry Potter sequels to mention one example (see also Copyright and Tables 16A and B).

**Claims**    are the concise written statements that define the invention covered by the patent application. What falls within that definition is protected by the patent-anything outside it, is not protected.

Whether a patent will be granted is determined, in large measure, by the choice of wording of the claims. The claims of a patent are somewhat like the legal description in a deed because they describe the metes and bounds of the invention.

**Complete Specification**    is the basis for a patent whereby the invention must be described fully, and putting the invention into effect must be outlined succinctly, while at least one Claim is to be put forward.

**Priority Date**    is established for an invention when one first files a patent application that describes the invention in detail.

This is used to determine if the invention is new. If the invention is known to the public before this date, one is not entitled to patent it.

**Path**    refers to the location of a file or directory on that system. On PCs using MS DOS® or Windows®, the path is as follows:

driveletter:\directoryname\sub-directoryname\filename.suffix

Windows calls the directory a folder but it means the same, in Unix systems the modified syntax is:

/directory/subdirectory/filename

**Payload**    is the load of a Virus or actions performed by the malware that typically are harmful. Also described as the effects that it produces on being activated, such as deletion of data, and formatting of disk drives.

**PBX bugging** transpires when flaws in a telephone system are exploited, thereby permitting somebody to listen to conversations when the phone is hung up.

**Peer Review** refers to the checking and review of work performed by one's peers (equals) in a working group. Hence, both systems analysts and programmers will have their work checked by each other and this forms a critical aspect to the quality process. Peers can usually identify each other's errors quickly and easily and this should result in elevated performance (see Research).

**Double-Blind Review** is process whereby neither author nor reviewer knows the identity of the author except for the editor or client. This process is often used in science before an article is being accepted for publication (see Research).

Without any doubt, this type of review process has advantages but sometimes it may also stifle innovation (see Invention).

**Peer to Peer or P2P** see Darknet, also Spoof

**Penetration** results in Intrusion, Trespassing, Unauthorised Access into a system. Merely contacting system or using a keyboard to enter a password is not penetration, but gaining access to the contents of the data files by these or other means does constitute Penetration (see also Tables 7B & 24D).

**Penetration Testing,** is the execution of a testing plan, the sole purpose of which, is to attempt to hack into a system using known tools and techniques (see also Table 14).

The evaluators may be assumed to use all system design and implementation documentation, that may include listings of system source code, manuals, and circuit diagrams. The evaluators work under the same constraints applied to ordinary users (see also Table 24D).

**People or End-Users:** The term people in this context encompasses legitimate (authorized employees) and non-legitimate users (Hackers). End-users are made up of legitimate system users only, either on the Intranet, the Extranets (e.g., dealers) and the Internet (e.g., firm's Web page).

**Peripherals** are pieces of hardware attached to a computer rather than built into the machine itself such as, printers, scanners, hard drive units and other items which can be plugged into a port.

**Personal Digital Assistant (PDA)** are being used by employees as portable mini filing cabinets, storing every essence of their personal and business lives on them. Unfortunately, users are often oblivious to the fact that, without password protection, anyone can access this information. Hence, PDAs have to be part of the firm's security policy or else why their use is not permitted must be explained (see also Table 6).

Companies should purchase PDAs for their employees rather than wait for employees to purchase their own. This way, the company has control over the data held on the PDA and can ensure that its policies are implemented.

The IT department has to set standards for PDA security and synchronisation, and should not allow users to install their own synchronisation products on their devices. In fact, some industry experts predict that through 2005, PDAs will be the biggest challenge to manage and control among end-user platform choices, and the hardest ones to show a return on investment.

PDA functions are also more and more integrated into Smartphones.

**Person-Computer Interaction**   —the more traditional term used is "man"-computer interface which has been replaced here with a gender-neutral term. Person-computer interface could be defined as encompassing the critical factors for success to be considered before and during the acquisition of new technology and making the necessary adaptations leading to organizational change (e.g., work flow, job related tasks and organizational structure). Thus, person-computer interface looks at the physical context of work (e.g., workstation design, illumination, ambient temperature, privacy and social interaction, and also visual and acoustical privacy) as well as ergonomics [e.g., ergonomics of hardware such as the visual-display terminal (VDT) and keyboard design, software ergonomics and user-friendliness of technology applications].

The difference between ergonomics and person-computer interface is that while the former looks at the physical and sensory-motor aspects, person-computer interface goes much further. It also considers ergonomics issues in the larger context of the work flow, work design and the work environment in general, as well as the individual's attentional and cognitive resources (e.g., knowledge, reasoning and information processing). Hence, successful person-computer interaction leads to a healthy work environment and supports the employee's and the firm's efforts toward a high quality of work life for technology users (see also Ergonomics).

**Pervasive Computing**   does not benefit from a precise definition but some would say that it encompasses all inclusive anywhere, any device and any time technology that includes mobile computing, mobile commerce, telematics and more (see also Privacy–Information Space, Tables 21A and 21B).

A more narrow definition would suggest that Pervasive Computing encompasses those technologies and applications that connect embedded devices in cars, at home and industrial plants that send specific information alerts to remote servers, which decide what action needs to be taken.

Rapid advances in digital electronics have made computers faster, cheaper, and smaller. Similar progress in communications technology has provided users virtually unlimited bandwidth, anywhere and at any time. The resulting combination of virtually free computation and ubiquitous network access has fueled the new domain of Pervasive Computing.

Much as the advancement of earlier technologies enabled pervasive access to water, gas, and electricity, it is now becoming increasingly practical to define similar environments for ubiquitous computation and communication.

Pervasive Computing envisions environments richly lathered with computation, communication and networked devices, mobile users interacting with their environment using speech and vision, with secure access to personal or public data.

Pervasive Computing environments are not just stand-alone vehicles for number crunching, rather they are progressing toward immersing users in a triad of

1) invisible computation,
2) communication and devices, and
3) working in concert to satisfy user requirements according to the facilities available in the environment.

Topics that relate to Pervasive Computing include:

- computer and network architectures,
- mobile computing mechanisms,
- human-computer interaction using speech and vision,
- pervasive software systems,
- location mechanisms, and
- techniques and systems for security and user-authentication.

**Ubiquitous Computing** is a term put forward by Mark Weiser in 1988, describing it as information technology's next wave after the mainframe and PC. In this new world, what Weiser called "calm technology" will reside around us, interacting with users in natural ways to anticipate their needs and supply the information they want wherever they are.

Pervasive Computing requires that computing devices are ubiquitious and if not invisible, at least handy for users and easy to take wherever one wishes to go (e.g., small cellular used for tracking location of person). Pervasive Computing envisions environments richly lathered with computation, communication and networked devices, mobile users interacting with their environment using speech and vision, with secure access to personal or public data. Pervasive Computing environments will not simply be standalone vehicles for number crunching, rather they will immerse their users in a triad of invisible computation, communication and devices, working in concert to satisfy user requirements according to the facilities available in the environment.

As such Pervasive Computing is a world saturated with computing and communication on the road to Ubiquitous Computing. The latter also gracefully integrates social and end-user issues including but not limited to Social Informatics and Social Securematics.

**Pervasive Computing**   and Privacy (see also Privacy)

**Pervasive Computing and Securematics**   (also Security)

**PGP**   see Pretty Good Privacy

**Phishing**   is hacker lingo for fishing, whereby a million hooks are put into the water using Spam to see who bites.

Phishing usually occurs by sending a bogus eMail or providing a URL for a web site that lures one into disclosing account or other private information. Phishing scam messages can be just as destructive as viruses or worms. Phishing (fishing), also known as carding, is the use of bogus e-Mails and web sites to lure unsuspecting users into revealing identity, password and credit card information.

If one receives such a message unexpectedly from one's bank or favorite e-commerce site where one has an account, the links in the message must be ignored. Instead, one should use one's browser, type in the link or click on the link stored in one's favorites one usually uses for reaching the website. One can protect oneself against this in two steps:

1) Never run attachments that come through email even if the message has a valid-looking return address and the logo and graphics of a legitimate company;

2) If one is asked to go to a Webpage, one must assure that the same information or details that are in the eMail message are also on the web site one navigates to; and

3) If one is asked to update one's information, a legitimate firm would do this by asking the customer to log into his or her account on the firm's secure web site with an SSL connection.

Phishing scams are becoming more popular because it only takes a few people handing over their credit card numbers to make the Spam pay for itself. Stopping this particular type of scam requires on-going education (see also Spam).

**MiMail**   is the blending of Phishing and a worm program that spreads itself via attachments to this eMail. Hence, a MiMail message might look as coming from a legitimate vendor or bank with a warning that one's account is to be terminated. To stop this, one is asked to run the program attached to the eMail.

The attached program will prompt the user to provide credit card account details that will be sent to the maker of this scam. Additionally, a worm might send the original file and message to all the people in one's address book, thereby spreading the bogus mail in a Worm fashion.

**Phone Phreak**   is a person who uses technology's weakness and the phone switching equipment's vulnerability to chat with others (preferably long-distance) at somebody else's expense by circumventing security measures with rudimentary technology.

P

**PHP**   is an HTML-embedded Web scripting language. Accordingly, PHP code can be inserted into the HTML of a Web page. When a PHP page is accessed, the PHP code is read or "parsed" by the server the page resides on.

The output from the PHP functions on the page are typically returned as HTML code, which can be read by the browser. Because the PHP code is transformed into HTML before the page is loaded, users cannot view the PHP code on a page. This make PHP pages secure enough to access databases and other secure information.

A lot of the syntax of PHP is borrowed from other languages such as C, Java and Perl (see Program—3GL). However, PHP has a number of unique features and specific functions as well. The goal of the language is to allow Web developers to write dynamically generated pages quickly and easily. PHP is also helpful for creating database-driven Web sites.

**Physical Attack**   means the act of physically stealing or damaging a computer, network, its components, or its supporting systems such as air conditioning and electricity supply (see also Attack–Tables 3A & 3B).

**Physical Protection Measures**   are used to safeguard against a physical attack. This may include but not be limited to restrictions on entry to premises, restrictions on entry to computer department, locking/disabling equipment, disconnection, fire-resistant and tamper-resistant storage facilities, anti-theft measures, and anti-vandal measures.

**Pickling**   means archiving a working model of obsolete computer technology so that a machine will be available to read old archive records which were created and stored using that machines' system.

**Ping**   stands for Packet Internet (or Inter-Network) Groper and is a packet (small message) sent to test the validity/availability of an IP address on a network. The technical term for 'ping' is the Internet Control Message Protocol. Maliciously sending large volumes of 'Pings' to cause difficulties for anyone else attempting to access that address is known as Smurfing.

**PKI**   see Digital Signature

**Plain Text**   also known as ASCII Text.

**Platform**   refers to the hardware and, by implication, the Operating System of a certain type of computer.

**Policies**   are an important tool to outline what is acceptable behavior and what is not (see also Information Security Policy, Password, see also Table 7A).

Table 21A outlines some of the policies including regulations the firm must submit to. The organization may prescribe the appropriate use of company resources for administration of private business ventures. Unfortunately, it may still not be allowed to check if an employee used company eMail facilities for moonlighting that are against the employment contract (private use and moonlighting that is). A French case protected a worker's rights during 2001, claiming that company policies violated his right for privacy, thereby making the firm at fault for having checked and discovered violations in email correspondence.

It may also have special policies that apply to internal issues as also outlined in Tables 20A & 20B, as well as particular Policies (see Table 6).

Security management activities require reviews of systems, sites and policies, hence key controls acting as a baseline must be established (see Key Controls).

**Polling**   in the IT Security context means checking the status of an input line, sensor, or memory location. This allows one to see if a particular external event has been registered. Typically used on fax machines to retrieve information from a remote source, the user, will dial from one fax machine to another, then press the polling button to get information from the remote fax machine.

**Polymorphic**   see Virus

**Population**   see Sample

**Port**   is a word that can have three different meanings in our context as outlined below.

**Internet Port**   is a number that indicates what kind of protocol a server on the Internet is using. Web servers typically are listed on port 80. Web browsers use this port by default when accessing Web pages, but you can also specify what port you would like to use in the URL like this: http://www.excite.com:80.

FTP uses port 21, eMail uses port 25, and game servers use various other ports. It is good to know what a port is, but one seldom has to specify it manually.

**Table 21A:** Policies and IT-Resources and Appropriate User Behaviors

| Tasks | Description |
|---|---|
| Acceptable Use of Facilities | Can include how email can be used and the World Wide Web from one's workplace (e.g., what sites, private versus corporate email/surfing, during or after working hours). |
| Using Facilities Means User Abides to the Following Laws | • Data Protection Legislation<br>• Spam Legislation<br>• Legislation pertaining to information and system security<br>• Privacy Legislation<br>• Trade Secrets Legislation<br>• Anti-Discrimination Legislation<br>• Obscenity/Pornography Legislation<br>• Cybercrime Legislation<br><br>In the European context, the above legislation may include national legislation as well as EU legislation (e.g., a Swiss firm following national anti-virus legislation as well as EU cybercrime legislation). Moreover, European Commission (EC) Directives must be incorporated into policies very quickly since they may enter local legislation within a few months anyway. |
| Policies and Agreements | Those may be industry standards, best practice and union contract the firm has to abide by. |
| Internet | Special ones the firm may have developed to protect its informational assets (see also Table 7A). |
| Anti-Chain Mail | Neither passing on email virus alerts, chain letters nor Hoaxes. |
| Anti-Spam | Forbidding employees to use organizational resources for dissemination of Spam, junk mail and other forms of inappropriate mass email for private or work-related purposes.<br>Listservers at work for particular purposes may be exempt. |
| Anti-Virus | Possible virus-related problems are to be reported to the call center or designated super user/security officer, and logged to the appropriately qualified person or team.<br>This team or individual finds out the validity of virus warnings before taking the necessary steps (e.g., informing workforce). Having Virus warnings sent out without being validated beforehand, causes unnecessary worry and resource consumption (see Anti-Chain Mail above).<br>Unqualified staff (probably including most support personnel) may not pass on warnings about Viruses, Trojan Horses and other security breaches without Authorization |

**Note.** This outlines some of the policies, readers are also referred to Table 7A (Critical Infrastructure Protection–Policies) where some of the specific security-related policies are outlined in detail (see also Tables 20A, 20B, 20C, 20D & 22D).

**Hardware Port**  refers to any one of the ports that are on the back of a computer where devices can be hooked up such as a keyboard, mouse, printer, ADSL modem and digital camera. Some common ports found on today's computers are USB (e.g., ADSL modem), Firewire, and Ethernet.

**Port**  used as a verb refers to the editing of a software program's code so that it can run on another platform. For example, to get Final Fantasy VII to run on a PC, programmers needed to port it to the PC from the Playstation. Popular Windows games are often ported to the Macintosh as well.

**Port Address Translation (PAT)**  is communication technology used by routers to allow multiple users in a local network to access—with their own IP address—the Internet or corporate networks via a single public address. PAT actually translates multiple private IP addresses to a single public address, or to a public sub network, recognized by the IP service provider. This function can reduce operating costs, increase security and simplify Internet access.

If an attacker wants to access ports connected to the 3Com OfficeConnect Remote 812 ADSL router the router will not allow this connection. However, firmware versions V1.1.9 and V1.1.7 had a confirmed vulnerability that if a connection is made to a redirected port using PAT and then to any port not redirected using PAT, the router allows the successive connections to any port. The problem exists with TCP and with UDP.

**Port Scan**  gives a list of all ports that are actually listening. The netstat command can be run locally to determine the open ports but an external port scan against the system is usually also needed. If the results of netstat differ from the port scanning results, validation of why each port is open, and what is running on each port is needed. Ports that cannot be validated or justified should be closed. The final list should be recorded and used to audit the ports on a regular basis, thereby making sure no extraneous ports appear (see also Cracker, Server).

Blocking ports is not a substitute for a comprehensive security solution. An attacker may have gained access via other means such as a dial-up modem, a trojan e-mail attachment, or a person who is an organization insider. Hence, the attacker can exploit these ports if not properly secured on every host system in the firm (see also Appendix-7, also Table 22E).

**Probing and Scanning**  of ports does not necessarily constitute an attack but, unfortunately, it is often the precursor to attacks. Hence perimeter protection to block all services not offered to external systems is needed and, as importantly, all attempts at probing and scanning must be logged. In turn, external IP addresses that are logged as having performed Port scans or probes are blocked by the Firewall that provides perimeter protection. An email should also be sent to the domain authority of the IP address notifying the party that such activity was undertaken.

**Postfix**   is Wietse Venema's mailer that started life as an alternative to the widely-used Sendmail program. Postfix tries to be fast, easy to administer and be more secure than others. Nonetheless, since it is quite compatible with Sendmail making it not too difficulty for administrators and users to adjust. Hence, the interface has the Sendmail-ish flavor, however the inside is completely different.

P

Postfix was formerly known as VMailer. It was released by the end of 1998 as the IBM Secure Mailer, living on beyond that date as Postfix.

**Prepender**   see Infection

**Pretty Good Privacy (PGP)**   is a software package permitting users to use encryption when exchanging messages, widely available. Export versions of PGP are different than versions used in the USA and Canada (see also Encryption).

**Prevalence**   see Survey

**Prevention**   is the major thrust of IT Security (see definition further below). IT Security aims at preventing unauthorized access and/or use (see Access) of processes, files, data and information, or data in transit (see also Attack—Tables 3A, 3B, 17D, 21A and also Risk—Tables 22C, 22D & 22E). The word can further be defined by making a distinction between levels of prevention such as:

**Primary Prevention**   is aimed at reducing the risk for and incidences of unauthorized access and/or use of processes, systems and files and virus infections.

**Secondary Prevention**   aims to reduce prevalence of unauthorized Access and/or use by shortening the duration (see Table 15A & 20A). This also encompasses reducing the prevalence of Malware found on systems or else PCs whose operating system still runs without having well-known Vulnerabilities fixed with released Patches.

**Tertiary Prevention**   is aimed toward reducing the number or the impact of complications caused by unauthorized access and/or use of system resources. Tertiary Prevention also addresses reducing the impact or Damages that might be caused by a Threat being realized or a yet unknown Vulnerability being exploited or Virus being spread (see also Figure 2, Transmission of Infection).

**Prevention and Awareness Advisory (P&AA)**   is an organization's or agency's effort (see also Table 5A) to use Primary, Secondary and Tertiary

Prevention to help users safeguard their systems and information including reducing possible Identity Theft. Here the target group is primarily home users and Small and Medium-Sized Enterprises (SMEs).

In contrast to a Technical Alert or Advisory a P&AA may offer the recipient such information or descriptions as:

- **What is the problem** (concise and easily understood description of about 30 words);
- What option is there to **fix the problem**, outlined in concise non-technical language;
- How is the Vulnerability or Threat being reduced means offering the User a **step-by-step solution** on how it can be fixed such as first do this, than the screen will show you X, click on why and so on;
- Feedback about success, ideally offering an **online test** that confirms that the problem has been fixed. To illustrate, Visibility = scanner from trusted source/ website reports to the user that his or her following the step-by-step list for fixing the problem was successful. Namely, when pinning his or her machine, the previously open port had been successfully closed and, as importantly, Firewall had been re-configured correctly as well.
- **Scenario** is no longer than 150 words explaining a home user what could happen if the Vulnerability or Threat is not being patched or fixed.

It is obvious that the above information and P&AA can be successful only, if the average not very technically versed person can read, comprehend the information within three minutes and fix the problem within five by following the very practical advise provided. In total, it is very unlikely that a citizen will spend much more than 10 minutes each time to do the job.

But the above also requires a Trust and a Trusted Source providing this information to End-Users.

**Prevention Paradox**   exemplifies the situation whereby preventive measures to increase security brings large benefits to the organization or society but little to most individual units or employees/citizens. An example might be whereby not having the authority to install any software reduces the risk of system problems or possible virus infections. To further illustrate, not being allowed to install a non-sanctioned screensaver, such as the digitized picture of one's child.

**Preventive Infrastructure Management (PIM)**   is the application of preventive measures by IT security experts. A specialized and newly emerging field of IT security practice composed of distinct disciplines that utilize skills focusing on the security of defined IT infrastructures. All undertaken in order to promote and maintain security and well-functioning systems, and preventing service disruptions, compromising of files, data and protecting confidentiality, integrity, accessibility and accountability of systems resources and processes as well as their use.

The knowledge of basic and applied computing science, informatics and information systems management are at the core of PIP, as well as the skills common to all IT knowledge workers. The distinctive aspects of PIP also encompass knowledge of and competence in statistics; conducting, evaluating and designing research projects, computing science; business administration, including planning, organization, management, financing, and evaluation of security programs; system design, and the application of primary, secondary, and tertiary prevention measures within IT security (see also Attack, Infection, Prevention).

**Primary Case**   is the incident that introduces the Malware/unauthorized tool into a large network, IP address or subnets including servers or PCs.

**Privacy**   could be defined as the individual's right to determine his or her own communication contacts and the right to control the use of personal information by others. Additionally, it should be made technically and economically feasible for the individual and for commercial organizations to control and protect their own private data to an extent that they determine themselves and, as importantly, with measures selected at their own discretion (see also Identity Theft, Pervasive Computing).

In practice, privacy policies have an opt-in or opt-out clause that permits the user to either refuse the mailing of promotional material from the firm/ organization one has contact with (e.g., being a customer or signing up for a service via the Internet) or its 'affiliates' (firms who might have purchased customer lists) or else opt in to receive such materials.

If a person has opted out of such mailings or no relationship with the sending party of a promotional email, not only may the recipient's privacy be violated but, spamming may also be an issue resulting in additional legal problems (see also Spam). The EU and most other countries (e.g., Canada, Japan, Brasil) have stronger or weaker privacy legislation (see Appendix 4) that is being strongly or less strongly enforced either by regulators and/or victims taking violators to court (e.g., especially in the US, see Appendix 5 for a link).

But even if a person may opt-out of receiving information from his or her bank and the latter sells the information to a telemarketer who than calls up the people on the list to sell other products, may have little recourse against this privacy violation. In April 2002 New York Supreme Court, Appellate Division dismissed a class action privacy lawsuit against Chase Manhattan Bank, finding the plaintiffs failed to show they sustained actual harm as a result of the bank's selling their personal information to telemarketers. The court said that the complaint failed to allege any instance in which a named plaintiff or class member suffered actual harm from the receipt of any unwanted telephone solicitation or junk mail and, therefore, the lower court properly dismissed the action. Case name is Smith v. Chase Manhattan Bank USA.

The above illustrates that privacy legislation in the USA may have little teeth if the courts do not protect invasion. If firms do what Chase did, we will have many annoying calls during the early evening hours trying to sell us stuff we do not want. Than it becomes a pest, maybe what is needed is that the victim does not have to claim damages but that the violator would face stiff fines and criminal penalties (e.g., for the Chief Executive Officer or CEO) as most anti-spam bills suggest (see also Spam, Viral Marketing).

For more information see also the Resource section with links to USA and EU privacy legislation (Appendices 4 and 5).

**Digital Privacy Rules**   came into force in the EU On October 31, 2003 (see Appendix x for link). The new laws require companies to obtain consent before (see also Pervasive Computing).

- sending e-mail,
- tracking personal data on Web sites, or
- pinpointing callers' locations via satellite-linked mobile phones.

**Information Space**   addresses issues related to transferring electronic data across networks and physically transporting these into possibly insecure places such as storing sensitive data on a laptop. The boundaries for which one can express and enforce permissions requires a context-aware system for distinguishing objects and actions along the boundaries that have meaningful privacy implications for the user of information and, most importantly, the owner such as the patient.

Table 21B defines **Information Asymmetry** and the principles for minimizing these. Table 21C outlines Properties of Information Space as well as its Boundaries and the Operations that might further enhance or decrease Privacy.

**Information-Theoretic Privacy**   is achieved when the messages or ballots are indistinguishable (i.e. cannot be attributed to a particular party) regardless of any cryptographic assumptions (see Tables 11A and 11B).

Information-Theoretic Privacy is privacy which cannot be broken by computation, even with unbounded time and resources. This is in contrast to systems that would only provide for Computational Privacy.

Information-Theoretic Privacy is exemplified by election systems in which there is no reliance on cryptography in order to protect privacy (e.g., reliance

**Table 21B:** Privacy and Asymmetric Information Spaces–Definition and Principles

| Tasks | Description |
|-------|-------------|
| Defining Information Asymmetry | Means that one party in a transaction has more information than the other. |
| Understanding Information Assymetry | can be assessed by studying three factors as outlined below. |

- **Social Norms**—are a cultural phenomenon that prescribes and proscribes behavior in specific situations. Hence while loude music during the night creates negative externalities for neighbors, social norms have evolved whereby most will turn down the volume of the stereo and close their windows. Violating this social norm may make one vulnerable to **social sanctioning** but also neighbors complaining to the landlord, nocking on one's door and much more.

  Social sanctioning is, however, contingent on easy detection of violations of social norms. Ubiquitous computing may result in situations, whereby the person may neither know who has violated one's privacy nor how it was done (e.g., hidden cameras, see Appendix 3).

- **Markets**—here asymmetry of information results in individuals experiencing significant cognitive costs involved in data exchanges. This negatively impacts their ability to make informed decisions. With Ubiquitous Computing, proliferation of data collection increases, whereby data owners' have to make ever more decisions about data exchanges.

- **Legislation**—must be such that transferability of information as a Property Right is limited because significant asymmetric information increases the complexity for Data owners. It is difficult to assess the Risks inherent when giving a Collector or User a license for further exploiting personal information (e.g., data obtained through a loyalty air line, credit card issuer or food store) as further outlined below. A **license scheme fails unless Data owners are informed about and can exert control over one's personal data**.

| | |
|-------|-------------|
| Principles of Minimizing Asymmetry | Means that the asymmetry of information held between data: |

- owners
- collectors, and
- users

is being minimized by:

1. **Decreasing** the flow of information from the data owner (e.g., individual) to collectors (e.g., credit card issuer, and government), to users (e.g., police, convenience store).
2. **Increasing** the flow of information from collectors, to users and back to data owners.

**Note.** This defines the principles of Information Asymmetry. Confidentiality, Integrity, Availability of Data, User Accountability, Authentication and Auditing (CIA-UAA) (see Table 5C) are highly interrelated with Privacy, whereby a database may meet CIA-UAA principles while the rights of the Owner of Data are still being violated by having an unsatisfactory level of information asymmetry.

In the above definitions, **data owner** represents the individual or **citizen**.

**Table 21C:** Privacy and Asymmetric Information Spaces—Properties and Boundaries

| Tasks | Description |
|---|---|
| Information Space and Properties | illustrates that there are three privacy-sensitive properties of data contained in an information space, namely: <br><br> 1. **Persistence of data** referring to the lifetime of data and whether their quality should degrade over time. To illustrate, a store video might be taped over after one week and making its contents unusable after 60 days when it is being destroyed and replaced. <br> 2. **Observational accuracy of data** means that a person's exact location in a building might be updated within certain time intervals (e.g., every 30 seconds). <br> 3. **Observational confidence of data** illustrates the certainty of data or Reliability of a visual identification whereby from a privacy perspective if Reliability is 90% it is riskier for the person to have such data released than if it were 30% reliable to be true. |
| Information Space and Boundaries | Focuses on the possible delimitations of information space that is not physical, such as: <br><br> A. **Physical boundaries** separate information space from another by physical parameters, such as having a calendar with important meetings and other dates at the work computer system or at the home PC. <br> B. **Social boundaries** could be illustrated whereby the work calendar is shared with co-workers who can schedule meetings based on one being available and accepting the time or files on an area on the server are shared and worked on by all group members <br> C. **Activity-based boundaries** are where a teacher's presentation slides are shared by all students whereby his or her elaborations about these are shared by students attending the lecture only. |
| Information Space and Privacy-Sensitive Operations | are those being applied to data stored within the space such as: <br><br> • **Addition/Deletion and Update** are information performed with databases <br> • **Authorization/Revocation** results from principals changing ownership and release policies regarding data in information spaces (e.g., based on boundaries); <br> • **Promotion/Demotion** means that data could be such that its persistence, observational accuracy and confidence are increased or decreased by the principal. <br> • **Composition/Decomposition** may result whereby location, time and activity data are combined or separated in a database; <br> • **Fusion/Inference** results whereby similar to Statistics, certain raw data such as a video image from a room can be used to infer that a meeting between four individuals is taking place at this moment. |

**Note.** The above identifies additional parameters for the Information Space that relate to the level of privacy desired.

In the above definitions, **data owner** represents the individual or **citizen**.

on Encryption, see Tables 11A and 11B). Information-theoretic systems include, for example, systems where:

1) parties share keys in advance and use one-time pads (which is impractical and in any case subject to collusion attacks where keys are revealed);
2) parties share physically protected channels (this fails against collusion attacks where the channel is compromised without detection);
3) parties share information (via secret-sharing techniques) and they are assumed not to pool it together (again this fails against collusion attacks).

Information-Theoretic Privacy cannot protect voter privacy in the case of a court order that mandates revealing all keys and secrets used in the system.

**Fail-Safe Privacy** defined here for election systems where voter privacy cannot be compromised even if everything fails including software and hardware, everyone colludes and there is a court order that mandates revealing all keys and secrets used in the system.

Current **paper ballot voting systems** provide for fail-safe voter privacy. Another example of a system with fail-safe voter privacy is by not revealing the private voter information to the voting system, in any form, and yet providing an anonymous control structure with the DVCs (Digital Vote Certificates) and the EBs (Electronic Ballots).

**Computational Privacy** is privacy which could be broken by computation, given time and resources. Computational Privacy means that privacy is guaranteed only with respect to databases that are restricted to polynomial time computations. It also cannot protect voter privacy in the case of a court order that mandates revealing all keys or secrets used in the system.

This concept is exemplified by election systems that rely upon a threshold of collusion in blind signatures, mix-servers or Homomorphic Encryption, such that not less than N people working together can compromise voter privacy. However, such systems rely not only on the flawless implementation of mathematical formulas but also on the absence of a compromise to the computational platform. An example might be a computer Virus that would record all N keys for later use, or a non-intrusive electromagnetic eavesdropping device that would record all N keys for latter reuse without ever penetrating the platform.

The majority of proposed voting schemes provide Computational Privacy only, often without even considering the lack of Information-Theoretic Privacy.

**Privacy and Positioning** allows to track people and equipment using, for instance, infrared. To illustrate, battery-powered badges worn by doctors and patients give off both infrared and radio frequency signals that are picked up by receivers connected to the hospital's computer network.

Web browsers can be used to search for items with tags or for people with the badges and to view diagrams of floors showing real-time locations of doctors, patients and equipment.

While the above has all its uses, including mobile phones that help parents determine their children's exact location, these technologies can also reduce our privacy further.

**Privacy and Spam** can be a major problem. The European Union has adopted the opt-in approach, which makes unsolicited e-mail illegal unless the recipient gives permission in advance to the senders. But many say the law will be ineffective because:

- firms like Amazon.de still ask their clients to uncheck a box and if the client forgets, he or she will receive Amazon mailings and newsletters. With the opt-in approach, however, these boxes should be unchecked by default;
- because spammers are so evasive it will be hard to catch them, and
- most of Europe's junk e-mail comes from elsewhere.

EU politicians have argued that unless the United States and Asia take a similar approach, the floodgates will remain open.

The trade in eMail names is not limited to the back alleys of the Internet. Big, traditional mailing list companies have been buying eMail addresses, often from contest sites, and linking them with their vast stores of other information about people. Then marketers can send eMail to people who, say, have certain diseases or own a specific car model.

The chain of permission can be stretched even further. Some come from customer lists of Internet firms that collapsed as the dot-com bubble burst. While those companies may have had clear privacy policies, their mailing lists were often sold to other firms along with the rest of their assets. And those companies could in turn sell the lists to other marketers.

Executives at many of the big companies marketing by e-mail acknowledge that the list companies are not always honest about the sources of their names. But they say there is no way to test the quality of a list other than to send e-mail to its addresses and see how many complaints result (see also Spam, Phishing).

**Private Key**   see Digital Signature

**Privilege**   is the term used throughout most (if not all) applications and systems to denote the level of operator permission, or authority. Privilege can be established at the file or folder (directory) level and can allow (say) Read only access, but prevent changes. Privileges can also refer to the extent to which a user is permitted to enter and confirm transactions/information within the system. In many systems, the security features will offer the ability to implement dual control or automatic escalation to the next 'highest' level, to assist with Information Security compliance and best practice.

Privileges are established at 2 levels:

1) at the network level, where the level of privilege is established with respect to general access rights and permissions;
2) at the application level where the user's job function and responsibility will determine the level of privilege required.

In general, a user of an organization's systems should be offered no more than is necessary to perform the function required (see also Role-Based Access).

**Probe** describes the attempt to access a target in order to determine its characteristics.

**Process** describes a program in execution, consisting of the executable program, its data and stack, program counter, stack pointer and other registers, as well as other information needed to execute the program. Sometimes attackers seek access to a process that operates (e.g., the shell).

**Process Bypassing** happens when the normal controls are circumvented, such as inventory control mechanisms.

**Processor Cache** see Cache

**Program** is a specific set of ordered operations for a computer to perform. Programs can be characterized as interactive or batch in terms of what drives them and how continuously they run. An interactive program receives data from an interactive user (or possibly from another program that simulates an interactive user). A batch program runs and does its work, and then stops. Batch programs can be started by interactive users who request their interactive program to run the batch program. A command interpreter or a Web browser is an example of an interactive program. A program that computes and prints out a company payroll is an example of a batch program. Print jobs are also batch programs.

Creating a program means using a computer language (e.g., Pascal) whereby the language statements are the source program. Using a language compiler, the source program is than compiled resulting in an object program. This term is synonymous with object module and compiled program. It contains a string of 0s and 1s called machine language that the logic processor works with.

The machine language of the computer is constructed by the language compiler with an understanding of the computer's logic architecture, including the set of possible computer instructions and the length (number of bits) in an instruction.

**Generation Language (GL)** is a term that represent major steps or "generations" in the evolution of programming languages.

- **1GL** was (and still is) machine language or the level of instructions and data that the processor is actually given to work on. In conventional computers this is a string of 0s and 1s.
- **2GL** is assembler language. A typical 2GL instruction looks like this:

  ADD 12,8

  An assembler converts the assembler language statements into machine language. Assembler uses Mnemonics to represent each machine language instruction.
- **3GL** is a "high-level" programming language, such as PL/I, C, or Java. Java language statements look like this:

```
public bookean handleEvent (Event evt) {
switch (evt.id) {
  case Event.ACTION_EVENT: {
    if("Try me".equald(evt.arg)){
```

  A compiler converts the statements of a specific high-level programming language into machine language. For Java, the output is called bytecode, which is converted into appropriate machine language by a Java virtual machine that runs as part of an operating system platform. A 3GL language requires a considerable amount of programming knowledge.
- **4GL** is designed to be closer to natural language than a 3GL language. Languages for accessing databases are often described as 4GLs. A 4GL language statement might look like this:

  EXTRACT ALL VIRUS INCIDENTS WHERE "COSTS" TOTAL MORE THAN $ OR EUROS 5000
- **5GL** uses a visual or graphical development interface to create source language that is usually compiled with a 3GL or 4GL language compiler. Microsoft, Borland, IBM, and other companies make 5GL visual programming products for developing applications in Java, for example.

Visual programming allows you to easily envision object-oriented programming class hierarchies and drag icons to assemble program components.

**Security**—See Security Review—Source Code

**Project Management** is used for tasks that are completed in a shorter period of time, making the establishing of permanent organizational units not effective. Hence, resources and personnel are assembled temporarily and once the task is completed the unit is disbanded.

The key for temporary projects to succeed is managers that can garner the resources, support while following the timetable as outlined in the Project Plan.

**Project Plan**    is a plan which specifies, to an adequate level of detail, the precise nature of the project about to be undertaken, the resources required, the responsibilities of each party, the tasks to be performed and the dependencies and constraints upon the project. Project plans are **much** more than a list of tasks presented in the form of a 'GANTT' chart.

The Project Plan helps in gaining understanding and agreement on project objectives, deliverables, scope, Risk, cost, and approach to be used.

Sometime it is necessary to re-assess the Project Plan by determining if the original business case is still valid. For instance, a project that requires 10,000 effort hours might make business sense. If the more detailed planning process results in a more refined estimate of 20,000 hours, the project may not make business sense any more.

The Project Plan also focuses on making sure the resources one needs are available when they are needed. Providing a high-level baseline, from which progress can be compared is also part of the Project Plan. Finally, the Project Plan is used for validating the processes and managing the project ahead of time with the client.

It should make sense that small projects need a shorter planning cycle, and larger projects need a longer planning cycle.

**Protection Limit Poking**    is when somebody checks the system for flaws in its protections.

**Protocol**    is a set of formal rules describing how to transmit data, especially across a network. Low level protocols define the electrical and physical standards to be observed, bit- and byte-ordering and the transmission and error detection and correction of the bit stream. High level protocols deal with the data formatting, including the syntax of messages, the terminal to computer dialogue, character sets, sequencing of messages etc. Protocols are, therefore, a set of rules that define how communications should take place, as they are common formulas that enable two separate computers to 'speak' with and 'understand' each other.

The first group of protocols includes the Transmission Control Protocol/Internet Protocol (TCP/IP) family, used for communication via Internet. Other examples are such as HTTP that is used for Web page communications, being a subset of TCP/IP.

**Protocol**    can also mean an algorithm, carrried out by more than one party. Here the aim is to maintain some form of security relationship between the parties.

**Prowler**    is a daemon that is run periodically to seek out and erase core files, truncate administrative logfiles, nuke lost and found directories, and cleans up.

**P**

**Proxy**   see Firewall—Application Filter

**Proxy Server**   is a computer server which acts in the place of individual users when connecting to Web sites. The proxy server receives requests from individual workstations and PCs and then sends this request to the Internet. It then delivers the resultant information to the requesting PC on the network.

When used in conjunction with a firewall, a proxy server's identify (and its connected PCs) is completely masked or hidden from other users. This is the manner in which secure sites operate (see Firewall—Application Filter).

**PsychoDoS**   see Denial of Service through Psychological Manipulation

**Public Domain**   is software that can be used by anyone, for any purpose, in any matter without restriction. In contrast to Freeware where the author still retains copyright and control, as well as Shareware that requires a small payment for continued use (see also Open Source).

**Public Key**   see Digital Signature

**Quality** is the process of identifying and administering the activites needed to achieve the quality objectives of an organization. Josep Juran, along with W. Edwards Deming and Philip Crosby, is one of the founders of the quality management movement. Deming and Crosby often spoke of quality in more philosophical terms, urging firms to adopt a quality vision. Juran concentrated on the problems of planning and implementing quality systems.

Juran sees quality based on two principles:

- Managers must realize that they shoulder most of the responsibility for performance of their organizations, not employees;
- Executives must understand the financial benefits that can be realized once quality is made a priority.

Quality is implemented in three stages, namely:

1) Planning stage—quality targets (e.g., Benchmarking, Standard) are set and resources allocated (see also Project Management, Reliability, Validity, Statistics);
2) Control stage—performance is evaluated and compared with goals (Metrics)
3) Gap management stage—quality improvement projects are set up to find ways of closing any gap (e.g., Security), while implementing the solution is launched and tracked as well (e.g., Audit to see if Security has improved or Policies are less often violated than before)

Quality regarding IT Security **is defined by the user** not the producer of the technology (e.g., hardware) or software (e.g., Windows and Microsoft). Therefore, if the customers do not perceive that a product or service delivers adequate security, then the firm has failed. Successful Assessment or

Cost-Benefit analysis requires that management must look outside the company as well as inside.

Assessing Quality regarding security is the first step before implementing a quality system (see Metrics, Benchmarks).

**Quadrature Amplitude Modulation (QAM)-VDSL** (Very-high-bit-rate Digital Subscriber Line) provides wire-speeds from 5 Mbps to 75 Mbps over single-pair copper telephone lines to support simultaneous broadband services such as video, interactive multi-channel television and voice.

QAM-VDSL and DMT-VDSL systems have the same rate/reach performance. QAM is a mature and robust technology & is used in virtually all VDSL systems and is today about 2 years ahead of DMT-VDSL.

Some suggest that today every electric signal in the air (e.g., fax machine is turned on or elevator passes by) or over the telephone wire shuts off the DMT-VDSL system.

But fax machine, stationary and cellular phone can ring, while a video conference is being held. On top of this, plenty of bandwidth is still available to send and receive e-mail if QAM-VDSL is used.

The concept of DMT-based VDSL is derived from the notion that VDSL is 'improved ADSL' (or ADSL plus) and, therefore, has to be based on the same line modulation technology as ADSL (which is DMT). But VDSL is an entirely new technology that has much higher bit rates and symmetric as well as asymmetric capabilities to name two. Reaching true VDSL requires a technology that can operate in a very noisy environment and still provide trouble-free communication. Hence, video, data and voice services over twisted pair copper wires is possible with VDSL.

While the rate/reach factor may be the same for DMT-VDSL and QAM-VDSL, the cost factor rules in favor of QAM and it is also simpler technology compared to DMT-VDSL (see also Asymmetrical Digital Subscriber Line (ADSL), Discrete Multi-Tone (DMT)).

**Rabbit**  is a program that generates multiple copies of itself without attaching to other programs. This type of program is a type of attack often a so-called Denial of Service attack (DoS) based upon excessive use of disk or memory space or CPU cycles.

**Random Access Memory (RAM)**  is the place in the memory where currently running programs are being stored. The Viruses have to infect a part of this memory if they are to remain active.

**Radio Frequency Identification (RFID)**  technology was used by Gillette in field tests for tracking packets of razors through its supply chain. Michelin plans to use vulcanizing to attach an RFID to a tire.

Benetton is another clothing manufacturer that tested RFID tags in some products, such as, by weaving the technology into the collar tags of clothes that cost at least $15 to keep track of them as they ship. Benetton pulled back from this RFID trial after a consumer group announced a global boycott of the clothing manufacturer.

The advantage of RFIDs over barcodes is that information can be collected without a line of sight to the tag, hence, a pallet of goods or a razor can just be scanned by passing through a radio field.

With location tracking chips in mobile phones and toll payment cards the technology can always provide information about where the product and its user are currently located.

This does not look good for data protection and Privacy and consumer advocacy groups have complained loudly and continue fighting for citizen's rights to privacy. The first result was that July 2003, WalMart announced dropping its RFID testing plans. Although WalMart (USA) claimed that this was due to technical problems, it was likely consumer resistance that convinced management to drop the technology.

Tesco (UK) set off a storm of protest during July 2003 after it emerged that the store was automatically photographing consumers as they took Gillette razors from the shelf in Cambridge, Eastern England. Customers were secretly photographed again when they left the store with RFID-tagged products.

It seems as if RFID tags have very few advantages for consumers. For instance, they may help find clothes faster in a store or even making it easier to return items without a receipt, since the store would have recorded the RFID tag. Challenge areas that need addressing are not limited to but including:

- today's political climate one could envision the scenario whereby police and government officials wanting to use this system to nab deadbeat dads, kidnappers and other fugitives of the law.
- All electronic equipment including wireless technology and mobile phones should offer users opt-out as default and even if consumer opts-in by choice, turning off this technology if desired should be a standard feature (see also Privacy–Information Asymmetry, Tables 21B and C)
- Any product incorporating RFID technology (e.g., Gillette shavers) or stores (Wal-Mart to improve logistics) should be de-activated by the time it leaves the store by default and even if the client chooses to keep the technology activated, one must be given the opportunity to deactivate it at a later stage if one wishes to do so.

Even with the above limitations, RFID technology raises security risks regarding Confidentiality, Integrity and Authorization to mention a few issues (see Table 5D). How these will be safeguarded is still unclear.

**RAT**   see Remote Access Tool

**Read Only Memory (ROM)**   is the memory that can only be read, but not written upon. But this has changed with the use of "flash" EEPROMs. ROM is primarily used for the bootstrap programming for PCs.

**Read**   means obtaining the content of data in a storage device, or other data medium.

**Read Only**   can mean two things, namely:

1. A disk, file, data, document etc., which can be viewed, possibly copied, but cannot be changed.
2. Items within a system, such as a ROM Chip, which the system can read from, but not write to.

**Reality Check**   can be described as two things:

(a)  The simplest kind of test of software; doing the equivalent of asking it 'what is $2 + 2$' and seeing if you get '4'. The software equivalent of a smoke test.

(b)  The act of letting a real user try out prototype software.

**Receptive Host**   see Host

**Records**   as a term describes books, papers, maps, photographs, machine readable materials, or other documentary materials, regardless of physical form or characteristics, made or received by an organization.

   To assure documentation and evidence records are being preserved as evidence of the organization's functions, policies, decisions, procedures, operations, or other activities of or because of the informational value of data in them.

**Recordkeeping Requirements**   means what statements, actions and particular records to be created and maintained by the organization to satisfy legislation (see also Jurisdiction, Tables 7A & 16A).

**Recordkeeping System**   is a manual or automated system in which records are collected, organized, and categorized to facilitate their preservation, retrieval, use, and disposition.

**Recovery**   see Redundancy (see also Business Continuity Plan)

**Recycling of Hardware and Media**   describes the process whereby old equipment is being replaced with newer hardware and software. In many countries this is strictly regulated and requires the appropriate disposal of equipment. Some suppliers or manufacturers take the equipment back, and after replacing some parts (e.g., hard-disk and disk drive/reader), may sell it as refurbished or "renew" at an attractive price. Non re-usable parts are disposed off in the appropriate manner.

   **Data Security**—is an issue that matters when a computer or server is returned to the supplier (see Security of Media for more information).

**Redundancy of System**   or System Redundancy is a form of protection against system failures hopefully improving IT Security. It is used to protect systems from failure, data from loss and corruption, and to ensure that communication systems stay online and provide a required amount of performance and assure availability and integrity of data (see also Table 5C, Information Security, Mission Critical).

   To illustrate, making sure having always power supply, one may set up a system whereby in case of failure of supply source A, a back-up generator may provide the energy needed to run the system. Moreover, critical information may be duplicated in order to provide enough bandwidth or failover in the event that primary communication link fails. Another example is whereby critical systems are segregated and run on Virtual Private Networks (e.g., a banks automated teller machines) while e-mails are handled by the firm's normal internet connection (see also Partitioning of Network).

Redundancy can also be used for validation purposes, whereby an additional check digit or bit is included to make sure the right process was being launched (see also Disaster Recovery).

Redundancy does cost and depends on how critical system operations are to the organization (see Critical Infrastructure Protection–CIP, Mirroring, Mission Critical, Multi Level Security).

Redundancy of System must also be supported from a Business Continuity Plan that has been exercised so that kinks may be worked out before the crisis hits. Furthermore, effective Patch management also reduces the Risk of a Threat or Vulnerability being exploited, necessitating the use of the Redundancy feature.

**Mirroring**   see Mirroring

**Recovery**   means recreating data on a computer system after a hardware failure or other disaster has happened.

**Redundant Array of Independent (or Inexpensive) Disks (RAID)**   is a technology for improving data resilience by writing data simultaneously on two disks

**Reference Monitor**   is a security control concept whereby an abstract machine mediates access to objects by subjects. It should be mediating every access, isolated from modification by system entities, and verifiable.

A security kernel is an implementation of a reference monitor for a iven hardware base.

**Registry**   see Windows Registry

**Regression Testing**   see Testing

**Reliability**   is the degree of stability exhibited when a measurement is repeated under identical conditions. Hence, it refers to the degree to which the results obtained by a measurement procedure can be replicated.

Lack of reliability may arise from divergences between observers or instruments of measurement or non-measurability of the attribute being measured.

**Inter-Rater Reliability**   is the degree of stability obtained with a measure between two different observers or raters.

**System Reliability**   describes the system's or its components' ability to perform as required within a specified period of time without having operations being interruped neither due to design, implementation, nor configuration errors.

**Remote Access Tools (RATS)**   enables a person to access a server remotely by using, for instance, a telephone modem or wireless access. RAT can drift in and out of legitimacy according to the prevailing legal climate and the ensuing degree of nervousness displayed by the legal department (see Malware).

Nonetheless, generally **RATS** are defined as being malicious programs that run invisibly on host PCs. They can permit an intruder remote access and if successful give him or her also control of the machine or PC. These programs are usually installed for stealth installation and the programs may by hidden via a Trojan Horse that is embedded in a game or another program. These are usually small files with a size of between 10 KB–30 KB.

An attacker may try to hide this program using a so-called Binder to combine a RAT with legitimate executables, thereby enabling the RAT to execute in the background while the legitimate application runs as well, thereby keeping the victim unaware of these undesirable activities.

Best known RATs are Back Orifice and SubSeven that can capture screen, sound and video content. These Trojans are key loggers, remote controllers, FTP servers, and HTP servers. Telnet servers and password finders are also part of their capabilities and RATS may also rogue mechanisms that hide the Trojans by using encrypted communication. Worse is if they also contain professional-looking APIs, thereby making it feasible for other attackers to insert additional features.

**Invisible Hosting**   could be described as having a Trojan released into the wild embedded in game software or another program for spamming purposes. The Trojan may have a built-in proxy server and sendmail server. The latest variant of the Sobig virus did exactly this. Infected machines can then be remotely controlled by the spammer, who typically uses them to originate spam and to thwart attempts to trace back to the web site where the products are sold. Employing their own DNS servers, the spammers continuously reroute traffic between their customer's web sites and thousands of hijacked PCs across the Internet, making it all but impossible to trace back to the real owner of the web site.

The above makes it more difficult to fight spammers. In the past one could force a web site caught selling products that were promoted by spam. One had to trace the route and who is to determine which ISP controlled the IP address of the offending web server. Informing the ISP permitted it to shut down the server. With Invisible Hosting things are far more difficult (see also Spam).

**Remote Data Storage**   can be described as off-site location, which means it is located in another building, devoted to the storage of computer media, and in particular backup files.

**Removable Storage**   is storage media—such as disks, tapes, and CDs that can easily be removed from a computer and moved to another location or used in another computer.

**Repair**   is a technique used to undo the damage done to a file by Virus infection and/or corruption. Most virus infections can be repaired automatically by an anti-virus program, but there are some, together with other types of (non-viral) data corruption that must be handled manually. Damaged files must be moved into a specially partitioned area while being repaired. Severe and extensive damage to numerous files might require the recovery of an earlier version that of which a backup is available (see also Damages).

**Replicate**   or Reproduce is often used to distinguish the clandestine copying action done by a virus from the normal and deliberate duplication performed by the user.

**Report**   is a free-text message providing the reader with an evaluative statement about IT and wireless security matters, such as benchmarks, good practice approaches and other pertinent information.

A report may range from describing a situation that may harm IT and wireless infrastructure and data and as such is in more detail than a brief. Its length will usually not go beyond 15-typed pages of text, excluding Tables, Figures and reference lists.

As well, reports are issued infrequently and contain information that should be acted upon in a firm's strategic context and/or by citizens with broadband access that may also run their own servers from home. Reports should only contain verified information and include a risk assessment by staff (see also Advisory, Alert, Brief, Scenario)

**Reporting Date**   represents the first date that the incident was reported to a response team or other organization collecting data.

**Reporting Format**   represents the standardized why of recording an incident (e.g., reporting date, site, severity, etc.) on how a corporation reports these internally and subsequently after verification (e.g., within an hour) to the appropriate outside organization (see Computer Emergency Response Team–CERT, Policies, Information Security Policy).

Standardisation regarding Definition and Exchange Format(s) (DEFs) is in the works (see Appendix 6B).

The reporting format and its use are assessed regularly (see Control—Baseline for IT Security, see also Tables 24E & 24F).

More on Reporting Format regarding Vulnerabilities is also provided in Table 22E. Furthermore, Appendix 6—Section B addresses these efforts and outlines some of the challenges for Reporting Format regarding Vulnerabilities.

**Reporting Mechanism** encompasses the Reporting Format uses and Date of the incident. For instance, if reporting is automatic or done according to the log file but again mechanized that is with limited human interference, accumulated numbers can simply be taken and reported (see also Appendix 6—Section B).

The important factor to be considered is the system administrators have rarely if ever time the manually go through log files. Hence, a little program flagging certain occurances and ringing an alarm while a human makes an assessment and than logs the incident and takes the necessary action if need be, seems far more accurate than anything else. If the administrator is later asked, he or she may have an opinion about it and a feel that could be highly accurate or way off the mark but there is no Data available to substantiate it unless a semi-mechanized Data Collection Method is being used (see Tables 24E, 25F and 25G).

**Reporting Sites** are those site names of sites known to have reported an incident.

**Reproduce** see Replicate

**Requests for Comments (RFC)** document series is a set of technical and organizational notes about the Internet (originally the ARPANET), beginning in 1969.

The official specification documents of the Internet Protocol suite that are defined by the Internet Engineering Task Force (IETF) and the Internet Engineering Steering Group (IESG) are recorded and published as *standards track* RFCs.

RFCs must first be published as Internet Drafts (see also Appendix 6, RFC).

**RFC Editor** is the publisher of the RFCs and is responsible for the final editorial review of the documents. The RFC Editor also maintains a master file of RFCs called the "RFC Index", which can be searched online. For nearly 30 years, *The* RFC Editor was Jon Postel; today the RFC Editor is a small group funded by the Internet Society.

**Research** is the systematic investigation of a subject aimed at new knowledge or information (discovering data) and/or interpreting relations among the subject's parts.

Research aims at increasing our understanding (the why) of the phenomenon or phenomena being investigated. It often analyzes primary data (collected by a Researcher) or secondary one (e.g., from others or public statistics). Research can consist of empirical observation or hypothesis testing. A preplanned research design such as a survey, experiment and archival data may be used depending on the topic of investigation.

**Inductive Research**   is primarily based on curiosity in an issue. We can also call it navel gazing, whereby a researchers presents a theory that predicts new relationships and generalizations not thought or considered of earlier. An example is when Albert Einstein came up with today's famous Relativity Theory.

**Deductive Research**   is based on analyzing previous research and finding a perceived need for providing additional answers to issues to be investigated.

**Proprietary Research**   is research conducted on behalf of a client and may not be released into the public domain. Hence, while quality may be good, the ultimate test of having it put to public scrutiny is missing (see also Cryptographer).

**Peer Review**   means that the research has been studied by knowledgeable peers, before it gets published and/or peers who read the published article. Hence, such peers comment on the work and may require changes, improvements or further clarification before it can be published. Naturally, the popular press does not count as peer review (see also Peer Review).

Reading about a research finding in the popular press, one should pay attention to the motivations of the researchers and the public relations people who convinced the reporters to write about it. If the press release is based on a publication or a research paper presented and distributed at a conference and/or published in Best Paper Proceedings, academic peer-review will happen in the subsequent months after the conference and publication date (see also Program–Peer-Review).

**Researcher**   are individuals that conduct research, that is ultimately reviewed by peers for its quality and merit and subsequently published or else published and reviewed and discussed by experts who read the material. As such similar to Open Source Code or Software, research becomes public by being submitted for review before being published either in a journal or on the Web (see Theory).

**Anti-Virus Researcher or Security Assurance Researcher**   may conduct his or her research in many ways. An example might be a lawyer searching among old court cases for legal precedents regarding Privacy and Hacking.

An epidemiologist studying age groups or cohorts and hip-fracture incidents to an Anti-Virus Researcher studying malicious code to discover programming patterns and characteristics (see Theory).

Often Anti-Virus Research is used synonymously with "product development." Sometimes, a "bonafide antivirus researcher's" role within his or her organization might be documented by independent examination (see also Appendix 3 and badguys website).

And while the media may claim that antivirus research is considered among the most advanced fields of software development, it is still questionable if it represents Research as understood in science or technician work that deciphers code and programs remedies against Malicious code as fast as possible.

**Resident**   means a program that stays resident in the memory of the computer, while other programs are running, waiting for a specific trigger even.

An anti-Virus program may be memory resident, continuously scanning all the elements involved in any operation, such as files, email messages with attachments, and loading a file from a removable diskette.

Viral programs often attempt to 'go resident,' and so this is one of the functions that an activity monitor may check.

**Resource Description Framework (RDF)**   uses the subject, verb, object structure of the simple sentence. RDF can link different pages, concepts and assertions in order to create relationships between—and make statements about—people, things and properties. It allows the formalization of reationships and begins to contextualize Web resources as more than just links. Hence, A is dependent on B is one condition while relationships beweent documents, documents and people, people and organizations, people and places is possible as well.

Hence, RDF allows defining in a machine readable form that the chief security engineer is the author of a particular article on a Web site (see also Semantic Web, Extensive Mark-up Language—XML).

**Response**   see CERT

**Restore Data**   function is usually only performed when data are lost, corrupted, or otherwise changed. It is extremely important to review and test the restore procedures, to ensure that, in an emergency, appropriate action can be taken. A real danger, when restoring files from the backup, is that of restoring additional files which then over-write newer files. Were this to happen to an order processing system, or other system which records transactions, such an error could result in severe loss.

To avoid even the possibility of such an error, files must be restored to a specific location that is separate from the live files. After having verified the integrity of the restored file(s), they may be copied to the required area; again, cautiously and with consideration for the risks involved (see also Backup).

**Revenues or Earnings**–describes the revenues generated by the firm through the sales of its products and services.

In the information system context, revenues might be generated from the firms e-Commerce site (e.g., sales leads and contacts) or advertising (pageviews, clicks on ads, etc.). The firm may also advertise on other sites such as web portals or internet search engines (See also Webpages–Unauthorized Embellishment).

**Hiding of Pop-Up Windows**   occurs with software that provides code that hides pop-up windows behind the windows already on screen. These pop-ups remain in place and are revealed only after one minimizes or closes the other windows on screen—by which time it is difficult to determine where the pop-ups came from. The solution, such as it is, is to disable JavaScript; alternatively, if one can locate the offending sites, one can put them on a firewall's or browser's exclusion list.

Other products may deliberately overlay banner ads. They insert their own choice of advertisement using exactly the same dimensions as the original banner ad and fix their substitute to the same place on the Web page, thus obliterating the original entirely (see also Firewall–Rejecting Ads, Spam).

**Other Ad-Blocking Software**   can perform the same function as above or even without Firewall capabilities blocking advertising. Many such tools are available even as freeware.

The problem is that a Webpage may include links and advertisements but a user may have installed software that alters functions and appearance of Web pages before the user can see the intended content or advertisement. While the individual has the liberty to install whatever he or she wants on his or her PC, things are different for corporate PCs (see Policies).

It is not even certain that ultimately individuals and firms that provide such software may not be liable (see Jurisdiction), because they provide the tool that modifies work (e.g., Web page design) made by others without their explicit permission. It is a bit similar to modifying an artists painting or music/song without securing a license beforehand permitting one to do so. Only case law will show how this will be played out.

**RFC**   see Requests for Comments

**RFID**    see Radio Frequency ID

**Rich Text Format (RTF)**   embeds complex formatting information as text tags readable by most word processors. Unlike Word documents, RTF documents do not support VBA macros. Nonetheless, there are circumstances in which an RTF document can be a virus transmission vector.

For security reasons, one should never distribute Word documents and if possible, delete most if not nearly all of the information saved. And even if one has succeeded in deleting most of the information, sending the Word document using Outlook eMail software may negate all these efforts by default up to and including Windows XP or 2003 versions (see Appendix 3 for more details and step-by-step guide to achieve greater privacy with Word).

Regardless of this success, any Webpage including the one managed by Microsoft should have files uploaded in pdf format only to really protect authors' privacy successfully.

**Rijndael Algorithm**   was finally chosen as the winner because it was the fastest of them all. The algorithm was broken shortly after its adoption by Mike Boyle and Chris Salter as well as by Phillip Rogaway within days of its publication as the accepted AES. However, academic breaks are the ones that force you to change things in the design process; practical breaks force you to change things in fielded equipment. This work is clearly of the academic-break variety (see Tables 11A & 11B).

**Risk**   entails a probability that something positive or negative might occur.

**Risk perception**   is a cognitive evaluation (what people *think* about risks)

Attitudes (see Attitudes) and behaviors have both *cognitive* and *affective* components. Cognitive evaluations of risk may diverge from affective, emotional reactions (not be correlated).

Table 22A outlines these issues in further detail

**Emotional component of risk worry**   or the affective emotions people have. Virtually all theories of choice under risk are cognitive (see Table 22A).

**Table 22A:** Cognitive and Emotional Components of Risk—Perception and Worry

| Name of Concept | Description |
| --- | --- |
| Risk Perception | Risk perception refers to a judgement about the presence and size of a risk. It is the cognitive component and represents what people **think about risks**. |
| Worry | Worry calls for emotional reactions to the Risk and represents how people **feel about risks**. |

Worry and Risk are only weakly related. People can perceive the risk of a certain event as particularly high, but not be worried.

On the opposite, people might see an activity as not risky, but be very worried that something might go wrong.

**Note**. While risk perception deals with the thinking about risks, worry addresses the person's feeling about risks.

**Table 22B:** Risk: Experts versus Lay-People

| Name of Concept | Description |
| --- | --- |
| Lay-Person | Judge risks associated with technologies based on factors such as: |
| | —certainty to be fatal, |
| | —newness, |
| | —catastrophic potential, |
| | —dread and |
| | —delay of the effects |
| Expert | Use probabilities and size of loss to assess the magnitude of risks |

Because of these different views on risks, network administrators that invest and make use of security technologies to tackle internet risks, don't necessarily construct an environment that is seen by the users as trustworthy.

The link between security technologies and confidence is in fact based on the unverified assumption that users will accept these technologies as substitute for trust. Internet security technology providers may fail to gain commitments from users even though all the conditions are present to assert that the system is technically dependable.

Note. How lay people differ in their assessment of risks compared to 'experts.'

This is also related to Trust, whereby a higher level could reduce Risk Perception (see Trust–Confidence).

**Risk Assessment**   determines the likelihood of negative events, and also assesses the extent of harm that could emanate out of such events.
As Table 22B outlines, experts assess the risk differently than lay-people.

**Risk Management**   is the decision making process that combines information about risks with economic, ethical, legal, and political considerations.
    Table 22C outlines how a business may assess or categorize Risks related to the internet.

**Risk Communication**   is the exchange of information and preferences between decision makers, investors, and other important stakeholders such as customers and suppliers.
    Table 22D focuses the Risk paradigm on the individual user such as the employee or grand-mother using her PC at home.
    Experts usually assess risk as a probability of an event to occur and distinguish between two types of risks namely:

1. **Systematic Risk.**   This type of risk can usually be controlled for and is reduced by, for instance, building investment portfolios holding stocks, bonds, treasury bills and other investment instruments—to reduce the potential for losses due

**Table 22C:** The Business Perspective of Internet and IT Security Risks

| Business risks | Examples |
|---|---|
| Financial loss due to fraud | An external or insider hacker wrongfully transfers funds |
| Theft of valuable information | An intruder gains access to confidential information on proprietary technology or marketing information |
| Loss of business opportunity through disruption of service | Deliberate attacks or accidental events halt internet services for long or unacceptable periods |
| Unauthorized use of resources | An attacker exploits services to which he/she has gained illegitimate access |
| Costs resulting from uncertainties | Technical failures add a burden of costs due to extra procedures and time needed for repairing, or due to disputes that have substantial costs |
| Loss of customer confidence or respect | Actual (or simply perceived) fallacy of a company's technology damage its image |

Note. The above Table illustrates that managers may focus on particular facets of risks as they pertain to operations.

to economic cycles. The risk for power outages may be managed by having a back-up generator, and by limiting access to confidential data to a group of people and/or machines that absolutely need that access to perform their tasks and duties. (See Risk).

2. **Unsystematic Risk.**   This is risk from which an investor (or information system specialist) cannot usually be protected (e.g., natural disasters looming in the future). (See Risk).

**Table 22D:** The User's Perspective of Internet and IT Security Risks

| User's Risks | Examples |
|---|---|
| Financial loss | The user loses money or a valuable information, either because he or she is victim of a fraud as result of an online purchase, or because a computer virus has infected the hard disk |
| Performance loss | Due to a bad connection, the waiting time to receive and send data lowers user's actions |
| Physical loss | A product purchased online results harmful or unhealthy, or the user gets in touch with potentially dangerous individuals |
| Psychological loss | An addiction to the use of internet applications, or the dissatisfaction with a product purchased online |
| Social loss | The interaction with people offline becomes less frequent and more difficult for the user, or online communication is misunderstood by the recipient |
| Time loss | Wasting time by browsing web pages and following hyperlinks to information not related to the original goal |

Note. The table outlines how users may focus on potential losses when trying to assess the risks that they might be exposed to by using the internet and IT technology.

Systematic and unsystematic risk together makes up 1.0, the total risk. We need to assess the probability of a risk actually materializing. For simplicity's sake we call it **Probability of Risk (PR)**. Accordingly, we can assess what the **PR** that a particular unsystematic event will occur is and what the costs culminating out of this occurrence is.

The above systematic or unsystematic risk needs to be ranked and assessed to determine the necessary countermeasures that are needed to protect the firm's Assets.

Finally Table 22E focuses on Risks in relationship with the visibility of a computer on the network (internal and external such as the internet) in conjunction with Vulnerabilities and how this may increase or decrease Risks regarding one's network resources.

**Risk Threat**   requires that the individual threats, their source and probability of occurrence must be identified. For instance, if the chief executive officer mails out an announcement about upcoming staff cuts, what is the possible threat that such information ends up with the media.

1) Hardly Detectable Threat
2) Low
3) Average Threat
4) High
5) Extreme Threat

There is probably at least a high threat that such information will be leaked to the press by one or more employees.

**Risk Consequence**   entails the consequence or harm caused to the system services or resources as result of the lost or compromise of an asset. Harm is not related to the threat likelihood. While the threat likelihood of loosing a proxy server due to an unstable operating system may be 'high', harm could be 'minor' if the proxy server supporting the service or resources is not viewed by the data owner or management as critical. Every rated threat could then also be rated as per its consequence using a scale similar to the one below:

1) Hardly Detectable Consequence
2) Minor
3) Average Consequence
4) Severe
5) Grave Consequence

**Table 22E:** Network Security Risks–Visibility and Vulnerability

| Technological Risks | Examples |
|---|---|
| Network Security Risks | Can be divided into two broad categories: Visibility and Vulnerability |
| Visibility | Is a problem when a private network service is inadvertently offered to the public. In these cases, the service is not the problem, but its Visibility is. Examples might be open ports on a home user that is online using broadband. |
| | It's relatively easy to test for Visibility issues: A simple port scanner will do. However, Visibility tests have to be done from outside the Firewall. This is especially important for home users with a broadband connection to check if their Firewall is configured properly avoiding Visibility where not necessary. |
| | Netbios, the Windows "Network Neighborhood" protocol is another Visibility example. Though NETBIOS is wonderfully useful, it should *never* be permitted to enter or leave an organization's network. Seeing NETBIOS open when performing a network security audit is a serious error, even if a Hacker were unable to leverage it for increased privilege. |
| | Even a perfectly patched and locked-down web server presents a Visibility problem if private content is reachable from the outside world (by mistake). The employee phone directory is not always public information. |
| Vulnerability | is a problem when a service is intentionally offered to the outside world, but the service has a flaw that grants an outsider greater access than was intended. Vulnerabilities from a Network Security Risk perspective can be divided further as outlined below. |
| | **Firewalls protect against Visibility issues, not Vulnerability issues**. Whether a Netopia router, BullGuard on PC, or ipchains in a Linux kernel, Firewalls selectively block traffic as it enters and leaves a system. |
| | A Firewall should block all traffic that is not specifically permitted. However, if the Firewall is programmed to allow inbound traffic to port 80/tcp—the web server—and it turns out that the web server can be exploited via the HTTP protocol, the Firewall will happily pass all traffic, good and bad. |
| | Only a few Firewalls (typically very high end ones) can filter some malicious traffic, but one should never rely on a Firewall to protect badly run public services. |
| | Testing for Vulnerabilities is an involved process. Also not all software vulnerabilities have to become a Vulnerability issue. For instance, with a properly configured Firewall installed on a network, other things considered being equal, it does not matter whether a server has a bug or not because the outside world cannot even attempt an exploit. |

(cont.)

**Table 22E:** (cont.)

| Technological Risks | Examples |
|---|---|
| General vulnerabilities | Examples might be such as default installs of operating systems and applications; accounts with no passwords or weak passwords; non-existent or incomplete backups.<br>A common vulnerability is an unpatched or misconfigured web server that can be fooled into running operating system commands. Exploiting a buffer overflow in *sendmail* to obtain a root shell is another common vulnerability fault. |
| Windows vulnerabilities | Could be such as Unicode Vulnerability (Web server folder traversal); ISAPI extension buffer overflows; NETBIOS–unprotected Windows networking shares |
| Unix vulnerabilities | could be such as, buffer overflows in RPC services; Sendmail vulnerabilities; Bind weaknesses |
| Categorization | Suggests that Vulnerabilities should be categorized according to least the following information shall be mapped to categories:<br><br>• reader audiences,<br>• vendor including product affected and platform(s) it is being used,<br>• vulnerability impact as well as<br>• attack vector,<br>• severity, and<br>• class of vulnerability. |
| Definition and Exchange Format(s) (DEFs). | to be used widely requires that they are standardized across groups (see Appendix 6B for an an overview). In order to parse this information using of Extensible Markup Language (XML) is required. Hence, DEF as well as Categorization of information stored about vulnerabilities is required to enable systems to parse out the information required to Patch Vulnerabilities or take other measures necessary to reduce Risks. |

**Note.** See also Figures 1–3

Considering the previous example of the lay-off notice by the CEO being passed on to the media, damage may be minor because the same news was also related to the media in a press release emailed and faxed the same day.

**Risk–Treat Countermeasure**    to be taken depends upon the threat level and consequence as rated beforehand by security officers and data owners.

**Robot**    is a machine which performs certain functions usually done by people (or, in a disparaging sense, it is a person that behaves like a machine.) In our vernacular it is the name used for any mechanical device that looks or behaves like a living entity; so a machine that looks even vaguely like a dog and emits a barking sound becomes a "dog robot," while a machine that talks is referred to as a "talking robot." The noun robot (without the use of any modifiers) is used to describe any machine with an external covering that gives it an anthropoidal appearance, or machines that simply move while in what appears to be an erect position.

In the IT Security context this term (sometimes abbreviated as Bot) can also describe little programs designed to perform automated tasks on the Internet, such as indexing, looking/watching for message contents, or to act as avatars (human surrogates). On IRC, Robots can be malicious by cloning themselves (clonebots), or flooding the IRC channels with garbage (floodbots). There are hundreds of different types of Robots or Bots including, by some definitions, Agents and Crawlers.

**Rogue** is a program with a bug, interfering with normal system operations. Any damage caused is unintentional. The term is used in the mainframe circles and not very often used these days.

**Role** is the functions that are to be performed and relates to positions that entail certain tasks and responsibilities. Using roles to control access can be an effective means for developing and enforcing enterprise-specific security poligies, and for streamlining the security management process (see also Access Rights).

**Role of User** is based on the analysis of the tasks that must be performed to fill a position. Hence, the analysis is the foundation for deciding about the person's authority or need for gaining access to data or information from the organization (e.g., customers, suppliers and employees) and processes to be performed such as entering, manipulating, storing, or retrieving data (see also Role of User, User, Superuser).

**Role-Based Access Control (RBAC)** means that access decisions are based on the roles the user has as part of tasks to be performed (see also Access Control).

The central notion of RBAC is that users do not have discretionary access to enterprise objects. Instead, access permissions are administratively associated with roles, and users are administratively made members of appropriate roles. This idea greatly simplifies management of authorization while providing an opportunity for great flexibility in specifying and enforcing enterprise- specific protection policies. Users can be made members of roles as determined by their responsibilities and qualifications and can be easily reassigned from one role to another without modifying the underlying access structure. Roles can be granted new permissions as new applications and actions are incorporated, and permissions can be revoked from roles as needed.

R

The association of operations with roles within an enterprise can be in compliance with rules that are self-imposed. For example, a health care provider may decide that the role of Clinician must be constrained to post only the results of certain tests rather than distribute them where routing and human errors can result in a violation of a patient's right to privacy. Operations can also be specified in a manner that can be used in the demonstration and enforcement of laws or regulations. For example, a nurse can be constrained to adding a new entry to a patient's history of treatments rather than being generally able to modify a patient record. A pharmacist can be provided with operations to dispense, but not to prescribe, medication.

**ROM**   see Read-Only Memory.

**Root**   is the name of the superuser on a Unix system and also the ancestor of all files on a Unix system.

**Root access**   means that the user has the same privileges as *super user*, on UNIX systems usually called *root*.

**Rootkit**   usually describes a set of tools used to replace system binaries on compromised UNIX systems.

Rootkit usually replaces useful and often used commands with versions that have built in *Trojans* and/or *backdoors*. The name rootkit probably comes from the fact that one has to have *root access* to replace such binaries. There are rootkits for Microsoft Windows available as well.

**Router**   is an interconnection device similar to a bridge but serves packets or frames containing certain protocols. Hence, Routers link Local Area Networks (LANs) at the network layer.

But with Home Users installing their own routers, Denial of Serive Attacks can become a nightmare. For instance, in May 2003, the University of Wisconsin–Madison found that it was the recipient of a continuous large scale flood of inbound Internet traffic destined for one of the campus' public Network Time Protocol (NTP) servers. The flood traffic rate was hundreds-of-thousands of packets-per-second, and hundreds of megabits-per-second.

The only recourse available to the University was to go to its ISP and asking it to null-route all this traffic to the university servers, meanwhile paying a huge increase in bandwidth costs—an increase that seriously hurt the university's IT budget, and would have quickly depleted it they ISP did not respond by null-routing the traffic.

While NetGear has "fixed" this problem in their latter router images, very few customers have bothered to update their firmware quickly, and the attack continues to this day. NetGear and others need to be given the necessary incentive (i.e., Risk being put out of business, and the management put behind bars) to actively induce all customers to update their routers ASAP, so that this Attack will be a thing of the past.

Other software has caused similar problems for other sites. For example, NetTime was the reason why ultimeth.net was taken off the air. Unfortunately, the owners of what is now ultimeth.com continue to see very high DNS traffic for the time servers which no longer exist at the original IP addresses, and where even the names were removed from the DNS long ago.

Many of the source IP addresses are generating queries on the order of one per second, which gets unbelievably high when considering thousands or tens of thousands of clients worldwide.

The issue is in part the many PCs running Microsoft Operating Systems, with seriously broken DNS resolvers, which don't do any caching and which can re-query for nonexistent data as quickly as the program can ask for the information. Since NetTime can be set to recheck the time sync every second, this causes very severe problems.

The above case also raises issues about Jurisdiction (Table 16A, can Net-Gear be sued for negligence as part of product warranty and Liability legislation, if not the USA in another country?) and did NetGear put enough state of the art technology, Quality Control efforts and more into the product to make it secure such as Best Practice or Benchmarks (see Swiss legislation–Appendix 5, also Table 16A–Liability, also Testing Testing Liability).

**Routing Information Protocol (RIP)** is defined by RFC1058 (version 1) and RFC1723 (version 2). It is UDP based protocol providing routing information exchange between routers.

**RSA** see Encryption (Table 3)

**RTF** see Richt Text Format

**Rule Based Detection** sometimes also called misuse detection, detects intrusions by looking for activity that corresponds to a known intrusion techniques or system Vulnerabilities.

R

**Safety**   see Security

**Safety Engineering**   see Security Engineering

**Sample**   is a subset of the population. On the basis of observing the sample, generalizations are made to the population. An example might be Home Users with Broadband access to the internet in Flanders region compared to those in Wallony region (both in Belgium) regarding Virus infections and prevalence of a certain virus that was released at date X (see also Acceptable Sampling).

**Representative Sample**   of the population (e.g., Home Users with Broadband access in Flanders) means that we need to have both women and men in the sample as well as older and younger respondents. We do not want a **biased** sample that will lead us to making erroneous statements about the population (see also Confidence Level–Table 15B, Statistics, Significance).

**Random Sampling**   means that every member of the population has an equal chance of being selected for the sample (see also Statistical Inference).

Hence, making conclusions about Virus Prevalence (see Tables 24E and 24F) based on a vendor A's customer sample in the USA may be misleading, considering that vendor's B primary Home User customer base is in Japan. Vendor A may have to limit his or her statement regarding Home Users in the US.

Unfortunately, sometimes neither vendors nor journalists seem to be considering these sampling issues carefully enough, thereby making Statistical Inferences and Generalizations based on Samples that do not meet usual requirements (see also Methodology, Reliability, Sample, Theory, Validity of Study)

**Satan**  is a freeware Security Administrator Tool for Analyzing Networks by remotely probing and identifying the vulnerabilities of systems or IP networks, helps identify system security weaknesses. It has been developed by Wietse Venema and Dan Farmer and its release to a public hands caused lot of controversies. It has not been maintained after the initial release and it's value is nearly zero nowadays.

**Satellite Broadband Access**  are high-speed satellite internet access services that propel themselves into markets where cable and DSL access are unavailable (see also Asymmetrical Digital Subscriber Line–ADSL or Digital Subscriber Line–DSL, Broadband and Cable)

**Scan**  happens when accessing a set of targets sequentially in order to identify which one has a specific characteristic (see also Vulnerability Scanner).

**Scanning**  is the activity aiming to collect wealth of information about the targeted network and host–scanning collects *IP address*es, open and closed ports, used services and operating systems of targets.

  Nonetheless, Scanning can mean different things to different people, such as:

1) allows a user to have a program try out a set of sequentially changing numbers or code (e.g., search for Viruses);
2) Using a peripheral device to 'capture' documents, text, graphics, etc., into a system to make the information available to users.
3) Taking a radio device to scan the airwaves for electronic transmissions with view to interception.

**Scanner**  see Vulnerability Scanner

**Scenario**  is a free-text description of approximately 200–400 words describing in non-technical language a security-related event affecting IT and wireless infrastructure.

  The audience for such a scenario may be an entrepreneur, business owner, private citizen or a policy-decision maker that uses the Scenario to get a better grasp of possible financial and social consequences if certain IT security-related decisions are being made. For instance, saving costs by not installing a firewall may result in risks that could damage databases. Not spending the time and resources to formulate, implement and enforce an eMail retention policy carries the Risk of being unable to produce certain viable documentation in case of a law suit against the firm (see also Forensics, Jurisdiction, Table 16A & 16B).

As the above suggests, a Scenario outlines what could happen and spells out the financial consequences, thereby making it easier for citizens and entrepreneurs to understand why certain investments in IT security may be important to prevent possible disaster (see also Advisory, Alert, Brief, Report, Tables 24E–24G).

**Scope creep**   occurs when users demand additional functionalities that are in excess of what was originally agreed. This normally results from a failure to establish clear requirements beforehand (see Project Management, User Acceptability).

Continually reviewing and altering direction in a project is not helpful. While the outcome may not be the perfect turnkey solution, a product will be available and can be tested against User Acceptance Criteria.

**Screen Savers**   are used as a means of both protecting the screen and also for preventing casual shoulder surfing. Screen savers do have a useful and valid Information Security role. Used correctly, they will blank the screen from view or put up a picture or other visual, in turn requiring a user or network Administrator password to regain access.

Provided the Screen Saver is set to trigger maybe two minutes of inactivity, and upon user request, it can provide a useful and effective means of diverting casual/opportunistic incidents. But it is by no means a secure measure to prevent somebody from getting access to the machine if given enough time (e.g., if machine is left on overnight).

Hence, Authorized screensavers should be used only since downloading others represents a Risk that seems unnecessary in a corporate setting.

**Script**   is a series of commands entered into a file that can be run or executed by an operating system shell, such as a Unix one. In the personal computer world, batch files are equivalent of scripts.

A script can also represent automatic command files that exist in different operating systems. There are many different types of scripts–some of which have been used for creating viruses.

**Script Kiddie**   is a derogatory term used by "real" Hackers and security professionals for less skilled hackers. These Hackers usually use scripts and tools from internet without appropriate knowledge. They often target Unix hosts with tools that are for targeting of MS Windows hosts and vice versa. It has been observed that these hackers are not having much knowledge and even simple system commands may pose a significant challenge to them. Unfortunately, these types of Hackers can cause as much harm as "real" Hackers can.

**Scumware** (sometimes called Thiefware) is any software that significantly changes the appearance and functions of web pages, without permission of Webmasters or Copyright holders (see also Firewall, Revenues/Advertising, Webpages-Unauthorized Embellishment). Hence Scumware:

- makes unauthorized changes in the appearance and content viewed on a Webpage affecting more than one user;
- could imply relationships or endorsements of products, services or advertising that is incorrect;
- affects the contractual relationships between content providers and advertisers (see Jurisdiction)
- may result in modifications of content that culminates in unauthorized derivative work.

For example, some products install themselves without warning users, others bury the details of their Web-page modifications in the extensive legalese of end-user license agreements. Some Scumware is difficult or impossible to uninstall, or it might introduce instability into the operating system, and conflict with other applications.

To illustrate, Microsoft announced the XP Smart Tags 'feature' permitting specific words in lists to cause pop-up menus offering options for useful functions, such as formatting a text. Nonetheless, critiques of Windows Explorer 6 stated that if Smart Tags were to be implemented, there would be an opportunity to hijack web content by showing extra hyperlinks. These would, of course, direct users to Microsoft-related sites or those that had bought advertising in the Smart Tag space.

Public pressure convinced Microsoft to withdraw its proposal for Smart Tags in the Internet Explorer (see also Click Wrap Agreement, License).

**Secret Key** is sometimes used to mean the private key of a public key system, and in other cases used, in contrast to Public Key, to refer to a symmetric key system (see also Digital Signature-Public Key)

**Sector** means pie-shaped slices and track that are concentric rings on a disk. A combination of two or more sections on a single track makes a cluster or block, the minimum unit used to store information. The number of sectors per track determines the size of each cluster. In turn, the number of clusters on a disk's surface decides the storage capacity of the disk.

The sector is the smallest unit that can be accessed on a disk and it has a size of 512 Bytes.

**Secure Area** (or sand pit–see Java) is an area on a system which is totally shielded and/or isolated, from the potential impact of any code which is executed there. Whilst the isolation of the system is a clear requirement, scanning software which is able to detect Malicious Code activity must also be used. Nonetheless, as Trojan code activity may go undetected.

Such an area is particularly useful for downloaded files from the Internet. Such a file should not be opened or executed in the normal filing space for live systems or on a user's PC. Instead, a Secure Area should be used.

**Secure Hash**   A process which reduces a message of arbitrary length to a fixed length fingerprint which is very unlikely to be the same for any other message. The word "secure" indicates that the algorithm has been chosen so that it is not possible to forge a message which to have given hash value, nor to create two similar messages with the same hash value.

**Securematics**   is the study of information, data and the ways to handle it in a secure way, especially by means of information, communication and computing technologies.

There is a growing interest and concern with the way in which information and information technology shape human behavior and, conversely, the way human behavior shapes our development and application of information and information technology, in particular, regarding security of information, data while protecting individuals rights and responsibilities. These interests and concerns have helped to define Securematics as a domain reaching well beyond a single discipline, such as computer science, engineering or management.

Securematics encompasses research and Inventions from the natural, medical and social sciences, as well as humanities and engineering.

Table 23A is an incomplete endeavor for outlining the disciplinary roots and foundations of activities related to Information Security. Domains of Information Security Space (DISS) (see below) lists various theoretical, conceptual, practical and applied issues regarding information security.

Table 23A tries to systematize these issues in more detail by moving from disciplinary and scientific roots (first column) to sub-disciplines, theorys and methods as well as applications.

While Securematics concentrates on three major domains—technology, information and people—the primary interest is the intersection of these elements.

**Domains of Information Security Space (DISS)**   means different things to different people but in some cases, certification bodies define DISS as containing 10 specific domains, namely:

1. Access control systems and methodology.
2. Applications and systems development.
3. Business continuity planning.

**Table 23A:** Schemata with the Scientific Roots of Information Security–The Birth of Securematics

| Scientific Disciplines | Scientific Sub-Disciplines | Concepts, Methods, Models or Theories | Securematics |
|---|---|---|---|
| Computing Science | —Data Communication<br>—Computer and Human Interaction<br>—Programming<br>—Software<br>—Computer and Society<br>—Theoretical Computer Science | —Software Design<br>—Computation<br>—Cryptography<br>—Electronic Commerce (eCommerce)<br>—Encryption and Keys<br>—Information theory<br>—Network security<br>—Identity Management Security | —Information retrieval and storage<br>—Informatics (social & structural)<br>—Privacy<br>—Prevention–technical measures<br>—Malicious Code and viruses<br>—Vulnerabilities<br>—Software metrics, reliability and testing<br>—Software engineering and programming<br>—Databases<br>—Secure Audit Logs and Computer Forensics |
| Engineering | —Circuits & Systems<br>—Communication<br>—Computing<br>—Informatics<br>—Information Technology<br>—Security<br>—Theoretical Computing<br>—Mathematical Computing | —Authentication theory<br>—Systems and methodology<br>—Applications and systems development.<br>—Cryptography.<br>—Physical security.<br>—Security architecture and models.<br>—Security management practices<br>—Social implications of technology<br>—Telecommunications, network and internet security. | —Disaster recovery<br>—Encryption and key management<br>—EpiSystemiology<br>—Identity management<br>—Physical and operational security<br>—Role-based access management<br>—Redundancy design and management<br>—System application and management<br>—User issues |
| Management | —Human Resource Management & Personnel<br>—Corporate Strategy & Policy | —Recruiting, selection, and career development<br>—Cognition | —Awareness raising<br>—Learning, skills training and continuous education |

(cont.)

**Table 23A:** (cont.)

| Scientific Disciplines | Scientific Sub-Disciplines | Concepts, Methods, Models or Theories | Securematics |
|---|---|---|---|
| | —Technology and Innovation Management<br>—Organizational Behavior (micro and macro)<br>—Organizational and Institutional Theory<br>—Management Information Systems (MIS)<br>—Communication Science, Technology & Society | —Innovation and adaptation of disruptive vs. continuous technologies<br>—System design, implementation and auditing<br>—Coordination and management within institutional structure (e.g., organizational structure)<br>—Using multiple communication channels<br>—Ethics<br>—Planning | —Trust and Confidence<br>—Return on Security Investment (ROSI)<br>—Business continuity planning and management<br>—Information security management<br>  —risk assessment, policy definition, planning and implementation<br>  —operation, audit, testing and certification<br>  —responding to an event, post-mortem and forensics<br>—Prevention management–human and institutional factors |
| Social Sciences & Humanities | —Information & Library Science<br>—Communication<br>—Philosophy<br>—Law | —Archiving<br>—Ethics, Morals and Justice<br>—Regulation<br>—Content, format and type of communication | —Data storage–access, preservation of media<br>—Copyright and software piracy<br>—Jurisdiction e-commerce<br>—Code of Conduct |

**Note.** The above contents are neither listed in order of importance nor all inclusive. Accordingly, there might be some additional material that should be included but was omitted due to space limitations.

The importance of the table is to illustrate that various major scientific disciplines are the foundation of information security-related activities. It suggests that an interdisciplinary approach is required, while simplistic training may result in technicians being able to use a brush approach instead of providing comprehensive solutions. However, System Complexity requires specialists with different educational backgrounds and experience to safeguard information and systems from Attacks. Accordingly, no human can possibly cover the whole spectrum of Securematics.

Accordingly, Securematics has Technical and a Social component (see also text for definitions) and while these may further evolve into sub-disciplines, their homes will in part decide about content and focus. Thus, attending a course about Social Securematics in a Communication Department will be different than if it were given in Computing Engineering or Psychology.

4. Cryptography.
5. Law, investigation and Ethics (see Table 16B) including Forensics.
6. Operations security.
7. Physical security.
8. Security architecture and models.
9. Security management practices.
10. Telecommunications, network and internet security.

During August 2003, the USA National Security Agency (NSA) announced its intent in offering a new certification level for its information technology staff. NSA's certification is supposed to build and expand upon other programs and does, therefore, go beyond the ten listed domains and culminate in the Information Systems Security Engineering Professional (IS-SEP) certification covering the following subject matters or Domains of Information Security Space (DISS):

11. Systems security engineering.
12. Technology management.
13. Certification and accreditation.
14. USA government information assurance regulations.

**Social Securematics (SS)** refers to the body of research and study that examines social aspects of security and information including the roles of technology in protecting information and data, the ways that the social organization of information and are influenced by social forces and social practices. Hence, SS represents the interdisciplinary study of security matters including design, uses and consequences of computing, communication and information technologies that take into account their interaction with institutional and cultural contexts.

SS studies aim to ensure that research agendas regarding information security is socially-driven rather than technology-driven based on two dimensions:

1. process whereby security is made relevant to the social dynamics of the situation or the institutional and regulatory context, and
2. substance involving the actual security design and system implementation and dynamics being made relevant to the end-user requirements

Based on the above Social Securmatics helps in setting priorities for design and implementation of security-related technologies, policies, systems and regulation. As such, SS has it its core social concerns that, in turn, define the technical work required for securing information and data.

Social Securematics focuses on safeguarding users' information assets and data while studying how technology, systems, procedures and behaviors can help to achieve security for safeguarding this connection (see Table 23A).

SS includes but is not limited to the studies and other analyses that are part of the security domain including awareness, confidence, ethics, information policy, prevention, privacy, regulation, risk assessment/management, worry, and trust (see also Table 23A).

**Secure Socket Layer (SSL)**   means that the communications between the client and the (host) web server are encrypted and, additionally, that the host web server may be validated by the client using a Digital Certificate on the server (see also Hyper Text Transfer Protocol). SSL is a protocol developed by Netscape. The most common application of SSL is https for ssl-encrypted http. Nowadays, many other protocols use advantages of SSL, such as POP, SMTP, and NNTP.

**SSLeay**   is a freely available implementation of SSL protocol and the cryptographic algorithms used by SSL, developed by Eric Young (AU). Available worldwide it never breached USA export legislation. While Eric withdrew from the project, development continued under the name OpenSSL by a team of developers.

**OpenSSL**   is the name used for the SSL library originally known as SSLeay (see above).

**Transport Layer Security**   (TSL) is the latest version enhanced version of SSL 3.0, and is a proposed internet standard (see RFC2246 ftp://ftp.isi.edu/in-notes/rfc2246.txt).

**Security**   means that the Confidentiality, Integrity, Availability and User Accountability, Authentication and Audit (CIA-UAA) of information and data including the Critical Infrastructure Protection (CIP) is to the satisfaction of stakeholders (e.g., customers, employees and suppliers). Accordingly, unauthorized use and alteration of data has been limited using various means that result in a level of Risk that is acceptable.

It can also be defined as the protection of confidentiality, control, integrity, authenticity, availability and utility of information. Within this framework, a poorly designed or sloppily documented or misunderstood feature can be as bad as a bug from a security standpoint.

Accordingly, Security is about making sure things work properly, while security measures are neither broken nor penetrated in the presence of Malicious Code or an adversary who does everything in his or her power to make sure that things don't work, in the worst possible way at the worst possible times (see Tables 23B & 23C).

This also means that a good attack is one that the engineers never even thought about. Hence, good attackers have, do and will cheat.

Because security has nothing to do with functionality, no amount of beta testing can ever uncover a security flaw. Security flaws in a piece of code are discovered during software evaluation. While Open Source (see Invention–Collective Invention) is no guarantee for good security, very likely many people have looked at a popular code for security flaws and found them quickly. Naturally these then need to be fixed.

For proprietary code, flaws are also found but at a slower speed. Primary reason is that many experts can look at Open Source code but only the originator's employee will probably check for security flaws in the proprietary one (see Linux).

Naturally, Security can also be improved by building Redundancy into systems, Separate Systems and use Multi-Layered Security as well as Multi-Leveled Security.

Computer Security has always been sold as "threat prevention." Encryption, firewalls, anti-virus, PKI are all technologies that prevent particular Threats. Threat Prevention is a cost, and if an organization does not understand the threats, the CEO is unlikely willing to pay for prevention. But IT security is about Risk Management, namely that if the organization can manage its risks better than another, this should be reflected on its bottom line.

Nonetheless, some have stated that there is no such thing as Security, just **levels of insecurity**. The latter need to be kept at acceptable levels (see also Tables 2A–2D)

**Security versus Safety**    differs in that the former addresses issues that prevent anything from going wrong while the other focuses on making sure that everything goes right.

This is outlined in detail in Table 23B (see also Table 23C).

**Language**    is an important issue here, several languages such as German and Danish do not distinguish between security or safety, instead the word "Sicherheit, Sikkerhed" encompasses both, security and safety. Hence, this semantical difference can result in difficulties in making sure that the meaning is shared (see also Trust)

**Security Architecture**    describes the detailed description of all aspects of the system that relates to security, along with a set of principles to guide the design. It describes how the system is put together to satisfy the security requirements.

**Security Awareness**    see Awareness

**Table 23B:** Defining Security and Safety for Information Systems-Related Products and Services

| Term | Definition |
| --- | --- |
| Security | usually refers to all precautions that have been taken to protect an organization, system, person or other things from being attacked or harmed. |
| | In the information security context, it is making sure things work properly, while security measures are neither broken nor penetrated in the presence of Malicious Code |
| | Or an adversary who does everything in his power to make sure that things don't work, |
| | —in the worst possible way |
| | —at the worst possible times. |
| | A good attack is one that the engineers never even thought about. Hence, good attackers |
| | 1) have, |
| | 2) do and |
| | 3) will cheat. |
| Security Risk | Could mean somebody or something being a security risk or threat to the safety of an organization or information system (see also Table 22E). |
| Safety | is the state of being safe or the probability of being harmed in a particular situation or due to the undertaking of a particular activity (e.g., sports). |
| | Deals with design and engineering issues that affect a technology or other product's, such as: |
| | • performance, or |
| | • what can be done regarding Risks and possible damages if a person performs actions they were not intended to be performed, when things fail, such as: |
| | —flat tire while driving on the freeway, |
| | —slippery road, or |
| | —kids playing with appliances, such as iron's electric cord. |

**Note.** This table outlines the difference between safety and security in the IT security domain and their correlation or link to each other (see also Table 24A).

**Security Assurance**   see Information Security

**Security Breach**   is where a stated organizational policy or legal requirement regarding Information Security, has been contravened. However every incident which suggests that the Confidentiality, Integrity, Availability and User Accountability, Autentication and Audit (CIA-UAA) of the information has been inappropriately changed, can be considered a Security Incident. Every Security Breach will always be initiated via a Security Incident, only if confirmed does it become a Security Breach (see also Data Leakage).

**Risk of a Security Breach**  is increased in cases were extra security precautions seem to fail such as when a person wants to transfer an account that is in joining names. For instance, wife and husband have a joint account but her having the maiden name on the account. Even though from the bank's perspective she could be a person with no relationship to her husband, the call to the bank's helpline might enable the husband to answer "extra security" questions such as:

- who is the other named account holder? Information is printed on the back of the statement;
- what is your overdraft limit? Information printed on the front of the statement.

In turn, the account can be closed and the rest balance transferred or paid out in cash. As the kid in Terminator 2 says . . . "easy money" . . .

If a Policy allows the scenario outlined above to occur, extra security measures are basically useless while security breaks are likely.

**Security Engineering**  differs from other engineering disciplines, most importantly it requires a certain kind of mentality to approach systems from an attacker's perspective. During World War II, the British found that the best cryptographers were chess players and musicians. Some have argued that good security people are D&D players and tinkers. The ability to find loopholes in a system, be they implementation, design or configuration-based vulnerabilities, mathematical, systematical, or procedural errors, is vital to a Security Engineer.

Most engineering involves making things work. Security Engineering involves making things not happen but, instead, figuring out how things fail, and then preventing those failures from occurring.

A more comprehensive definition and distinction is also given in Table 23C below (see also Table 23B above).

**Safety Engineering**  see Table 23C above.

**Security Engineer**  (also called Security Administrator) should have the skills outlined under Security Engineering. He or she is responsible for all security aspects of a system on a day-to-day basis. The Security Engineer takes primary responsibility for the IT security related affairs of the organization. Regardless of size, a firm should designate an individual who becomes accountable for the Information Security of the organization (see also Skills).

The Security Engineer should be independent of both development and operations staff. The most sensitive activities can only be undertaken with a combination of both Security Engineer and the System top-level passwords (see also Table 20A and 20B, Skills). If the Security Engineer is not

**Table 23C:** Security Engineering versus Safety Engineering

| Term | Definition |
| --- | --- |
| Safety versus Security Engineering<br>Security Engineering | Most engineering involves making things work.<br>    Security Engineering involves making things not happen requires a certain mentality, such as:<br><br>—WW II best cryptographers were chess players and musicians<br><br>Accordingly, for a successful or effective security engineer it is important that the person finds loopholes in a system, be they:<br><br>—implementation,<br>—design or<br>—configuration-based<br>—vulnerabilities, mathematical, systematical, or procedural errors.<br><br>It requires figuring out how things fail, and then preventing those failures from occurring. |
| Safety Engineering | Safety Engineering could be described as safety being rooted or grounded in a well designed and programmed system of which software is one key element, as well as:<br><br>• necessitating the design of some level of redundancy into a system,<br>• using separate and isolating safety-critical aspects of a system,<br>• making predictability a key element for safety engineering, while<br>• violating assumptions may occur in some instance of use.<br><br>The above illustrates that much if not all aspects of Safety Engineering are also part of or at least linked to Security Engineering (see also text). |

**Note.** Defining Safety and Security Engineering (see also Table 23B) is also linked to what security engineers look for when talking about internet vulnerabilities (see Table 22E).

In many languages, safety and security are not separate words but one term encompasses both such as in in German "Sicherheit," in French "sécurité", and in Danish "sikkerhed." Hence, in these languages it is more difficult to explain and distinguish between security and safety at least in layman's terms.

independent of these departments, such as Auditing from Accounting, otherwise it is similar to the fox guarding the chickens.

**Security Filters**   can be installed between two separately classified systems, thereby permitting controlling the flow of classified or confidential data that is presented for transmission across the interface. This action has to be part of the Information Security Policy and could be used to deny any executable files to reach users. It may also be an anti-virus scanner (see Virus) that scans any files for viruses that leave and are sent to users behind the Firewall.

**Output Filters** can work if it is possible to rely on the classification label of data presented for transmissions. Hence, the classification label received by the filter must be the same as the one affixed by the individual classifying the document, and no more highly classified information was attached to the data as it passed through the transmitting computing entity (see also Spam Filter).

**One-Way Gateways–Diodes** may be used to protect a connection, whereby information can be transferred from the lower classified system to the higher one only (see also Multi Level Networks).

**Perimeter Based Security** controls access to all entry and exit points of the network. Usually linked with Firewalls and/or Filters.

**Security Incident** is an Alert to the possibility that a Security Breach may be taking, or may have taken place (see also Attack, Incident, Risk, Security Breach).

**Security of Media** is an issue when a hard disk or other storage media is being replaced. Besides total destruction that will completely remove all traces of the information borne by memory devices, including volatile storage such as Random Access Memory (RAM) or magnetic media. Several methods can be used (see also Hard Disk, Security of Media, Electronic Shredding), such as:

- Degaussing also called demagnetizing is a procedure that reduces the magnetic flux density to zero by applying a reverse magnetizing field. Hence, it renders any previously stored data on magnetic media unreadable. Degaussing is the most reliable method of purging magnetic media short of destruction;
- Magnetic Media Overwrite describes overwriting by replacing every addressable location with one pattern (usually binary 'ones') and then with the complementary pattern usually binary 'zeros.' This procedure is best implemented following these three steps (see also Electronic Shredding):
- Overwrite all data bit locations with a pattern such as binary zeros, verify that it has occurred;
- Overwrite data bit locations with binary ones or the complement of whatever pattern was used during the previous step while verifying that it has occurred. Verification is accomplished by reading all, or a sample of the overwritten media. How much depends on a risk assessment. Check if no other characters can be detected.
- Repeat the above steps based on the risk assessment requirements (see Electronic Shredding)
- Laser Printer and Copier Drums can be sanitised by printing a quantity of blank pages designed to exercise the whole drum after its last use.
- Volatile Media can be sanitised sufficiently by the removal of all power including battery power and earthing the device.

- Physical Security and Destruction Methods using an approved method must be applied for paper, microfiche, microfilm, CDs and related storage media since they cannot be sanitised properly. Hard disks and volatile memory should be destroyed by melt, smelt, grind, or smash method. Floppy disk media should also be destroyed by an approved method (see Security of Media, Electronic Shredding).

The above issues may also become a problem if equipment is being Recycled (see Recycling of Hardware and Media).

**Security Patch**   see Patch and Table 19B

**Security Patch Management**   see Patch Management and Table 19B

**Security Policy**   see Information Security Policy, also Policies

**Security Review**   sometimes also called security audit is an expensive, time-consuming, manual process that covers

- specification,
- design,
- implementation,
- source code,
- operations, and so forth.

Functional testing cannot prove the absence of bugs. Similarly, a Security Review cannot show that the product is in fact secure.

If a Security Review on a software product or operating or information system was done in isolation or the laboratory, the results may not be replicated in an operational environment or a different operational setting. Accordingly, the more complex the system is, the harder a security evaluation becomes and the more security bugs there might be found (see also Testing).

**Source Code**   flaws are liked easiest if many people have looked at a popular code for security flaws. For proprietary code, only the originator's employee will probably check for security flaws in the proprietary one while in Open Source Code many experts can look at it (see Linux, Security).

When checking for errors in Source Code, some experts suggest a set of questions for determining how much time it might take for reviewing the code. The more "yes" answers to these questions, the more time might have to be spent looking at the source code of a program for finding problems. Questions could be:

- Does the code run by default?
- Does the code run with elevated privileges?
- Is the code listening on a network interface?

- Is the network interface unauthenticated?
- Is the code written in any 'language' that might be more likely to cause problems such as C/C++?
- Does the code have a prior history of vulnerability?
- Is this component a proprietary code and thus under not open for scrutiny by the 'scurity community?'
- Does the code handle sensitive or private data?
- Is the code reusable (for example, a DLL, C++ class header, library, or assembly)?
- Based on the threat model, is this component in a high-risk environment or subject to many high-risk threats?

The above was in part inspired by the fact that Microsoft published a white paper about its approach to security and code testing that can be found here: http://msdn.microsoft.com/msdnmag/issues/03/11/SecurityCodeReview/default.aspx

**Security Solutions** can be delivered, offered, designed, developed, implemented or provided depending on the latest buzzword being fashionable. The may range from ready meal solutions (my pre-cooked frozen TV dinner sold at Aldi, Safeway or Carrefour), lawncare solutions (where I still need to use a lawnmower to cut the grass), or an agile collaborative network security suite. But solutions require a clearly defined problem that can also be isolated/located easily, such as a person's ingrowing toe nail that must be removed to get rid of the pain and infection.

Accordingly, Security in the IT domain is neither a product nor a solution to a specific problem but, instead, the **process** of watching systems carefully for any signs of attacks. For instance,

- does the Firewall's, Unix or NT servers' logs give raise to concern?
- What about the routers and network servers?

A Security Engineer has learnt how to read these logs daily and understands how an attack may look like and knows how to recognize it (see Security Engineer). A Security Engineer knows that any product helping reduce the Risk for Threats to materialize requires time and expertise to make the tools work properly. Daily baby-sitting is at the core of this process.

**Security Space** see Domains of Information Security Space (DISS)

**Segregation of Duties** (and/or **Tasks**) occurs when tasks are apportioned between different members of staff, thereby reducing the scope for error and fraud. For instance, the person who creates data is not permitted to authorize processing or distribution, or system development staff are not permitted to get involved with live operations.

This approach will not eliminate collusion between members of staff in different areas, but is a deterrent. In addition, the segregation of duties provides a safeguard to staff and contractors against the possibility of unintentional damage through accident or incompetence.

Again the above relates to the independence required for Security Engineers (Auditors) from IT services/system department (Accounting) to assure that the work can be performed well (Security Engineer).

**Self-Signed Certificate**   means that the owner of a certification (e.g., citizen) signed the message herself instead of having a recognized Certification Authority do so. This is unlikely to be trusted by anyone wishing to use the certificate as proof of ownership of the corresponding Public Key (see Digital Signature–Public Key)

**Semantic Web**   is the way the technology is expected to go. Hypter Text Mark-up Language, and Extensible Mark-up Language are already used to help computers figure out if a text is supposed to be shown on the browser in bold and how information on a page is structured. The Resource Description Framework (RDF) uses the subject, verb, object structure of the simple sentence, a first bloc of the semantic Web. Hence, RDF links pages and concepts, making statements about people, things and properties such as this Dictionary was written by and published by on this subject.

However, the Semantic Web requires artificial intelligence tools, notably the concept of ontologies. These create the taxonomy or ordered classification system, and their relationship with rules such as, football or soccer in the UK is a game, and a footballer is a person who participates in the game. It is played with a ball and a game requires 2 teams, 10 field players, and a goalie each.

Vital to the concept of the semantic web is the use of software agents. These are programmed or learn how to seek out relevant ontologies to aid the understanding. Hence, the aim is to populate the web with "Dictionaries of Meaning" that agents can refer to as they traverse cyberspace.

Early implementation of the Semantic Web will focus on e-Commerce applications such as procurement. Since June 2002, anyone wanting to create a Web-based catalogue using this standard coding needed for the Semantic Web has been able to download free catalogue-building software from the Electronic Commerce Code Management Association (ECCMA). It was established in 1999 to create open technical dictionaries for commercial Web content.

ECCMA's software attaches Extensible Mark-up Language (XML) codes to every item loaded into a catalogue, which is then placed on a corporate Web site. While today this requires a plug-in to be used with one's browser, the future will be machine-to-machine searches where it will go and search the Web:

"Find and list any Identity-Theft insurance provider (not broker) for private party, total coverage 1 Mio Dollars, at monthly subscription price of Euro 10–15."

**Semaphore**   means a switch in an operating system program

**Sendmail**   is one of several implementations of the Simple Mail Transfer Protocol (SMTP). Sendmail is the Unix program implementing the internet standard for email. While it is the mostly used implementation, unfortunately it is also the one that has been targeted for many exploits. For alternatives see Postfix

**Server**   describes a computer which supplies (serves) a network of less powerful machines such as desktop PCs, with applications, data, messaging, communications, and information. The term is replacing 'host' in many situations since the processing power of a desk top server is such that one machine is sufficient to run the computing requirements of a corporation or department.

When configuring servers, only essential services should be active, and precautions should be taken with those that by default, leave more than one port open (see also Cracker).

**Server Signature**   is the string usually returned as part of servicing each http request that gives the name and version of the web server software being used (See also Active and Passive OS Fingerprinting).

**Service Level Agreement (SLA)**   is a contract between a client and the vendor of a particular service (e.g., anti-virus scanner) or systems. SLAs specify precisely type of support service purchased including minimum standard. The latter should include a maximum response time after a call to the service desk has been logged, such as until when a security engineer should be on-site or the patch should have been delivered.

It is very important to discuss the details of the SLA with the vendor because, often, the only time when the client will use it, is when things have gone wrong (e.g., system breakdown). Hence, this is the time when the customer depends upon the 'fine print' of the SLA.

**Session Hijacking**   transpires when an attacker is taking over an authorized user's terminal session.

**Session Key**   is the key being used for just one message or a set of message. A typical system would generate a random session key for use with

Symmetric algorithm to encode the bulk of the data. Only the session key itself is communicated using public key encryption (see Digital Signature–Public Key)

**SET**    is a secure protocol designed by MasterCard and Visa to facilitate financial transactions over the Internet. Compared with SSL (see Secure Socket Layer), it places more emphasis on validating both parties to the transaction.

**Shareware**    is software being supplied on a 'try before you buy' basis. Shareware is produced by software companies and independent programmers and supplied to users through a variety of channels including magazine cover disks, e-mail, mail order, and internet downloads. The basic idea is that users will try out the software (which is sometimes, but not always crippled or limited in some way) and will like it so much that he or she will pay a relatively small registration fee to become an authorized user of the unrestricted program.

Many times Shareware depends on the honor system. If you like the program and use it, payment is required. It is also the 'right' thing to do since these limited revenues permit the developer to continue fine-tuning the program. In turn, new releases and often free upgrades offer users additional benefits.

Companies with policies which permit the installation and use of such material should restrict it to stand alone test or development machines, where the software behavior and the programs claimed benefits can be examined fully before being installed as registered version on live machines. Hence, users should only be permitted to install pre-approved/tested shareware on machines (see also Freeware).

Unlike Freeware that is distributed for free on the web, Shareware is not free while registration and paying of a small fee is often required (see also Invention–Collective Invention, Open Source Code).

**Shell**    can be a command interpreter in a system such as Unix.

**Short Message Service (SMS) Flood**    means a cell or mobile phone being flooded by receiving too many SMSs in a very short time, thereby making it impossible for the owner to receive or call a party.

Generally SMS is being used for sending a short message to a mobile phone via a wireless. Such a message could also contain a news item (e.g., stock quotes) or a virus alert. Since wireless carriers may pay just about 1 cent but charge a multiple of that to users, SMS is a highly profitable service. In Europe users pay for sending an SMS while receiving one is free. However, in the USA the recipient of an SMS also pays a fee.

During late 2003, some experts raised the issue about using SMS as a way to launch a denial-of-service attack against cell phone users. The attacker could use his or her own phone or those of co-workers, while these 1,000 messages are sent instantly and anonymously.

Such an 'SMS Flood' can render a person's cell phone unable for making or taking calls. Apparently, cellular carriers such as T-Mobile are still struggling to stop or block such SMS-type floods. Hence, an SMS Flood could be very costly for a recipient living in the USA, since he or she would have to pay for each of those SMS received during an SMS Flood. Hence, adding insult to injury is when the victim is being charged for each SMS received during such type of an Attack. Only the future will tell us how wireless service providers will deal with this security issue.

**Shoulder Surfing** happens when somebody watches a user entering a user-name and password to gain authorized access to certain system resources (see also Screen Saver).

**Shrink Wrap Agreement** see Click Wrap Agreement

**shttp** or **https** see Hypertext Transfer Protocol

**Signature** represents a virus' special pattern or infection routes. A series of letters or numbers within the virus code often serve to identify it. This string is called a signature and can be considered as being the digital fingerprint of the virus. The latter permits creating a method to detect this particular virus. We can create signature files containing the signatures of all known viruses although worldwide there does not exist one list that is nearly as complete as one might wish (see also Digital Signature, Trojan, Virus, and Worm).

Signature is also unique "fingerprint" used in Intrusion Detection. Each possible Attack has its own signature/fingerprint and using pattern matching software, known attacks for which exist signatures can be easily detected, for example by analyzing packets on wire.

**Signature Based Intrusion Detection Systems** are matching collected data against known set of signatures of known attacks. This means that these systems are only as good as their patter/finger print/signature database. These databases have to be continuously updated and maintained to as-sure their currency. This is a tedious task and there are recently attempts to create central repository and unified descriptive language for these systems.

**Significance** is the degree to which a research finding is meaningful or im-portant (see also Statistics).

**Significance Testing** requires using tests such as chi-square, $t$ test or $F$ test to determine how likely it is that observed characteristics of samples have occurred by chance alone in the population from which the samples were drawn (Statistical Inference).

**Statistical Significance**   said of a value or measure of a variable (e.g., gender) when it is ('significantly') larger or smaller than would be expected by chance alone. A very large sample size very often leads to results that are statistically significant, even when they might be inconsequential (see also Sample).

**Simple Mail Transfer Protocol (SMTP)**   is is an inherently insecure protocol. Everything is transferred in clear text and subject to easy sniffing. Passwords travel unencrypted on the wire. For an alternative see Postfix.

**Simple Network Management Protocol (SNMP)**   is a protocol defined by RFC1157 (version 1), RFC1446 (version 2) and RFC2570 (version3). This protocol is mainly used for management of network devices. It is one of the least secure protocols available.

**Simulation Exercise**   can be used to offer staff and system personnel the opportunity to test behaviors in an emergency-type situation, such as a major Virus Infection, or sudden loss of system. This can be extremely useful in monitoring organization performance during the emergency, as well as providing data for how procedures could be improved.

Similar to a fire drill, people need to acquire automatisms to perform excellently during emergencies. While there is never a good time to run such an exercise, the lessons to be learned from such a simulated disaster can prove invaluable should a real emergency ever arise.

**Single Sign-On**   see Password–Single Sign On (SSO)

**Site**   is the organizational level with responsibility for security events, the organizational level of the site administrator or other authority with responsibility for the computers and networks at a particular location.

**Site Name**   (see also Domain Name).

**Sizing Exercise**   is an activity that analyzes the demands to be placed upon a system, in terms of concurrent users, data types and quantity, storage requirements, expected response times and a possible Denial-of-Service Attack. It stipulates the minimum specification for the system.

**Skills**   see Learning

**Small and Medium-Sized Enterprises (SMEs)**   are also heavy users of information technology but do often lack the in-house know-how or permanent staff for Information Security. Moreover, cash flow problems may not permit the outsourcing of such activities.

The most dangerous Risk and Threat for an SME regarding the internet occurs when switching from a dial-up connection to a broadband one. For instance, while many SME's stay online maybe two hours a day when using a dial-up connection, having a Digital Subscriber Line (DSL), a cable connection via the TV cable supplier or any other broadband access means that the firm might now be on-line between eight to nine hours daily (i.e. as long as people work at the office). It might well be 24 hours a day, seven days a week if the modem is not turned off after working hours.

This gives more time for hackers and automated programs, or 'bots', to find and abuse the company. Even having the Internet Protocol (IP) address dynamically assigned when the connection is made and not changed until the connection is dropped does not necessarily help. A dynamically assigned IP address is effectively like a static IP address, because broadband connections tend to stay up longer than dial-up accounts. This means a spammer or hacker can find a company again once it has identified it as a soft target.

If a connection is left on 24/7, attacks can happen at night when nobody is there to notice. An example was the Blaster worm, which is able to access unprotected machines, and install itself on many networks overnight. Most SME staff will only know they are infected because their machine operates slowly and crashes, behavior which is sometimes difficult to detect.

Beyond the simple Risk of being online for longer than is necessary, there are other issues with broadband. Spam can be a problem: if a mail server is not adequately protected, a spammer can re-route his or her messages via the SME's server within just about 10–12 hours.

As well as using bandwidth, this can mean that the innocent company is branded as a spammer and blacklisted by its Internet Service Provider (ISP) or by Realtime Black Lists (RBLs). Again, a dynamic IP address does not protect the firm from having its server used by a spammer for a few hours a day or over the weekend if it is online (see Table 23D).

Table 23D outlines some of the issues that should be addressed by a SME to improve Information Security while reducing the Risks. Additional information can be found throughout this dictionary (see also Trust, Table 20D).

**Smart Cards** contain a chip with information stored about the individual usually using Biometrics (e.g., picture, fingerprint, iris, and other) (see also Access Control, Tables 4A, 4B and 4C).

By 2004, the USA Department of Defense (DOD) intends to have issued smart cards to all active-duty and civilian personnel, as well as military reservists, sub contractors and eventually all others connected to the department

**Table 23D:** Security Engineering for a Small and Medium-Sized Enterprise (SME)–Check List

| Security Step | Description |
|---|---|
| Basics must be in place | A Firewall is best accompanied by: <br><br>• Intrusion Detection System if there are any services running on the network, <br><br>• anti-Virus protection, and <br><br>• spam filtering (server but as importantly, each PC/notebook as well). <br><br>IDP and content/spam filtering need to be updated regularly (see also Table 23D–Visibility). |
| Broadband connection | Must be turned-off overnight and at weekends if it is not needed (e.g., best if web pages for clients are hosted out-of-house on a virtual server). <br> All PCs should be shut down (turned-off) when user is not at work. This saves energy and, most importantly, reduces Risk for a successful Attack during those hours. |
| Very slow network or system | This may be an indication of an unauthorized intrusion, system personnel must investigate. |
| Remotely managed security system | This should improve the Risk ratio by having problems spotted and blocked overnight. As importantly, maintenance and rapid update of security patches and virus signatures is maintained by the service provider. <br> This approach might be beneficial (see Costs and Benefits, Tables 1–3D for a systematic calculation) and an economically viable option. For instance, having security maintained and patches installed during long weekends when SME staff may not be available could be advantageous from a Risk Management perspective. |
| Security Policy-implementation and Monitoring (see also Table 20B) | Develop the appropriate security policy and ensure that it is adhered to by everybody (see also **ES**[3]). <br> Monitoring should also be through **social means**, whereby workers monitor and improve their own security behaviors and help colleagues' improve their's. For instance, P2P or Kazaa technology should not be used to share music files, since this is neither relevant to one's job nor legal by violating copyright. <br> Using P2P to access or share files (e.g., audiofiles from the USA Supreme Court are available via P2P technology) should, however be used if it helps to improve quality and sales. Such issues cannot necessarily be addressed by a security policy but through discussions and social monitoring it is more likely that workers **understand and agree** with the merit of an item in a security policy, thereby, making the following of policies more easy. <br> The above indicates that intermittent training for raising awareness could be the key for a successful implementation that results in encouraging findings during the monitoring phase. |
| **ES**[3] (ES three) | Ensuring staff comprehend–and therefore carry out–your plan of action regarding IT Security demands a sure touch. Moreover, employees must not only understand the communication in the policies but believe in them. Otherwise they are unlikely to follow through. <br> Using memory aids–phrases or combinations of letters and numbers (mnemonics) helps remind everybody about how important information security and safety are, namely: <br><br>—**Everyone knows our information security policy,** <br>—**Everyone improves information security, and** <br>—**Everyone safeguards information (e.g., customer data, R&D).** |

**Note.** The above outlines some of the Security Engineering issues for an SME (see also Table 20D). The approach focuses on reducing Risks and Costs (see also Tables 2D, 7A and 15C)

(e.g., retired employees and family of staff). This will bring the total number of cards in circulation to about 4 million for that biometric system along. New security issues are surely to arise

During 2002, a smart ID card trial was launched by the airline industry including the Air Transport Association. The project is sponsored by the European Commission and Swiss Office for Education and Science. The project tests a card carrying biometric data (Biometrics) based on facial recognition. The information is being matched with evidence collected by cameras at key points in an airport. This could be used to speed passengers through check-in and security procedures. The aim is to develop industry standards making the card usable worldwide. Meanwhile, Scandianvian Airlines launched a test during 2002 with a smart card that carries details of a passenger's fingerprint.

The advantages and disadvantages of smart cards including costs and False Rejection Rate (FRR) and the False Acceptance Rate (FAR) are outlined in Tables 4A, 4B and 4C (see also Access Control). For instance, facial recognition technology does not seem to work well in airport settings (see Table 4C).

**Smart Mobile Phones**   are handsets with multimedia applications, such as games and photos. The number of handsets shipped using the Symbian operating software rose from 230,000 to 2.68m in the six months to June 30 in 2003. Globally, about 11.5m Smart Mobile Phones were sold during 2003 worldwide and about 8m were fitted with the Symbian system.

In comparison Microsoft sold about 200,000 copies of its system software for Smart Mobile Phones during the same period. Each manufacturer pays Symbian a royalty of between $5 and $7 depending on the terms of each contract, on top of consultancy fees for implementing the software.

Smart Mobile Phones are taking away sales from Palmtop Digital Assistants (PDAs) since they can perform many functions of the latter as well (e.g., calendar, and address book) and than some.

**Tidbit**   of interest here is that for a Smart Mobile Phone costing around € 700 a piece, software costs paid by the consumer for the Symbian operating system is about Euro 30 maximum, including the profit margin, just about 4.25% of the sales price. For a Euro 1200.00 notebook, however, the Windows operating system is a bit more expensive and represents a low 2 digit percentage.

**Smart Phones**   see Smart Mobile Phones

**Smog**   see Electro Smog

**Smurfing**   is an attack that exploits features of the IP protocol within the TCP/IP protocol used for internet communications.

A smurf attack causes a victim's computer to become completely 'way laid' with answering fictitious network requests ('Pings') that it grinds to a halt and prevents anyone else from logging on (see also Denial of Service Attack-DoS, Ping).

**Sniffer**   is software designed to look at and/or to collect traffic on the wire. Sniffing tools are built into majority of UNIX type systems and there is wealth of free tools available on the internet for other platforms. Majority of them are designed around the libpcap library and tcpdump tool. Some Intrusion Detection Systems have option of being run as a sniffer too.

**Social Engineering**   is a technique where persuasion and/or deception are used to gain access to the systems. This is typically implemented through human conversation or other interaction. Typical example of this is an attack where a hacker pretends to be a high positioned IT executive traveling on company business and having problems to connect to the organization's information system through its remote access point.

The person may gradually succeed in persuading the Help Desk operator to tell him or her all the necessary details for the connection set-up. Later on attacker calls again, complaining that his password for some reason does not work and persuades the Help Desk to change it to a password of her or his liking. Hence, the person may gain unauthorized access (see also Denial of Service through Psychological Manipulation).

The term can also be applied to exploiting the victim's good intentions and lack of in-depth technical knowledge in order to inspire fear and confusion. This process is often considered in the context of 'memetics', which deals with the transfer of memes (the 'unit of cultural inheritance') from brain to brain.

Where social engineering is linked to an IT security issue or hoax, it nearly always trades on technophobia (see also Technophobia)

**Social Network Analysis (SNA)**   is the study of social relations among a set of actors. SNA maps and measures relationships and flows between people, groups, organizations, computers or other information/knowledge processing entities. The nodes in the network are the people and groups while the links show relationships or flows between the nodes. SNA provides both a visual and a mathematical analysis of complex human systems.

The unit of analysis in network analysis is not the individual, but an entity consisting of a collection of individuals and the linkages among them. Network methods focus on dyads (two actors and their ties), triads (three actors and their ties), or larger systems (subgroups of individuals, or entire networks). (see also Network, Local Area Network–LAN)

SNA in the information technology context, means that computers are scanned for contact information in electronic calendars and address books of users, such as stored in Outlook. It tallies whom the users have e-mailed and how long it took for the recipients to respond.

The real power of such methods and software is that after scanning all contacts and digital address books in firm A, the software can than scan a supplier or client's employees' address books if these firms agreed to have their contacts linked with firm A.

If supplier B has an employee with a contact to a possible client an employee from firm A would like to contact, the software emails the guy, telling him somebody is seeking an introduction to his contact. The ad guy could decline to help without letting the inquiring person know she was the one who rejected the request. But the software would take note, and possibly downgrade its assessment of the relationship between these two people.

So what does this have to do with security? Intelligence and law enforcement agencies crave tools that help them link suspects in new ways. Moreover, companies can take advantage of their employees' business connections.

But networking prowess may also invite unauthorized scanning of contacts from a person. An example might be scanning the firm A, its contacts and all the others linked to the firm (e.g., firm B see above). A hacker could than use mimick agreement to share or respond positively to a help request, and important contacts.

In another scenario, a court order could allow law enforcement to use this software to establish contact patterns (e.g. in alleged cases of insider trading).

Privacy concerns may also matter. For instance, anybody giving somebody information for their address book may now also have to fear that their unlisted phone number or email address could be inadvertently shared with a person they do not want to have it shared with. Customers might be worried that through a security breach their information is shared with government officials (e.g., tax authorities). Hence, there are productivity gains from the use of such Social Network Analysis tools but a Cost-Benefit Analysis (see Table 2A) may reveal that the Risks for breaching Confidentiality and Trust might be too great (e.g., Unauthorized Access–see Figure 1) to warrant their corporate use or a private person's participation in such a system.

**Social Harvesting of Community Knowledge (SHOCK)** is a way whereby a computer develops a private profile of its user's interests, based on her email and web browsing. The idea is to give access to such information to a search engine in the computer network.

Cell or mobile phones could perform similar information-sharing for networking or dating applications. If person A's device could discover person B has many similar phone numbers in his or her contact list, A and B might be interested to meet.

However, an incautious application of such tool by a provider could hurt the field with a big breach of Privacy (see also Social Network Analysis for further security concerns).

**Socio-Technical System Approach:**   Takes into consideration social issues (e.g., interaction between users, decision-making and structure of groups) as well as technical ones (e.g., type of technology, ergonomics, performance and software) when addressing the application of technology at work and during leisure time. In conjunction with the communication process, it reveals information about who communicates with whom, closeness between members of the network, as well as communication style and semantics used, including software and hardware offered by the information systems assessed.

**Social Informatics**   see Informatics

**Software Imaging**   see Imaging Software (Table 19B)

**Software Hacking**   is hacking into one particular software application using intimate knowledge of such application.

**Software Inventory**   provides the firm with two things:

1) A detailed list of all software licensed to the corporation, listing such information as, license number, program name, version/release number, cost, location(s), user(s), and asset reference number (if appropriate); and
2) A detailed list of hardware in order of machine and user(s). This sheet may be used for Audit checks to confirm that any given user machine still has the software detailed and no unauthorized additions, removals, or modifications have been made (see also Jurisdiction).

**Software Piracy**   happens when a user copies without authorization a copyrighted software package or a firm uses more software licenses than it has actually paid for in its agreement with the vendor (see also Copyright, Software Inventory).

**Source Code**   see Security Review–Source Code

**Spam**   can come via email and, therefore, be a variant of bombing; it refers to sending email to unwitting recipients. This can be a nuisance for users since it clogs their email in-boxes. The practice is known as "spamming." Email spamming can be made worse if recipients reply to the email, causing all the original addressees to receive the reply. It may also occur innocently, as a result of sending a message to mailing lists and not realizing that the list explodes to thousands of users, or as a result of an incorrectly set-up responder message (see also Remote Access Tools–RATs–Invisible Hosting).

Some suggest that it was May, 1978 when electronic Spam got started. This first spam ever is attributed to have been a pitch from Digital Equipment Corp. sent, literally, to everyone on the fledgling internet. At that time recipients thought it was a little bit annoying but sort of amusing. But things have changed.

If one has opted-out of receiving marketing information from a vendor, receiving it anyway means the latter may have violated the recipient's privacy (see Privacy-Spam). But in most cases, the sender has received the message from a party with whom he or she has no apparent link. The violator may have collected the eMail from a web page or an eMail directory. In some case the address may have been purchased the address from a service that is free to recipient (e.g., mail forwarding or reminder service) in return for permitting the firm to sell one's eMail address. With the increasing amount of spam, however, it is nearly impossible for the user to determine exactly if the sender got the eMail in a way that meets normal Privacy standards (see also Spam).

To avoid this problem, firms have tried to use different approaches, whereby customers are engaged to help an organization reach more potential clients (see Viral Marketing). Another way is if a free service, such as an eMailed newsletter (also called ezine) one has subscribed to may carry some commercial information or advertising similar to the newspaper one purchases at the newstand. But here, the individual subscribed to the service and, most importantly, knows that the advertising is in part the reason why the service is free.

But all of the above cases, Spam increases eMail volume that must be processed by an eMail gateway. In fact, some Spam may be sent by gaining unauthorized access to a server permitting the processing and mail out of Spam to many recipients. In turn, the server or Domain Name could be blacklisted or get negative publicity by inadvertently being blamed for the Spam mailed to thousands of recipients.

One approach, favored by the **European Union**, is to allow companies to send unsolicited e-mails only to individuals who have already consented to receiving the messages. This is commonly referred to as "opt in." This approach was used effectively a decade ago to eliminate junk faxes that were clogging up fax machines and wasting ink and paper. Such faxes are now mostly a thing of the past.

During 2002, the European Commission passed a law on data protection that mandated the "opt in" approach for unsolicited e-mail. European Union member countries had until October 2003 to adopt and enforce the law. But a few are behind and might not be able to deliver on this score until sometime later in 2004.

The **U.S.** has taken a different approach. There, lawmakers are leaning toward what they call "opt out," meaning companies can continue to send unsolicited eMail to anyone provided a person has not specifically said he or she does not want to receive it.

- 'Opt in' assumes that permission (for companies to send junk e-mail) is not given and must be requested.
- 'Opt out' assumes that permission (to send junk e-mail) is (already) there and can be withdrawn unless there is an objection that has been posted in some recognized public place.

Supporters say the "opt out" approach gives better protection to companies, but detractors say it is unworkable in practice. Pessimists claim that an individual could conceivably spend most of his or her life writing eMail to opt out of receiving spam.

Another problem is that the trade in eMail names is not limited to the back alleys of the Internet. Big, traditional mailing list companies have been buying eMail addresses, often from contest sites, and linking them with their vast stores of other information about people. Then marketers can send eMail to people who, say, have certain diseases or own a specific car model. The chain of permission can be stretched even further. Some come from customer lists of Internet firms that collapsed as the dot-com bubble burst. While those companies may have had clear privacy policies, their mailing lists were often sold to other firms along with the rest of their assets. And those companies could in turn sell the lists to other marketers. . Executives at many of the big companies marketing by e-mail acknowledge that the list companies are not always honest about the sources of their names. But they say there is no way to test the quality of a list other than to send e-mail to its addresses and see how many complaints result.

**Hormel Foods Corporation** is the maker of Spam, the luncheon meat, whose name is now synonymous with junk email as a result of the Monty Python skit in which the Viking chorus of 'Spam, Spam, Spam' eventually drowns out everything. The company's Website http://www.spam.com/ci/ci_in.htm has its 'Position Statement on Spamming,' which says:

*'We oppose the act of 'spamming' or sending unsolicited commercial e-mail. We have never engaged in this practice, although we have been victimized by it.'*

**Spam Filtering** is a process and not a one-day event. Various techniques exist to combat the problem;

- keyword-based filters,
- source blacklists,
- signature blacklists,

- source verification, and
- combinations of these to name a few.

All of them have problems, such as:

- keyword filters need to be constantly updated manually and are not very accurate, while
- blacklists also need to be constantly updated, and will always lag behind spammers.

Spam filtering is a subset of text classification, which is a well established field, but the first papers about Bayesian Spam filtering per se seem to have been given at the same conference in 1998, one by Pantel and Lin, and another by a group from Microsoft Research.

Bayesian filters are based on Statistical Methods which give a probability for an email belonging to a given class, such as Spam and not-Spam. The beauty of Bayesian filtering is that the filter can be trained by each individual user simply by categorizing each received email as either Spam or not-Spam; after the user has categorized a few eMails the filter will begin to make this categorization by itself, and usually with a very high level of accuracy. If the filter makes a mistake, the user re-categorizes the email; the filter learns from its mistakes. No complicated maintenance is required after the filter is installed.

One method is to consider the following before classifying a message as either spam or not spam by a Spam filter. False positives (e.g., rating something as junk while it is a friend who is writing the message) are a different kind of error from false negatives (e.g., a person who writes a chain letter all typed using capital letters). Filtering rate is a measure of performance. False positives are something like a bug. The filtering rate is similar to optimization, and decreasing false positives is similar to debugging (see also Filtering Software).

**Spam–Spim**   see Spim

**Statistical Filtering**   such as using Bayesian filtering should work if we calculate probabilities based on each **individual user's mail**. These can be much more effective, not only in avoiding false positives, but in filtering as well. For instance, finding the recipient's email address base-64 encoded anywhere in a message is a very good Spam indicator. Most important is that using individual filtering means that everyone's filters have different probabilities. Hence, it will make the spammers' optimization loop, what programmers would call their edit-compile-test cycle, appallingly slow. Instead of just tweaking a spam till it gets through a copy of some filter they have on their desktop, they'll have to do a test mailing for each tweak. It would be like programming in a language without an interactive top-level, a tough task to accomplish.

**Network-Level Type of Filters**   using Statistical Filtering do not offer much promise. When there is a static obstacle worth getting past, spammers are pretty efficient at getting past it. They may be enough to kill all the "opt-in" spam, meaning spam from companies like Virtumundo and Equalamail who claim that they are really running opt-in lists. One can filter those based just on the headers, no matter what they say in the body. But anyone willing to falsify headers or use open relays, presumably including most porn spammers, should be able to get some message past network-level filters if they want to.

**Phishing**   see Phishing

**Spim**   also called **Spam–Spim** are unsolicited instant messages. Unlike e-mail, which people can check at their leisure, spim is an intrusion that presents itself on the desktop with all the annoyance of an unexpected pop-up ad.

**Spim**   see Spam

**Spoof**   describes the masquerading that occurs by assuming the appearance of a different entity in network communications (see also Darknets).

**P2P Spoofing**   means that an attacker could have anonymously tricked an innocent P2P user into downloading a contraband file from another user on the P2P network. This can occur by having an attacker modify search requests and search results in transit by, for instance, placing the innocent user's IP address in the search result packet that lists a contraband file. Another way might be whereby a search request for music has a hop count set to 255. The flawed P2P application permits the attacker to set the hop count value back to zero, thereby making the innocent user be seen as the originator. Changing the search string *church hymns* to Rolling Stones makes an authority assume that the innocent user went out to search for illegal content.

The difficulties for authorities is to prove that the apparent offender was the actual offender, in turn this would require that the agency proofs that there were no malicious users on the P2P network at the time while the apparent offender's P2P application had no implementation flaws that are possible.

**Spot Check**   represents the need to validate compliance with procedures by staff and suppliers. It requires the performing of impromptu checks on vouchers, records and other files that capture the corporation's day to day activities.

**SSL**   see Secure Socket Layer

**SSLeay**   see Secure Socket Layer

**SSO**   see Password–Single Sign On

**Stability** describes the situation where Reliability of a system requires a stable environment. Hence, corporate users will rarely purchase a 1.0 software version instead of a 1.3 where some bugs have already been worked out. For instance, during 2002 Windows XP system administrators were still reluctant and concerned about the program's stability and design bugs, hence many firms continued running on older version, such as Windows 2000 or even 1998 on their networks.

Stability signifies that it may be used, as intended, without crashing, freezing or displaying other adverse characteristics (see also Down Time).

**Stack Fingerprinting** see Active Fingerprinting

**Standard** is usually an industry-wide, national and/or international standard (e.g., International Standard Office = ISO) that outlines which standard must be used (e.g., by government contractors) for a technology (e.g., servers, or software). (see also Benchmarking, Best Practice, Security Guidelines).

Sometimes, a market leaders product may de-facto become a kind of standard (e.g., Windows Operating System).

**S**

**Starting Date** is the date of the first known incident activity, that is when it was reported as having occurred by a site (see also Expiry Date).

**Statistical Significance** see Significance (see also Sample, Statistics)

**Statistics** provides tools that formalize and standardize our procedures for drawing conclusions (see also Acceptable Sampling, Significance, Table 15B–Confidence Level).

**Descriptive Statistics** are those describing a population or a Sample, such as using the mean, standard deviation, and also maximum and minim values.

Statistical Inference (or Inferential Statistics) is concerned with two types of problems

1) estimation of population parameters, and
2) tests of hypotheses

Statistical inference investigates how to draw conclusions about a large number of events on the basis of observations of a portion of them (i.e. a Sample of the population). Hence, Acceptable Sampling techniques must be used, otherwise, inferences made from a Sample are meaningless.

**Parametric Statistics** uses population values to obtain 'parameters' while making many assumptions about the nature of the population from which the scores are drawn. Parametric statistics can be used with scores that are truly numerical.

**Non-Parametric Statistics** do not make numerous or stringent assumptions about parameters. These techniques result in findings that require fewer qualifications or meeting of assumptions. Many non-parametric tests focus on the order or ranking of the scores, not on their 'numerical' values.

The **sign test** is probably one of the oldest Non-Parametric tests whereby the statistic is computed from data in the form of plus and minus (+ and −) signs. In a two group experiment the researcher could simply assign a + to each case where a known Vulnerability led to Unauthorized Access and a–where a known Vulnerability did not result in Unauthorized Access

Finally, a Parametric test may focus on the difference between the means of two sets of scores. The equivalent Non-Parametric test may focus on the difference between medians. The computation of the mean requires arithmetic manipulation (addition and than division); the computation of the median necessitates only counting.

**Steal** takes place when possession of a target is accomplished without leaving a copy in the original location.

**Stealth Bomb** see Virus

**Steganography** ("hidden writing") is a form of data hiding. Unlike cryptography, which creates an unreadable version of a message for anyone without the key, Steganography conceals even the existence of secret messages. One of the earliest forms of Steganography is spread-spectrum radio transmissions, in which parts of a message (even parts of individual bits) are sent on pseudo-randomly varying radio frequencies; without the right equipment, the signal is merely electronic white noise.

Steganography circumvents restrictions on encryption and prevents SIGINT (signals intelligence) personnel from detecting encrypted traffic. Digital watermarks and copy-protection schemes are forms of Steganography used to reduce the ease of illegal copying of intellectual property and to trace the origin of files (see also Invention, Copyright, Jurisdiction).

There are many tools available for embedding secret messages in other files; for instance, MP3STEGO modifies MP3 audio files to hold messages. Steganalysis tools look for tell-tale patterns in changed data when looking for concealed messages

**Stream Cipher** encrypts in small units, often a bit or a byte at a time. Unlike a basic block cipher, a stream cipher will have output corresponding to a given input will depend on where in the message it occurs. The simplest type of stream cipher uses a complicated function, which retains state, to generate a pseudo-random sequence which is then combined with the input using a simple operation such as bytewise addition.

**Submarine Warfare**   has been touted by some as a new paradigm for security, stating that we no longer have a well-defined entry point, such as a going across the drawbridge (head-end router), portcullis (firewall) and guards (IDS) into a castle (Local Area Network–LAN) with impregnable walls.

Submarine Warfare is based on the situational analysis that attacks can come from anywhere, at any time. There's no well-defined perimeter, and it's often difficult to tell friend from foe. Defenses should focus on hardened, well-protected assets–not bigger, stronger fences.

Stealth, intelligence gathering and deception play increasingly critical roles in enterprise security.

Accordingly, more layers of firewalls, Intrusion Detecion Systems (IDSs), and network components but instead, a change in thinking and strategy requires that the focus is on ready-to-use "combat tactics" suited for Submarine Warfare such as:

- Using internal Firewalls and changing control where trust zones and production and development zones are clearly separated (System Separation).
- Hardening of all servers and workstations, not just Demilitarized Zone (DMZ) type of servers.
- Confusing and misleading the enemy while if necessary, trapping him or her.
- Drilling Security teams to produce a high state of readiness and security Awareness.
- Adopting a zero-tolerance stance for rogue servers and hacker software on the organizational network.
- Employing Asset management approach for protecting critical components and expending resources efficiently.

While Information Warfare is being sold by some consultants as the new buzzword, it does not really represent a Paradigm shift in Information Security but possibly a slight shift in emphasis toward Prevention and possibly Active Defense (see Table 7B) instead of just Passive Defense.

**Super User**   is a privileged user who has access to all resources being used by any authorized user, plus all system files and processes

Super User privileges should, however, be under dual control because such users can, if they so wished, destroy the firm's systems maliciously or simply by accident.

**Survey**   is a research design in which a sample of subjects is drawn from a Population and studied. Methods could be interviewing or else a paper-and-pencil survey. This design is often contrasted with an experiment, whereby subjects are assigned at random to different conditions or treatments.

**Prevalence Survey** is a term often used in conjunction with Virus statistics. Reporting prevalence of Virus threats for home users is substantially different than reporting corporate/organizational prevalence. For a prevalence estimate of a group to be meaningful, one should expect similar behavior within each group. It would be stretching all expectation to assume that security-related behavior with virus threats for a 10 year old would be similar to that of a 17 year old or a 45 year old parent as home user.

Therefore, prevalence estimates for home users regarding computer Viruses or hacking Attacks against their servers must be calculated for logically homogeneous groups. Most estimates are for the home user without distinguishing between such factors as single person household or more members in a household, including children or others.

There is also some question as to how to define security-related problems for a home user. For instance, Virus prevalence is often defined as a case whereby within the last Quarter the home-user had an occurrence of a virus on his or her machine (see Eurobarometer studies for European Union). Unfortunately, distinguishing between an occurrence of a virus as reported by the anti-virus software as having 'cleaned' a file infected by a computer Virus and those that actually caused damages is usually lacking.

Making Prevalence data useful requires that Statistics, Acceptable Sampling and so on are described and carefully outlined for the reader's benefit. And whilst a list of top Threats or "10 Most Prevalent In-the-Wild Malware Surveyed by XYZ US" on a web site is possibly interesting, without careful distinctions (e.g., across countries, type of user groups and software platforms) these 'rankings' do not allow generalizations as should be possible from scientifically sound data sets (see Methodology).

**Sustaining Technology**   (see Invention)

**Symmetric key** is one in which the same key is used for encryption and decryption (see also CAST, Cipher, Digital Signature, Session Key)

**Sympathetic vibration** occurs when the use of packet feedback mechanisms in network protocols cause the network to overload.

**System Documentation** specifies and documents the technical operation of a specific hardware and/or software system.

**System Development** is the term used to describe the function of designing, coding, testing and updating software programs and other code such as scripts. The roles within Systems Development, will be

- systems analyst,
- programmers and, if needed
- other technical specialists.

**System Hacking**   is hacking into the particular system. It is usually based on the intimate knowledge of targeted operating system as well as knowledge of that particular system's weaknesses and security problems (see also Hacker).

**System Load**   refers to the demands placed upon it including such factors as:

- storage capacity for programs and data,
- number of programs that can run concurrently,
- total number of concurrent users, peaks, and
- average number of peripherals being used in total, such as using a file server as a print server–this increases demand since each to be printed document must be 'spooled' to the server's disk before being queued and thereafter being printed.

The above must be compared to the expected response times and performance that is needed.

**System of Record**   describes a system of record is an information storage system (likely to be a computer system) which is the data source, for a given data element or piece information. The need to identify the Systems of Record can become acute in large organizations, where Management Information (or MIS) systems have been built by taking copies of output data from multiple (source) systems, re-processing the data and then re-presenting it for their own business uses.

Where the Integrity of data, in particular the element is vital, they must either be extracted directly from the System of Record or be linked to it (see also Table 5B). Where there is no direct link with the System of Record, the integrity, and hence validity, of data is open to question.

**System Operations**   generally refers to the team of individuals who are responsible for running the system.

Systems Operations personnel have 3 main types duty, namely, they will:

1) run the day to day procedures for each of the main systems. Whilst these operations may well be automated, a systems operator will execute and oversee the operation.
2) perform routine housekeeping procedures on the systems, reviewing error logs and responding to any problems which occur day to day.
3) Carry out the end of day and 'end of period' (e.g. monthly) procedures; these will include the creation of backup copies of all the key data files across the systems.

Systems Operations personnel do not concern themselves with development, testing or the functionality of the various software applications being run. Their task is focused upon maintaining maximum 'up-time' by keeping all system and networks running efficiently.

**System Redundancy**   see Redundancy

**System Requirements**   are outlined in a document produced by, or on behalf of the organization/client. It documents the purposes for which a system is required, including its functional specifications usually all listed in order of priority.

**System Software**   is the general term used to describe the many software programs, Drivers and Utilities which **together** enable a computer system to operate. One of the main components of system software is the Operating System of the computer, for instance, Microsoft Windows® 2000 Professional, Windows XP and Longhorn.

**System Testing**   see Testing

S

**Target**   is the computer or a logical entity of the network (e.g., account, process, or data) or physical entity (e.g., component, computer, network or other infrastructures).

**Taxonomy**   is an agreed upon terminology and principles to classify information in a field of inquiry. An effective taxonomy should entail the following characteristics

1) *mutually exclusive* whereby categories do not overlap;

2) *exhaustive* in that taken together categories include all reasonable possibilities;

3) *unambiguous* (meaning high inter-rater Reliability), whereby two people will categorize incidences the same way (see also Reliability)

4) *repeatable* (= Measurement Reliability) resulting in the same classifications if done several times over by same or different people (see also Reliability)

5) *valid* in that the taxonomy helps categorize what it is supposed to be assessed or measured (see also Validity)

6) accepted and useful to security experts and system administrators,

7) allows the automatic collection of real data that was generated based on categorizing incidents using the taxonomy, and

8) permitting the collection of a sample that is representative of the larger population, thereby permitting the making of inferences (or conclusions) about a population or about how likely it is that a result could have been obtained by chance (see Statistics).

The taxonomy will meet some of the above criteria better than others. Hence, it is an approximation of reality being used to gain better understanding of a field of inquiry.

**TCP/IP**   see Transmission Control Protocol/Internet Protocol

**TCP Three-way Handshake**   is the basic principle of establishing a TCP connection. It consists of the exchange of three special packets called SYN (synchronize), SYN/ACK (Synchronize and Acknowledge) and ACK (Acknowledge).

**TCP Wrapper**   usually means a group of programs (e.g., Wietse Vensema's tcp_wrapper) that 'wraps around' the traditional tcp/ip utilities, such as finger, telnet, rsh, and ftp. It allows an administrator to make origin-based decisions about network requests. For example, all 'finger' requests could be denied or 'telnet' sessions could be restricted to certain remote users or sites.

**Team Collaborative Applications (TCA)**   provide an integrated set of web-based tools for collaboration; core integrated functionality areas are shared work-spaces for posting and exchanging files, tasks, and other project/team information.

**Technical Note**   usually provides advice on specific aspects of protective security to IT security personnel. This may provide further information regarding an Alert or an Adviscory (see also Alert, Advisory and Briefing Notice).

**Technology**   see Invention – Disruptive Technology or Sustaining Technology

**Technophobia**   is people's Angst that may result in them passing on hoaxes (see Hoax) or urban legends (UL) (see Urban Legend) to others out of fear of suffering some negative outcome if they fail to do so.

**Telecommunication Market**   see Market

**Telework**   describes individuals who may be working from a satellite office and/or home, or another location than the main office part or all of their working hours.

Telework can be defined as work performed with the help of computer-based communication technology. Accordingly, it does not imply that the employee has a constant on-line connection with his or her main office but, instead, it may simply mean that one uses computer technology for performing tasks, while being geographically in a different location than head-office.

Nonetheless, Telework does raise security issues. For instance, the design of an organization's infrastructure usually creates a safe, 'hard-shelled' perimeter in which users can operate laptops and desktops with little or no security technology installed locally. When these devices are taken out of this secure perimeter they are highly vulnerable and, in some cases, contain the corporate crown jewels.

A stolen corporate laptop not only offers locally stored data but in many cases passwords to other systems, a history of visited websites, some personal correspondence, an email system with contacts and much more. If possible, systems should contain firewalls, access control and encryption software that is supplemental to the corporate, server-based protection.

Accordingly, simple security measures on portable technology, such as disk or file encryption, can greatly reduce the risk of company data being compromised.

Personal firewalls and **biometric login/access control** are useful additions to any laptop or PC used at home to do work-related tasks, including logging into the corporate network.

**Tempest** see Transient Electro Magnetic Pulse Emanation Standards

**Terena** see Tables 5A–5C

**Terminate and Stay Resident (TSR)** is the property of many DOS programs that allows them to remain in the computer's memory even after they are no longer running. TSRs can include all sorts of functions.

**Testing** refers to the testing of the system in artificial conditions to ensure that it should perform as expected and as required (see also User Acceptance). Errors or Bugs are noted, analyzed and interfaces for export and import routines must also function as required (see also Patch).

Testing neither addressed the functionality of the system nor if it meets the user's needs.

**Regression Testing** in this context, is renewed testing due to a hardware or software upgrade, ensuring that the system is still functioning as expected and according to specifications. With a software upgrade, the regression testing plan helps making sure that the reports, screen, scripts and user options are all functioning as expected. While some bugs and errors are likely to be discovered, this process also helps to avoid a situation whereby the system could fail upon upgrade (see also Patch, Table 19B).

In statistics the term has a vastly different meaning such regression on the mean or multiple regression (see a Statistic Dictionary).

**Testing Software** and the results are often published in magazines or even touted in advertising by the respective firms. Usually, such tests are being conducted by either comparing a software package or hardware such as servers with others. Sometimes some type of Benchmark tests may also be used.

The difficulty can arise, when it is not obvious what testing Methodology has been used in case of, for instance, Anti-Virus software.

The Hamburg Virus Testing Center (VTC) not only publishes its Methodology but provides vendors also with examples of the code where their software may have failed or underperformed (see also Security Review).

Hence, VTC uses Methodology that can be checked by others, while also making it possible for others to replicate the findings, as should be possible with any high quality Research. Others including news media often fail to provide such information, thereby making it impossible for another party to check the findings by, for instance, replicating the test (see also Testing and Liability below).

Another concern is who might be liable for testing incorrectly or using the wrong criteria (see below).

**Testing and Liability**   could become an issue when a test result is neither meeting Reliability nor Validity and Methodology-type of requirements that is expected of scientific Research. For instance, on August 21, 2003 the University of Wisconsin-Madison revealed that beginning in May, it discovered being the recipient of a continuous large scale flood of inbound internet traffic destined for one of the campus' public Network Time Protocol (NTP) servers. The university determined the sources of this flooding were and continued in being literally hundreds of thousands of real internet hosts throughout the world. What was thought to be a malicious distributed denial-of-service (DDoS) attack, turned out to be a serious flaw in the design of hundreds of thousands of NetGear platinum products, including the RP614 and MR814.

These are low-cost internet routers targeted for RESIDENTIAL USE. IT press has provided awards and favorable reviews for these products. The impact of this product flaw is compounded by the fact that hundreds of thousands of HOME and SMALL BUSINESS USERS own these routers and are unaware of the flaw and the problem it is causing the University of Wisconsin- Madison. The issue that will have to be addressed is if product Liability applies here for:

- the manufacturer of such defect products,
- the IT magazines and newspapers publishing articles recommending such flawed products, and

Where does the Home User fit in with all this. With the rapid diffusion of bradband services and routers in residential settings having millions of servers online, such equipment may be misused for Distributed Denial of Service (DDoS). Is the home-user then possibly liable (see also Liability, Copyright, Jurisdiction—see also Table 16B).

For years some security experts have been talking about the concepts of:

- downstream liability, and
- attractive nuisance

as being existing legal concepts that could be applied to enterprises that leave their computer systems in vulnerable condition.

This issue become a major concern considering also Software Testing, whereby a magazine supposedly tests anti-Virus software without necessarily neither telling what criteria is being used nor basing the confidential criteria on any kinown or generally accepted standard. For instance, are certain criteria used for anti-virus software important for home users versus people working on a network with 10,000 PCs being connected?

Hence, new legislation (e.g., Switzerland—see Appendix 5) requires that firms proof that the security protection and Hardening of Operating System do meet Best Practice standards. What about the firm being fined for failure to have the best anti-virus software subsequently suing the software vendor?

These issues still await testing in the courts by downstream liability and attractive nuisance are concepts here to stay and are likely being more and more adhered to by courts whose judges are becoming ever more Information Security savvy.

**TFTP**  see Trivial File Transfer Protocol

**The Coroner's Toolkit (TCT)**  is a tool developed by Dan Farmer and Wietse Venema for analysis of file systems, originally targeted for post mortem investigation of cyber crime. These tools can also be used for data recovery outside of the *forensic computing* domain.

**The @Stake Sleuth Kit (TASK)**  is a refinement of the original *TCT* and a tool called TCTUTILS. It builds heavily on TCT but has many refinements. It can be used in command oriented mode or together with *Autopsy Forensic Browser* it provides GUI interface. Its main advantage against the original tools is that it enables investigation of other than UNIX file systems—notable NTFS, FAT and PALM.

**Theft of Service**  happens when the unauthorized use of computer or network services without degrading the service to other users is happening.

**Thesaurus**  can be described in several ways, namely as a:

1) A lexicon, more specifically where words are grouped by ideas or sets of concepts.
2) A grouping or classification of synonyms or near-synonyms.
3) A set of equivalent classes of terminology.

Within the context of a data base management system, a thesaurus facilitates access to data by defining key indexing and search terms.

**Thiefware**   see Scumware

**Theory**   could be defined as a set of interrelated constructs or concepts, definitions, and propositions presenting a systematic view of the phenomenon while specifying relations among variables. The purpose is to explain and predict the phenomenon. Generalizability of a theory is obtained by having it predict the phenomenon in various settings (e.g., organizations, countries and fields). A theory answers the what and how of these relationships but only the why explains in the context of who, where, and when an Attack happened.

Hence, a theory about computer Viruses would provide us with a statement or group of statements about how some part of the world works, often explaining relations among phenomena such as maybe Programming, Vulnerabilities and Hardware. Practitioners may distinguish between theory and practice but, a good theory about Information Assurance, Information, Computer Viruses and so on is probably the most practical way in explaining the why, how, when, where and when context of the phenomena investigated.

Research can be conducted in many ways such as a lawyer searching among old court cases for legal precedents regarding software Liability. Another example is an epidemiologist studying age groups or cohorts and hip-fracture incidents or an Anti-Virus Researcher studying malicious code to discover programming patterns and characteristics to develop taxonomies.

But in all cases, theory is the basis for Research and the **why** of the context must be explained, in order to generalize to other contexts (see Research).

**Anti-Virus Theory**   if it would exist would be based on Inductive or Deductive Research outlining phenomena and their relationship to other issues. Hence, investigation of the subject aimed at uncovering new information in a systematic way, while permitting a group of statements about how some part of the world works, in this case Computer Viruses. A good Anti-Virus Theory would allow us to generalize from one virus to the next (see Tables 19A and 19B).

**Threat**   A threat is the potential for having accidentally or deliberately compromised the availability, confidentiality and integrity of a system/database. For instance, data may be released to other parties who should not have access to the information. Moreover, data may be compromised by having it altered, after which time it is no longer authentic. Table 24A outlines the two main types of threats.

**Table 24A:** Differentiating Threat, Visibility, Vulnerability and Risk at One Glance

| Type of Threat | Description |
|---|---|
| A Threat | can be defined as a potential for the accidental or deliberate compromise of the fundamental security objectives including Confidentiality, Integrity, Availability, User Accountability, Authentication and Auditing (CIA-UAA) (see Table 5B) regarding data and their use. |
| | A threat is an external security issue represented by a natural or man-made attack. For example, a lightning bolt is a natural attack, since the lightning can threaten the safety and security of a data network. |
| | Likewise, an external intruder is a human-made threat that attempts to compromise a network. |
| A Visibility | is a problem when a private network service is inadvertently offered to the public. In these cases, the service isn't the problem, but its visibility is. |
| | The best example of a visibility issue is NETBIOS, the Windows "Network Neighborhood" protocol. Though NETBIOS is wonderfully useful, it should *never* be permitted to enter or leave your network. Seeing NETBIOS open when performing a network security audit is a serious error, even if a hacker is unable to leverage it for increased privilege. |
| | Firewalls protect against Visibility issues, not vulnerability issues. Firewalls selectively block traffic as it enters and leaves a system. A firewall should block all traffic that one does not specifically permit. However, if one left port 80/tcp open for inbound traffic—the web server—it might turn out that the server can be exploited via the HTTP protocol—a Vulnerability. In short, the Firewall will happily pass all traffic, good and bad. |
| | To discover if Sandra Random User can see a particular machine, one must perform the Visibility test from outside the Firewall. Important is also to consider that if the corporate firewall permits traffic from a home based PC, the latter is still "trusted." Accordingly, Visibility testing must be done from another machine. |
| A Vulnerability | Is a specific degree of weakness of an individual computer or network exposed to the influence of a Threat. |
| | Vulnerability is a problem when a service is intentionally offered to the outside world, but the service has a flaw that grants an outsider greater access than was intended. |
| | A common vulnerability is an unpatched or misconfigured web server that can be fooled into running operating system commands. Exploiting a buffer overflow in *sendmail* to obtain a root shell is another common vulnerability fault. |
| | To illustrate, not having applied the latest security patch to the operating system of a web server means that one has a Vulnerability. Reason being, that computer system is exposed to potential intruders. |

(cont.)

**Table 24A:** (cont.)

| Type of Threat | Description |
|---|---|
| A Risk | Is the degree of probability that a disaster will occur in light of the existing conditions, and the degree of vulnerability or weakness present in the system (see also Table 22B). |
| | A risk entails a person's judgment about the presence and size of a risk (see also Table 22A). |
| | The **key difference** between a Threat and a Risk is that a threat is related to the potential occurrence of a security issue. In contrast, a risk is the probability of an incident occurring based on the degree of exposure to a threat and the cognitive assessment of the presence and size of a risk. |
| | A Vulnerability can **increase the Risk for a Threat actuation** against information Assets (see Table 18A). |
| | Risk, for security purposes, is usually calculated in dollars and cents. |
| | But as Tables 1, 2A–2D & Table 15C indicate, such assessments are subjective and open to questions because ultimately it is the cognitive component or what a person thinks about risks that lets one decide to either do something or leave it be (or not worry, see Table 22A). Hence, security budgets are not always based on rational risk assessments. |

**Note.** The above can also be compared to Figures 1–3 (attacks) and Tables 3A and 3B, as well as Tables 22A, 22B, 22D, & 22E).

**Table 24B:** Typology of Threats: Two Main Types

| Type of Threat | Description |
|---|---|
| | A threat can be defined as a potential for the accidental or deliberate compromise of the fundamental security objectives including Confidentiality, Integrity, Availability and Accountability of data and their use (see Table 5). |
| | A Vulnerability can **increase the Risk for a Threat actuation** against information assets (see also Tables 3A & 3B). |
| Structured Threats | Is a planned methodical attack focusing on a specific computer or information system for the purpose of compromising, corruting or disrupting services. |
| | Methods could be hacking, malicious code or electronic warfare. |
| Unstructured Threats | Remote penetrations by exploiting systems vulnerabilities to initiate random, often unrelated events that may cause the compromising or disrupting of system operations. |
| | Methods could be such as hacking, freaking, viruses or Malicious Code. |

**Note.** The above can also be compared to Figures 1–3 (attacks) and Tables 3A and 3B, as well as Tables 22A, 22B, 22D, & 22E and also Table 24A.

**Table 24C:** Taxonomy for Structured and Unstructured Threats

| Threat Taxonomy | Domain Category | Sub Category | Description |
|---|---|---|---|
| | | | Structured and unstructured threats (see Table 24B) can be further divided as follows: |
| Fundamental Threats | Information leakage | | Whereby information is disclosed or revealed to an authorized person or entity. |
| | Integrity violation | | Data consistency is compromised through unauthorized creation, alteration, or destruction of data (Table 5D). |
| | Denial of Service (DoS) | | Legitimate access to information or other resources is deliberately impaired. |
| | Illegitimate use | | Resource is used by an unauthorized person or in an unauthorized way. |
| Primary Enabling Threats | | | These are significant because their realisation can lead to the cognizance of any of the fundamental threats as outlined above. These are comprised of main penetration and planting threats (see below). |
| | Main Penetration Threats | Masquerade | Person or system pretends to be a different entity. |
| | | By-Passing Controls | In order to acquire unauthorized rights or privileges, an attacker exploits system flaws on security weaknesses. |
| | | Authorization Violation | Authorized system user performs unauthorized use, thereby making it an inside threat. |
| | Main Planting Threats | Trojan Horse, Virus | See definitions for terms and Malicious Code (see also, Virus, Figure 4). |
| | | Backdoor or Trapdoor | See definition for Backdoor. |
| Underlying Threats | | | Fundamental and Primary Threats should be analyzed to identify the "Underlying" Threats. The latter may result in several additional threats. For instance, the Fundamental Threat of information leakage might have several underlying threats apart from the Primary Enabling Threats, such as: <br><br> —Eavesdropping <br> —Traffic analysis <br> —Indiscretions by staff, and <br> —Media scavenging |

**Note.** The above can also be compared to Figures 1–3 (attacks) and Tables 3A and 3B as well as Table 21A.

**Table 24D:** Further Classification of Typology of Threats and their Taxonomy

| *Type of Threat* | | *Description* |
| --- | --- | --- |

Using the Typology from Table 24A, Structured and Unstructured Threats can be further analyzed and distinguished by using the typology presented in Table 24B.

Table 24C outlines Fundamental, Primary or Underlying Threats. Furthermore, Merging of Attack Technologies has led to Blended Threats as defined below.

| | | |
| --- | --- | --- |
| Blended Threat (see also Hybrid Threat) | | A blended threat utilizes multiple methods and techniques to transmit and spread an attack. Effective protection from blended threats requires a comprehensive security solution that contains multiple layers of defense and response mechanisms. |
| | Characteristics are: | **Causes harm** by, for instance, launching a Denial of Service (DoS) attack at a target IP address, or defaces web servers while leaving Trojan horses behind for later execution. **Multiple methods of propagation** means that the threat scans for vulnerabilities it understands to compromise a system, exemplified by embedding into the html files of infected server, infecting visitors to a web site or sending emails with a Worm attached from a compromised server. **Multiple points of attack** as illustrated by Nimda, injects Malicious code into each .exe file on a system, raises the privilege level of the guest account while creating world read and writable network share. It is also making numerous registry changes and injecting script code into html files. By damaging many points in an information system, the necessary clean up is more difficult. |
| | Spreading automatically | means a Blended Threat continuously scans the internet for finding vulnerable servers that than will be attacked. |
| | Exploiting of Vulnerabilities | Means that by taking advantage of known Vulnerabilities, such as buffer overflows, http input validation Vulnerabilities, and known default Passwords as common points of exploitation, unauthorized Access can be gained on a server (see Figure 1–3). Hence, information stored at the root level can be opened thereby violating Confidentiality, Integrity, Availability of Data, User Accountability, Authentication and Auditing (CIA-UAA) principles. |

Nimda and Code Red are examples of Blended Threats

**Note.** The above can also be compared to Figures 1–3 (attacks) and Tables 3A and 3B as well as Tables 24A, 24B and 24C. Vulnerability is defined in Table 26 as well.

A threat can be magnified by the vulnerabilities with which a system may be faced (e.g., users with limited knowledge or being careless with passwords). Accordingly, a system's vulnerability may increase the likelihood of a threat materializing and result in a compromised information system.

Table 24B outlines Unstructured and Structured Threats. Table 24C explains how these can be further divided into Fundamental, Primary Enabling, and Underlying Threats.

But even these threats may become Blended Threats as outlined in Table 24C, whereby multiple methods are used to spread an attack.

**Threat in Cyberspace**    differs compared to a threat in a physical settings, especially as far as fraud, theft and terrorism are concerned by enabling:

1) automation, thereby making attacks more profitable,
2) actions at a distance, and
3) easier and more raped technique propagation and possible diffusion amongst users (authorized or non-authorized) (see also E-Voting).

**Threat Level Definition**    defines the severity of a Threat. A Threat Level is based on the security experts (e.g., CERT) assessment of the possible impact from recently discovered vulnerabilities. It is also influenced by the availability of patches, descriptions of workarounds and if workable exploits exist.

The Threat Level is usually assessed for vulnerabilities and security flaws in commonly used systems such as:

• Apache webserver,
• most widely used products (e.g., Microsoft operating systems, software and servers, Cisco routers)
• Linux and Unix server operating systems,
• antivirus products and firewalls.

Significant vulnerabilities in the systems mentioned above leave many corporate networks open for attacks, leaving the internet exposed (Table 21D).

**Blended Threats or Hybrid Threats**    as outlined in Table 24D can be extremely dangerous and some argue that it is getting increasingly difficult to protect systems against such types of Threats. One of these is also the Project Injecting Trojans that may come in various forms including as a Blended Threat, below is just one example.

**Process Injecting Trojans**

**Threat Level Definition—Criteria**    is at least until now not an exact science. As Table 24E suggests various factors may play an important role.

**Table 24E:** Definition of Criteria to be Used for Evaluating Threat Level for Malware and System Vulnerabilities

| Criteria Used to Obtain Assessment Level | Question to be Answered | Description |
|---|---|---|
| Diffusion or Prevalence | How widespread is the malicious code or vulnerability? | Vendors' assessment of this criterion reflects the number of incidents, such as Blaster or Slammer, reported by customers. Accordingly, depending on the profile of the user database, assessment of this indicator could differ across vendors or service providers (e.g., Message Labs versus Outbound) (see also Sample, Statistics). |
| Potential for Damage | What happens when the vulnerability or malware is being exploited by a hacker? | Unforeseeable Damage—The virus redistributes confidential data to third parties, or destroys an entire network.<br>Very Serious Damage—The virus manipulates data silently.<br>Serious Damage—The virus deletes many files, formats hard drives, deletes Flash BIOS.<br>Medium Damage—The virus deletes individual files, or renders the computer temporarily unavailable.<br>Little Damage—The virus generates bogus text or generates sounds. |
| Commonality of the infection vehicle | How common is the platform (e.g., Windows), program, or software that the malicious code targets as its entry point for infection?<br><br>Some use Speed of Distribution here but it is obvious that the speed is highly correlated with the commonality, hence, it appears more useful to use this as an indicator. | Very common Operating Systems: Microsoft Windows (e.g., 95, 98, NT, and XP, 2003, Longhorn) Applications: Word, Excel, Email, Newsgroups.<br>Common Operating systems: Mac-OS Applications: Windows Scripting Host (for Visual Basic Script and Java Script).<br>Less common operating systems: Unix, OS/2 Applications: Access, Corel Draw (Corel Script). |

**Note.** The above outlines how viruses and vulnerabilities may be ranked (see also Tables 24F, 24G and Tables 26, 25, and 29).

## Threat Level Definition—Malware

**Table 24F:** Threat Level Definition—Malware

| Level of Threat | Description of Malware Characteristics | Degree of Diffusion (DD)[1] | Potential for Damage (PD)[2] | Speed of Distribution (SP)[3] |
|---|---|---|---|---|
| Level 1 (Very Low) | —poses little threat to users, <br>—malware not necessarily in the wild (i.e. no reported citings of virus outside the laboratory setting) | L | L | L |
| Level 2 (Low) | —reasonably harmless and containable. | L | L/M | L |
| Level 3 (Moderate) | —potential damage and speed of distribution | M/H | L/M | M |
| Examples: W32/Sobig.e@MM, JS/NoClose | —software heuristics may still identify and eliminate this type of malware <br>—immediate signature update of anti-virus software used is highly recommended | | | |
| Level 4 (Severe) Examples: Mylife, Klez | —serious threat type and difficult to contain <br>—could have high damage potential, or <br>—great SP (especially worrisome if currently prevalent in one region only), <br>—most anti-virus packages may require virus signature update to make sure that disinfection of media or data can be secured | M/H | M | H |
| Level 5 (Red Alert/ Very Severe) Examples: Nimda, LoveLetter | —severe type of threat that is difficult to contain, anti-virus heuristics likely not able to catch code, <br>—hence, signature update required for effective defense | M/H | H | H |

**Note.** Threat Levels are difficult to define and based on criteria and various sources of information. Often, the final assessment and ranking depends upon the assessor's perception and is, therefore, subjective.

Below are three main metrics describing different facets that influence classifying a virus or malware threat anywhere from Low Level up to Red Alert.

While at a certain point DD, DA or SD may be judged as being M, they could change rapidly to H or High status due to changes (e.g., a few very large organizations are being infected and the virus spreads amongst their respective employees located around the globe within a few minutes and from there to their many suppliers and customers).

Degree of Diffusion is an arbitrary number and while some anti-virus vendors might state that if the percentage of computers examined by their software on clients' machines reports these as being infected by the virus is between 2.5% and 3.5%, this might be considered widespread, others do not even provide such numbers.

Low = L; Moderate = M; High = H; Epidemic = E

[1]**Degree of Diffusion (DD)**—extent to which a virus is already spreading among computer users, how many cases have been reported from outside the laboratory (also sometimes called in the 'wild'), how prevalent is the virus (low, moderate or high).

[2]**Potential for Damage (PD)**—addresses the potential degree of damage an infection could cause to the user resources (e.g., hard disk) (low, moderate or high).

[3]**Speed of Distribution (SD)**—measures how fast a program spreads itself (low, moderate or high). This is very critical criteria, because the faster Malware may spread, the less time system administrators have to respond for reducing the chances for damages to occur if any hardware is being infected, such as through email.

## Threat Level Definition Vulnerabilities

**Table 24G:** Threat Level Definition—Software/Operating System Vulnerabilities

| Level of Threat | Description of System Vulnerability Characteristics | Degree of Diffusion (DD)[1] | Potential for Damage (PD)[2] | Speed of Distribution (SP)[3] |
|---|---|---|---|---|
| Level 1 (Very Low) | —vulnerabilities that could be exploited have not been published recently; <br>—minor vulnerabilities have been published in limited numbers, while patches are available; | L | L | L |
| Level 2 (Low) | —minor vulnerabilities leaving certain configurations open to attack; <br>—patches or work around approaches are available; | L | L/M | L |
| Level 3 (Moderate) | —easy to exploit vulnerabilities exist <br>—patches and work around approaches are available <br>—vulnerability exploits are in the wild | M/H | L/M | M |
| Level 4 (Severe) | —easy to exploit vulnerabilities exist <br>—work around approaches are available but no patches yet <br>—work around approaches require good technical skills <br>—limited public awareness <br>—vulnerability exploits are in the wild | M/H | M | H |
| Level 5 (Red Alert/ Very Severe) | —easy to exploit vulnerabilities exist <br>—patches and work around approaches are still being fine-tuned or not yet available <br>—public awareness is raising but patches for easy installation are not yet available <br>—vulnerability exploits are in the wild and used successfully by some. | M/H | H | H |

**Note.** Threat Levels regarding Vulnerabilities are difficult to define and based on criteria and various sources of information. Often, the final assessment and ranking depends upon the assessor's perception and is, therefore, subjective. We have also not given specific examples since these might be primarily attributed to one vendor.

Below are three main metrics describing different facets that influence classifying a virus or malware threat anywhere from Low Level up to Red Alert.

While at a certain point DD, DA or SD may be judged as being M, they could change rapidly to H or High status due to changes (e.g., a few very large organizations are being infected and the virus spreads amongst their respective employees located around the globe within a few minutes and from there to their many suppliers and customers).

Degree of Diffusion is an arbitrary number and might be simply pre-determined by the prevalence of a particular software or hardware.

Low = L; Moderate = M; High = H; Epidemic = E

[1]**Degree of Diffusion (DD)**—extent to which a prevalent among computer users due to the wide use of a system, software or hardware.

[2]**Potential for Damage (PD)**—addresses the potential degree of damage that could be caused on a firm's information assets if a vulnerability is being successfully exploited by an unauthorized party.

[3]**Speed of Distribution (SD)**—measures how fast an attack exploiting this vulnerability might spread.

**Three Strikes**   describes the method, whereby users who fail to provide a valid password within three attempts are locked out.

**Time Bomb**   is a logic bomb whose condition is based on time.

**Timing Attacks**   transpire when they are taking advantage of timing of computer processes and operations (see also Attack).

**Tinkerbell Program**   is a monitoring program used to scan incoming entwork conenctions and generate alerts when calls are received from particular sites, or when logins are attempted using certain ID's.

**TLS**   see Secure Socket Layer (SSL)

**Tool**   is a means of exploiting a computer or network vulnerability.

But a tool can also just be a utility program used primarily to create, manipulate, modify, or analyze other programs, such as a compiler or an editor or a cross-referencing program, or perform maintenance and/or repairs on system hardware or application software.

Tools include such as, Hex editors, disk checkers, file backup and recovery programs. Tools are powerful pieces of software and the use of tools within an organization should be restricted to those employees, who have either received the proper training or have otherwise proven their competence in the use of such software.

**Toolkit**   is a software package that contains scripts, programs, or autonomous agents that exploit vulnerabilities (see also Rootkit).

It can also describe a collection of tools with related purposes or functions, such as, Anti-Virus Toolkit, and Disk Toolkit.

**Topology**   is the map or plan of the network. While the physical topology describes how the wires or cable are laid out, the logical or electrical topolgy outlines how the information flows.

**Total Cost of Ownership (TCO)**   is an annual cost representing the actual 'all in' cost of 'end user computing'. Some estimate that a networked PC can cost about $13,200 per node annually for hardware, software, support and administrative services and end-user operations.

Hardware costs have come down but end-user costs, particularly support continue to stay high.

**Tracking Process**   see Disruption Management

**Traffic Analysis**   is the collection and analysis of information, particularly through the analysis of message characteristics and content (e.g., filtering or scanning).

**Training**   see Learning—Skills & Knowledge

**Transient Electro Magnetic Pulse Emanation Standards (Tempest)**   is the study of electro-magnetic signals bearing compromising information emanating from electronic processing equipment and cabling. All IT-related hardware and communication equipment produce unintended electro-magnetic emanations that are related to the information being processed or communicated. Analysis of these emanations may allow the recovery of the original information, which can then be exploited. Certain measures can be used to counter these effects such as:

- Enclosing systems within a screened room or building and managing the con-trolled space, thereby preventing unauthorized physical access near classified systems.
- Using Tempest rated or tested equipment which is, however, costly;
- Fiber optic cabline elminates cable Tempest conduction and radiation
- Filters (e.g., telephone or electricity) will reduce Tempest conduction, and
- Separation of equipment and cabling of differently classified systems (e.g., low security).

**Transmission Control Protocol/Internet Protocol (TCP/IP)**   is the suite of protocols establishing the principle method of communication on the Internet.

**Transmission of Infection**   is the mechanism which an infectious agent is spread from a source or reservoir to another program or system (see also Infection). These mechanisms can be described as:

1) **Direct** and essentially immediate transfer of a virus infection to a receptive portal of entry through which the virus infection may take place such as exchanging files

2) **Indirect** transfer may be

   a)   **Vehicle-borne**, whereby the virus is transported and introduced into a sus-ceptible host through a suitable portal of entry, such as a Windows virus infecting another Windows system

   b)   **Transmitting host borne** whereby, for instance, a Windows virus is first being channeled through a Unix system. The latter is an environment where the virus cannot be executed but it passes it on to another vulnerable system passively instead of by self-replication (sometimes also called heterogenous virus transmission).

**Transmission Parameter**   describes the proportion of total possible contacts between infectious PCs or systems and susceptible ones that lead to new infections.

**Transport Layer Security**   see Secure Socket Layer (SSL)

**Trap Door**   see Backdoor

**Trasher**   or cyber-terrorist (see also hacker) is an attacker that will damage data or infrastructure and habitually modify data, thereby damaging data's integrity (e.g., modifying patient records).

**Trigger**   see Virus and Table 13

**Tripwire**   is a software tool that uses a database that maintains information about the byte count of files. If the byte count has changed, it will identify it to the system security manager.

**Trivial File Transfer Protocol (TFTP)**   is a program for transferring files between computers on a network. This is one of the least secure protocols ever known—it does not provide for any authentication. Accordingly, it should simply not been used.

**Trojan**   is usually a program that seems to do something very useful. It often does, but often also does other things behind the scene.

Trojans take their name from the mythical Trojan horse built for getting behind enemy lines and which, under the guise of a harmless gift, concealed in its interior a group of Greek warriors. The programs grouped under this heading share the same philosophy. Under the guise of harmless utilities, they conceal damaging code that is entered into affected computers with the goal of obtaining confidential information or destroying important data. **Unlike worms, true Trojans are not capable of replicating** (see also Signature, Virus, Worm).

**Trojan Horse**   is a term was coined by Hacker, turned spook, Dan Edwards. A Trojan Horse is a malicious, security-breaking program that is disguised as something benign, such as a directory lister, archiver, game or, in one notorious 1990 case on the Apple Macintosh, a program to search and destroy viruses (see also Table 19A, Figure 5).

Trojan Horse is a program that performs like a real program a user may wish to run. Unfortunately it also performs unauthorized actions (see also Signature, Virus, Worm (Tables 18A and 18B).

**Mockingbird**   is a special type of a Trojan Horse, namely software that intercepts communications (especially login transactions) between users and hosts, and provides system-like responses to the users while saving their responses (especially account IDs and passwords) for later transmission to, or collection by, a third party.

**Process Injecting Trojans**   see Trojans are a new generations of this type of Malware. To avoid detection these Trojans attach themselves to a process that forms a key part of the Windows operating system itself.

In the case of The Beast, the processes chosen for infection are winlogon.exe and explorer.exe. These have been selected because they are always present on any 2003/XP/2000/NT-based PC.

This stealthing approach makes The Beast (see Appendix . . . ) particularly hard to detect. Certainly a normal process scanner will notreveal its presence and almost all common anti-Virus scanners will miss it as well.

Killing or deleting the Trojan is also difficult as it resides within a process essential for the operation of Windows. Hence, removing the Trojan may in fact render the Windows operating system useless.

And if you think that the .dll checksum feature in a firewall will protect your assets, it may not. Some version are able to pull down 32 of the most popular Firewalls and anti-Virus scanners and many anti-Trojan monitors as well.

Some test results with this type of Trojan indicate that Norton Anti-Virus 2003 disappears, closely followed by a Sygate Personal Firewall Pro and the BoClean anti-Trojan monitor. Not only were these defenses pulled down, they were permanently destroyed so they could not be restarted.

If a Trojan, such as beast, has infected your PC the attacker essentially has complete control. He/she can view, upload or erase any of your files and log all your keystrokes including your all your passwords. Worse still, you may not even know your PC is infected.

There are some tips about how one can protect oneself against such types of Malware while doing safe computing (see Appendix 7) but total safety is, of course, a dream. Nonetheless, being cautious helps.

Trojans are becoming ever more sophisticated. Each new Trojan generation becomes more difficult to detect and is armed with ever more aggressive weapons aimed at a system's defenses.

Some anti-virus software does address the above issues but most failed to do so at least in early 2004.

**Trolling**   describes the baiting of readers on Usenet newsgroups whereby a posting is put up designed simply to incite a large volume of angry responses.

Posts such as those that scream out racist epithets are common trolls. This activity is not normally a problem for companies - unless the person trolling happens to be using an organization's machine. The likely result may well be mail-bombing or other denial of service activity (Denial-of-Service, Mail-Bombing).

**Trust**   as defined in dictionaries is something similar to assured reliance on the character, ability, strength, or truth of someone or something—as well as a person or party in which confidence is placed. In fact a thesaurus will probably indicate that Trust and Confidence are synonymous (see also below).

In the context of information Security, eCommerce and eGovernment, Trust consists of two dimensions, namely:

1. **Perceived Credibility** which is related to the objective credibility of the product offered such as the expectancy that the customer can rely on the seller's word or written statement about the security product's or service's performance, and
2. **Benevolence**, which is related to the information security service provider's interest in the Alert recipient's or client's welfare and motivation to seek a joint gain.

**Confidence**   is exemplified in users that trust the merchant's competence, integrity and benevolence to perform the intended behavior in the transaction such as shipping the goods after payment has been received. Users should also have Confidence in the dependability of information technology. This latter condition, in turn, entails that the technology is perceived as secure, safe, reliable and available.

Hence Users' Confidence that the anti-Virus software or Firewall will function properly, or that any willful and malicious acts won't succeed is an important factor that influences users' Risk perception and Worry (see also Table 22B).

Finally, Confidence is considered a synonym of Trust in the English language.

**Trust and Confidence**   are considered synonymous terms and in relationship to Information Security, these two 'concepts' can be defined as done above and further expanded upon just below.

**Trust Level**   depends on the information that the trustee has on the trusted person. A person who has

- **imperfect information** is more likely to perform a decision based on trust and may gather information from trusted information sources. People with imperfect information need to trust the provider of the information and put more importance on evaluating the information in order to make the decision.

In contrast, the individual who has:

- **perfect information** about a product can decide solely on this information and does not need to revert to trust developed in past transactions. People with perfect information put less importance on trusting information.

Accordingly, trust in Security or Securematics is **situation specific, depends on the actual level of information available** to the parties involved and **develops over time**. Specifically, through relationships people begin to trust each other's knowledge and advice regarding Information Security.

**Repeated Transactions—Trusted Source for an Alert or an Advisory**
is one that people have come to trust as having proven in the past of being
correct (e.g., government, CERT, anti-virus vendor, and CASES).

For repeated transactions credibility and benevolence are continuously
evaluated and if the source of an Alert or Advisory fails to keep an agreement, such as delivering the alert in a timely fashion, credibility might be
lowered.

**Trusted Information Sharing Network (TISN)**   for Critical Information
Infrastructure (CII) (see also Critical Infrastructure Protection) allows owners
and operators of such infrastructure to share information on vital issues, such
as:

- Business Continuity Management
- Attacks
- Vulnerabilities
- Incidents
- Threats
- Technical Advice and Research

Table 5A outlines various organizations might provide information regarding
Vulnerabilities and Incidents while Table 5B focuses specifically on TISN
(see also Social Networks).

**Trusted Operating System**   is one that has been specially modified to be
secure, thereby affording maximum security for those systems which require
it. One reason for this development is due to the substantial rise in concern
over the apparent ease by which hackers are able to gain access to seemingly
**secure** systems.

A number of vendors have developed variations on mainstream version of
UNIX and Windows® which go well beyond the standard Operating System
hardening which is advisable for all and any desktop and server systems.

However, the deployment of a trusted Operating system, does require substantially more training of your systems operations staff as, no longer does the
Administrator necessarily have 'ultimate power'. Henceforth the functions
which control say, file, print or network access, are now split into separate
'sandboxes' which permit only a subset of actions to be performed by one
systems administrator. It will be apparent that a substantially higher degree of
coordination is required with the systems Operations team, and also a much
deeper level of planning before any changes are made.

Whilst this may appear to be a high overhead; it does prevent a system
from gradually being changed over time by a single systems' Administrator
making small changes 'here and there'. In effect the Operating System is

locked down and such Trusted Systems lend themselves to any e-commerce business where maximum security is paramount; say e-banking.

**Trusted System**   see Trusted Operating System

**Trusted Third Party Encryption (TTPE)**   see Key Recovery

**Tunneling**   is a term that describes the use of one data transfer method to carry data for another method.

It may also involve tracing the system interrupts to the final programming, as used by both, viral and antiviral programs in order to detect or disable opposing programs.

To illustrate, file operations performed on the computer are analyzed by the Resident anti-virus program. The latter intercepts the actions that the operating system carries out before they are executed and checks if is is malware. If the virus intercepts these requests first, the anti-virus program will fail to detect the presence of the malicious code. Accordingly, tunneling in this context means that the anti-virus software's interrupt routines are avoided, thereby enabling the virus to use its own interrupt system. But anti-virus software detects viruses using this technique.

T

**Ubiquitous Computing**   see Pervasive Computing

**Unauthorized**   describes a not approved or sanctioned action by the owner or administrator.

**Unauthorized Result**   transpires when an unauthorized consequence of an event occurs.

**Unicode**   is an international character set. Similar to American Standard Code for Information Interchange (ASCII), Unicode provides a standard correspondence between the binary numbers that computers understand and the letters, digits, and punctuation that people understand.

Unlike ASCII, however, it seeks to provide a code for every character in every language in the world. To do this requires more than 256 characters. ASCII is based on the 8-bit character set while Unicode uses 16-bit characters as the default.

With thousands of characters and new characters being added all the time, it will be extremely difficult to categorize all the possible characters consistently, and where there is inconsistency, there tends to be security holes. Hence, an Intrusion Detection System (IDS) probably won't be able to get a consistent definition of what to accept, what is a delimiter under what circumstance, or how to handle arbitrary streams safely.

Accordingly, it could happen that simple validators pass data and upper layer software, trying to be helpful, attach magic-character semantics, and a brand-new variety of security holes or vulnerabilities might just be ready to happen.

In the early 1990s, various software suppliers started developing a 16-bit character standard, called 'Unicode'. This could have resulted in a de-facto standard that competed with the ISO standard, but the development of the two has long been harmonised. The Unicode standardisation can be seen as the industry standard implementations of character encodings compatible with Unicode. Although it is commonly 16 bits, there are 32-bit Unicode standards (UTF-32, as opposed to UTF-16). Note that although 16 bits might be thought to only allow $2^{16} = 65536$ characters, it is possible to extend this (see also ASCII).

**Uniform Resource Locator (URL)**   is the technical term for the location of a file or resource on the Internet. The URL will always include the type of protocol being used, such as http for a web page or ftp for the address of a specific file which is to be downloaded.

An example URL using the http protocol is: http://Security.WebUrb.org

**Uninstall**   is the process whereby a program is being removed from a system. Instead of simply deleting files in a program directory, an uninstaller is being used. Best is if this program was active at the time of installation, thereby enabling it to record ALL changes made to disk and file contents.

**Uninterruptible Power Supply (UPS)**   is a vital piece of hardware that during, a power 'outage' or even a surge prevents the system from being shut down. For PC owners this might not be too severe. Nonetheless, when running Windows® NT, 2000 or UNIX, while experiencing a sudden loss of power, the consequences can be quite serious. Potentially, hundreds of files can be left in an "open" state. This, in the worst scenario, could prevent the system from rebooting properly—or even at all.

Because a UPS contains its own battery(ies) it can not only prevent damage from sudden power surges, but it can continue to run your systems for between 15 minutes and 1 hour (or more), thus allowing an orderly, but speedy, close down.

A UPS is, however, not supposed to allow the system to be operated for any length of time. Hence, to provide a greater degree of protection against power cuts, a backup power generator should be considered.

Unfortunately, backup generators are intended to supply power for a limited amount of time but as the Province of Quebec (Canada) found out a few years back over a two week winter period with a power failure, generators were not able to cope with running at full tilt, 24 hours each day during the power outage. Hence, they broke down. Accordingly, Disaster Management requires that the firm's power requirements (e.g., air circulation system and information systems) are assessed carefully and the backup systems are designed accordingly.

Lightning can result in a falling tree interrupting power supply from Switzerland to Italy, causing the latter's energy grid to fall apart. Happened in September 28, 2003. This was also Rome's museum night and by 3 am the city was dark, subways did not work nor the mobile phone network. If such a power interruption is a problem than the firm must protect itself.

**Unix**   is an operating system that was developed by Ken Thompson and Dennis Ritchie in 1969; it is the predominant operating system for high-performance computing.

**Up or Uptime**   means that the system is running and accessible in the usual manner. Uptime, refers to the period during which the system is up such as in between maintenance or system Updates.

**Updates**   means that the archive containing all the signatures needed to detect viruses is being updated. While usually only the Virus Signature File needs to be updated oven (e.g., daily), an Upgrade may be less frequent.

**Upgrades**   are the release of new software (or hardware) which genuinely fixes old problems and introduces new (and tested) functionality.

Unfortunately, upgrades can become a clever means of charging customers for the functionality that they should have gotten in the first place when they purchased the product. Normally, where a product has reported bugs and problems, the software vendor will release a patch (e.g., in 2001, Microsoft released over 120 patches for Windows products), in 2003 these vulnerability patches were over 100 again (see also Patch, Releasing of Security Patch)

**Urban Legend (UL)**   is a slightly amorphous class of fantasy/seem-fantasy by

1) appearing and spreading spontaneously in various forms;
2) encompassing either humor or horror, in the latter case a person flouting society's conventions might be 'punished;'
3) telling a good story
4) having a core of truth, possibly based on fact but in regards to point 2 and 3 above their life after-the-fact makes them particularly interesting

Urban Legend may also carrry an implied moral subtext (see also Virus Hoax).

The difference between an Urban Legend and a Chain Letter may be that the latter includes an explicit replicative mechanism.

**URL**   see Uniform Resource Locator

**Usenet**   describes the part of the internet populated by Newsgroups, defined as Network News Transfer Protocol or NNTP. The term 'news' is a little misleading since these groups are more in the nature of discussion groups. Usenet is relatively harmless, but access to newsgroups, as opposed to Email, is largely unnecessary for organizational users, except possibly for some of the groups dedicated to technical computer matters.

**User**   is the individual that uses, changes, or views information and data (See also Role of User, Superuser and Help Desk)

**User Involvement**   see Invention—Collective Invention

**User Command**   is a means of exploiting a vulnerability by entering commands to a process through direct user input at the process interface. An example is entering Unix commands through a telnet connection, or entering commands right at an SMTP port.

**User Acceptance Testing**   is the test procedures that lead to formal 'acceptance' of new or changed systems. The final part of the UAT can also include a parallel run to prove the system against the current system.

   The above including the User Acceptance Test Plan (see below) should help in reducing Downtime. This approach is also highly recommendable if a Patch needs to be installed. Hence, before installing the Patch, it should be tested in a safe environment making sure that any conflicts do not result in affecting the system negatively (see also Table 19B).

   User Acceptance may also be linked to Project Management and the plan.

**User Acceptance Test Plan**   outlines the requirements and performance bechmarks that are planned in order to provide a realistic and adequate exposure of the system to all reasonably expected events. The testing can be based upon the user requirements specifications to which the system should conform. An evaluation scheme is needed with whose help the system performance is evaluated such as:

- **Show Stopper**—means that it is impossible to continue with the testing because of the severity of an error or bug in the system;
- **Critical Problem**—testing can continue but going live is not possible because of this problem discovered during the test;
- **Major Problem**—testing can continue but going live would mean that this error or bug could cause severe disruption to the business process;
- **Medium Problem**—testing should continue, going live with the system might result in minimal departure from agreed processes and performance standards; and

- **Minor Problem**—more testing is needed while going live is pretty safe since if the bug occurs, only minimal disruptions are envisaged; and
- **Cosmetic Problem**—minor visual issues that are rated as being of little significance while being easily fixed within an agreed period.

To make this testing evaluation process effective, however, a range of examples must be agreed upon in advance, reducing the risk for disagreements (see also Acceptance Criteria).

**User Acceptance Criteria**  are the key parameters and indicators agreed between users and a system supplier. Hence, they must agree on the maximum number of acceptable 'outstandings' for each particular category. Users may agree to accept and sign off on a system, subject to a range of conditions.

**User Group**  is often formed in order to enable users a venue for exchanging issues and solutions common amongst them. The User Group can also act as a common voice from the User Group to the vendor, thus offering the possibility of consensus and focus where competing priorities could otherwise exist.

**User ID**  is the backbone of most system's access security. The ID can be any combination of characters and is normally issued with a password. The (user) ID will usually remain fixed and is often the user's name or perhaps job title. Linked to the ID will be a Password which should be changed in accordance with your Information Security Policy.

Having a User Name of 'UrsG' or 'MaraikaDahl' is also reducing the effectiveness of one of the main security safeguards for all system's access; the User ID and password. If the User ID is already known, his name is Urs Gattiker or Maraika Dahl, this allows a hacker to concentrate upon the password, in the certain knowledge that the User ID is correct.

**User Interface**  is the way in which a system presents itself to, and interacts with, a human user. In today's Graphical Windowing environments the User Interface is a combination of the look, feel and overall logic of the 'human machine interface'.

**User Requirements Specification (URS)**  documents the purposes for which a system is required—its functional requirements—usually in order of priority/gradation.

Whilst the URS will not usually probe the technical specification, it will nevertheless outline the expectations and, where essential may provide further detail, such as the User Interface (e.g., Microsoft Windows®), and the expected hardware platform.

The URS is an essential document which outlines precisely what the User (or customer) is expecting from this system. The term User Requirement Specification can also incorporate the functional requirements of the system or may be in a separate document labelled the Functional Requirements Specification—the FRS.

**Utility** is a specialized program designed for more technical users as a tool, or set of tools, for checking the system, housekeeping, monitoring system health/status, repairing files, etc. Access to utility programs by non-technical users should be restricted.

**Validiation** is the process of establishing that a method is sound (see also Mathodology, Statistics, Survey, Validity, Confidence Level–Table 15B).

**Validity of Measurement** is derived from the Latin *validus*, strong. In general the term means the degree to which a measurement measures what it purports to measure. The term is usually accompanied by a qualifying word or phrase such as:

**Construct Validity**—encompasses the **degree to which the measurement corresponds to theoretical concepts concerning the phenomenon under study**. For instance, if on theoretical groups, the phenomenon should change with age, a measurement with construct validity would reflect such a change (e.g., riskier behavior by younger employees, more likely to violate policy).

**Content Validity**—the **extent to which the measurement incorporates the domain of the phenomenon under study**. For instance, the measurement of functional IT security status should embrace activities of daily use, data groups, access restrictions and other factors.

**Criterion Validity**—is the extent to which the **measurement correlates with an external criterion** of the phenomenon under study, such as Vulnerability metric of a system with number of Pin attempts recorded against system every day.

**Concurrent Validity**—how well the measurement and the criterion refer to the same **point in time**. To illustrate, the person's knowledge about the firm's

IT security policy assessed in a discussion is compared with his or her log of visiting unauthorized web sites.

**Predictive Validity**—encompasses the **measures ability to predict the criterion**. For instance, how well a person does on a few questions regarding the firm's IT security policy is validated against subsequent user behavior regarding security matters in using system resources.

**Validity of Study**   refers to the degree to which the inference drawn from a study, espcially generalizations extending beyond the study Sample (e.g., system administrators in Fortune 500 firms = 500 largest USA firms), are warranted. Here account is also taken of the study methods, the representativeness of the study Sample (see also Statistical Inference), and the nature of the population from which it is drawn. Two varieties of study validity are distinguished:

**Internal Validity**—assesses how index and comparison groups are selected and compared in a way that the observed differences between them on the dependent variables under study may, apart from sampling error, be attributed only to the hypothesized effect under investigation (e.g., PCs infected by new virus)

**External Validity (Generalizability)**—is achieved if the study permits the production of unbiased inferences (see also Statistical Inference) regarding a target population. For instance, based on a sample taken from information assurance or security officers in Fortune 500 firms, can the inferences made be generalized to

- other Fortune 500 firms (e.g., banks vs. retailers),
- the 500 largest European firms, or
- to Small and Medium-Sized Enterprises (SMEs) in California or Bavaria?

As the above would suggest, it is very difficult to achieve External Validity and most of the time it is safer to limit one's statements to a particular group of respondents or type of firms instead of making sweeping statements, such as damages caused by a virus cost organizations about Euro 5,000 to 25,000 for each PC unless one can show with a thorough costing system (see Tables 2A–2C) that this is a valid statement. Lawyers talk about proof meaning "beyond reasonable doubt". Calculating damages requires the same to make these numbers valid.

**Value-chain integration**   *is* a process of collaboration that optimizes all internal and external activities involved in delivering greater perceived value to the ultimate customer. Hence, a supermarket chain may allow hundreds of suppliers to access its data warehouse, giving them real-time information about how each of their products is selling in every single store. This enables suppliers to tailor production to demand and shifting tastes while enabling the store to never run out of stock. On the selling site, the supermarket may use the website for remote shopping and electronic cataloguing while also collecting customers' preferences from the site to personalise promotions.

**Van Eck Radiation**   describes the electronic emanations surrounding a computer, in particular the monitor.

**VDSL**   see Very-High-bit-rate Digial Subscriber Line

**Version**   identifies a variant of the original value of an object.

1. In terms of records, successive copies of an original documents to which changes have been made.
2. In terms of software programs, successive releases usually providing enhancements and improvements over the previous release or version.

**Very-High-bit-rate Digital Subscriber Line**   (VDSL) can reach 30 to 40 Mbps (with Quadrature Amplitude Modulation (QAM)-VDSL about 75 Mbps), which is about 1,000 times faster than a classical dial-up connection. In comparison, Asymmetrical Digital Subscriber Line (ADSL) offers up to about 6.11 megabits per second (Mbps). Moreover, VDSL is symmetric, whereby in contrast to ADSL, upload and download speeds are identical (see also Asymmetrical Digital Subscriber Line–ADSL).

To get the full benefits coming with VDSL, however, integration of Discrete Multi-Tone (DMT) modulation is sometimes used but Quadrature Amplitude Modulation (QAM)-VDSL) allows users to reap the full speed rewards and help avoid interference from other technologies (e.g., ringing mobile phone).

**Video Viewing**   occurs when somebody is monitoring video signals on a network. Some people also call this Sniffing (see Sniffer).

**Viral Marketing**   was coined after the way viruses multiply rapidly in a cell, commandeering the cell's resources to do the virus' bidding. The classic example is HotMail.com, a free email system. Each email message (sent by definition to a person's own friends and associates) carries a message encouraging the recipient to sign up for a HotMail account, too. This technique lifted HotMail's user base from 3 million two months after launching to 10 million at the end of 1997 with a marketing budget of just $500,000. The company finished 1998 with more than 30 million users, a feat that simply has no equal in Net history. Microsoft spent more than $400 million to acquire HotMail in late 1997.

Reportedly coined by venture-capital firm Draper Fisher Jurvetson in 1998, "viral marketing" is synonymous with advocacy marketing, which harnesses the evangelical zeal of customers. Budweiser was likely the first consumer brand using viral marketing techniques to promote its TV commercial via the Internet.

Users are becoming increasingly concerned about viral marketing efforts. For instance, in the case of Ikea's tell-a friend campaign in the USA 2001, consumers who received animated postcards from their friends about Ikea cried "spam." The promotion got stopped after 37,000 messages. So while viral marketing attached to Hotmail might be acceptable, a more obvious promotional effort as in Ikea's case may not.

Viral marketing efforts from free services offered by portals may be attached to any email sent from such a service, three examples are listed below from hotmail, Yahoo! and Web.de

- Get your FREE download of MSN Explorer at http://explorer.msn.com
- Do You Yahoo!? Yahoo! Sports—live college hoops coverage http://sports.yahoo.com/
- Darf es ein bisschen mehr sein? Mehr Speicher, mehr Mail, mehr Erlebnis, mehr Prämie, mehr WEB.DE. Der WEB.DE Club—http://club.web.de

In the above case, viral marketing through the customer may be accepted because it is in return for a free service. Nonetheless, the recipient may have given consent to the above when ticking on the Condition of Service—Accepted button when signing up for the service. Accordingly, viral marketing may reflect various levels of choice including those for getting free service (see also Spam).

With free Short Messaging System (SMS) services to cellular/mobile phones this may also be used by entering to the bottom of the message something similar like:

- Powered by Bluewin

Whereby the provider gets anywhere from 10–30 spaces of the 160 spaces used for an SMS.

**Virology**   is the science of viruses, the branch of medicine concerned with the study of viruses and the diseases they cause.

In Virology, Viruses are often referred to whether they have or have lost some aspect of their biological activities rather than referring to living or dead viruses. Accordingly, one can talk about the number of infectious particles, or number of plaque forming particles rather than number of living particles.

Virology distinguishes between primary classification such as nucleic acid and virion structure of a Virus. Secondary classification deals with the replication strategy of a Virus.

In practical virology, it is useful to have reference types. These are particular isolates of a Virus that is a member of a species. One can think of it as being representative of a particular species and its genus. Cultures of reference types can be exchanged between laboratories so as to enable direct comparisons to be made with any novel isolate.

A reference type is therefore fundamentally distinct from a Type Species, which as a species is an abstraction and not a virus culture. In bacteriology, a "Type Strain" is defined as the type of a species where there is a living culture. Reference isolates or reference strains of Virus species are thus directly analogous to these "type strains".

**Computer Virology** is still a fledgling field of science whereby the creation of the computer Virus is a specific variety of human creative work. It has originated almost simultaneously with the creation of the first computer program.

Its "negative" realization is found in the possible destruction, unauthorized use and intrusion in computers around the world.

While the idea of the biological behavior of the computer viruses and genetically borrowed mechanisms for propagation may be seen as helpful by some, it is far from reality. Self-encoding and self-mutating algorithms are still not comparable to infectious particles or number of plaque forming particles as is the case in Virology.

Computer Virology is the study of computer viruses, their environment, and relation. The primary interests are viruses and Virus detection.

**Detection Problem** see Virus Detection Problem

**Virtual Private Network (VPN)**   is a network which emulates a private network, although runs over public network lines and infrastructure. Using specialist hardware and software, a VPN may be established running over the Internet. The use of encryption and a 'tunnelling protocol' maintains privacy. Because public networks are used, the cost of a VPN costs a fraction of that of a traditional private network. VPN is set up to provide a seure channel using public communications networks such as the Internet. Because the channel is encrypted, data are not likely to be compromised through lack of confidentiality, integrity, or accessibility protection measures. Nonetheless, it is subject to the same availability problems as the public communications network (see Critical Infrastructure Protection).

The encrypted data shares the public communications media, but is logically separated from the public network by encryption. End-users are unaware of the encryption process. The VPN tunnel eliminates the cost of dedicated encryption links between different communicating sites.

**Virtual Private Network-Gateway**   are the vulnerable end of a VPN. If any element in a trusted relationship between two systems has been compromised, naturally the entire network on wether side of that relationship is potentially open to a Hybrid threat infestation.

Poorly Secured or configured remote/mobile access points such as laptops, personal digital assistants (PDAs) or mobile phones may themselves be compromised. Thereafter their trusted relationship to the VPN gateway may be used to transmit hybrid threat directly into a corporation's network.

**Virtual Server**   is a server that is not directly attached to the hardware. One hardware unit can run several virtual servers under the umbrella of one operating system. Such a system can run even different versions of operating systems on each virtual server. The term is often associated with web servers.

**Virtual Web Server**   is a one particular web server that runs on hardware that provides more virtual servers. This improves utilization of powerful hosts and makes life easier for ISPs. They can have tens of virtual servers on one physical server and they will all appear as unique servers to the outside world. Virtual Web Servers can be either IP address based or name based.

**IP Address Based Virtual Web Server** is a physical server that has more than one network card with different IP addresses, or one network card is serving several different IP addresses using aliasing in network setup.

**Name Based Virtual Web Servers** are distinguished only by their fully qualified domain name (FQDN), however, they do have same IP address. This is achieved by creating aliases (CNAME entries) in DNS database.

Both options mentioned above have each their advantages and disadvantages.

**Virus**   is a segment of a computer code or a program that will copy its code into one or more larger 'host' programs when it is activated. Unfortunately, it also may peform other unauthorized actions at that time (see also Merging of Attack Technologies, Trojans, Virology).

To illustrate, virus is a program that searches out other programs and infects them by embedding itself in them, so that they become Trojans. When these programs are executed, the embedded virus is executed as well, thereby propagating the "infection". This process tends to be invisible to the user (see also Malware, and Ghost Positive).

**Hybrid** see Hybrid Threat (Table 24D)

**Legal Issues**—see Damages

**Virus antivirus** represents a virus that searches for one particular virus or several types of viruses and, hopefully, eliminates the viruses.

To illustrate, a so-called "good Samaritan" worm (W32/Nachi.A) rooted through networks looking for the Blaster worm that debilitated so many networks. The virus found the Blaster, removed it and fixed it by automatically downloading the Microsoft patch. Unfortunately, it did so at the expense of processing speed and bandwidth. When the new worm got inside the USA Navy Marine Corps' Intranet network, it ate up huge amounts of bandwidth by sending out pings to locate instances of the Blaster worm during August 2003. In turn, sending out a Patch against the "good Samaritian" worm was much delayed, further exacerbating the problem.

Incidentally, Nachi.A is designed, like the infamous Blaster worm, to exploit the RPC DCOM Vulnerability that affects some versions of the Windows operating system. Nachi.A does not spread by e-mail. It incorporates a TFTP (Trivial File Transfer Protocol) server that allows it to attack remote computers via TCP/IP in order to cause a buffer overrun in the targeted machine. As a result, the affected computer will download a copy of the worm. Nachi.A, whose origin seems to be China, can also exploit the WebDav Vulnerability.

Nachi.A has an unusual feature, it uninstalls the Blaster worm from computers affected by this malicious code, killing its processes and deleting the file that contains the worm. Besides, it downloads and installs the Microsoft security patch that fixes the RPC DCOM vulnerability. Finally, it deletes itself when the year of the system date is 2004.

**Virus scanner** is a program designed to detect and destroy known computer viruses based upon signatures. Virus scanners must be updated regularly as new viruses and virus strains become prevalent.

**Virus writer** is an individual who programs a virus but may use a kit to do so or else

Table 25 outlines the various category of viruses that are known at this point building on the more general definitions in Tables 18A and the example of how much more difficult the challenge is becoming as outlined in Tables 18B and 18C.

**Virus Detection Problem (VDP)**    is the main issue whereby given a program, does the program contain a virus? Additionally, what kind of viruses are detectable? What type of viruses are undetectable?

Issues su.ch is if an algorithm can carry out effective virus testing like human experts is also of concern (see Virology)

Sometimes terms such as, Virus detection theory, Virus analysis, Virus modeling, Virus detection methods, Viral algorithms, are also discussed but because of their very fuzzy definition and use they are not defined here.

**Table 25:** Types of Viruses-Categorization

| Name of Category | Definition of Category |
|---|---|
| Boot Sector Virus (BSV) (sometimes known as a boot-sector infector–BSI) | Is a virus that replaces the original boot sector on a floppy or hard disk.<br>Sometimes, a BSV attacks the first physical sector of the disk, regardless of disk type. Hence, by attacking the master boot record on hard disks makes it a BSV of the master boot record type. |
| Cluster Virus | infect hard or floppy disks modifying their file systems in such a way that all file entries are redirected towards the virus code. This virus code only exists on a single location on the disk but on running any file the virus is automatically run as well. This way it appears to infect all programs on the disk. |
| Fast Burner Virus | mails itself to everyone in the victim's address-book (see also Heuristics). A fast burner hoax virus that 'gets lucky' can go global within hours or minutes of its introduction 'into the wild.' The above can mean that by the time the vendors have a fix, melted down mail servers and oversubscribed vendor web-sites constitute serious obstacles to distribution of updates and patches. |
| Companion Virus (also referred to as Spawning Virus) | A type of viral program that does not actually attach to another program. Instead it interposes itself into the chain of command<br>It exploits the Disk Operating System (DOS) file naming extension property that if two programs with the same name exist, the operating system will execute a .COM program in preference to an .EXE file. |
| Hoax Virus (also referred to as Virus Hoax) | Depends on the gullibility and lack of technical expertise of the victims. As such they depend on the recipients' altruistic urge to warn as many people as possible about what they believe to be a genuine danger.<br>A number of close-related or derived hoaxes (e.g., Irina, PenPal Greetings, Deeyenda, It takes Gut to Say Jesus, and Join The Crew) are 'Alerts' about viruses (Meta Viruses) using a very similar array of 'special effects.' These are described as spreading over the internet and having some destructive effect when email or newsgroup postings are read.<br>The hoax victim is warned not to open mail with a specific Subject: field and asked to pass on the warning to as many people as possible (see also Hoax, Social Engineering)<br>While hoax virus warnings may not carry an actual malicious payload, they do carry the threat of bogged down servers and embarrassment of those who have forwarded the message. |
| Germ Virus | Is a viral program that does not directly attach to programs (see also Bacterium, Figure 5). Sometimes also used to describe a generation-zero virus, one that has not yet infected its first sample. |
| Latent Virus | See Infection—a virus that is an environment in which it can neither execute nor self-replicate. |

V

(cont.)

**Table 25:** (cont.)

| Name of Category | Definition of Category |
|---|---|
| Macro Virus (see also Macro) | Exploits the application's ability to automatically execute the macro when opening or closing a document. The macro is a small piece of programming, used to perform a simple, repetitive function. Microsoft's WordBasic and VBA macro languages can include macros in data files. Hence, a Macro Virus uses the original document or application (e.g., Word or Powerpoint file) as the agent to execute the code and spread. |
| Media Virus | Describes a virus being hyped up by media and/or in part due to over-estimating the impact of a particular threat or due to being overzealous to gain a marketing advantage as a vendor. Wanting to be the first with the news might trigger a too quick or hyped up news release by a vendor being carried by many media (see also Alert and Expert) |
| Meta Virus | Usually an 'alert' about a virus that turns out to be a hoax (see Heuristics). |
| Multipartite Virus | Traditionally a viral program that will infect both boot sectors (Master Boot Sector (MBR)) and files. Today, the term is sometimes used to refer to a virus that will infect more than one type of object, or that reproduces in multiple ways. |
| Overwriting Virus | Is a file virus that overwrites part of a file with itself. Some are memory resident while others are not. Infected files cannot be recovered, thereby making it necessary to delete the original file and replace it with a previous version as generated by backup. |
| Polymorphic Virus | Applies a technique that permits the changing of the 'form' of the virus on each infection. Done in the hopes that signature-scanning software will not be able to detect all instances of this virus since it changes its signature each time. Encryption is not the only way in which to 'morph.' Moreover, an encrypted virus is not necessarily polymorphic. |
| Script Virus | The virus is written in VBScript and JavaScript programming languages. It uses Windows Scripting Host to go into action and infect other files. Usually this type of virus will run automatically upon launching VBS and JS infected files. This type of virus usually includes the following letter in its name such as VCS or JS—VBS/LoveLetter.D |
| Stealth Virus | Hides the modifications it has made in the file or boot record. This is usually done by monitoring the system functions used by programs for reading files or physical blocks from storage media. The stealth virus is also forging the results of such system functions; hence programs that try to read these areas see the original uninfected form of the file, instead of the actual infected form. |

**Note.** This taxonomy provides an overview. While it includes the major categories of Viruses, it is not all inclusive. Individual types or names of viruses have been omitted.

The above list is in alphabetical order but not necessarily in order of importance.

Additional information is also given in Tables 18A & 29 as well as Figure 4.

**Visability**   see Vulnerability

**Visual Basic for Applications (VBA)**   is the scripting and macro language in current Microsoft Office products allowing macro viruses to operate. The first generation of Word viruses, however, was written in the closely related WordBasic dialect.

**Visual Basic Script (VBS)**   is a scripting language similar to VBA (see above), used by a number of virus/worm authors.

**Voice Mail**   enables clients and employees to leave phone messages. Protecting information stored in a voice-mail system should be part of the enterprise systems security mandate. This system may contain orders left by clients or other important information such as executives discussing highly sensitive matters.

- Use voice-mail password rules that follow other Password rules but do not permit the password to be the phone number itself or another Canonical Password (see Password–Canonical), definitely not even as per default.
- Make sure that the PBX does not have any suspicious accounts and if it does, remove them.
- Synchronize the list of passwords with the human resource information system, permitting the removal of voicemail accounts and access for employees who have left
- Remote-access features should never be turned on, unless for maintenance purposes
- PBX maintenance accounts must be properly safeguarded by security mechanisms such as cryptographic tokens or biometric identification systems.
- Regular checks for unauthorized voic-mail boxes must be done

The PBX and voice-mail system must be part of the firm's Information Security Policy and regular audits are also required (see Information Security Audit)

**Voice over the Internet Protocol (Voice over IP or VOIP or VoIP)**   is a term used in IP telephony for a set of facilities for managing the delivery of voice information using the internet Protocol (IP).

In general, this means sending voice information in digital form in discrete packets rather than in the traditional circuit-committed protocols of the public switched telephone network (PSTN). A major advantage of VoIP and internet telephony is that it avoids the tolls charged by ordinary telephone service.

**Security and VoIP** means that in itself, VoIP represents a new "vector" for potential security issues but does not introduce any Vulnerabilities that have not been seen before. Some experts have argued that digitizing voice and placing it on a data network makes voice communications more accessible and easier to intercept.

In a traditional, analog environment, physical access to a switch or wiring closet is usually necessary to intercept communications between two parties. By placing voice traffic on a data network, one could intercept a voice communication by capturing the associated packets as they traverse a large network.

**Law and VoIP** raises a few new issues. For instance, Edison, N.J., USA-based Vonage tells its VoIP customers that they may not transmit or receive "any illegal, harmful, threatening, abusive, harassing, defamatory, obscene, sexually explicit, profane, racially or ethnically disparaging remarks or otherwise objectionable material of any kind. . . ."

In contrast, when it comes to traditional phone service, one may swear like a sailor unless one says things that the law defines as "obscene," or one is behaving in a way that harasses or threatens someone.

Vonage, however, is not considered a phone company (a "common carrier") according to USA law because it is an Internet-based service. That means Vonage can define its terms without any meddling from Federal Communications Commission (FCC), even if it means banning blue language.

Internet phone conversations are supposed to be private, but are governed by legal agreements suited to public forums like internet chat rooms. But if a firm as Vonage would try to exercise its right to terminate service, would a judge back the company's right to do so? That is the sort of question privacy and civil liberties advocates want answered.

**Market and VoIP** could mean that if the infrastructure or the last mile for VOIP is separate from the telecommunication carriers' infrastructure, competition will further accelerate price erosion for voice telephone. Already, in Eastern Europe price differentials between mobile/cellular and stationary calls are being reduced through competition (see Market).

**Voice-over-IP (VoIP) over Wireless Local Area Network (WLAN)** allows a user with the help of a handset to take advantage of the firm's WLAN to place phone calls. In a hospital this might allow a nurse to call for a specialist to get advice or being reached by the administration while working on the floor.

Demand for Voice over WLAN will increase because it permits users to take advantage of an organization's infrastructure namely its WLAN. VoWLAN handset prices will drop and the voice portion of 802.11x technology will move into the mainstream business environment.

Security issues have yet to be fully addressed but as with every emerging technology, challenges will occur and solutions will be offered in the market place.

**Volume Testing**   describes the purposely subjecting of a system (both hardware and software) to a series of tests where the volume of data being processed is the subject of the test. Such systems can be transactions processing systems capturing real time sales or could be database updates and or data retrieval.

Volume testing will seek to verify the physical and logical limits to a system's capacity and ascertain whether such limits are acceptable to meet the projected capacity of the organization's business processing.

**Vulnerability**   is a hardware, firmware, or software flow that leaves an information system open for potential exploitation (see also Figures in Appendix–Attack Taxonomy). It can be:

- Implementation,
- design, or
- configuration vulnerability

The above creates a Risk that results in a potential Threat that if realized results in unauthorized Access (see Access) resulting in a root or account break-in.

The Weaknesses materializing from the above are based on a weakness in a automated system security procedures, administrative controls, physical layout, internal controls, and so forth. All these could be exploited by a threat to gain unauthorized access to information or disrupt critical processing. Vulnerability and therefore the Risk for a Threat being realized can be reduced by Partitioning of Network or Redundancy built into the system (see Table 26).

**Vulnerability Audit** see Audit

**Vulnerability Assessment** tries to proactively identify possible or potential security exposures. Unfortunately, this process is time-intensive and requires substantial technical expertise that might not be available in a small or medium-sized enterprise. Having discovered a vulnerability, however, means that prioritization and of corrective action for weaknesses found is a necessity.

**Vulnerability Attribute** cab be numerous whereby one can find a particular vulnerability including software name and version number.

The term can also be defined as a weakness or lack of controls that would allow or facilitate a threat actuation against a specific asset or property (see also Threat, Risk).

**Vulnerability Consequence** can be such that it affects a range of outcomes such as availability, confidentiality, integrity, security protection to root/user level and other access.

**Table 26:** Taxonomy of Vulnerabilities

| Type of Vulnerability | Sub-Category | Description of Vulnerability |
|---|---|---|
| | | Vulnerability is the weakness or lack of controls that may permit or facilitate threat actuation against a specific asset or target. As such it is a quantifiable and **threat-independent attribute** of an information system or component that enables assets to be compromised by allowing illegal state changes to occur within the system. |
| Technical | | |
| | Implementation | For instance, not well documented system implementation |
| | Design | Examples might emanate from connectivity, compatibility, operability and fragility. |
| | Configuration Vulnerability | This could be represented by visibility and audibility of system. |
| Procedural | | These might be inherent in the manual or automated interfaces and conventional security measures used. |
| Operational | | Procedures and practices built into the inadequate asset valuation, insufficient auditing of policy compliance. |
| Attitudinal and Environmental | | Behavior by employees and other stakeholders such as suppliers, customers and governmental authorities. |

**Note.** These types of vulnerabilities can be used to exploit a system (see also Figures 1–3, Table 24D).

**Vulnerability in Design (Design Vulnerability)** is inherent in the design or specifications of hardware or software, whereby even a perfect implementation will result in a vulnerability (see also Table 26).

**Vulnerability Mapping** is a process of discovering what versions of services are running on particular (usually UNIX) host. For example by discovering that server is running Apache 1.3.9 that has known vulnerability attacker can deploy particular attack.

**Vulnerability of Implementation (Implementation Vulnerability)** results from an error made during implementation of the software or hardware that is otherwise correctly designed (see also Table 26).

**Vulnerability Patch** (sometimes also called bug fix) is usually the fix for a known vulnerability. The vendor or the Open Source community generally issues the patch. Unfortunately, patches never get installed. This is why most systems on the internet are vulnerable to known attacks for which fixes exist.

Being vigilant, as a System Administrator or Security Engineer requires the installation of bug fixes the soonest but definitely before a long weekend may be over.

**Vulnerability Scanner–Network, Server and Desktop** are products that permit staff to pro-actively identify potential avenues of attack in a regular fashion. Most important, appropriate measures to ensure the security exposure are properly repaired are needed and based on findings produced by these scanners.

Whereas an Intrusion Detection Scanner (IDS) looks for patterns of unauthorized network traffic that might signal a break-in, Vulnerability Scanners are geared toward detecting whether or not a computer's current configuration is inherently vulnerable to attack.

The difference between an IDS and Vulnerability Scanning is similar to trying to lose weight by taking either little bunch of pills or better, starting to eat right and exercise appropriately.

IDS is all about listing and alerting attacks that have happened, whereas Vulnerability Scanning or assessment will tell users what is wrong before the fact.

**Vulnerability(ies)–Server-Side Script** occurs when server-side scripts languages are not validated for correctness regularly. Some server-side scripts may not properly check the expected input of the script and it is possible to cause affected scripts to run operating system commands as the web server is user. Daily checks for input validation including allowed parameter values and parameter length of servier-side scripts should be performed. Most Websites have several updates a day and script errors may expose a website to an attack whilst it was a low risk just ten minutes before (see also Common Gateway Interface—CGI standard, PHP).

**Vulnerability Type** could be classified as access or input validation error, exceptional condition, environmental error, race condition, design error or other error.

**War Dialer** or **War Dialing**   see Demon Dialler

**Warhead**   see Payload

**Warning, Advice and Reporting Point (WARP)**   are specifically conceived to fill the enormous gaps in coverage of warning, advice & incident reporting services, a gapt that existing CERTs cannot possibly meet. Hence, WARPs are complementing CERTS

WARPs may focus on a particular region and/or service a specific constituency such as an industry (e.g., travel agents). While the provide information they do not offer incident response services to any significant level as CERTs do.

Tables 27A and 27B outline in more detail how a WARP may function. Each WARP is generally oriented toward a specific group of entities with common interests, ensuring that only applicable security information will be passed along to WARP members. The WARP network can be extended to include private sector as well as public ones such as school districts.

**WARP**   see Warning, Advice and Reporting Point

**Warranty Disclaimer**   are often used for Security Alerts and Advisories mailed out to subscribers and one could look something like this:

NO WARRANTY

Any material furnished by Carnegie Mellon University and the Software Engineering Institute is furnished on an "as is" basis. Carnegie Mellon University makes no warranties of any kind, either expressed or implied as to any matter

**Table 27A:** Constituencies for a WARP

| Constituencies | | Explanation |
|---|---|---|
| Geographic | Region City | This could be a region within a country A large city or a group of smaller cities |
| Organisations | Public | This includes such organisations as federal, regional and other government agencies, as well as universities, schools and hospitals. |
| | Private | A company may decide to run a WARP for itsclients (e.g., online banking customers), or even as a service to their employees (and their families). |
| | Non-Governmental (NGO) | These may include a variety of different types of NGOs building their own WARPs |
| Associations | Industry | This could be illustrated by an association of employers or an industry or chamber of commerce. |
| | Trade Union | Including a federation of unions and/or its members |
| | Citizen Groups | This could include, such as the various chapters of the Internet Society (ISOC), the Association of the Elderly, and Association of Taxpayers. |

**Note.** This table outlines focus and type of constituency a particular WARP might serve.

A WARP has to focus on a particular group of users and their prevalent operating system and software such as home users with PCs running on the Windows operating platform. Moreover, a WARPs mission is not to duplicate a CERT nor to compete with private firms providing on-site services. Instead, a successful WARP provides help by raising awareness and allowing greater success for prevention.

Accordingly an effective WARP does not duplicate such services and instead of Alerts provides checklists, best practice guides and other material focusing on its target group including assessing CERT or anti-virus vendors' Alerts for their relevance regarding the WARPS constituency.

**Table 27B:** WARP Focus and Functions

| Description of Functions |
|---|
| Receive warnings/advisories from other WARPs/CERTs and other sources, filter and assess them, and reissue to their community the ones which are relevant, perhaps with increased priority. |
| Provide e-mail and/or telephone advice to community members on Internet-related security matters. |
| Solicit and record IT-security incident reports from community. |
| Share (sanitised) incident reporting data with other WARPs/CERTs etc with whom a sharing agreement has been reached (formal or informal). |
| Contribute incident data, resources and/or expertise/knowledge to other information sharing network nodes to help deal with widespread problems. |
| Participate in 'networking' and sharing of experiences and knowledge with other information sharing network nodes. |
| Develop close links with selected WARPs/CERTs for support and collaboration on problems. |

**Note.** The pros and cons of the new protocols and encryption methods can be argued for a long time. However, for most businesses, time is probably better spent fixing more basic security weaknesses of today's Wi-Fi networks by turning on WEP, for instance.

including, but not limited to, warranty of fitness for a particular purpose or merchantability, exclusivity or results obtained from use of the material. Carnegie Mellon University does not make any warranty of any kind with respect to freedom from patent, trademark, or copyright infringement.

For further information on a related issue regarding email see also Disclaimer.

**Waste Electrical and Electronic Equipment Directive (WEEED)**   in the European Union is likely to have a huge impact on the way companies dispose of unwanted or used IT and, for some small and medium sized firms, the cost and complication of complying with this directive could prove to be a nightmare.

The directive will require that end-of-lifecycle equipment is collected for recovery, recycling and re-use. Fines are likely to be imposed on businesses not complying with the directive, which is expected to become law between 2002 and 2004. Even companies with a turnover of less than Euro 3 million and fewer than 10 employees are not excluded.

WEEED does address an important problem since of every three new computers built, two become obsolete and by 2005 that figure will be one to one. In the USA alone that means 150 million PCs in the next few years looking for landfill homes-enough to fill a hole one acre in area by three and a half miles deep and the problem is just as bad in Europe.

Most organizations currently call their supplier, order the latest equipment, write off the old kit and chuck it into the garbage. However, throwing away old IT equipment not only causes environmental damage, it wastes potentially valuable assets and, it can be a security risk (see also Security of Media, Electronic Shredding).

Computers contain heavy metals like lead, cadmium, mercury and chromium. These chemicals cause health problems and pollute the environment. Moreover, much end-of-lifecycle equipment can be refurbished and then re-used.

**Wave of Computing**   can be put into five waves each encompassing a major development in computing and IT. They are as follows:

1) **Mainframe computer** represents the first wave, enabling organizations and universities to process certain tasks (e.g., analyzing data using statistics) with computing power (e.g., punching code on a keypunch card that is being read by the system that subsequently executed the tasks and provided a hard print-out for students doing an assignment);

2) **Personal Computer/Desktop** provided individuals with access to computers starting in the late 1970s with such products as the Apple IIe, enabling them to

do word processing, spreadsheet and other work at their desk or even at home or university;

3) **Client Server** put information technology at everyone's fingertips.

4) In the commercial world, the **internet** was the fourth wave. It was a move greatly accelerated by Ohio State University establishing a relay between CompuServe (now part of AOL Time Warner renamed Time Warner during 2003) and the internet by 1989. By 1993, the Los Angeles Times stated in one of its final editions during that year making its New Year Predictions that for California's Young Upwardly Mobile Professionals (Yuppi's) home internet access would be a must by the end of 1994..

Most academic employees (teaching and other staff) had already had email access since 1988 or even earlier (e.g., ARPANET established connections to England and Norway in 1973). They started using the Mosaic browser to search the web by 1990, long before Netscape appeared on the scene.

This wave gave everyone access to information stored digitally on any server or Website anywhere in the world. Communicating quickly and cheaply via the internet by either using email (see Email) or the internet phone (see Voice Over the Internet Protocol VOIP) have become ubiquitous in offices and households.

5) **Distributed Computing or Grid Computing** will give individuals and organizations access to nearly unlimited computing power anywhere in the world and any time (see Grid Computing).

**Web**—This term implies using a graphical software browser such as Microsoft Explorer or Netscape to answer email or using such free email services as Hotmail.

**Web-Based Standards**  see Open Source Software (see also Longhorn)

**Web Cache**  see Cache

**Web page**—can offer anything from a simple 'electronic brochure', to an engaging experience of a product or service 'on line'. In just a few years, web sites have grown from being static and 'flat' pages, to those with animated 3-D graphics and sound and many pages are being built dynamically depending upon selections made.

The web is what most people mean when they mention the 'the Internet'. Most Webpages are used to generate some Revenues (e.g., through advertising) or E-Commerce possibilities (see Revenues–Ad-Blocking Software).

**Web portal**  is a web site with quite substantial traffic with extensive content and hyperlinks. With the latter users can connect to other sites which might have content of interest to them. The idea of a web portal is to become the starting point for a user when logging onto the web with a graphical browser such as Netscape or Microsoft Explorer. The user begins the journey on the web by connecting to his or her favorite web portal. In turn, the latter usually attracts advertisers which want to target the consumers or clients visiting this site. Especially if the site has areas which are of interest to particular groups of users such as a site on growing flowers in one's garden including a chat and advice forum dealing with fertilizer, seed and pesticide issues.

Accordingly, such mega sites may be in direct competition for content providers such as AOL. But their services may be for free and paid by advertisers and purchases made by visitors, while services such as AOL also ask for a monthly fee.

Recently however, it appears as if users have become less keen on internet portals. In fact, British Telecom (BT) itself admitted in 2002 that 60% of Open-world users reset their home page rather than rely on the BT portal they are paying for.

**Web Services**   permit the free flow of traffic across an effectively unbounded, seamless network. This is in contrast to conventional web applications that usually operate at the boundary of the corporate network. They employ technological mediators, such as email and web servers, in order to carry traffic in and out. Hence, strict security controls can be established at various types of 'boundaries' (e.g., mail server).

Most firms deploy web services in only a limited way within the organization. But the real advantage of web services lies in opening up networks to the free exchange of information. This requires that security issues are addressed in two ways:

1) Sweeping local networks to monitor for any security anomalies. This is analogous to the security provided by virus scanners, thereby enabling the stopping of anomalous activity at the boundary.

2) Attach security to the individual web services themselves and maintain security piecemeal. This is usually done with a dedicated network within which web services alone operate.

Hence, under point 2, the application is done within a dedicated network, in an analogous way to Virtual Private Networks (VPNs)

**Web Services Network (WSN)** provides a secure environment for common applications for users of the network such as billing, whereby the provider of the network can act as a trusted third party for auditing and non-repudiation (see also Trust).

While Authorization and Authentication would work, firewalls are likely not to work well with a WSN. Firewalls monitoring the passage of traffic between web services may miss Malware or Viruses. The potential conflict is that to work across multiple system environments, Authentication and Authorization require the integration between applications, a thing that web services are designed to sidestep. Hence, integration-demanding Authentication and Authorization technology is still undermining some of the flexibility that is at the core of the benefits to be gained whilst using web services

One possible way to reduce the above conflict is to shift security provision to security management tools with a lighter touch, such as:

a) dynamic threat, and

b) risk management behavior

to supplement basic technology control.

Another issue is that web applications run along an outsourced model (i.e. WSNs frequently run as outsourced applications) and public facing servers. The odds of a hack-attack occurring in this area are, therefore considerably increased over an in-house application. Hence, additional security coordination and integration is needed to manage a disaster (see also Disaster Recovery)

Unauthorized Embellishment of Webpages occurs when baby:

a) using particular software, ordinary words are underlined or keywords are highlighted, making them hyperlinks to other sites, or

b) the browser plug-in can give Internet Explorer the ability to show additional links underlined in yellow lines, this type of software can also be bundled with other software [e.g., the KaZaa Peer-to-Peer (P2P) file sharing software].

During Spring 2002, it was estimated that about 500,000 users had Surf+ installed (see a), while approximately 2 million had eZula (see b category) on their PC. In the case of eZula, through the Click-Wrap (see Jurisdiction) agreement approves that this is a legal method being used for increasing business to paying clients. The latter, in turn, with their fees are paying for the free service that the user is taking advantage of with this software.

But again, certain types of software or services provided for free or that require advertising to pay for themselves may include in the End-User License Agreement (EULA) that the use of software blocking pop-up advertising is not allowed.

**Weeding**   means the selective stripping of records, files, data, etc. More refined than 'stripping' which is more wholesale in nature, weeding can be as precise as removing one particular field from a database.

**Whitehat**   is a computer/information systems/network security professional (see also Hacker).

**Wide-Area Network:**   Connects several LANs (see Local-Area Network) or other wide-are networks to each other; the internet is a huge wide-area network.

**Wide-Area Information Server (WAIS)**   describes a program that can search dozens of databases in one search.

**WildList**   was founded in 1994 in is an early warning system for computer viruses. It was launched by Shane Curson and Willy Wilder on a not-for-profit model with some vendor support. The two individuals took virus sample that they received from WildList reporters (vendor employees, researchers, IT security experts, lists, etc.) and verified these according to type, severity and degree of 'newness.'

The WildList proper consists of viruses that have been reported by at least to qualified reporters. The supplemental list consists of viruses that have been reported by one qualified reporter. The WildList was almost entirely PC-centric. Similar lists for Trojans and for Macintosh malware have yet to be developed

But support for the WildList coordinators has always been a challenge. In March 2002 the list announced that it might cease to exist due to funding difficulties. It was than taken over by TrueSecure and how this will affect its work is still not certain at this stage.

**Wide Area Network**   connects several Local Area Networks (LANs) or other wide area networks to each other, as such the internet is a huge wide area network.

**Windows Registry**   is a database holding system start-up, configuration, security, and file-association information in Microsoft Windows 9x, Me, NT, 2000 and XP systems. It represents Windows' central repository of all such information, replacing the old CONFIG.SYS, AUTOEXEC.BAT, and .INI files (they still exist and are sometimes used).

The Registry is an enormous object, often holding megabytes of data making searches difficult. It can be used to start viruses when the machine is being booted, without placing the viruses in identifiable start-up directories. Viruses affecting the Registry can be seen as system infectors. Compared to the old MS-DOS system infectors and the programming that was required, changing the Registry is easier.

**Windows Script Host (WHS)**   is a utility that runs scri+pting languages such as Visual Basic Script (VBScript) on certain Windows systems in a way somewhat similar to DOS batch files, but with more versatility.

The Love Bug virus (a.ka. LoveLetter) was a Windows script virus using VBScript. It relied on the presence of WSH that may be installed on all versions of Windows since Windows 95. Many organizations disable WSH to reduce to impact from VBSCript malware.

**Windows Update**   for XP and Windows 2000 offers an automatic update feature for users whereby a pop up screen informs them of new updates available for their systems. During Spring 2002, users complained that Windows Update is unreliable (see also Patch-Windows Update). It sometimes says systems are adequately patched when they are not, it doesn't report failed patch installations, and it doesn't always display the most current patches and worst, some patches are making systems unstable. One fundamental property of "patch and fix" is that the solution becomes the problem. That said, Time Warner (formerly AOL) manages to update their very intrusive client without generating complaints (see also Down Time and what happens with error reports sent to Microsoft).

**Wireless** means using the radio-frequency spectrum for transmitting and receiving voice, data and video signals for communications [Electro-Smog, Multiple-In, Multiple-Out (MIMO), Fixed Wireless Access and Market, Wireless Local Area Network (WLAN), Wireless Local Loop (WLL)].

**Wireless Local Area Network (WLAN)** permits transmissions using radio frequency methods, and obviate the need for expensive cabling infrastructures [see also Local Area Network, Fixed-Wireless Access, Multiple-In, Multiple-Out (MIMO)].

**Access Point (AP)** sends and receives local area network traffic via radio. Is the interface between the wireless network and a wired one. It acts as the method by which wireless computers communicate with the wired network infrastructure. A typical AP may function at distances of up to a few hundred meters. Access points combined with a distribution system such as Ethernet support the creation of multiple radio cells (BSSs) that enabling roaming throughout a facility such as an office building or Starbuck's coffee shop.

The Institute of Electrical and Electronic Engineers (IEEE) (USA) has developed the IEEE 802.11 as an international standard for WLANs. The standard specifies a number of technical parameters for operation of WLAN compliant devices. (see also Hotspot)

**Bluetooth** see Bluetooth

**802.11** is a family of specifications developed by the USA Institute of Electrical and Electronics Entineers (IEEE). Ther are currently three specifications in the family (802.11a, 802.11b, and 802.11g), with more being developed

The 802.11b standard often referred to as Wi-Fi (short for "wireless fidelity") is currently the most widespread. Nevertheless, hardware manufacturers are increasingly offering multi-standard equipment that can work with various standards.

**802.15.3** or **Ultrawideband (UWB)** is a faster wireless standard than Bluetooth. Texas Instruments, Intel and Motorola are pushing UWB. It has the potential to replace both Bluetooth and Wi-Fi but will more probably complement them with cheap last-mile links for broadband newtworks from the road to the house's front porch. There is no single standard for the technology

**802.15.4** or **ZigBe** is a relatively low-speed, low-power consumption wireless network technology thereby particularly suitable for devices requiring a long battery live. Examples would be remote controls or sensors. Therefore ZigBe is likely to complement rather than compete with Bluetooth.

**Lightweight Access Point Protocol** (**LWAPP**) lets the emerging class of wireless LAN "switches" or gateways or whatever-they-are communicate with various brands of stripped down, simplified **WLAN** radios. July 18, 2003, the Internet Engineering Task Force (IETF) voted to go ahead with creating a working group charge with finalizing the Lightweight Access Point Protocol, or LWAPP, as an IETF standard.

Regarding WLAN support, a vendor could be asked:

- If WLAN is supported, how will the firm's WLAN infrastructure be upgraded with LWAPP?
- If no WLAN support is forthcoming soon, what will this mean in case the firm wishes to deploy larger-scale WLANs sometime in the future?

It is not clear if LWAPP creates an undeniable, and important, benefit for enterprise WLAN users. Most WLAN deployments so far seem to be

- standardized on a single vendor for the infrastructure—the access points, and
- the same or another vendor for the client wireless adapter cards.

The chief benefit may be for the WLAN switch vendors, who desperately want to fit into existing Ethernet and WLAN infrastructures as fast and as smoothly as possible and need, therefore, to work with an array of existing hardware.

The LWAPP protocol is specific to the 802.11 wireless LAN space; however, a superset of the effort dubbed the Control and Access Provisioning of Wireless Access Points can be applied in any wireless network, say those involved in the effort. These include, for example, short-range, high-speed ultrawideband wireless networks and the emerging 802.16a and 802.16e standards for fixed and mobile metro-area wireless networking.

**Multiple In, Multiple Out** (**MIMO**) also known as space time coding, is based on the idea of using multiple antennas on both transmitter and receiver. MIMO promises to give a huge fillip to radio speeds without needing any more radio spectrum.

The basic idea with MIMO is that the use of multiple antennas at both the transmitter and the receiver opens up multiple parallel spatial data pipes within the same bandwidth and allows linear (in the number of antennas) capacity increase provided rich enough scattering is present.

The increased capacity in MIMO radio links is due to two effects. First, by increasing the number of channels mean capacity is increased almost linearly with the number of antenna elements. Second, by providing temporal, transmit, and receive diversity channel reliability is highly improved for higher data rates. Consequently, the outage capacity for high availability will increase with a rate higher than the number of created channels. Outage capacity for 90 per-cent availability at SNR of 10 dB has been reported to reach an order of 40 b/s/Hz with eight element antennas at both transmitter and receiver. This rate is almost 40 times higher than the achievable rate in a single-element antenna link (see also Information Theory—Shannon).

**Security Threats** through a WLAN are several (see also Information Security Guideline, Information Security Policy, Policies, Security), such as:

a) **Confidentiality and Integrity** points out that an attacker could intercept communications between a mobile computer and the AP. Thereby, sensitive or classified information may be captured. Normal Local Area Networks (LANs) also work in this 'broadcast' mode, although intercepting communications on a standard LAN requires physical access to the cabling infrastructure. Converseley, it may also be possible for an attacker to insert information into an authentic transaction, without the knowledge of the legitimate users [see also Confidentiality, Integrity, Availability of Data, User Accountability, Authentication & Audit (CIA-UAA)— Table 5C].

b) **Authentication** means that mobile platforms must use Authentication (see Autenthenciation), otherwise an attacker may simply connect the WLAN using an 802.11 compliant device and become an 'authorized' station or user on the WLAN.

c) **Availability** can be an issue because 802.11 compliant devices operate either in the infrared or the 2.4GHz radio frquency range. The 2.4GH range is a frequency band set aside for use by industrial, scientific or medical equipment. As such, it is possible that an attacker could either 'jam' the band or communciations may be inadvertently disrupted by another device operating in this band. Hence, compliance of equipment and pre-tests are needed to avoid disruptions (e.g., of medical equipment).

802.11 compliant devices operate using infrared or 'spread spectrum' communication which are direct sequence and frequency hopping. Spread spectrum methods provide a degree of protection against Denial Service Attacks. Unfortunately, they may not provide sufficient strength against attacks on confidentiality or integrity of WLAN traffic. Wired Equivalent Privacy may help but not eliminate the problem for all communication situations (see Table 28).

**Table 28:** Leaks and Security Lapses in Wi-Fi 802.11

| Type of Wi-FI Vulnerability | Description of Security Problem |
|---|---|
| Authentication | The traditional method of authenticating who gets into a network is based on a unique ID, called Mac address. This address is hard-wired into each Wi-Fi card. However, Mac addresses can be intercepted, thereby allowing a hacker to pretend to be an authorized user. To solve this identity problem, smart card vendors are promoting smart cards such as using a W-Lan enabled Sim card that identifies the W-Lan user and holds the security keys needed to access the corporate network over a secure Virtual Private Network (VPN). |
| Connection | The details on such a Sim card can be read using either a W-Lan adapter with Sim slot or by a card reader that plugs into the laptop. |
| Firewall | Another effective way is to use firewalls to crate a "demilitarized zone" (DMZ) that separates the Wi-Fi network from the main corporate network. |
| Wired Equivalent Privacy (WEP) | This is built in to Wi-Fi products. WEP can be cracked by determined hackers as the standard is broken in four places. However, using WEP is better than nothing at all. WEPs biggest shortcoming might be that it encrypts data transmitted over the air using a shared key (see below shared key) |
| Service Set Identifier (SSID) | Network administrators may not have changed the default network name, known as the SSID. Some Wi-Fi networks even broadcast the SSID to any person who wants to listen. The SSID broadcast feature can be turned off and instead it can be programmed into laptops and other access devices. Another option is to change the SSID regularly and avoid easily guessed names. |
| Shared Key | The WEP protocol uses a shared key because it assumes that only authorized users will have access to the WEP key. However, stolen laptops will have the key inside, while former employees and guests or temporary workers may make a note of the key and use it once they have left. A determined intruder may also crack the key by analyzing the encrypted data transmitted over the airwaves. |
| Wi-Fi Protected Access (WPA) | To avoid proliferation of proprietary initiatives to boost security, vendors support this new standard. Here the flawed WEP protocol is replaced with a stronger encryption method. WOA has the advantage that it is compatible with current technology, so firms can improve security of existing Wi-Fi networks by upgrading the software—assuming the manufacturer supports WPA. |
| Wi-Fi Signal | One of the most effective ways to improve security is to reduce the Wi-Fi signals leaking out of a building. One can relocate the access points or use directional antennas to focus the signal inside the building, thus reducing leakages outside. |
| 802.11i | Is a stronger standard with USA government approved encryption. However it will require companies to buy new hardware. |

**Note.** The pros and cons of the new protocols and encryption methods can be argued for a long time. However, for most businesses, time is probably better spent fixing more basic security weaknesses of today's Wi-Fi networks by turning on WEP, for instance.

**Wired Equivalent Privacy (WEP)** is the optional encryption algoright for IEEE802.11 standard when communicating on Wirless Local Area Networks. It is designed to mitigate the risk of compromise by eavesdropping on the network's traffic. The algorith is not designed for a very high or ultimate level of security but, instead to be 'at least as secure as a wire.'

Accordingly, WLAN may not necessarily be as secure as some users require.

**Voice-over-IP (VoIP) over Wireless Local Area Network (WLAN)** see Voice over Internet Protocol

**Wireless Local Loop (WLL)** is a technology that in its latest version no longer requires a line of sight, or outdoor installations.

For instance, some hardware is similar to a mobile phone in that it can be carried around and used from other points within radio range of a service provider's base-station. Such a terminal is little larger than a video cassette but it has to be plugged into an electric outlet.

Interesting is that WLL devices may permit users to receive up to 12 megabits per second which is about 10 times faster than most DSL connections and more than 200 times faster than a dial-up system (see also Broadband).

Interesting is that WLL is generally being priced based on service guarantees and peak speed, not volume of data or time spent online. Similar to the so successful short-test messaging (SMS) on mobile phones, data travel over spare network capacity not used by telephone calls.

**Wireless–Fixed Access** see Fixed Wireless Access and Market

**Wireless Smog** see Electrosmog

**World Wide Web (WWW)** was invented by Tim-Berners-Lee at the European Particle Physics Laboratory in Geneva; the WWW is somewhat similar to the WAIS. However it is designed on a system known as hypertext; that is, words in one document are "linked" to other documents. It is sort of like sitting with an encyclopedia-you read an article, see a reference that intrigues you, and so flip the pages to look up that reference (see also HTML, XML).

**Worm** is a software program that propagates by itself, across a network. Unlike a virus or a Trojan, it executes on a system without human intervention. Typically, it performs a task in which it attempts to find other potentially vulnerable (Vulnerability) systems. It enters a system by exploiting bugs or overlooked features in commonly used network software already running on the targeted system. It uses an automated approach very similar to those employed by human attackers. Worms often exist purely in memory, thereby avoiding the file system and, most importantly, making themselves invisible to file-scanning anti-virus software (see also Trojan).

**Table 29:** Worms

| Type of Vulnerability | Sub-Category | Description of Worm Characteristics |
|---|---|---|
| Worm | | Replicates and sends copies of itself across network from one machine to another, they can be distinguished by: |
| | Transport | a) Email worms spreading via **email**, or<br>b) Arbitrary protocol worms spreading via **protocols**, such as TC/IP sockets) |
| | Launching Mechanisms | 1) Program that is **self-propagating** across the internet exploiting security flaws in widely used services, not requiring interaction with the victim, such as the Morris or Internet Worm, and<br>2) **User-launched** worms that require him or her to do something involving a degree of social engineering, thereby making the worm propagating more slowly. |
| Magnitude of Threat | | Internet-scale worms have been known for a while but their severity due to the threat is been magnified quickly with the increasing degree of making the internet part of the country's critical infrastructure (e.g., emergency services). |
| | Hit-List Scanning | May use a simple list of machines running a particular server type. The worm begins scanning down the list and when it infects another machine, it divides the hit list in half, communicating half to the recipient worm, keeping the rest. |
| | Permutation Scanning | Here all worms share a common pseudo random permutation of the IP address space, whereby using a 32-bit block cipher and pre-selected key is being used. Each worm looks like it is conducting a random scan, but it attempts to minimize duplication of effort. Hence, if the worm discovers and already infected host, it knows that the original infector of the host is already working along the current sequence in the permutation, hence it changes the sequence to avoid duplication. |
| | Warhol Worm | This requires the combining of hit list scanning and permutation scanning, making the worm seem capable of infecting many vulnerable targets in a few minutes to perhaps an hour.<br>Hit list scanning improves the initial spread, where permutation scanning keeps the worm's infection rate high for much longer when compared with random scanning. |
| | Flash Worm | The attacker could plausibly obtain a hit list of most servers with the relevant service open to the internet ahead of the time of the worm's release.<br>This greatly speeds up the infecting of the vulnerable population in 10s of seconds, thereby making a human-mediated counter response impossible while necessitating an automated response to protect the IT infrastructure (see Critical Infrastructure Protection). |
| | Surreptitious Worm-Contagion | Spreads more slowly but is harder to detect since it masquerades as normal traffic (contagion). In early 2002, based on simulation data researchers suggested that it could subvert upwards of 10,000,000 internet hosts.<br>Such worms are very difficult to detect and counter, permitting a patient attacker to slowly but surreptitiously compromise a vast number of systems. The contagion model represents a latent threat for peer-to-peer (P2P systems executed on users' desktops with less security than servers, being interconnected with many different peers, used to transfer large files including 'grey content' making P2P users less inclined to draw attention to any unusual behavior of the system that they participate in. |

**Note.** Additional material can also be found in Tables 18A and 25 as well as Figure 4.

Although the different types of viruses seem to be clearly defined, it is common to come across simplifications. Papa, considered to be Melissa's successor, was presented in numerous sources as the "Papa virus" so as not to cause confusion among users. In reality, Papa is a worm, since the Excel document that contains the malignant macro is limited to making copies of itself.

The denomination problem exists because damaging programs usually inherit the characteristics of a number of the different organisms described above. As a rule, in addition to their own characteristics, viruses generally incorporate the possibility to propagate through networks like worms, to disguise themselves as harmless applications like Trojan horses, and to trigger their payloads when specific conditions are met, just like Logic Bombs (see Virus, Tables 24G and 25).

In cases where several characteristics are manifest, the most outstanding of them is generally used to describe the attacking entity. For example, in the 1999 case of the notorious I-Worm.ExploreZip, this worm was presented under the guise of a compressed archive, in the Trojan horse style. However, it was described (correctly) as a worm, as it replicated following the traits of this type of infector (see also Figure 5, Table 1).

Table 29 outlines these issues in somewhat additional detail.

**Worm and Prevention** can be illustrated with Slammer, where Infrastructures that did not expose UDP port 1434 to the Internet were not infected by the worm.

Further back, systems running IIS 4.0 disabling ida/idq script mappings were not infected with Code Red.

The above are not necessarily Zero-Day Exploits, but these Worms do illustrate that lack of vision and prevention can result in undesirable outcomes.

**Worry** denotes the preoccupations, anxieties or fears that people may feel when considering, or having effectively to deal with, uncertain and unpleasant events. Worry is a common response to Risks that produces strategies for coping with possible negative events. Accordingly, behaviors change when people worry about perceived or actual risks. The extent of this change is however unknown, for past research on worry is scarce (see Table 22A).

In psychometric risk literature worry is a narrowly defined concept, distinguished from concerns and fears. Whereas "*concern*" is restricted to a specific object, worry can be referred to general and complex situations (e.g., worry about having one's hard drive infected by a virus). Worry occurs well before an event such as being infected by a virus. "*Fear*", on the contrary, is initiated by the event, causing physical responses such as tension and sweat (see also Risks, Table 17A).

**X.509**  is an International Telecommunication Union (ITU) recommendation for the format of Digital Certificates (see also Certification Authority)

**XML**  see Extensible Mark-Up Language

**XGA**  eXtended Graphics Array

**Zero-Day Exploit**  can be defined as the case where a system ('in the wild') is being compromised before the vulnerability was known to exist by most security professionals (not published on public security mailing lists, such as CERT, Bugtraq, and Full Disclosure, Vendors.

During 2003, WebDAV and Dave Aitel's Real Server exploit were considered Zero-Day Exploits.

**Zippo Framework**   see Jurisdiction

**Zip Disks**   was introduced by the Iomega corporation. They have become a de-facto standard for transportable data storage. Being physically a little large than a 3.5' floppy disk, and yet able to store 250MB (or 100MB in older versions).

However, it is precisely **because** such large amounts of data may be easily copied and transported, that the use of such devices needs to be carefully controlled within the organization.

10 years ago, 250MB was equivalent to the total storage capacity of most organization's data, and whilst this may appear small by today's standards, it's capacity ensure that ensure client databases, product details, plans and charts can be reliably copied onto a disk that fits into a shirt pocket.

# Epilogue: Critical Infrastructure Protection (CIP)—We All Do Care

Several days after the August 14, 2003 power failure and massive outage in New York and Toronto it was still unclear what might have caused it. One theory on the Northeast blackout attributes what started the cascade effect to human failure to respond properly to an alarm denoting the failure of transmission lines (including a tree in contact with a power line) near Cleveland at 3:06 pm—over an hour before the massive nine-second propagation. It is not clear whether the problem with the alarm delayed action by the utility, FirstEnergy Corporation, or the consortium that controls the regional grid, the Midwest Independent System Operator.

One lesson that can be drawn from incidents like the power outage is that decreasing margins in all our infrastructures place critical societal functions at greater and greater risk of significant disruptions from rare accidental and Malicious acts. Redefining acceptable levels of Risks and protections as the world changes is hard work, but must be done.

Cost pressures and tight engineering under benign assumptions lead to thin margins. Safety Engineering leads to most events being of small consequence whereby the system can tolerate them. Unfortunately, in some rare events they can cause massive disruption. It would be 'bad engineering' to over-design a system to tolerate very rare events, if that tolerance costs more than the failures it would prevent (in expected value to customer terms). Fragility to extremely rare events can be seen as good business. It would be surprising if there were not rare disruptions, such as power outages in highly optimized Infrastructures.

But the invisible hand of economics and good engineering leave systems designed and optimized under assumptions of relatively benign environments at great Risk if new or unexpected Threats arise (e.g., 9/11 event or Lockerbie attack against Pan Am jet). However, computer and information systems change rapidly and manufacturers and people running cyber infrastructure are obviously subject to the same economic motivations as described above. So they are already and will become even more fragile to rare or unexpected accidental or Malicious events. This makes business sense but it also paves the road to new Vulnerabilities in Microsoft software or other operating systems being developed and exploited overnight.

Government procurement practices, software Liability and other mechanisms will have a profound impact on the Reliability and Cost (see Asset Value) of cyber infrastructure, as well as economic matters.

Hence it is of utmost importance to continuously define and redefine old and changing Threats. Getting a handle on possible new Threats and Risks is a must. To define and quantify cyber threats and their impact, particularly in combination with coordinated physical and psychological attacks and effects, requires contemplative research, development, large experimentation, and most, importantly, financial resources to pay for it.

Once new Threats and Defenses (see Tables 3A, 3B and 7A & 7B) are defined, all the costs associated with deployment of those mechanisms can be at least partially quantified (see Tables 1–2D & Table 6). The latter is difficult to resolve when human lives are involved (e.g., critical IT system breaks down at a hospital). To illustrate, Libya offered $10 Million to dependents of each of the 270 passengers that died at the Lockerbie Pan Am airplane disaster from December 21, 1988. This encouraged the USA to ask the UN Security Council to lift the trade embargo. But France resisted for a long time in part, because Libya paid France $3,000–$30,000 for each of the 170 victims of the UTA plane that was shot down by terrorists over Niger on September 19, 1989.

So what is a well-reasoned decision regarding various Risks, costs justifying which appropriate levels of protection is a risky and morally difficult business (see Table 16B). The pace of technology change and societal reliance on these systems amplify the uncertainty, urgency, and magnitude of risk here (see Tables 13A, 13B & 13C). It is almost unthinkable that western societies would not put very large resources against a problem of this grave potential.

This issue will become ever more important for Information Security because the emergence of few large information utility companies that supply IT infrastructure. Hence, such developments concentrate vast resources in a few hands. What suggests that 250 IT utility- infrastructure firms in the USA will spend more between them over the next decade than just three equivalent companies in the UK, thereby setting the stage for a disaster to happen in one region? Remember, investigations of August's blackout and aftermath revealed that exactly this represented reality, according to industry experts!

This blackout disaster reminds us of massive USA West Coast grid blackout on 2 July 1996. Than a tree touched a power line, and the operator who had detected an anomaly could not find the phone number required for the manual alert. Thereafter, there were numerous claims that such a massive outage could not happen again until an eight state collapse on 10 Aug 1996 and now this also affecting Canada. Blackouts also highlight our inability to heed earlier warnings and whilst Europeans enjoy better maintained grids, who knows but a freaky cascade of events might result in power shortages in Europe or elsewhere down the road. Incidentally, during October 2003 lightning hit a tree that knocked out vital power lines from Switzerland to Italy which meant the latter was without power for several hours on a Sunday. The lack of supply and some human errors let to the system shutting down in Italy leaving people without electricity.

This time server systems drew immediately on battery power for a few seconds, at which point major generators kicked in at ISP operations, thereby allowing normal operations. Hence, customers suffered "no disruptions whatsoever" to their Internet service resulting from the electrical system failure. Nonetheless, because home-users and SME's had no power, they could not connect.

But what can be done if such a type of blackout goes on for several weeks instead of a few hours or a day? In deep winter Quebec's 2-week power forced generators to run at full capacity to supply hospitals and other critical systems with adequate power levels. Since generators were not designed to run over extensive period of times at full speed, many broke down forcing hospitals to be closed down as well.

Hence, blackouts should have taught us the following 2 lessons from the Critical Infrastructure Protection (CIP) and Information Assurance 101 course at university or college:

Q. What is the infrastructure warranting special Critical Infrastructure Protection (CIP) efforts upon which all the others depend?

A. Electricity and ever more information systems (see hospitals, airports, stores/retailers, public transport systems cannot function without)

Q. What is its most salient feature?

A. Nobody knows what could result in a situation in which electricity grids and information systems including that the internet do not work properly for an extensive period, such as three weeks.

Hence, Information Assurance and Information Security warrant continued but, most importantly, serious attention something it currently does not get enough today.

---

All this supposedly happened in nine seconds, and yet
the cause is still unclear!

---

The book provides readers with information regarding IT Security but it should help especially in becoming more aware about the issues involved.

Below there are various links to help raise **AWARENESS AND PREVEN-TION** further by giving readers links to:

- encyclopedias and dictionaries,
- digital libraries and specific materials on legislation,
- government documents including but not limited to EU directives and regulations,
- standards and best practice guides and handbooks,
- tools and utilities for system administrators,
- tools and utilities for PC at home and in schools, and
- awareness raising and skill development including free newsletters.

Some of these sites may be busy during regular business hours (consider time differentials, US sites are quick to access from Europe in the early morning). Others may have a relatively slow connection because they are run by volunteers with limited resources. Hence, it is advisable to connect with a computer that has broadband connection with unmetered access to enjoy the experience to the fullest.

Finally, some of the links may no longer work properly and this might be the case because the webmaster moved things around. However, using the title one might still find the document or else go to an internet archive such as the one listed here: http://security.weburb.dk/frame/show/news/2480 or else to find the site and link as it existed when this book was written.

# Appendices

# Suggestions for Additional Resources

Readers wishing to consult information security, vulnerabilities, hacking, computing virus texts to supplement their information available in this dictionary have *many* works from which they can choose. Not only are there printed works available but also many online options are open and can provide one with additional insights just a mouse click away.

The following brief list focuses on books or internet sites with information about these issues that are especially clearly written, and/or widely cited "classical" accounts, and/or representative of some of the many disciplines in which these methods are used.

Please remember, the list is neither complete nor comprehensive but represents a snapshot only. The list also includes only English resources and, thereby, ignores many other high quality ones.

Finally, while we provide some comment about the site we have found all of the links given below as helpful in one or another instance. But it is subjective and therefore requires that you make your own final choices.

# Appendix 1   On-Line Databases for Vulnerabilities, Security & Miscellaneous

| Name of Standard | Description and Comments | URL |
| --- | --- | --- |
| Bugtraq Archive | This lists all the past messages about vulnerabilities. In addition, you can also access tools and look at the library. If you wish you can subscribe to Bugtraq but be aware that it might result in more than 30 messages daily. | http://www.securityfocus.com/archive/1 |
| Cassandra | This tool allows you to create saved profiles of the services and applications running on your networks, typical (standard configurations) hosts or important hosts. Cassandra can then notify one by email of new vulnerabilities relevant to one's profiles. Queries (including incremental queries) can also be performed live through SSL. | https://cassandra.cerias.purdue.edu/main/ |
| CERT/CC Vulnerability Notes Database! | Descriptions of vulnerabilities are available from this web page in a searchable database format, and are published as "CERT Vulnerability Notes."<br>One can search or browse Vulnerability Notes by several key fields, including name, vulnerability ID number, CVE name, date updated, date public, or metric. One can also customize database queries to obtain specific information, such as the ten most recently updated vulnerabilities or the twenty vulnerabilities with the largest metric score. | http://www.kb.cert.org/vuls |
| COTSE (Church of the Swimming Elephant) | Provides Bugtraq Archives, NT Bugtraq Archives, CERT CC Archives, CIAC Archives, as well as Bulletins Released Today. | http://www.cotse.com/ (see security list rectangle, top and middle of screen) |
| DOVES: Database of Vulnerabilities, Exploits, and Signatures | This is an ongoing effort to collect and cross-index vulnerabilities, attack tools ("exploits"), and signatures (traces of the attack used for intrusion detection and/or system forensics). Part of this will be public, but part of it will have limited distribution. It will provide a historical record of vulnerabilities, as well as a database against which theories of vulnerabilities and vulnerability analysis. | http://seclab.cs.ucdavis.edu/projects/DOVES/ |

(cont.)

Appendix 1: (cont.)

| Name of Standard | Description and Comments | URL |
|---|---|---|
| Grep the Net | Is a search engine which searches several different security sites for information on a vulnerability, threat or other news including tools and utilities. | http://gtn.host.sk/ |
| ICAT Vulnerability Index Common Vulnerabilities and Exposures (CVE) number | For each vulnerability this site keeps an id, object, class, CVE number, remote and/or local, and the date when it was published and if necessary the update dates for each. | http://icat.nist.gov |
| | *ICAT* is a searchable index of information on computer vulnerabilities. It provides search capability at a fine granularity and links users to vulnerability and patch information. | |
| | You can also download CVE here: | http://icat.nist.gov/icat.cfm |
| Internet Security Vulnerabilities | A list of the most critical vulnerabilities including general, Windows and Unix vulnerabilities. | http://www.sans.org/ top20.htm |
| Opensec: The Open Security Project | Offers the Common Vulnerabilities and Exposures Database (CVE) in Extensible Markup Language (XML) with a CVE RSS Feed | http://www.opensec.org/ cve/ |
| | Additionally, this group also works on the Advisory and Notification Markup Language (ADML) (see also Appendix 6) that should further facilitate the exchange of information regarding vulnerabilities and managing the Patching and Updating process | http://www.opensec.org/ standards/ |
| Open Source Vulnerability Database (OSVDB) and OSVDB ID | The folks at the OSVDB have been busy building a database and system to catalog and explain thousands of vulnerabilities. This is a system based on volunteer effort. Volunteers are expected to update at least **one vulnerability per day over a period of a month**. | http://www.osvdb.org/ index.php |
| | On average the OSVDB folks claim that it only takes between 15 to 30 minutes to complete a vulnerability. | |
| | The database is quite user friendly and works well, definitely a tool security experts are advised to consult and contribute to. | |

(cont.)

Appendix 1: (cont.)

| Name of Standard | Description and Comments | URL |
|---|---|---|
| Packet Storm | This is security tool resource dedicated to providing the information necessary to secure the World's networks publishing new security information on a worldwide network of websites. | http://packetstorm.icx.fr/pssabout.html |
| Security Tracker | Organizing advisories by category, cause, impact, reported by, target, underlying OS, and vendor is offered here. | http://www.SecurityTracker.com |
| The Internet Ports Database | This database tracks which network services TCP and UDP ports are used and for what services. | http://www.portsdb.org/ |

## Appendix 2  Dictionaries & Encyclopedias

| Title | Description | Location/URL, Publisher, ISBN |
|---|---|---|
| COTSE (Church of the Swimming Elephant) | Dictionaries and encyclopedias, searches for definitions of items similar to a meta engine, bringing back definitions for an item or string of words from several sources (e.g., Webster and Jargon File). Definitions sometimes a bit general and not technical enough but a good start. | http://www.cotse.com/cgi-bin/Dict |
| Cyber Rights And Digital Liberties Encyclopedia (CRADLE) | An interactive dictionary of censorship-related terms developed to help young people understand the sometimes complex legal and legislative issues related to free speech in cyberspace | http://peacefire.org/cradle/ |
| Dictionaries and Glossaries | Bookreviews of various dictionaries and glossaries regarding the IT and telecommunication fields. | http://victoria.tc.ca/int-grps/books/techrev/mnbkdc.htm |
| Dictionary—Computer User | Provides definitions to more than 7,000 high-tech terms | http://www.computeruser.com/resources/dictionary/dictionary.html |
| FOLDOC | A free online dictionary to computing, can be downloaded as a zipped text file, quite large :-) | http://foldoc.doc.ic.ac.uk/foldoc/index.html |
| Glossary of Communications, Computer, Data, and Information Security Terms | Online dictionary in progress, but full of interesting information and links | http://victoria.tc.ca/int-grps/books/techrev/secgloss.htm |

(cont.)

Appendix 2: (cont.)

| Title | Description | Location/URL, Publisher, ISBN |
|---|---|---|
| Internet Security Dictionary | Handbook defining security terms. | Berlin: Springer Verlag<br>ISBN 0-387-95261-6<br>http://www2.latech.edu/<br>~phoha/home/admin/<br>DictBooks.htm |
| IT-Security.com | This is an ongoing dictionary project. | http://www.itsecurity.com/<br>dictionary/dictionary.htm |
| Mobile Computing | Provides definitions of abbreviations and terms in wireless, mobile communication and computing | http://www.pcwebopaedia.<br>com/Mobile_Computing/ |
| Security | Online resource for general security terms, click on term to get concise definition written by different individuals (styles change and quality not uniform across dictionary but still great source) | http://www.yourwindow.to/<br>information-security/ |
| Telecom Glossary | Development Site for proposed Revisions to American National Standard T1.523-2001, provides 2000 glossary plus additional information about proposed changes. | http://www.its.bldrdoc.gov/<br>projects/devglossary/ |
| Telecom & Wireless Industry Acronyms | Provides a comprehensive list of these. | http://www.mob1le.com/<br>acronyms.html |
| The New Hacker's Dictionary | Full of jargon translation<br>Text version can be downloaded or else viewed as html document online (huge file) and the online version is called the Jargon File. | Boston, MA: MIT Press<br>ISBN 0-262-68092-0<br>http://www.elsewhere.org/<br>jargon/ |
| TechTarget | Definitions for the most current IT-related words | http://whatis.techtarget.com/<br>whome/0,289825,sid9,00.<br>html |
| Virus— Encyclopedia | Panda software's on line encyclopedia. | http://www.pandasoftware.<br>com/library/<br>http://www.pandasoftware.<br>com/virus_info/encyclopedia/ |
| Virus— Encyclopedia | Symantec's on-line encyclopedia for exploits, macros, Trojan horses, viruses, vulnerabilities, and worms. | http://securityresponse.<br>symantec.com/avcenter/<br>vinfodb.html |
| Web Dictionary of Cybernetics and Systems | This dictionary is a combination (with permission) of the ASC Glossary, Krippendorff's Dictionary and Hornung's Glossary. | http://pespmc1.vub.ac.be/<br>ASC/indexASC.html |
| Wireless Dictionary | Provides a wireless dictionary and information about the field's terminology online. | http://www.agilent.com/cm/<br>wireless/dictionary/c.html |

# Appendix 3    Miscellaneous Resources

| Title | Description | Location/URL, Publisher, ISBN |
|---|---|---|
| @-nough | This website is a short cut for anyone who needs a day in the reference library or in cases where a search on Google results in either very technical or too popular terms and descriptions than what one needs.<br>This service is efficient, helpful and prompt and, as importantly, free. It is a shared reference service among libraries throughout the US. Logging onto the service one might get a librarian that is working at a library at the time or else one who is working from home. Regardless it surely helps and they do know how to search on the Web for the best IT security info. | http://247ref.org |
| Bad Guys | Sarah Gordon's site with much material about anti-virus including what a "real anti-virus researcher" does or is, such as:<br><br>—proficient with computers<br>—handling viruses in secure environment<br>—has ethical responsibility to act and behave accordingly, and more.<br><br>The above outlines how the industry might see an anti-virus researcher including his or her activities.<br>The site wisely refrains from addressing what anti-virus research might contain of to contribute to science. This has been a heated topic in the anti-virus field. | http://www.badguys.org/researchers.htm |
| Computer Science Reference Sources | List of Computer Science and Security resources in printed and online format | http://www.ulib.iupui.edu/subjectareas/compsci/reference.htm |
| Crime | An excellent parody of computer crime and paranoia | http://www.digicrime.com/dc.html |
| Cybercrime, Copyright and Software Piracy Issues | Social Control Theory and Moral Developmental Theory can be used to explain software and music piracy (Cybercrime) to some degree.<br>However, these links show that if the majority does not care, enforcing the norms becomes a loosing battle. | http://security.weburb.dk/frame/show/news/3096<br><br>http://security.weburb.dk/frame/show/news/3155 |

(cont.)

Appendix 3: (cont.)

| Title | Description | Location/URL, Publisher, ISBN |
|---|---|---|
| Cyber Security | The Washington Post has compiled a list of IT security resources for those who want to know more about cyber security. | http://www.washingtonpost.com/wp-dyn/articles/A29557-2002Apr22.html |
| Full Disclosure Policy (RFPolicy) v2.0 | Even-handed way to manage disclosure of problems to vendors and the community by Rain Forest Puppy (better known as rfp). This RFPolicy can be used as a guideline for how researchers or security experts should deal with vendors when they find a security problem. | http://www.wiretrip.net/rfp/policy.html |
| Handbook— Computer Security Incidence Response Team (CSIRT) | West-Brown, M. J., Stikvoort, D., Kossakowski, K. P. (December 1998). Computer Security Incident Response Teams (CSIRTs). Pittsburgh: CERT. This is a source for people who are active in the incident response business. | http://www.sei.cmu.edu/pub/documents/98.reports/pdf/98hb001.pdf |
| Idea Finder | This site helps to find out about innovations or inventions, myths and new products. It allows the visitior to take a glimpse into the past at some of the more unusual inventions and fascinating inventors. | http://www.ideafinder.com/home.htm |
| Information Theory | A cite with many interesting links and resources regarding information theory and communication. | http://datacompression.info/InformationTheory.shtml |
| | Information Theory is an umbrella term for the scientific disciplines that attempt to codify the mathematical underpinnings of data. In particular, Information Theory is interested in topics such as data compression, data communications, and error correction. Mathematicians see Information Theory as The branch of mathematics dealing with the efficient and accurate storage, transmission, and representation of information. However, as our definition in this dictionary indicates, Information Theory goes way beyond the above definition. Nonetheless reading sources linked to on this site will give one this more comprehensive understanding for sure. | http://mathworld.wolfram.com/InformationTheory.html |

(cont.)

Appendix 3: (cont.)

| Title | Description | Location/URL, Publisher, ISBN |
|---|---|---|
| Information—How Much | This study is an attempt to estimate how much new information is created each year.<br>The researchers looked at several media and estimate yearly production, accumulated stock, rates of growth and other variables of interest about information growth.<br>The reported published in 2000 was the first one and used 1999 data. | http://www.sims.berkeley.edu/research/projects/how-much-info/ |
| | The group produced an update releasing the report on July 2, 2003 (How Much Information—2003). The 2003 study—has revised certain of the 1999 estimates where the researchers have found new and better data sources. | http://www.sims.berkeley.edu/research/projects/how-much-info-2003/index.htm |
| Internet Archive | This site is building a digital library of Internet sites and other cultural artifacts in digital form.<br>Like a paper library, it provides free access to researchers, historians, scholars, and the general public.<br>The archive has a so-called Wayback Machine that makes it possible to surf more than 10 billion pages stored in the Internet Archive's web archive. | http://www.archive.org/ |
| Internet Protocol version (IPv6) | This site provides FAQs to the IPv6, implementation help areas, discussion forums and much more. | http://www.ipv6.org/ |
| Jargon File Resources | Printed version also available from MIT Press.<br>Text version can be downloaded or else viewed as html document online (huge file).<br>The Jargon File, version 4.4.3 was released during Spring 2003. | http://catb.org/esr/jargon/ |
| Netiquette | Has links to many documents ranging from ethics to netiquette | http://www.cpsr.org/publications/newsletters/issues/1998/NetiquetteURLs.html |
| Penetration Testing | Wayne's Windows Administrator Support site for Windows NT/Windows 2000/Windows XP/Penetration Testing/Firewalls lists over 200 free resources in this area, definitely worth a visit. | http://is-it-true.org/pt/ptips13.shtml |

(cont.)

Appendix 3: (cont.)

| Title | Description | Location/URL, Publisher, ISBN |
|---|---|---|
| Privacy and Cameras | How to find hidden cameras, practical advice and illustrations on how to safeguard one's own privacy | http://www.tentacle.franken. de/papers/hiddencams.pdf |
| Privacy and Word/Outlook | Word reveals much information about the history of any document including authorship, comments, sections copied from other documents and so on. There is a way to make sure that one's template prevents this from occurring or else one can manually fix documents as outlined with this link. Sending the file via Outlook by default adds new information to the Word file about the sender which might be undesirable, hence use of another eMail program is a must to avoid canceling out previous efforts regarding one's privacy. | http://security.weburb.org/ frame/show/news/3193 |
| Safe Computing | For general tips on safe computing for home users. | http://news.weburb.dk/frame/ columns/ISSN16009665 V2N8.html |
| Safe 'Hex' | This is a free guide to what's involved with safe 'hex.' | http://www.claymania.com/ safe-hex.html, |
| SANS Security Reading Room/Library | Full of interesting material that is down to earth and very practical | http://www.sans.org/rr/ |
| Security & Cryptography | Links to papers, other data sources and libraries including cryptography standards. | http://lasecwww.epfl.ch/ links.shtml |
| Security & Virus Related Books | Provides reviews of many books in this area, helpful if you want to purchase | http://victoria.tc.ca/int-grps/ books/techrev/mnbksc.htm |
| SecurityPointer.com | Provides links to various Web sites dealing with Internet, IT and Wireless security | http://www.securitypointer. com/web_sites.htm |
| Sharpened.net Computer and Internet Glossary | Provides general definitions about computers and the internet. | http://www.sharpened.net/ glossary/index.php |
| Ubiquitous Computing | Mark Weiser, a researcher in the Computer Science Lab at Xerox Palo Alto Research Center, first put forward the notion of ubiquitous computing in 1988, as information technology's next wave after the mainframe and PC. In this new world, what Weiser called "calm technology" will reside around us, interacting with users in natural ways to anticipate their needs such as using one's digital assistant in a shopping mall, asking it to locate store XX. | http://www.ubiq.com/ hypertext/weiser/ UbiHome.html |

(cont.)

Appendix 3: (cont.)

| Title | Description | Location/URL, Publisher, ISBN |
|---|---|---|
| Virus Myths | Is a site that keeps you on top of the latest computer virus hysteria as it happens. | http://www.Vmyths.com |
| Viruses and Worms | Wayne's Windows Administrator Support site for Windows NT/Windows 2000/ Windows XP/lists many free resources in for virus protection including FAQs. | http://is-it-true.org/ antivirus.shtml |
| WI-FI Security | List of resources and checklists regarding wireless networks | http://www.informationweek. com/story/showArticle. jhtml?articleID=10808750 |
| Worms | Frequently Asked Questions (FAQ) about Worms, very extensive and well done indeed. | http://www.networm.org/faq/ |

# Appendix 4   Legislation and Regulation—European Union

| Name of EU Regulation, Law or Directive | Description and Comments | URL |
|---|---|---|
| Consumer Legislation | Provides links to EC directives regarding consumer legislation, laws, directives and arbitration procedures. | http://europa.eu.int/comm /consumers/cons_int/index_ en.htm |
| Data Protection Directive | Proposal for a Directive of the European Parliament and of the Council concerning the processing of personal data and the protection of privacy in the electronic communications sector. | http://europa.eu.int/information _society/topics/telecoms/ regulatory/new_rf/documents /com2000-385en.pdf |
| | By December 2003, 14 of the 15 member states (except for Spain) had began to transpose the Directive into their local laws. The Directive itself required implementation by 31 October 2003. | |
| | But by year-end, besides the UK and Italy, national legislation had yet to reflect and integrate the directive that would, in turn, help much in fighting spam. | |
| | The final directive is here: | http://register.consilium.eu.int/ pdf/en/02/st03/03636en2.pdf |

(cont.)

Appendix 4: (cont.)

| Name of EU Regulation, Law or Directive | Description and Comments | URL |
|---|---|---|
| Digital Signature Directive | Full Document as published in the Official Journal of the European Communities. | http://europa.eu.int/information _society/topics/ebusiness/ ecommerce/3information/ law&ecommerce/legal/ documents/1999_93/1999_93 _en.pdf<br>http://europa.eu.int/eur-lex/en/ com/greffe_index.html |
| eEurope 2005 | The plan for Europe's information society including trust and confidence issues. | http://europa.eu.int/information _society/eeurope/2002/news_ library/documents/eeurope 2005/eeurope2005_en.pdf |
| Framework— electronic communication infrastructure and associated services | New Regulatory Framework for electronic communications infrastructure and associated services. | http://europa.eu.int/information _society/topics/telecoms/ regulatory/new_rf/index_en. htm |
| Access and Interconnection Directive | The above framework carries with it several Directives as listed in the left column. | |
| Authorisation Directive | All were to be implemented and applied in all EU Member States | |
| Universal Service Directive | by 25 July 2003. For links to all of these go to hyperlink provided | |
| Consolidated Directive on Competition in the Market for Communication Services | on the right.<br>However, Spring 2004 showed that several countries have yet to adjust their national regulation to reflect this directive and some | |
| Regulation on unbundled Access to the Local Loop | will take until 2005. | |
| Safe Harbour Agreement | The Safe Harbour Agreement was proposed in 2000 to facilitate exchange of data between EU domiciled firms and US counterparts regarding privacy and data protection. US firms who signed the agreement are able to exchange a variety of data (e.g., customer information) with European firms. This was needed because EU legislation is more restrictive than US Privacy legislation (see also below). | http://europa.eu.int/comm/ internal_market/en/ dataprot/adequacy/0177- 2000en.pdf |

(cont.)

Appendix 4: (cont.)

| Name of EU Regulation, Law or Directive | Description and Comments | URL |
|---|---|---|
| | Is the Safe Harbour Agreement working—a report Feb. 2002 from the EC can be found at this link. | http://europa.eu.int/comm/ internal_market/en/ dataprot/news/02-196_ en.pdf |
| Patent Directive | The European Parliament has voted to approve a controversial proposal that governs patents for computer-related inventions. The approval also included several amendments, however, which may make it difficult for the directive to become law. EU Commissioner Frits Bokestein might instead try to scuttle the directive in favor of an intergovernmental treaty. Consolidated directive at: | http://swpat.ffii.org/papers/ eubsa-swpat0202/ plen0309/resu/index.en .html |
| The Radio Equipment and Telecommuni-cations Terminal Equipment Directive (1999/5/EC) | On 9 March 1999, the Council and the European Parliament adopted a Directive, defining new rules for the placing on the market and putting into service of Radio Equipment and Telecommunications Terminal Equipment. This Directive abolishes former Directive 98/13/EC and national approval regulations. This regulation affects mobile communication equipment. | http://europa.eu.int/comm/ enterprise/rtte/index.htm |
| Security and Legal Aspects with Digital Signature | Issues on Digital Signature addressing Security Issues. | http://europa.eu.int/ information_society/ topics/ebusiness/ ecommerce/3information/ keyissues/security/print_ en.htm |
| Information Society— E-Commerce Information | Legal documents from European institutions including e-commerce, mobile communication and cybercrime. | http://europa.eu.int/ information_society/ topics/ebusiness/ ecommerce/3information/ law&ecommerce/legal/ index_en.htm |

(cont.)

Appendix 4: (cont.)

| Name of EU Regulation, Law or Directive | Description and Comments | URL |
|---|---|---|
| E-Commerce Law | Most important is here that a dispute between a consumer in one EU contry and an online retailer in another, the consumer is able to sue in a court in his or her own cuntry. The EU hopes that this will help consumer confidence and trust in e-commerce (see also Jurisdiction, Zippo) | http://europa.eu.int/ information_society/ topics/ebusiness/ ecommerce/3information/ law&ecommerce/legal/ index_en.htm |
| Rome II | The European Commission has adopted a proposal for a regulation to harmonize the law applicable to non-contractual obligations, known as "Rome II". | |
| | Consultation information here: | http://europa.eu.int/comm/ justice_home/unit/civil/ consultation/index_en.htm |
| | The regulation, if implemented, would ensure that the same rules apply to cross-border disputes involving non-contractual obligations in all EU member states and would facilitate mutual recognition of court rulings within the European Union. | |
| | The draft calls for disputes to be settled in the country where the injury occurs, typically the home jurisdiction of the consumer, except where different cross-border rules have been adopted. | |
| | Draft here: | http://europa.eu.int/eur-lex/ en/com/pdf/2003/ com2003_0427en01.pdf |
| | That exception effectively creates a carve out for e-commerce, which is subject to the e-commerce directive's law of the supplier or Web site approach. | |
| | The business community has expressed concerns about the potential effect of the regulation. The proposed regulation would affect the treatment of claims involving defamation, advertising, intellectual property rights and product liability. Companies providing services to customers outside the European Union could be sued under a variety of laws, depending on where the claimant happened to live or simply has a product. | |

(cont.)

Appendix 4: (cont.)

| Name of EU Regulation, Law or Directive | Description and Comments | URL |
|---|---|---|
| | For online transactions involving consumers, industry suggests that the law that should be applied is that of the country where the provider is physically located or has sold the products or services. | |
| Waste Electrical and Electronic Equipment Directive (WEEED) | The directive will require that end-of-lifecycle equipment is collected for recovery, recycling and re-use. Fines are likely to be imposed on businesses not complying with the directive. Even companies with a turnover of less than Euro 3 million and fewer than 10 employees are not excluded. Directives have to be implemented in local laws by August 13, 2004. | http://europa.eu.int/comm/ enterprise/electr_ equipment/eee/ |
| | For advice about how to recycle effectively the Council For Electronic Equipment Recycling has established a resource site in the UK that is interesting to organizations. | |
| | This site relates to security regarding of recycling of old PCs, disk-drives and other hardware whereby data must be deleted to avoid its use by unauthorized parties using recycled equipment. | http://www.icer.org.uk/ legislation.htm |

**Note.** The above regulations affect the selling of software, hardware and security services including outsourcing of these across borders. Especially, contracting obligations, privacy and other regulations when contracts across EU member states are involved as well as other countries (e.g., Canada and India).

These links might no longer work because the EC has a tendency of moving things around or even removing them. You can usually find the document by using an Internet Archive, see http://security.weburb.dk/frame/show/news/2480 to find the document by turning the clock back.

# Appendix 5   Legislation and Regulation

| Name | Description and Comments | URL |
|---|---|---|
| CyberLaw | Find US legislation about e-biz, malware, infrastructure protection and others. | http://www.findlaw.com/ |
| Privacy Act of 1974 5 U.S.C. §552A as amended | The US. Privacy legislation. | http://www.usdoj.gov/04foia/ privstat.htm |

(cont.)

Appendix 5: (cont.)

| Name | Description and Comments | URL |
|------|--------------------------|-----|
| Law | One of the larger Internet law libraries with cases and other documents | http://internetlaw.pf.com/ subscribers/html/Digests .asp |
| Law Dictionary | Comprehensive online dictionary for legal terminology including e-commerce and security issues | http://dictionary.lp.findlaw .com/ |
| Privacy and Security | Several good sites including but not limited to the one of Canada:<br><br>Schlewswig Holstein, Germany:<br><br>New Zealand: | http://www.privcom.gc.ca/ index_e.asp<br><br>http://www.datenschutz-zentrum.de/<br><br>http://www.privacy.org.nz/ top.html |
| US Laws | The TV show Frontline from PBS has produced a page linking to US laws related to cyberspace (e.g., crime, privacy, etc.) | http://www.pbs.org/wgbh/ pages/frontline/shows/ hackers/blame/crimelaws. html |
| Swiss Law Art. 100quater StGB | Fighting terrorism and Denial of Service Attacks. In case where an individual perpetrator cannot be identified, the organization may be held liable. This could culminate in a stiff fine for the organization (see also Damages)<br>"...das es nicht alle erforderlichen und zumutbaren organisatorischen Vorkehren getroffen hat, um eine solche Straftat zu verhindern."<br>(...that it has not installed all needed and expected organizational mechanisms that would prevent such an illegal act = free translation).<br>This passus still awaits being put to the test by case in a Swiss court. A definition or case law regarding what can be expected and what represents standard regarding security (e.g., limiting the risk for unauthorized access to a firm's servers in order to use these for a Denial of Service (DoS) Attack) is still left primarily to the interpretation if the judge(s) (see also Damages).<br>For more information see also Table 16A. | http://www.admin.ch/ch/d/as/ 2003/3043.pdf (German)<br>http://www.admin.ch/ch/f/as/ 2003/3043.pdf (French)<br>http://www.admin.ch/ch/i/as/ 2003/3043.pdf (Italian) |

**Note.** The above list is not complete but was chosen to make some additional points. How Swiss legislation handles malicious code or hacking attacks is outlined in the Dictionary itself (see Damages). The above 'terrorism law' went into force by October 2003 and puts the onus on the organization to be able to proof that it did the necessary work to protect information assets. Rather unique but might be followed in other countries as happened with the law about computer viruses that was put into force by 1995 (see Damages).

# Appendix 6    Standards and Best Practice—A

| Name of Standard | Description and Comments | URL |
|---|---|---|
| AES. FIPS-197 | Was signed on November 26, 2001, after a multi-year evaluation process by NIST NIST special publication SP 800-38A, "Recommendation for Block Cipher Modes of Operation," is also available. The initial modes are ECB, CBC, CFB, OFB, and CTR. Other modes will be added at a later time. There are many more standards listed on this site and also best practice guides a rich place for information. | AES info: <http://csrc.nist.gov/ encryption/aes/>AES info FIPS-197: <http://csrc.nist.gov/ publications/fips/fips197/ fips-197.pdf SP 800-38A: <http://csrc.nist.gov/ publications/nistpubs/ 800-38a/sp800-38a.pdf> Key-management info: <http://csrc.nist.gov/ encryption/ kms/> |
| Australian Communications— Electronic Security Instruction 33 (ACSI 33) | This standard was developed by the Defence Signals Directorate (DSD) to provide guidance to Australian Government agencies wishin to protect their information systems. Again, a bit cumbersome to download since every single chapter needs to be downloaded but information is free. | http://www.aisep.gov.au/ library/acsi33/acsi33_ draft_information.html |
| Etrust—Comité Européen de Normalisation (CEN)—European Committee for Standardization | CEN's mission is to promote voluntary technical harmonization in Europe in conjunction with worldwide bodies and its partners in Europe. It is currently proposing an e-commerce standard that can be found with the link on the right. | http://www.cenorm.be http://www.cenorm.be/isss/ Projects/c-ecom/ |
| Guidelines for the Security of Information Systems | On 26 November 1992, the Council of the OECD adopted the Recommendation of the Council Concerning Guidelines for the Security of Information Systems and the 24 OECD Member countries adopted the Guidelines for the Security of Information Systems. | http://www1.oecd.org/dsti/ sti/it/secur/prod/e_secur .htm |

(cont.)

Appendix 6: (cont.)

| Name of Standard | Description and Comments | URL |
|---|---|---|
| IEEE 802.11 | Intitute of Electrical and Electronic Engineers (IEEE) (USA) developed the 802.11 as an international standard for WLANs. It specifies a number of technical parameters for operation of WLAN complaint devices. | http://www.IEEE.org |
| | Find out all about 802 standards here | http://standards.ieee.org/getieee802 |
| IETF—LWAPP | Lightweight Access Point Protocol (LWAPP) proposed standard (expires Dec. 2003) | http://www.legra.com/downloads/draft_calhoun_seamoby_lwapp_033.pdf |
| | David Molnar (July 18, 2003) CAPWAP security issues. Presented at 57th IETF meeting in Vienna. | http://www.legra.com/downloads/IETF_CAPWAP_Legra_security.pdf |
| Internet Engineering Task Force (IETF) | RFC 2350—Expectations for Computer Security Incident Response | http://www.ietf.org/rfc/rfc2350.txt?number=2350 |
| | RFC 3013 Recommended Internet Service Provider (ISP) Security Services and Procedures | http://www.ietf.org/rfc/rfc3013.txt?number=3013 |
| | General Site is here | http://www.ietf.org |
| IT Security Protection Manual | This site provides Germany's standard security safeguards for IT systems of all types. A bit cumbersome to download since every single chapter needs to be downloaded but information is free. | http://www.bsi.bund.de/gshb/english/menue.htm/ |
| Privacy and Data Security Seal | This site runs a privacy seal program including certification of software, hardware and procedures. | http://www.datenschutz-zentrum.de/guetesiegel/index.htm |
| | Audit certificates are also offered: | http://www.datenschutz-zentrum.de/audit/index.htm |
| Requests for Comments (RFC) | RFC editor page, hosts all information about RFCs | http://www.rfc-editor.org/ |

(cont.)

Appendix 6: (cont.)

| Name of Standard | Description and Comments | URL |
|---|---|---|
| Software Development Standards—Life Cycle Approach | This link is chalked full of valuable information regarding the Software Development Life Cycle (SDLC). The USA's Department of Justice is now involved in software development so much that they are dictating software development standards and practices. The best part about this standard is the January 2003 release that has information security integrated throughout. | http://www.usdoj.gov/jmd/irm/ lifecycle/table.htm; |
| US—National Institute of Standards and Technology (NIST) | Computer Security Resource Center (CSRC) provides access to standards regarding security and best practice/benchmarks as well as metrics from the security committee | http://csrc.nist.gov/ publications/nistpubs/ index.html |

# Standards and Best Practice—B

Ideally, information sharing formats are based on **Extensible Markup Language (XML)** to facilitate the exchange and sharing of **Definition and Exchange Format**(s) (**DEF**s). Generally, it is suggested that four basic DEFs should be considered, namely:

1) Intrusion Detection DEF (IDDEF)
2) Incident Object DEF (IODEF)
3) Penetration Testing DEF (PTDEF)
4) Vulnerability and Exploit DEF (VEDEF)

The following Table summarizes the current status of work pertaining to the above four basic DEFs and how they are progressing. The following Table does neither claim to be complete nor offer these initiatives in order of importance.

A1  Definition and Exchange Format(s) (DEFs)

| Initiative(s) | Standards[1] | Group | Comments | URL—Progress Reports |
|---|---|---|---|---|
| Intrusion Detection Message Exchange Requirements (IDMEF) | Internet Engineering Task Force (IETF) | Intrusion Detection Exchange Format (IDWG) | This evolved from the earlier Common Intrusion Detection Framework (CIDF). Despite years of effort, this initiative is still not fully mature, but does have enough support suggesting that a result will be forthcoming sometime in the future. | http://www.ietf.org/html.charters/idwg-charter.html http://www.ietf.org/internet-drafts/draft-ietf-idwg-requirements-10.txt |
| Incident Object Description and Exchange Format (IODEF) | IETF | Extended Incident Handling (INCH) | Not really ready yet for use as a User Interface. The XML 'X-Forms' package is not sufficiently mature and bugs still need to be ironed out. | http://www.ietf.org/html.charters/inch-charter.html |
| | | Task Force (TF)—CSIRT | Current design reflects the 'Techie' heritage. Its applicability to business processes is still not obvious to all. | |
| Vulnerability Assessment Report Format (VARF) | IETF | I²CWG (abbreviation stuck from earlier name) | Some early work on Vulnerability Assessment Reporting Format is being done here. Unfortunately, it a mystery how far along this initiative is and if it will ever be implemented. | Only available internally |
| | | NATO Consultation, Command and Control Agency (NC3A) | The discussion list on the NATO VARF is in a closed military network. | |
| Advisory and Notification Markup Language (ANML)[2] | Not Known | OpenSec: The Open Security Organization | This group is working on developing ANML using an XML-based standard to describe security advisories. It is already distributing the CVE database in XML format (2nd link) | http://www.opensec.org/articles/00003.html http://www.opensec.org/cve/ |

**Note.** The above Table is not complete but lists some of the important work going on in this area while below two more abbreviations are spelled out. This Table benefited greatly from the initial work by Ian Bryant, Head of Research & Technology, National Infrastructure and Security Coordination Centre (NISCC), UK which I expanded upon. All possible errors, omissions or misrepresentations are mine.

[1] Standardisation Approach

[2] ANML is supposed to also help in developing a consistent Advisory Format
Computer Security Incident Response Team (CSIRT)

**A2** Definition and Exchange Format(s) (DEFs)—Continued

| Initiative(s) | Standards[1] | Group | Comments[2] | URL—Progress Reports |
|---|---|---|---|---|
| Common Advisory Interchange Format (CAIF) | Internet Engineering Task Force (IETF) | Task Force (TF), CSIRT—Rechenzentrum Universität Stuttgart (RUS-CERT) | At this stage the group has identified certain issues and is conducting field tests. | http://cert.uni-stuttgart.de/projects/caif/ |
| European Common Advisory Format (ECAF) | None | TF-CSIRT—European Information Security Promotion Program (EISPP) | This program was funded under Framework Program 5, better known as FP5 from the European Commission. Funding expired during 2003. Last document outlining the ECAF was published March 2003 (see 2nd link). But format is not yet machine-readable and further development seems to have ceased. | http://www.eispp.org/links.htm http://www.eispp.org/commonformat_1_2.pdf |
| 2 Versions a) Web & b) Application | Not Known | Organization for the Advancement of Structured Information Standards (OASIS) The OASIS Application Vulnerability Description Language[3] (AVDL) | This group's objective is to produce a classification scheme for web security and application software vulnerabilities. With the help of a model the scheme is to provide guidance for initial threat, impact and therefore risk ratings. XML will be used to describe web security conditions that can be used by both, assessment and protection tools. | http://www.oasis-open.org/committees/overview.php http://www.oasis-open.org/committees/tc_home.php?wg_abbrev=avdl |

**Note.** The above Table is not complete but lists some of the important work going on in this area while below two more abbreviations are spelled out.
For all the above efforts, the main challenge is that if a simple text editor is used to report and then prepare advisories and documents thereoff, this conflicts with automatic distribution requirements. The latter necessitate easy parsing and the implementation as in XML. Structural information has to be in XML documents.

This Table benefited greatly from the initial work by Ian Bryant, Head of Research & Technology, National Infrastructure and Security Coordination Centre (NISCC), UK which I expanded upon. All possible errors, omissions or misrepresentations are mine.

[1] Standardisation Approach

[2] Although there is a de facto standard for storage of Vulnerability information [Mitre's Common Vulnerabilities and Exposures (CVE) see Appendix 1 for link), there seems to be a perception, judging by the existence of competing initiatives as outlined above that this does not meet the needs of the CSIRT or security engineering community.
It is yet unclear how these different initiatives will eventually stack up in the field. Some have yet to move beyond the paper stage and even implementations and field tests are scarce.
It is also possible that one or two of the initiatives will build upon each other's work and thereby leap ahead of the pack.

[3] AVDL is used to create an XML definition for exchange of information relating to security vulnerabilities of applications exposed to networks.
Computer Security Incident Response Team (CSIRT)

# Security and Utility Tools

Readers wishing to consult information security, vulnerabilities, hacking, computing virus texts to supplement their information available in this dictionary have *many* works from which they can choose. Not only are there printed works available but also many online options are open and can provide one with additional insights just a mouse click away. The following brief list focuses on books or internet sites with information about these issues that are especially clearly written, and/or widely cited "classical" accounts, and/or representative of some of the many disciplines in which these methods are used.

## Appendix 7 'Nearly' or Outright Free Security Tools for System Administrators

| Name of Tool(s) | Description and Comments | URL |
|---|---|---|
| Apocalypse Online | Provides news, latest security tools and hacking news daily including security programs. | http://www.apocalypseonline.com/security/index.asp |
| CERIAS—Center for Education and Research in Information Assurance and Security—Purdue University | Tools, software, standards, policies and papers are offered on this site | http://www.cerias.purdue.edu/tools_and_resources/ |

(cont.)

Appendix 7: (cont.)

| Name of Tool(s) | Description and Comments | URL |
|---|---|---|
| Computer Forensic Analysis | Free tools including the Coroner's Toolkit. Dan Farmer and Wietse Venema put their work here. | http://www.porcupine.org/forensics<br>ftp://ftp.porcupine.org/pub/security/index.html<br>http://www.porcupine.org/satan/ |
| Free Internet Scanner— Vulnerabilities | To test how a system fears according to vulnerabilities listed in the SANS/FBI Top Twenty list, a free scanner can be downloaded from the Center for Internet Security | http://www.cisecurity.org |
|  | Here Bob Todd's free Internet Scanner SARA can also be downloaded testing for a variety of vulnerabilities | http//:www.cisecurity.org |
| Is it true | Over 200 free tools such as scanners, sniffers, network analyzers, traffic monitors, and port scanners. | http://is-it-true.org/pt/ptips13.shtml |
| Password Strengthening | Computer programs are available to reject any password change that does not meet security policy<br>UNIX_Npasswd/Sun OS 4/5, Digital Unix, HP/UX, and AIX<br>The programs assure that when passwords are modified, they will be of the length and composition required to make guessing and cracking a bit more difficult. | http://www.utexax.edu/cc/unix/software/npasswd |
| Free Security Tools-Toolbox— System Administrator | Visit this newsboard—toolbox provides you with descriptions and URLs for download to more than 200 free tools regarding security and utility-related matters for networks and PCs. | http://security.weburb.org/frame/newsboard/other/toolbox.html |
| Tucofs—The Ultimate Collection of Forensic Software | This site provides complete sources and software help for forensic tools and law enforcement efforts ranging from anti-virus, steganography to biometrics and data recovery. | http://www.cybersnitch.net/tucofs/tucofs.asp?mode=mainmenu |
| 75-tools | List of software that can be used for intrusion detection (open source and commercial) with rating by various types of users for Windows, Linux and Unix platforms | http://www.insecure.org/tools.html |

# Appendix 8   'Nearly' or Outright Free Security Tools for Home Users

| | | |
|---|---|---|
| Cleaning Hard Disk | This is a good program for getting rid of left over files. It warns the user about deleting certain files and makes sure that with its backup, inadvertently deleted Windows System files can be recovered. There are other programs but they do not appear to have as many checks and balances protecting the user from making severe mistakes when cleaning up a PCs hard disk. | http://security.weburb.dk/frame/show/news/3259 |
| File Shredder | This program (freeware) permits the user to do electronic shredding overwriting multiple times with varying bit patterns. The program exceeds US federal standards for Media Safety.<br>This is particularly important considering that hard-drives are being recycled and information recovered on these may be misused or violate other regulations such as customer privacy. Here is Sure Delete V5.1 a free package (see also Recylcing below). | http://www.pcworld.com/downloads/file_download/0,fid,22393,fileidx,1,00.asp |
| Free Security Tools-Toolbox—PC | Visit this newsboard—toolbox provides you with descriptions and URIs for download to more than 200 free tools regarding security and utility-related matters for PCs. | http://security.weburb.dk/frame/newsboard/other/toolbox.html |
| Hard Disk and Computer Protection/Encryption | For locking down one's computer securily while encrypting part or all of one's hard-disk, thereby preventing unauthorized parties from getting access. | http://security.weburb.dk/frame/show/news/3197 |
| Open Ports | Some claim that 1 in 6 PCs are without protection which is like securing the front of your house (PCs at work) with the latest alarm but leaving your back door open (PCs used by road warriors and from home to log into system). | http://www.testmysecurity.com/index.php |
| | This tool provides a summary about a PCs vulnerabilities such as open ports. What a port does is described as well. | http://www.portsdb.org/ |
| | In case some ports are open unnecessarily, this link provides a step-by-step guide on how to close these. | http://ntsecurity.nu/papers/port445/ |

(cont.)

Appendix 8: (cont.)

| Password Checker | If you want to check how secure a password is or how long it might take to figure it out using a program, this site allows you do check and assess if your proposed changes improve anything. | http://security.weburb.dk/ frame/show/news/3204 |
|---|---|---|
| Password Encryption | This program is also freeware that enables one to store all passwords on one's hard disk in encrypted form. Hence, accessing the Internet bank site or a a shopping Webpage where one needs to log in with username and password. A good way to store one's many passwords while making them unusable to somebody getting inadvertently access to the hard drive | http://security.weburb.dk/ frame/show/news/1759 |
| Recycling PC | If you recycle your PC make sure nothing can be read on your hard-drive. While damaging the hard-drive might be best, a less drastic solution is offered by the program offered on the right, called de-Gaussing if used it makes all deleted files actually unreadable to subsequent users (see also File Shredder above). | http://www.pcmag.com/ article2/0,4149,25745,00. asp |
| Window Alternatives | The user may choose to save money but, more importantly reduce risks by avoiding the most popular programs such as the Windows Operating System The programs presented here are often Windows compatible, have a very similar interface and do the same jobs, such as Word, Powerpoint but for much less money. | http://security.weburb.dk/ frame/show/news/3128 |

# Awareness Raising—Skill Development

Readers wishing to consult information security, vulnerabilities, hacking, computing virus texts to supplement their information available in this dictionary have *many* works from which they can choose. Not only are there printed works available but also many online options are open and can provide one with additional insights just a mouse click away.

The following brief list focuses on newsletters with information about these issues that are especially clearly written, and/or widely cited "classical" accounts, and/or representative of some of the many disciplines in which these methods are used. Again the list does neither to be comprehensive nor inclusive it just provides a limited selection.

Below we have only listed resources that

- — are free to subscribe and,
- — public, that is not private requiring, for instance, an invitation or referral to join.

## Appendix 9    Newsletters

All the newsletters listed below are being moderated, i.e. the editor checks what material is being included. The best way to find out which of these are best for you, we suggest that you subscribe to three newsletters listed below that are most interesting to you. Why not try them out for a few weeks. **All newsletters are free!**

Daily or Sometimes More than Once a Week—Newsletters

| Name | Short Summary about Content, Focus and Other Aspects |
| --- | --- |
| BNA Internet Law News | Primarily US/Canada news pertaining to legal issues and the Internet, privacy, e-biz. Each story is very short and sometimes links to sources that cannot be accessed without subscription (e.g., Wall Street Journal), about 30% of stories link to original court verdict, legislation or corporate statement or research report.<br>Visit http://ecommercecenter.bna.com to get subscription |
| InfoSec News | E-mail distribution list for information security news<br>To subscribe to ISN, send mail to majordomo@attrition.org with "subscribe isn" in the BODY of the mail.<br>Provides also a weekly Linux, Windows security newsletter as part of the list, including re-posting of articles from some magazines.<br>High traffic about 40 messages each week but worth browsing through the headers. |
| SecurityFocus | Has various newsletters, discussion list and other news sources on IT security.<br>For registering visit: http://www.securityfocus.com/subscribe |

Weekly Newsletters

| Name | Short Summary about Content, Focus and Other Aspects |
| --- | --- |
| EPIC ALERT | Provides information about privacy-related matters including legislation, e-marketing, cybercrime and much more.<br>http://www.epic.org |
| INFORMATION SECURITY THIS WEEK | This European newsletter provides a weekly summary of IT, e-biz and wireless security regarding: critical infrastructure protection, anti-virus, privacy, hacking, legislation, free security software & utility tools, and vulnerabilities.<br>Provides brief and concise interpretation of stories, no advertising, 3-pages in length of text format news with very HANDY links.<br>Archive Search is possible by going to the newsboard.<br>Subscribe sending empty e-mail to: security-subscribe@WebUrb.dk<br>Back issues are available at:<br>http://security.weburb.org/frame/newsletters/other/information_security.html |
| LE FORUM DES DROITS SUR L'INTERNET | This is French newsletter that covers all legislative issues pertaining to the Internet primarily in France but also how EC Directives are being implemented across Europe. This public interest group also invites comments about documents written by the group pertaining to legislation affecting Internet use e-government, etc.<br>http://www.foruminternet.org<br>Site is lobbying French government and its legislation and case summaries are very insightful. |

(cont.)

Weekly Newsletters (cont.)

| Name | Short Summary about Content, Focus and Other Aspects |
| --- | --- |
| Linux Advisories This Week | This is a comprehensive newsletter that outlines the security vulnerabilities that have been announced throughout the week. It includes pointers to updated packages and descriptions of each vulnerability.<br>To subscribe send an email to: vuln-newsletter-request @linuxsecurity.com with "subscribe" in the subject of the message. |
| Linux Security This Week | The LinuxSecurity.com weekly newsletter summarizes the most notable security issues that concern Linux and open source security administrators and security professionals. It is distributed Monday mornings by Guardian Digital.<br>To subscribe send an email to: newsletter-request@linuxsecurity.com with "subscribe" in the subject of the message. |
| Network World | This printed publication has various online newsletters focusing on but not limited to such topics as wireless, LAN, anti-virus and home network issues.<br>To subscribe or unsubscribe to any Network World e-mail newsletters, go to:<br>http://www.nwwsubscribe.com/Default.aspx |
| Risk Forum | This is an international forum on risks to the public in computer and related systems (moderated). Sometimes links are merely to newspaper articles, other times to very insightful research and from time-to-time a story may be tongue and cheek or even chatty. Worth checking out.<br>http://www.CSL.sri.com/risksinfo.html<br>Subscribe sending one line email with 'subscribe' as text to: risks-request@csl.sri.com |
| SANS Newsbites | This newsletter provides about 10–20 stories or more a week. Sometimes the link is to an original source or security patch, often it is to a news item only, thereby requiring some digging to find the original document. |
| The SANS Weekly Security News Overview | http://www.sans.org/sansurl<br>SANS also has alerts and other news products that are insightful |
| Scambuster | Reports about telemarketer, Internet, wireless and other scams, primarily US focus.<br>To subscribe, visit: http://www.scambusters.org/ |
| Vmyths.com 'What's New' Newsletter | Tells subscribers what's going on at the vmyth about viruses website, from recent virus hoax trends to the newest editorials & resources.<br>http://www.vmyths.com |

Monthly (or greater interval between issues)

| Name | Short Summary about Content, Focus and Other Aspects |
| --- | --- |
| CRYPTO-GRAM | A free monthly newsletter providing summaries, analyses, insights, and commentaries on computer security and cryptography. Shorter stories with several links, as well as in-depth articles by editor or contributors on very pertinent topics for IT security.<br>To subscribe, send a blank message to:<br>crypto-gram-subscribe@chaparraltree.com<br>Back issues are available at: <http://www.counterpane.com/crypto-gram.html> |

# Appendix 10   Alerts and Advisories

All the newsletters listed below are being moderated, i.e. the editor checks what material is being included. The best way to find out which of these are best for you, we suggest that you subscribe to three newsletters listed below that are most interesting to you. Why not try them out for a few weeks. **All newsletters are free!**

Alerts and Advisories (General)

| Name | Short Summary about Content, Focus and Other Aspects |
| --- | --- |
| Avert Labs | Provides a free advisory service whereby advisories are ranked. Tough to sign up and navigate so follow suggestion below.<br>http://vil.nai.com/vil/default.asp click on Subscribe to Avert Virus News (or search on the site for this to find it, otherwise time-consuming to find sign-up page). |
| CERT—CC Advisories | Provides subscribers with advisories as they occur regarding vulnerabilities and threats.<br>http://www.CERT.org<br>http://www.cert.org/advisories/ |
| Vmyths.com Virus Hysteria Alert | Keeps subscribers on top of the latest computer virus hysteria as it happens.<br>http://www.vmyths.com |

**Note.** There are many additional alert services, some are available for customers only (e.g., some anti-virus vendors) others are offered by private firms to subscribers for a fee (e.g., Securia and Outpost). For brevity's sake, the list is limited to free services only.

Daily or Sometimes More than Once a Week—Newsletters or Advisories

| Name | Short Summary about Content, Focus and Other Aspects |
| --- | --- |
| Oxygen3 24h-365d Alert | Panda Software's service provides daily virus news, weekly summaries and other information. It sometimes has short but insightful definitions, news summaries and explanations that help one make sense out of complex material mailed by others. To sign on send e-mail to: oxygen3com-SIGNon-REQUEST@oxygen3.pandasoftware.com or visit http://www.pandasoftware.com/ |
| Secunia Weekly Alert | Provides services similar to Bugtraq but is a firm specializing in this service. Its mailing lists are moderated and certain services are not free. However, their weekly summary is free. To sign on visit: http://www.secunia.com/secunia_security_advisories/?menu= |

**Note.** All anti-Virus vendors offer some type of alert or advisory service, some of them free, others as weekly summaries and so on. The above lists three samples without any claim to being comprehensive.